TRUST AND PARTNERSHIP

Founded in 1807, John Wiley & Sons is the oldest independent publishing company in the United States. With offices in North America, Europe, Asia, and Australia, Wiley is globally committed to developing and marketing print and electronic products and services for our customers' professional and personal knowledge and understanding.

The Wiley CIO series provides information, tools, and insights to IT executives and managers. The products in this series cover a wide range of topics that supply strategic and implementation guidance on the latest technology trends, leadership, and emerging best practices.

Titles in the Wiley CIO series include:

The Agile Architecture Revolution: How Cloud Computing, REST-Based SOA, and Mobile Computing Are Changing Enterprise IT by Jason Bloomberg

Architecting the Cloud: Design Decisions for Cloud Computing Service Models (SaaS, PaaS, and IaaS) by Michael Kavis

Big Data, Big Analytics: Emerging Business Intelligence and Analytic Trends for Today's Businesses by Michael Minelli, Michele Chambers, and Ambiga Dhiraj

The Chief Information Officer's Body of Knowledge: People, Process, and Technology by Dean Lane

CIO Best Practices: Enabling Strategic Value with Information Technology (Second Edition) by Joe Stenzel, Randy Betancourt, Gary Cokins, Alyssa Farrell, Bill Flemming, Michael H. Hugos, Jonathan Hujsak, and Karl Schubert

The CIO Playbook: Strategies and Best Practices for IT Leaders to Deliver Value by Nicholas R. Colisto

Enterprise Performance Management Done Right: An Operating System for Your Organization by Ron Dimon

Executive's Guide to Virtual Worlds: How Avatars Are Transforming Your Business and Your Brand by Lonnie Benson

IT Leadership Manual: Roadmap to Becoming a Trusted Business Partner by Alan R. Guibord

Managing Electronic Records: Methods, Best Practices, and Technologies by Robert F. Smallwood

On Top of the Cloud: How CIOs Leverage New Technologies to Drive Change and Build Value Across the Enterprise by Hunter Muller

Straight to the Top: CIO Leadership in a Mobile, Social, and Cloud-based World (Second Edition) by Gregory S. Smith

Strategic IT: Best Practices for Managers and Executives by Arthur M. Langer and Lyle Yorks

Transforming IT Culture: How to Use Social Intelligence, Human Factors, and Collaboration to Create an IT Department That Outperforms by Frank Wander

Trust and Partnership: Strategic IT Management for Turbulent Times by Robert Benson, Pieter Ribbers, with Ronald Blitstein

Unleashing the Power of IT: Bringing People, Business, and Technology Together by Dan Roberts

The U.S. Technology Skills Gap: What Every Technology Executive Must Know to Save America's Future by Gary J. Beach

TRUST AND PARTNERSHIP

STRATEGIC IT MANAGEMENT FOR TURBULENT TIMES

Robert J. Benson

Pieter M. Ribbers

with Ronald B. Blitstein

WILEY

Cover image: © iStock/PixelEmbargo
Cover design: Wiley

Library of Congress Cataloging-in-Publication Data:

Benson, Robert J.
  Trust and partnership : strategic IT management for turbulent times / Robert J. Benson.
    pages cm. – (Wiley CIO ; 575)
  Includes bibliographical references and index.
  ISBN 978-1-118-44393-4 (cloth); ISBN 978-1-118-85350-4 (ebk); ISBN 978-1-118-85352-8 (ebk)
1. Information technology–Management. 2. Strategic planning. 3. International business enterprises–Communication systems–Management. I. Title.
  HD30.2.B4577 2014
  004.068'4–dc23

2014005245

Printed in the United States of America

10 9 8 7 6 5 4 3 2 1

CONTENTS

PART TWO—Principles for Transforming Business in Turbulent Times   139

CHAPTER 7   Requirements for Strategic IT Management   145

CHAPTER 8   The Service Relationship   171

CHAPTER 9   The Partnership Relationship   197

PREFACE

We began this book with the goal of describing information technology (IT) and business[1] solutions to turbulence and uncertainty, while at the same time finding solutions to the weak relationships and frequent mistrust that exists between IT organizations and their business "partners." We presumed these problems were rooted with the IT management and its governance processes; therefore, our Strategic IT Management solution would be better IT processes and organizational structure. Examples of these "better" processes include strategic IT planning, scenario planning, portfolio management, project development, and operational excellence, all of which we discuss in Part III. We characterize them as basic competencies every enterprise needs in order to cope successfully with turbulence and uncertainty. However, this is an overly IT-centric and very mechanistic view of the problems and their solutions.

As we worked through the book, we realized that the lack of trust and ineffective business–IT partnerships—together with systemic turbulence and uncertainty—are really the fundamental problems. These must be understood before we can begin to discuss how to improve the management and governance processes. Consequently, we describe (and justify the need for) a set of Strategic IT Management capabilities as building blocks for partnership and trust as well as a means to provide solutions for turbulence and uncertainty. We thought we had zeroed in on our target. However, the road to this book proved more circuitous.

The problem proved to be much more fundamental. Partly, the silos separating IT and business are an issue; Ron Blitstein talks about "breaking down the barriers" between the two. More fundamentally, though, the problem transcends IT and is actually an enterprise problem. Consequently, the Strategic IT Management solution is a systemic enterprise solution, *engaging business and IT in partnership*. We characterize the solution as a set of *enterprise IT capabilities*, bringing together business and IT and (perhaps as importantly) challenging both to view their world from the other's perspective. In particular, IT needs to embrace the business view fully, as it participates in the enterprise to deliver powerful IT capabilities that represent new sources of business value. And by the way, when we say "IT," we do not mean just "the" IT organization; we mean all sources of IT to the business, including the "IT organization" but also the in-business IT activities, sourcers (e.g., cloud), and "do-it-yourself" IT. Our definition of IT spans the value chain of the enterprise—from raw materials to cash, from content creation to cash, and from service design to cash. All streams are comprehended.

Through our personal experiences (as consultant, CIO, professor) we've come to understand that we're dealing with business functions and IT organizations as well as individuals, collectively as cultures and individually in terms of personal behaviors and beliefs. While improved management and governance processes may be critical in their own right, our objective is to create partnership, trust, and joint actions that can accelerate the needed organizational responses to business turbulence and change. This new foundation allows the full realization of IT's transformative power on the business.

We believe the nature of economic, societal, and, accordingly, business turbulence is fundamentally different than we have seen in the past. This brings new levels of uncertainties that alter the environment and place demands on all concerned. These heightened demands require new levels of speed and adaptability for both IT and business. This combination of culture/organization, turbulence/uncertainty, and speed/adaptability is something of a perfect storm that can either invoke damage control behaviors or unleash the grace and speed of surfing for a management team. Our book reflects a choice: Maintain the status quo or change. So while Strategic IT Management does indeed ultimately consider the mundane things like planning, portfolio management, project development, and operational excellence, among many other things, it does so in this significantly different context, a quickly and continuously changing business landscape. In response, Strategic IT management offers a different perspective. Ours is a holistic enterprise view that encompasses the actions required by all parties to deliver Enterprise IT capabilities that are necessary for success.

Strategic IT Management meets a critical need. From the IT perspective, much has been written elsewhere about the future of IT, the IT organization, and, by extension, the CIO. A lot of this information has a "strategic" bent— exploring how various technical and organizational future trends will transform the business, its IT, and the CIO. IT, of course, can be transformative to the business. Certainly IT, the CIO, and the IT leadership team face significant changes.

While this description may seem primarily focused on IT, we treat the business side as "co-dependent"—an equal partner and an equal contributor to the problems, as well as their solutions. The explosion of information and IT opportunities, and the means for acquiring them, demands an effective enterprise management framework. Thus the CEO, business executives, and leadership teams have responsibilities for change as well. This merger of business and IT responsibilities is the intention for *Strategic IT Management*.

It cannot be said that business–IT relationship is in good shape now. In fact, inadequacies in IT management practices often prevent the evolution of trust, competency, and confidence that is required to build effective, enduring, and resilient business relationships.[2] Please note that business management does not escape scrutiny; there are plenty of gaps and necessary improvements in business attitudes and practices as well. This joint responsibility is an important and parallel theme of the book.

The book's subtitle is *to Transform Business in Turbulent Times*. This is a bit misleading, for our focus is on enabling the business (and government) to *adapt* successfully (and continuously) to turbulent times. This surely has some considerable transformation in it—but the point we make is not based on a perspective of strategic planning toward specific new business opportunities. Rather, it is the perspective that planning (and everything else) has to occur under conditions of turbulence and change. Unlike other books, we do not intend to inventory all the possible sources of turbulence or the menu of possible business and IT responses; others do this well. We start with these opportunities as a given; the problem here is exactly how business and IT executives will deal with these opportunities successfully. So while "transformation" is in the picture—and transformation is certainly occurring—it is a consequence of turbulence, not a traditional catalog of possible business and IT innovations.

Strategic IT Management is about the seven critical enterprise IT capabilities every business and government organization must have, especially under conditions of turbulence. It is about the environment of trust, partnership, and leadership required for success. These core capabilities are particularly necessary today, as turbulence and change increasingly characterize the landscape for businesses, governments, and the global economy. It is a handbook for both IT and business professionals expecting to enhance shareholder value and to do so while recognizing IT as a full partner in achieving competitive and mission performance goals, achieved in the face of increased turbulence and uncertainty.

Strategic IT Management enhances the enterprise's systemic capabilities for exploiting IT. It not so much a set of methodologies; rather it is a set of mind-sets, mental models, and management commitments to creating the environment in which the potential of information technology is fully exploited by the enterprise. It moves IT and the enterprise from reliance on individual capabilities and efforts—its heroes and gurus that have single-handedly moved the enterprise's IT forward—to reliance on partnership, trust, and individual managers and professionals with the skills to work in this new context. Individual technical and business skills remain important and need to be upgraded; we provide the roadmap. Overall, *Strategic IT Management* upgrades the ability of the enterprise as a whole to cope with rapid change, business environmental challenges, and turbulence. *Strategic IT Management* also upgrades the ability of individual managers and professionals to contribute significantly to the success of IT in the enterprise.

What is new about this book? Among the three of us, we have read hundreds of books on management theory, IT's role in the enterprise, and so on—all the "classics"—and countless journal articles and doctoral dissertations on the subject of business and IT. They have all made great contributions, so it is a challenge to do more. What is new here?

1. We define the firm's IT capability as an organization-wide capability that depends on competences of both business and IT functions. As a consequence, creating business value with IT is an enterprise-wide responsibility, where business and IT functions have their distinct roles to play.

2. We understand that turbulence, change, and transformation are occurring rapidly, and are a critical component of enterprise management challenges. We also understand that IT is both a consequence (providing responses to turbulence) and a cause (creating new opportunities, new transformations).[3]

3. We establish the fundamental importance of trust, partnership, and leadership. This is equally a business and IT issue, and affects every manager and professional.

4. We address business and IT issues as a holistic enterprise issue. At the same time we emphasize the need for effectively dealing with the silos of individual business units and their distinct requirements for IT.

5. We apply IT in a business service framework with the attendant business-oriented Service Management implications.

6. We emphasize strengthening the relationship between business and IT. This is done in trust/partnership terms as applied in seven enterprise IT capabilities.

7. We address the increasing turbulence in IT, its effects on organization, the emergence of new IT sources, and the rapid evolution of new business capabilities and hence demands on IT. Our slogan here is "dynamic IT capability," an IT requirement.

8. We provide a wealth of self-assessment tools to permit the reader to apply the concepts of Strategic IT Management to his/her enterprise, together with a clear roadmap for addressing the self-assessment results. These tools and roadmaps are simple and practical. They also apply to every reader by providing individual self-assessment.

9. We understand that IT governance is woven through every aspect of Strategic IT Management. While we do not have a governance chapter, the business-engagement, decision-making, and organizational issues of governance are discussed throughout.

Who is our audience? Business and IT, CEOs, CIOs, and all level of management. This is not a "role of the CIO" book; it is about how everyone in the enterprise plays the roles needed to create business value and respond to turbulence and uncertainty. So, in effect, we're writing to the enterprise in describing the systems capabilities it requires; we're also writing to every individual involved, suggesting that all stakeholders—both business and IT—get their collective and individual houses in order in these difficult and challenging times.

Important Message to the Individual Reader

This book talks about large-scale ideas such as enterprise-wide issues, organization, and culture. It has, for example, chapters for the CEO and CIO. The primary messages seem to be targeted on the enterprise as a whole, for example, "Enterprise IT Capabilities." However, the individual reader—perhaps a project manager, a student, a business supervisor—should ask "How does this apply to me?" More the point, "What can I do? What should I do? What's the lesson I should be learning?"

The answers: The individual reader should think about the skills and capabilities he or she has or needs to develop, particularly focused on trust and partnership. Focus on behavior, values, personal objectives. The reader should consider how best to contribute as an individual professional, as a project leader, a supervisor, to the goals. The important questions: How can I help improve my company's *Service & Operational Excellence*? How can I best contribute to our *Development & Transformation*? To our *Cost & Performance*? How should I behave? The answers are in this book.

The point is *not* to emphasize technical or management processes or methods, or to train the reader in any given methodology. *The point is to have the reader understand the underlying values, cultures, goals, objectives, behaviors, and the imperatives of working well together with counterparts within IT, within the business, with sourcers*. So, ultimately, this book is directed at the individual and his/her role in partnerships. Yes, it would be good if the CEO and CIO and other executives could initiate appropriate actions. But in fact, the message for every reader is "It is up to me." And at the appropriate points in the book, we will have sections about "what this means to me."

A Note on Vocabulary and Cultural Differences

Our audience is not limited to North America and Europe. While English is a common business language in all areas, significant differences in usage of common words can lead to confusion. We adopt several specific conventions as follows.

IT, I/T, ICT, IS, IT/IS, MIS

The distinctions among these alternative names and acronyms are sometimes obscure and, without taking care, can be understood as synonyms. In some areas (e.g., Europe), *IT* is a narrow name covering just the technology and *information systems* (IS) covers the use of the technology via applications and information management.[4] Some use *information and communications technology* (ICT) rather than IT. Often the term *IT* is understood to be the organizational unit responsible for IT or ICT or IS or MIS and so forth.

For our purposes, we use IT as the single name for all these variations. We also include all forms of information technology—for example, communications and its application in manufacturing. We use specific modifiers when a narrower meaning is intended (e.g., "IT Organization"). IT also includes "IS" as it is being used in Europe.

IT Demand and IT Supply

These terms describe the organizational relationships between IT organizations (and more broadly, the external or internal source of any IT services) and the business organization—the consumers of IT. *IT Demand* engages the business in working with the IT organization(s) to express requirements, whether for applications, projects, or user services, of information for analysis . . . anything that the IT organization(s) are prepared to provide as a service. IT Demand engages the IT organization(s) in communicating with the business, in processes like planning or prioritization or project requirements. Artifacts used may include service-level agreements, IT budgets, priority lists, and so forth.

IT Supply consists of the processes and organizations used to produce the IT services, such as infrastructure, projects, and IT architectures. IT Supply can be an internal IT organization, an external IT provider (e.g., a third-party cloud provider or outsourcer), an internal-to-the-business group, or individuals in the business using do-it-yourself IT facilities.[5]

The connection between IT Demand and IT Supply—in effect, the connection between business and IT—begins to describe what we will be calling *Strategic IT Management*.

Differing Perspectives on the Management of IT Demand and Supply

Who is responsible for managing the IT Demand and IT Supply connections between business and IT? This is not the question of who manages the technology of IT, but rather of who manages the performance of the connective links of demand and supply: ensuring their performance, ensuring outcomes.

Different practices exist. In Europe, the chief information officer (CIO) tends to represent the demand side, and consequently is a lynchpin between the business organization and IT. As a matter of fact, (s)he is responsible for managing the business–IT linkage. The supply side then is the responsibility of a chief technology officer (CTO) or IT director.[6] In contrast, in the United States, the CIO tends to be more technology-focused. Of course, these distinctions are company-specific, particularly given the global environment in which companies operate.

On some level, it does not matter who is responsible, as long as someone is. Our focus is on the business–IT connection itself and how the relationships can be strengthened to deal effectively with the issues of turbulence, change, partnership, and the related matters that are the subject of this book. Again, the goal is to transcend these forces to deliver superior business results.

Capability, Total Value Performance Model, Competency, and Culture

We use four distinct concepts to characterize the connection of business and IT.

Capability is introduced in Chapter 1 and describes the systemic ability of the enterprise as a whole to perform the partnership roles and tasks necessary to 1) create superior business value from investments that exploit IT, and 2) produce superior response to turbulence and uncertainty. "Capability" includes all the systemic elements that make up this overall ability. For example, in describing the enterprise IT capability for *Planning & Innovation*, the elements may include an organization's:

- *Ethos* (can it be accomplished within the current business and IT cultures?)
- *Leadership* (is there appropriate business and IT leadership for the efforts and tasks?)
- *Partnership and trust* (can the business and IT groups work together in performing the efforts and tasks?)
- *Organization* (are the skills and accountabilities available in business and IT?)
- *Resources* (are the funds and staff available?)
- *Opportunity* (is there acceptance of the need to perform the tasks in the current business and IT context and the courage to execute?)

Capability is a characteristic of the enterprise. Capability, as we use the term, describes the enterprise IT capabilities.[7] It is instructive to note the definitions others have used.

Hagel and Brown say, "We use the term *capabilities* broadly to refer to the recurring mobilization of resources for the delivery of distinctive value in excess of cost . . . . We use the term *capability* rather than *competence* because the latter's common usage has tended to denote technology and production skills. For example, we could say that Dell has a distinctive capability in organizing pull-based production and logistics processes on a global scale."[8]

Teece, in defining dynamic capabilities, says they are "the ability of an organization and its management to integrate, build, and reconfigure internal and external competencies to address rapidly changing environments . . . and the essence . . . is resident in its tacit knowledge and its organizational processes and in the leadership skills of its top management . . . and display the ability to learn and adjust."[9]

The *Total Value Performance Model (TVP M)* is introduced in Chapter 2 and describes the current success (of lack thereof) of the enterprise in producing the actual outcomes required to achieve superior business value from investments in information technologies and, perhaps more importantly, the specific performance outcomes and therefore credibility that is the foundation for business–IT trust. The TVPM describes this for both business and IT, and also reflects an ordering of these outcomes (performance and trust is built up from step to step in the model).

Competency is introduced in Chapter 7 and describes the specific knowledge, skills, and experience foundation needed for actually performing the processes and methodologies required. Competency is the demonstrated command of tasks producing the specific outcomes expected. So, for example, the enterprise IT capability for *Planning & Innovation* depends on all the resources necessary, including the culture, leadership, partnership/trust, organization, and assets that join business and IT. The specific competencies required may include command of the specific methodologies and tasks required, such as Strategic IT Planning, Scenario Planning, or Innovation Planning. Competency is a characteristic of the specific organizations (and individuals) charged to perform the tasks, processes, and methodologies. These may be business and/or IT organizations, including those external to the enterprise (e.g., suppliers).

Our use of capability, competency, and the TVPM is completely consistent with these definitions, as we apply them to the task of achieving superior business value from IT and superior response to turbulence and uncertainty.

Culture is discussed throughout the book. It is a term we use to describe the context in which process/decisions/behaviors occur and the conflicts that may exist within and between the business and IT silos in the enterprise. Culture is a slippery word, though; Leidner and Kaywroth wrote an extensive review of culture applied to IT, laying out the many definition and application permutations.[10] For example, they report 164 different culture definitions. Their review focused on basic assumptions/belief systems and values. This is the context in which we apply the term *culture*—in terms of basic assumptions and beliefs (e.g., in business, in IT organizations) and values (e.g., what is good behavior). In this sense, we apply Schein's recent statement: Culture is the "pattern of shared basic assumptions learned by a group as it solved its problems . . . which has worked well enough to be considered valid . . . as the correct way . . . to think."[11]

A Note on Our Perspectives and Prior Work

The three of us have had a terrific time working through this book and its content, conclusions, and recommendations. We bring very different perspectives to the subject: Ron has very extensive CIO and consulting experiences worldwide; Piet has a leading Netherlands- and European Union–based academic research and teaching career; Bob has extensive academic, CIO, and consulting experience, largely in the United States, Netherlands, and Mexico. The point is that these three perspectives do not always match, as the practices and mental models used in the United States, European Union, and elsewhere are not always comparable. These differences have enriched the book but, perhaps, may lead to somewhat different vocabulary and perhaps conclusions. We worked very hard to reconcile these, and hope we have succeeded for every reader.

This book builds on our prior work. Bob Benson and Pieter Ribbers in their professional lives share an interest in the impact of IT on business organizations. Bob Benson's earlier publications focused on the business–IT relationship, particularly how to improve it. He co-developed the concepts of business–IT alignment and impact; the former ensuring that IT supports the existing strategy and structure of the business, the latter shaping the enabling impact of IT on new strategies and structures. The economics of the IT decision-making process has been a key element of his approach. *Information economics* in this regard is a multicriteria decision-making method to prioritize among competing IT investment proposals. These approaches were developed in the following books:

- *From Business Strategy to IT Action* (Wiley, 2004), with Tom Bugnitz and Bill Walton
- *Information Economics* (Prentice Hall, 1988), with Marilyn Parker and Ed Trainor
- *Information Strategy and Economics* (Prentice Hall, 1989), with Marilyn Parker and Ed Trainor

Bob has since written well over 100 monographs, articles, and management advisories further developing the ideas underlying these approaches.

In his earlier publications, Pieter Ribbers studied the impact of IT on business models. Key issues he addressed include the implications of changes in marketplace structures on trade with customers and other partners; which business models and revenue models to consider to exploit the Internet; and the importance of online marketplace hubs or exchanges to the business. In line with this, one of his areas of interest concerns outsourcing and insourcing of IT and its impact on business models. These studies were published in the following books:

- *E-Business: Organizational and Technical Foundations* (Wiley, 2006), with Michael Papazoglou
- *Managing IT Outsourcing*, 2nd ed. (Routledge, 2011), with Erik Beulen and Jan Roos

Notes and Acknowledgments

Note from Bob Benson

The road to this book has taken many turns. My business partner in our consulting firm, The Beta Group, Tom Bugnitz, has been a supportive and integral part of my thinking and practices for more than 30 years now. My academic partner, Piet Ribbers, has been equally supportive and a crucial contributor to my thinking. He contributes substantially to this current book. We have worked together for almost 30 years as well. I have been fortunate to work through Cutter Consortium for the last several years, with its unique business plan of engaging leading practitioners as associates. One of them, Ron Blitstein, with a CIO's wisdom drawn from experience, is also a major contributor to this book.

Many individuals contributed to the process and review of our thinking and writing on this book, among them Carlos Viniegra, Cuitlahuac Osorio, Kevin Guenther, Charles Bartels, Bill Keyworth, Mike Rosen, and Charmane May. Thanks to all.

Without question, the most important support and encouragement comes from my wife, Noreen Carrocci. Efforts like this could not be done without her limitless affection and support.

Note from Pieter Ribbers

In 1987, when I started the executive master program in Information Management at TiasNimbas, the executive business school of Tilburg University in the Netherlands, I got in touch with Bob Benson. At that time, Bob was the dean of the School of Technology and Information Management at Washington University in St. Louis, Missouri. We both shared a passion for the impact of IT, particularly on business organizations. Our relationship has survived almost 30 years of discussion. During our yearly meetings, a recurring theme has been "We have to write a book about this." However, we seemed better at discussing than writing; our wives, Lia and Noreen, smiled at us each time we brought up the subject. Eventually, two years ago, we picked up the challenge. What you hold in your hands is the result of all those years of discussion and a lot of hard work. It has been a challenging journey, and it still causes lively discussions between us, as our European and U.S. views on the topic do not always match. An important contributor to the discussion and its outcome has been Ron Blitstein. His analysis and opinions, based on his many years of experience as an IT leader, CIO, and consultant, continuously forced us to sharpen our ideas. Ron, thank you for your tireless perseverance when critically "fileting" my views.

During my years as a professor at Tilburg University, I have had the privilege to be able to stand on the shoulders of a few strong leaders in our field, two of whom I particularly want to acknowledge for this book. My thoughts have been shaped by Professor Chris Nielen, who has been my lecturer, colleague, and friend. He loved to pioneer with groundbreaking controversial views. His passing away left an empty space.

Through Bob Benson, I also met Marilyn Parker; Marilyn and Bob coauthored *Information Economics*, published in 1988. I had the pleasure to work closely with Marilyn when "supervising" her Ph.D. at Tilburg University—I use quotes here, as one can hardly supervise a strong leader. Our long discussions in Tilburg and Florida have also shaped my ideas for this book.

Writing a book is in itself an intensive process; it is all the more if you do that with authors located on different continents. As Skype meetings prove to be useful but certainly not sufficient, the more we appreciated the support and hospitality of Bentley University in Waltham, MA, which allowed us to have week-long face-to-face meetings in one of their offices. In particular, our thanks go to our colleagues Professor Nader Asgary and Mrs. Patricia Foster who have made this possible.

Finally, Lia, my wife, said, "I hope this is your last book for the time being." However, I am not sure. Whatever comes, I still hope I can count on your support.

Note from Ron Blitstein

I wish to acknowledge the patience of my coauthors as we "actively" explored the various themes developed in this book. I would also like to acknowledge some exceptional leaders from whom I have learned much. These include Pat Cusick, Peter Dew, Lynne Ellyn, Fred Purdue, and Michael O. Sawyer. Lastly, I would like to thank my wife, Harriet, for her boundless support; after our many years of marriage, she continues to steal my heart.

Notes

1. We use the term *business* with the understanding that turbulence and uncertainty—and Strategic IT Management—apply equally to government and nonprofit agencies.
2. See, for example, Paul A. Strassmann, "In Search of Best Practices," in *The Squandered Computer: Evaluating the Business Alignment of Information Technologies* (Information Economics Press, 1997): 135.
3. See John Hagel III, John Seely Brown, and Lang Davison, *The Power of Pull: How Small Moves, Smartly Made, Can Set Big Things in Motion* (Basic Books, 2012): 3: "we face two challenges: making sense of the changes around us, and making progress in an increasingly unfamiliar world."
4. For example, the U.K. Academy of Information Systems (UKAIS) defines information systems as the means by which people and organizations, utilizing technology, gather, process, store, use and disseminate information. See J. Ward and J. Peppard, *Strategic Planning for Information Systems* (Wiley, 2002).
5. Marianne Broadbent and Ellen S. Kitzis, *The New CIO Leader: Setting the Agenda and Delivering Results* (Harvard Business Press, 2006): 32.
6. A recent (2011 and 2012) study by the Business School INSEAD in collaboration with CIONET (a network of over European 3500 CIOs, CTOs and IT directors) revealed that only one third of the participating CIOs see their strategic roles as primarily technology-driven; instead, they see their roles as more business process– and client-driven. Moreover, the findings indicate that almost a quarter expect their roles to change from either technology-driven or client-driven to business process–driven in the next three years. See Fonstadt, "E-Leadership Skills," in *e-Skills for Competitiveness and Innovation: Vision, Roadmap, Foresight Scenarios* (Final Study Report, 2013).
7. See also the discussion in Joe Peppard and John Ward, "Beyond Strategic Information Systems: Towards an IS Capability," *Journal of Strategic Information Systems* 13 (2004): 167–194, and John Ward and Joe Peppard, *Strategic Planning for Information Systems* (Wiley, 2002).
8. John Hagel III and John Seely Brown, *The Only Sustainable Edge: Why Business Strategy Depends on Productive Friction and Dynamic Specialization* (Harvard Business School Press, 2005): 17.
9. David J. Teece, *Dynamic Capabilities & Strategic Management: Organizing for Innovation and Growth* (Oxford University Press, 2009): ix.
10. Dorothy E. Leidner and Timothy Kayworth, "A Review of Culture in Information Systems Research: Toward a Theory of Information Technology Culture Conflict," *MIS Quarterly* 30, No. 2 (June 2006): 357–399. This article provides a thorough discussion and extensive bibliography about culture.
11. Edward H. Schein, *Organization Culture and Leadership*, 4th ed (Wiley, 2010): 18.

PART ONE
The Challenges

CHAPTER 1

Business and IT in Turbulent Times

C hapter 1 introduces the basic challenges facing business and IT management. These range from business and technology turbulence and uncertainty to the critical need for transformed relationships and management processes between business and IT. Mutual trust and partnership establishes the foundation for the transformation, and applying strategic management principles to the business–IT relationship and processes provides the means.

However, in addition to these factors, every enterprise must also overcome a number of existing challenges successfully. First, the relationship between business and IT organizations has not been functioning well. Second, business managers do not understand their responsibilities for their part of the relationship with IT. Third, IT managers and professionals do not have the needed competencies for successful delivery of business transformations based on developing and maintaining trust and partnership relationships. These three challenges combine to create inadequate governance and IT management processes that do not deliver a closer linkage between IT and the business. Without significant changes and improvements, neither party will achieve its aims.

Our goals are simple: superior business value from the use of information and IT, and superior business responses to turbulence and uncertainty.

Turbulence and Uncertainty Challenge Enterprises

We write this book at a time when turbulence appears rampant and is increasing throughout the world. It affects all domains: government, economics, society, individuals, and of course the ways in which information technology plays a compelling and leading role in business and government. To be fair, IT is both causing some of the turbulence (e.g., social media, big data, the ubiquitous Internet) and enabling enterprises to craft practical responses to the turbulence (i.e., enabling stronger and more adaptable enterprises). Perhaps it is this duality that adds a degree of tension to the mix. Inarguably, IT is the only enabling function that serves the business by facilitating its current goals and strategic ambitions, while at the same time acting as a disruptive force that challenges existing business models and enlarges the plate of future opportunities. In 1942, Joseph Schumpeter[1] coined the term "creative destruction" to describe the "process of industrial mutation . . . that incessantly revolutionizes the economic structure from within, incessantly destroying the old one, incessantly creating a new one." The rapid advances in information technology continuously force successful business leaders to reexamine business models and the basis for competition. They also serve as an epitaph for those businesses, no longer relevant, that failed to stay current.

Turbulence affects everything and compels effective, continuous, adaptive, and swift responses from both business and IT management. But achieving this goal is difficult, in that the trust and partnership gap that separates IT and business prevents the necessary effective and continuing responses; they simply are not adequate to the challenge. "Best practices" must evolve into forms that build trust and partnership (in our terminology, bridging the gap between IT and business) while also enabling businesses and government to adapt rapidly to the turbulence and change that surrounds them.

We have revisited hundreds of books, numerous professional articles, and countless research reports, adding this knowledge to our many industry contacts and direct hands-on experiences. In the process, we have found that it is easy to be overwhelmed by the volume and noise of the recurring theme; we are in a period of intense turbulence—represented by concepts like dynamic capability, rapid innovation, "outside-the-company" sources of value, nimbleness, and implications of dispersion and networking of enterprises. Uncertainty due to government actions and regulatory changes only adds new spice to the turbulence. One only has to have a subscription to popular business journals (e.g., *Bloomberg*) and professional journals (e.g., *HBR*, *Sloan*), and even such outliers as *Foreign Affairs* to increase that sense of being overwhelmed.

And then there is the turbulence present in technology itself. From a relatively stately sense of regular process to lurching and breathtaking leaps, every year technology offers us the promise of bigger, faster, cheaper versions of essentially the same stuff. However, it also provides a sense that a whole new dimension is coming at us, and a lot of it is already here. One only has to look at the web sources reporting on the Gartner Hype Cycle[2] for just a taste of this.

All this puts great pressure on enterprises to find ways in which to cope with the turbulence. It also puts great pressure on them to deploy IT effectively, a task made considerably harder when there is a lack of trust and partnership between IT and business/governmental enterprises. Many of these challenges have been with us for a long time (e.g., "alignment," effective planning and deployment, etc.). But—and this is fundamental premise of this book—turbulence and resulting requirements for change and adaptability have the potential to render much of the current "best practices" ineffective and perhaps dangerous to the enterprise. Equally compelling are the historic gaps between business and IT, which have in the best of times made it difficult to perform and now, under conditions of turbulence, degrade the ability of enterprises to respond effectively.

This Is Not about Alignment (Entirely)

IT has grown up in a context that emphasized the need for supporting business objectives. The tools and methods for doing so have been bundled under the term "alignment." Alignment has proved a satisfying way to think about and deal with many of the business and IT relationship problems successfully.

Alignment, however assumes the enterprise management knows what it is doing. Surely it does, with respect to its strategies and operational activities that carry them out.

The problem, though, is that enterprise management may not have a clear view of the business opportunities afforded at a strategic and an operational level. Exactly how would business strategy and/or business operations change, if the possible IT innovations were fully understood and expressed in business terms?

Exhibit 1.1[3] has done well over the years as a vehicle for explaining the relationship between these two factors: one of alignment and one of innovation/transformation. The diagram itself began life as an explanation of *enterprise-wide information management*, developed through a joint-study research project between the IBM Los Angeles Scientific Center and Washington University's Center for the Study of Data Processing. The diagram has been

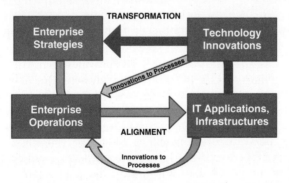

Exhibit 1.1   Business and IT Cause-and-Effect Connections

modified and adopted by others, including Henderson and colleagues,[4] as a way to express strategic IT and business relationships. Over the years, the terminology has changed slightly (e.g., "Transformation" started out as "Impact" and then became "Innovation") but the meaning did not. The two factors of alignment and transformation do state exactly what is needed: to have a common view of the manner in which IT supports the business strategy and operations, and at the same time to provide a clear path to finding transformational opportunities. Turbulence and uncertainty, as we will see, make this even more important.

Unfortunately, one side effect has been to emphasize the separation of business and IT. For a long time we described the gap between them as being overcome through the processes of alignment and of transformation (e.g., strategic planning.) This represents part of the objectives of Strategic IT Management, to eliminate more directly the gap through trust and partnership relationships.

We will refer back to this two-factor relationship in subsequent chapters, particularly highlighting the responsibilities of CIOs and CEOs to fully understand and communicate the transformational potentials provided by IT. And certainly (as we will show in Chapter 5), those potentials have been often realized as contributors to business turbulence, namely big data, the Internet, the collapse of supply chains, and so forth.

The Problem of Business and IT Relationships

In most enterprises, the business–IT relationship is not functioning well. This has been the case for a very long time, all the way back to the origins of data processing. Every enterprise of any size has a history of establishing IT as a separate organization and then trying many different processes of governance, planning, and performance management to bridge the gaps between business and IT. Every so often, new organizational approaches are tried (e.g., centralization, decentralization, federation), new forms of governance attempted (e.g., prioritization, planning, service management), new technologies and methods adopted (e.g., green screens, Internet, thick or thin PCs, agile development, enterprise architecture). Despite these interventions, the relationship continues to function poorly, as we will describe in Chapter 2.

Everyone has anecdotal examples of the relationship problems. When we do group exercises with IT managers, typical concerns they express include 1) we're always asked to corral increasing IT costs; 2) business executives are dismayed with IT performance; 3) they don't believe we can get projects done on time on budget, and when we do, business does not use the result or does not like the result; 4) there's no strategic direction; 5) we need modernization but there's no support for it; and 6) we're simply not at the table. When we do group exercises with business managers, their typical concerns include 1) IT does not speak our language; 2) IT does not understand the business; 3) IT cannot produce good business outcomes; and 4) each business unit has distinct requirements.

Clearly, these perspectives describe a union that will be hard-pressed to create successful business outcomes and perhaps achieve successes in spite of itself, which is the functional equivalent of the adage that even a blind squirrel can find an acorn. This does not factor in the effect of turbulence and uncertainty, which creates even greater need for strong, effective, and trusting relationships.

If the problem has been recognized for so long, why haven't we solved it? Based on our observations and experience, buttressed by comments in the press, books, and articles, we can conclude that neither IT nor business is ready to address the problem successfully.[5]

IT Is Not Ready

In most enterprises IT (as an organization) typically just is not ready to do what needs to be done, at three levels. As the issues are discussed with business and IT managers, we emphasize necessary behaviors (for both business and IT):

- Think strategically about the business and how technology change can be exploited to enhance business outcomes
- Nurture a partnership and trusting relationship between business and IT
- Build the ability to respond quickly ("Dynamic Capabilities") and build flexibility

Think Strategically

Mention the term "strategic" to IT professionals and the conversation may turn to the latest developments in cloud, data visualization, business intelligence, or various platform and network developments. Alternatively, IT leaders may respond with structural responses inherent in the mantra to run "IT as a service business." The importance of IT to the business underlies the conversation, particularly as it relates to providing flexibility, enhancing the user experience, improving competitiveness, and the like. However, these same IT leaders are typically unable to answer fundamental questions about the business that can guide the strategic use of technology, such as:

- What are the most profitable and least profitable products or services and why?

- Who are the most profitable customers and least profitable and why?
- Why do customers buy our products or services?
- When we lose a customer, why?
- When we lose in a proposal competition, why?

The truth is that much of this "strategic" conversation will be limited to issues of IT Supply—how the IT organization will effectively develop and provide leading-edge capabilities and the "strategic" means for supplying them to the business. This *Supply* view is largely inward-looking—inward to the IT organization and the technologies, services, and management processes it embraces. This inward view does not account for the general business performance or turbulence facing every business, not-for-profit, and government organization.

The IT Supply view includes external organizational factors like the cloud, outsourcing, and so forth; these represent alternatives to more traditional means of providing IT services to the business. It is all inward-to-IT focused. The typical IT manager or professional rarely "thinks strategically" from the business perspective.

Nurture the Partnership

The IT culture tends to look inward to the technology and seeks stability and control over unanticipated change. Most IT professionals do not have a firm grasp of the business, other than at the transactional level. These blinders do not make a partnership easy.

Respond Quickly to Turbulence

In most enterprises, the perception of IT processes, including governance, is that of bureaucracy. Whether true or not, the tendency for IT to resist unanticipated change can be high (unless of course it comes in the form of interesting new technologies). Even IT areas like new development processes or "efficient" architectures can be a barrier. Much of IT has been built on engineering concepts and the goal of stable results, which does not make rapid response a natural outcome.

However, there is also a more fundamental problem that highlights the message of this book. The essential conflict is between well-defined methodologies and processes, which attempt to produce well-engineered IT solutions and well-structured governance (read "bureaucracy") on the one hand, and the requirement for rapid innovation, quick response, and learning-while-doing (e.g., the use of agile in development)[6] on the other. This conflict between structure and certainty (which has typically characterized IT management from the beginning) and innovation, speed, and flexibility is the inherent challenge we face. It is not that engineered/structured approaches are incompatible with innovation, turbulence, and change. And we realize not everything can be done quickly (e.g., enterprise resource planning, or ERP, deployments). Indeed, our message is that we need to have both; this is defined in the enterprise IT capabilities, and it takes trust, partnership, and leadership to attain them.

Business Is Not Ready Either

In most enterprises, business management is only loosely engaged with IT. Governance processes are not strong, and managers at all levels are not clear on their responsibilities for developing a trusted relationship with IT. The problems range from difficulties in establishing measurable business cases and requirements for projects to overall governance of the total IT spend. As turbulence increases and new technologies become available in new ways, business management is not clear on the consequences of ignoring or bypassing the more traditional IT organization and, IT processes.

The outcome becomes silos of thinking and practice. Breaking down the walls between business and IT is a fundamental goal and critical to "transforming business in turbulent times."

Current Practices, Architectures, and Organizations Get in the Way

The 50 years of IT growth in business has produced much process and many organizational structures. In spite of them, problems persist. Certainly the details of management and governance processes are important but they are just one component of a two-part problem. The other part is the organizational milieu, culture, and behaviors in which management processes operate. This context sets the stage for the degree of partnership and trust that will result. These attributes may allow processes to work well in periods of relative stability but unless they evolve will prove to compromise the enterprise during times of significant business turbulence and change. Our case for this is based on history and observation, applying the thoughts and experience of a great many leaders in business and IT management and organizational design and development. The key point is to think of these problems in terms of organizations and people, and not solely management and governance processes.[7]

Through the years IT has always been challenged by perceived failures in business partnerships and trust, and IT has always been challenged to respond quickly and nimbly to turbulence and change. One only has to review the books and journals of the last 50 years to see the consistent and recurring concerns about these challenges. The current heightened economic turbulence and transformational technology changes significantly exacerbate this 50-year pattern of failure and disappointment.

Business brings its own myopia to the stage. While it is an easy target to focus on the IT side of trust, business has its own culture, processes, and barriers to the partnership. This is an equal opportunity discussion.

Overcoming the barriers, really "breaking down the walls," means establishing the partnership, the close relationships between IT and business. It means opening up the silos between and among business and IT. This will allow the business and IT to overcome turbulence and change with effective management and governance processes. In this way, IT and the business, working together, can successfully pursue the opportunities this affords the business.

Business and IT: A Complex Relationship

In its most simple form, the IT organization and an individual business unit have a complex relationship within the enterprise. For example, at one level, the IT organization provides IT services and capabilities to the business unit. This is a service relationship, with IT providing IT services and business consuming them. At another level, the IT organization and business unit must work together to create business value for the enterprise. This is a partnership relationship, in which business and IT work together on common goals. The multiple aspects of the relationship range from planning through operation. Exhibit 1.2 shows seven of those aspects (such as *Planning & Innovation*) that are the subject of Strategic IT Management.

Reality brings complexity to this simple model. While we may speak of "the IT organization" and "IT service providers" (and, of course, the "business

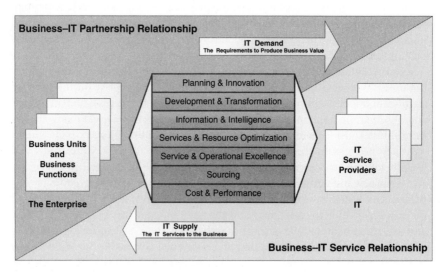

Exhibit 1.2   Strategic IT Management

unit"), in fact, IT is delivered to the business in many ways. For example, delivery is achieved through enterprise-level IT organizations (perhaps one or more separate organizations for network, ERP, corporate e-mail), outside providers (e.g., application-specific services like sales force automation), inside providers (e.g., specialized units within the business unit such as market/design support groups), and even individual providers (e.g., acquiring and using PCs/workstations/other technologies). Furthermore, the IT actually delivered across business functions is comprised of several specific services: applications (including data management), infrastructure (e.g., e-mail, Internet), projects, support (e.g., help desk), and management (e.g., assistance in acquiring PCs and tablets, etc.). Of course, the business unit itself is made up of a plethora of individuals, functions, and organizational subunits, all of which have various needs and opportunities for the IT being provided to them.

Having said all that, if we step away from the messy details of multiple IT sources and multiple business units and the many processes required to provide required IT services, such as planning, governance, operations, and the like, we can generalize with the simple statement that business and IT are linked in a relationship bound by partnership. They do things together, depend to various degrees on one another, and mutually work toward overall business goals such as competitiveness and operational excellence, measured ultimately by bottom line (or for government, mission) performance. Business and IT are, or at least should be, in a partnership relationship—one that is hopefully mutually successful. Understanding this allows principles to be defined that can help create and sustain that mutually successful goal. We expand on the nature of this partnership in subsequent chapters, and introduce and describe the full meaning of the Total Value Performance Model. Here, its message reinforces the concept of mutual interest, common goals, and the partnership between business and IT.

Overall, of course, our story is based on two concepts. First, that turbulence and its cousins uncertainty and change greatly affect the success or failure of the relationship. Second, that the existing "best practices" that characterize the operational aspects of the relationships (e.g., planning through operational excellence) must accommodate turbulence and uncertainty and also build partnership and trust in the relationship.

Our goal is to describe how IT organization(s) develop the capabilities to participate in and strengthen the relationships with business and, in so doing, better contend with the turbulence and uncertainty that plagues everyone. However, we go beyond thinking that this is just an IT problem; it is an enterprise-wide problem, equally involving business and IT. As a consequence, the business is as challenged to develop the respective capabilities to participate and strengthen the relationship with IT as IT is with the business.

IT's Value Is a Core Issue

Since the 1960s everyone, it seems, has been working on the problem of linking IT to business organizations and the bottom-line outcomes produced. Much of the literature back then talks about the same issues of partnership, trust, and the gap between business and IT.[8] More than 50 years have lapsed and we are still talking about the same things.

Part of the problem is the age-old "IT value" issue. Paul Strassmann devoted considerable research since the 1980s to the basic proposition that there is no correlative relationship between IT spending levels and business performance. In other words, enterprises that spend more on IT do not show higher profitability or returns.[9] Faisal Hoque,[10] in his descriptive book on consulting frameworks, presents some arguments that increasing maturities lead to better performance, but the connection is not causative. Simply put, there is little real data in the literature, other than Strassmann's, that talks to the issue of IT's value in meaningful financial or value terms.[11] Yes, business cases are constructed for individual investments. However, there are still many open questions. How reliable are the results; what is included and what is not; what about intangible benefits and costs; how is the uncertainty of future outcomes accounted for, and so on? So far, for *ex ante* business cases, the *ex post* realization of the business case is rarely confirmed, let alone controlled.

This is simplistic, of course, because IT is certainly the heartblood of most business. Most industries could not function without IT—but the same can be said of electricity and other infrastructures. This is what led Nicholas Carr to argue that IT does not matter in competitive or distinctiveness terms: IT is simply a commodity, something that has to exist in order to do business.[12] So the business–IT relationship, affected by barriers, poor partnership, and lack of trust, is also challenged by a poor understanding of IT's value. This, along with lack of credibility about IT's operational and project-development performance, erodes the relationship.

Challenges to Overcoming the Barriers and Walls

Finding new ways of managing IT and the business partnership is critical for all IT organizations and managers. It is difficult to imagine an industry that has not experienced IT-sparked transformations in how business is done, for example in working with customers, managing supply chains, providing insight into competitive and customer behaviors, and so on. Overall, there can be little question about the ongoing absorption of IT into the business. Demand for agility and speed, the use of information for strategic purposes, the role of the Internet in enabling this—all of these signal the incredible potential for even greater investment in IT. These transformative qualities are coming along faster, as Chapters 3 and 4 point out, requiring the enterprise leaders to raise their game.

The challenges of addressing these transformations are reflected in five fundamental barriers to partnership and trust—and barriers to the ability to respond faster and better to turbulence and change:

- *IT's Culture and Processes.* Several factors play into this barrier, but it can be summed up as being IT-centric rather than business-centric.
- *Business Failure of Accountability.* While the IT function may be IT-centric, business management does not understand its role or responsibilities in the partnership. The entire business, not IT alone, is responsible for applying information technology effectively within the business.
- *CIOs Are Not Providing the Leadership.* The CIO sets the tone and substance for the business and IT relationship. Without this, the partnership and trust suffers.
- *CEOs Are Not Setting the Stage.* Similarly, the CEO sets the tone for the enterprise as a whole, ranging from acknowledging IT's role through encouraging business management to take notice and play their role effectively.
- *Lack of Capabilities.* Both the business and IT sides lack the capability to anticipate and manage change. In particular, there is a lack of *Dynamic Capability*.

In many ways, these barriers are opposite sides of the same coin.

So Why Haven't These Problems Been Solved?

Where have the failures been?

A major problem is trust. Our premise is that a large part of failing to solve the problem is failure of trust between business and IT. This chapter lays out the groundwork, and we will return to this theme in Chapters 5 and 6. A second major problem is bureaucracy and associated time delays in performance. A third problem is the false notion that "one size fits all"—despite which, best practices and methodology seems to operate as though one size does in fact fit all.[13] But fourth—and this is the most important—the prescriptions and processes that others have developed are mostly IT-centric, always focused on how to fix IT. In truth, it is a combined problem of both business and IT. And there is a fifth problem, voiced by Nicholas Carr. Maybe IT does not matter; maybe IT is really a commodity, and there is no competitive distinctiveness involved. We have always had these problems. But lack of trust, partnership, and the increase in turbulence and change make it worse.

We characterize the business–IT relationships, and the best practices that connect them, as the management of IT Supply and Demand. We will elaborate on these ideas a bit later, but these form the foundation of the relationship and practices that must evolve to contend with the kind of turbulence, change, uncertainty, and distrust we have identified and will discuss in coming chapters. We have seen many of these ideas since the publication of Bob Benson's book a decade ago, *From Business Strategy to IT Action*.[14] In the last decade, IT has become so much more of a "given" in business—something that every enterprise has to have, simply to play. Whether back-office or customer-facing or in the supply chain, IT is in the fabric of the business. And there are considerable new possibilities for every business to exploit IT, whether the application is business intelligence, a radical change to customer experiences, restructured supply chains, or any other use.

Exhibit 1.2, earlier in this chapter, shows one view of the partnership and service connections between the enterprise and IT. As we have emphasized previously, by *IT* we mean all sources of IT, whether internal to the business unit, a corporate IT organization, an external provider such as outsourcers and cloud-based services, or "do-it-yourself" IT developed by individual business activities or individuals. The connections exist for all, and all must be a part of developing an effective business–IT relationship.

To Solve These Problems, We Apply the Concepts of Strategic Management to Business and IT

We adapt the terminology and definitions of *Strategic Management* to the specific problem of effectively and efficiently supporting the business with information and IT. We base strategic IT management on the strategic management frameworks developed in the 1970s and thereafter. Their core idea is that management has to take a holistic view of the assets and resources available to the business and optimally deploy these assets and resources in pursuit of the strategic objectives and outcomes desired. One need only recall the introduction of Design for Manufacturability concepts in the 1980s to appreciate that leaders can overcome seemingly intractable divisions. When approaching IT, the same core idea applies. Management has to take a holistic view of the IT assets and resources available and optimally deploy them in pursuit of the business strategic objectives and outcomes desired.

This is a direct assault on the silo approach that infects business and IT. In IT in particular, it is so easy to separate the technology issues from the organization that it is perhaps understandable when a bureaucratic collection of turf and technical visions is produced (e.g., infrastructure, software development, data management, architecture, operations, etc.). The same applies to business organizations, where functional areas become silos, as do individual lines of business. In both cases, the silo approach restricts flexibility and speed in responding to business requirements and turbulent change.

But what is *Strategic Management* exactly? Broadly, it is end-to-end planning and management of a business's strategies and strategic goals from initial planning through the organization and implementation processes, as well as the required management actions to deliver them successfully. Strategic Management takes a holistic view of the business, its competitive and operational strategies (mission and mission strategies in the case of government), and the complete set of decisions and actions necessary to achieve those strategies.[15] When applied to IT, the same definition applies. The strategic management concept is a new framework for managing the IT and business partnership, and is critical for all IT organizations and managers. Note that Strategic IT Management is *not* "treating the business as IT's customer." It is a partnership, with all that implies.[16]

The Emergence of Strategic IT Management

Influential authors[17] on management of (or management *and*) information strategy and systems discuss a "three-era model," which consists of a data processing (DP) era, a management information systems (MIS) era, and a strategic information systems (SIS) era. The DP era was a period where IT was efficiency driven and mainly function in a support role to improve existing data-intensive business processes. In the MIS era, focus of IT was to support management decision making (e.g., by providing exception reporting). During these eras, the objective of the application of information technology was to improve the internal functioning of the firm, either by adapting or changing business processes or by providing adequate management information to managers on all levels of management. The latter was made possible by new database concepts like the relational database.

The current SIS era has a fundamentally different view on the impact of IT, as it perceives the enterprise as an *open system*, contrary to the former views that looked at the enterprise as a *closed system*, the internal functioning of which had to be improved by IT. The open view included the notion that IT might have an impact on the (competitive) market position of the business. IT applications were to support that existing market position, or had the enabling possibility to shape new strategies. IT could dramatically change the firm! IT could offer a competitive advantage or could be a competitive necessity because of competitors who develop new IT-based concepts. For each era, practices, methods, and tools were developed and applied to support IT planning.[18]

The three eras have in common that the IT function is positioned as a separate function that maintains relations with business functions; the role of the IT function is to support the existing business organization or to enable new strategies and structures. Steering committees and linking roles are needed to shape the business–IT collaboration at all levels.

In their analysis of strategic planning for information systems, Ward and Peppard[19] conclude that a subsequent era has emerged: the era of the organizational IS capability. They define the IS capability as "the ability of an organization to deliver business value from investments in IS/IT continuously." According to Ward and Peppard, this capability goes beyond seeking alignment and opportunities for competitive impact of IT. It is a capability that is ingrained in the activities of the organization.

Our book builds on this view and moves forward to Strategic IT Management. We define the firm's IT capability as an organization-wide capability that depends on competencies of the business and IT functions. As a consequence, creating business value with IT is a business-wide responsibility, in which business and IT functions have distinct roles to play. In this book, we analyze the elements that compose the IT capability and the required competencies of business and IT functions upon which the IT capability depends.

Strategic IT Management Is a New Approach to Old Problems

Strategic IT Management is based on seven enterprise IT capabilities every enterprise must have. These capabilities connect business and IT; they are not specifically IT or business; rather they represent capabilities that the business and IT must have together.

The Enterprise IT Capability for Strategic Thinking and Action about IT in the Business

Planning & Innovation. An enterprise requires the capability for business and IT (together) to define the future of the business and its use of information and IT.

This capability requires the ability to establish strategies, products/services, and business models; to describe the turbulence and uncertainty affecting the business; to forecast its requirements or means for reacting to uncertainty; to understand competitive and performance requirements; and to respond to its requirements and uncertainty with viable plans, goals, and roadmaps for all its IT, as well as to do so successfully in conditions of turbulence.

The Enterprise IT Capabilities to Deliver Value through IT

Service & Resource Optimization. An enterprise requires the capability to optimize the sourcing, development, and application of all its IT services and resources, from all sources: internal IT, business-unit IT activities, suppliers, and do-it-yourself IT activities.

Development & Transformation. An enterprise requires the capability to develop, implement, and apply information and IT capabilities to change and transform the enterprise so that superior returns can be achieved.

Information & Intelligence. An enterprise requires the capability to acquire, manage, analyze, and apply the vast information sources at its disposal in all relevant enterprise areas.

The Enterprise IT Capabilities to Execute IT in Partnership with the Business

Service & Operational Excellence. An enterprise requires the capability to perform its IT services with operational excellence and the right balance of adaptability/flexibility toward standards and stability (and, overall, holistically covering the enterprise and all its IT).

Sourcing. An enterprise requires the capability to define, plan, acquire, manage, and effectively employ IT services from all sources: internal IT, business-unit IT activities, suppliers, and do-it-yourself IT activities.

Cost & Performance. An enterprise requires the capability to capture and analyze the complete IT costs from all sources and applications of information and IT, and to describe its IT performance requirements and metrics, from the business perspective

Taken together, these seven capabilities create a systemic capability for the enterprise to exploit IT for maximum value and response to turbulence and uncertainty.

Enterprise IT Capabilities Cannot Be IT-Centric: They Require a Partnership

Enterprise IT capabilities are the essence of Strategic IT Management—mobilizing and directing all relevant enterprise resources to achieve strategic purposes, namely achieving superior business value and enabling superior business responses to turbulence. All IT resources, however sourced (e.g., internal, external), and all business resources (e.g., process management, planning and decision-making, product and customer activities, etc.) are engaged in the process of "transforming business in turbulent times." This is a concertedly holistic approach.

The enterprise IT capabilities are those of the business and IT partnership. Again, these seven capabilities are not simply reworked IT processes. Enterprise capabilities are not focused solely on IT. These capabilities are at the enterprise level, with all stakeholders, in a trusting partnership.[20]

Enterprise IT Capabilities Focus on the Enterprise's Ability to Produce Value and Respond to Turbulence

We frame these capabilities in the seven-part perspective shown in Exhibit 1.3. These seven capabilities reflect the required management and governance activities that—fully engaging both business and IT—effectively enable the full power of IT to improve and transform the business. In subsequent chapters we'll explore each of these in detail, including the idea that it is not critical who acts as pilot and copilot in performing the processes; rather, it is important is that they occur in a climate of trust and partnership with the requisite speed and flexibility[21] to respond effectively to turbulence and change in the business and technology environments.[22] This requires both business and IT to take proactive steps together rather than simply react to circumstance. These connections can exist in informal relationships and in formal organizational structures and processes. For example, the first, "Planning for the Use of Information and IT," can be as simple as having conversations between an IT manager and a business manager or as complex as a multistep strategic planning process. Perhaps IT is involved in the business strategic planning itself. All kinds of patterns exist: The hope is that the function is satisfied, namely that the process will "find and implement the best business opportunities for applying information technology to transform the business," as shown as the first element of Exhibit 1.3.[23]

Some of these enterprise IT capabilities deal mostly with IT Demand. Some of the connections deal with day-to-day activities, or the relationships between IT service providers. Critically, each of these connections has a "dynamic capability" component requiring the ability to respond effectively to turbulence and uncertainty.

As shown in Exhibit 1.3, each enterprise IT capability does include traditional IT-centric topics, but with the specific additional focus on business-centric issues. New in our approach is the combination of a thorough examination of the management and governance activities together with a clear assessment of the reasons they currently do not work well. At the same time, we are mindful of the stage theory for the effectiveness of IT organizations as presented in Chapter 2: the notion that what an organization is ultimately capable of doing is dependent on its success in performing more foundational tasks, such as operational excellence, software development, and so forth.

We package the end-point characteristics into overall solutions and specifics of the seven areas of management governance as shown in Exhibit 1.3, and in the process address barriers with restructured governance and management processes. We focus on planning, financial management, accountability, operational excellence, and development. We use tools like portfolio management, PMOs, and governance structures. These are described in Part III. Their

Exhibit 1.3   Seven Enterprise IT Capabilities and Outcomes

Enterprise IT Capability	The Enterprise—business and IT working together—is capable of this: (IT Perspective)	The Enterprise—business and IT working together—is capable of this: (Business Perspective)	The Enterprise is capable of this: (to deal with turbulence and uncertainty)
Planning & Innovation	1. Plan for the Use of Information and IT 2. Match IT Supply to IT Demand	1. See the potentially massive disruptions in business and technology 2. Understand the potential for IT as transformational force 3. Move beyond business as usual 4. Take a holistic perspective of the business; overcome the silo mentality. 5. Ensure that business and IT work in partnership 6. Understand the business 7. Think strategically 8. Find business innovations through the use of information and IT 9. Adopt "sense and respond" to fast moving business requirements 10. See and understand industry patterns 11. Rise above the IT-centric perspective 12. Plan for adaptive/dynamic IT (*These apply to all seven IT Enterprise Capabilities*)	• Perform faster, produce quicker responses, enable dynamic business changes • Adopt enabling architectures and capabilities necessary for dynamic IT
Development & Transformation	3. Maximize Project Value		
Information & Intelligence	4. Apply Analytics and Data		
Services & Resources Optimization	5. Manage IT Assets 6. Strategic Sourcing		
Sourcing	7. Make the Best Decisions among the Alternatives for IT Sourcing 8. Manage Sourcing Decisions		
Cost & Performance	9. Know and Manage Costs 10. Understand the Cost and Value of all Information and IT		
Service & Operational Excellence	11. Perform Service Excellence in all Five IT Service Portfolios 12. Deliver IT Services to the Business		

power lies in how they address the fundamental issues of trust and turbulence. Overall, these represent the capabilities and capabilities the enterprise (IT and business) simply must have to address current challenges in business and technology.

Note that we do not call for the "integration" of business and IT. Rather, we look for IT to take its place as one of the core business functional areas. Like any other business function, information and IT are used in the business, however supplied. This makes the concerns as to how IT is supplied simply a supply problem, unrelated to the specifics of how to use it effectively in the business. Other than details like cost, reliability, and flexibility, no one really cares about the details of supply. This is not an integration issue; it is a relationship within the business issue.

But look carefully at the *business perspective* column in Exhibit 1.3. While many of these capabilities have the characteristics of a process (e.g., partnership, planning, overcoming silos), most focus on the attitude that business executives and professionals take about IT. For example, the capabilities raise the expectations for understanding the transformational role of IT, understanding the industry disruptions, and generally thinking strategically about IT. This is major, and it describes much of the capabilities gap between IT and business. Indeed, it underlies the importance of fully developing the enterprise IT capabilities, with IT and business working together. This is not an IT problem; it is equally a business problem.

Of course, identifying the issue as a problem for both business and IT also emphasizes the challenges of accomplishing this in the context of turbulence in IT itself, particularly given the organizational changes in how IT is supplied to the business. Again, this emphasizes the need for thinking holistically about the capabilities the enterprise requires.

Strategic IT Management Changes the Mental Models about IT in the Enterprise

A mental model is a representation of how things work, the relationships of things, "the ideas and beliefs we use to guide our actions . . . we use them to explain cause and effect as we see them, and to give meaning to our experience."[24] Peter Senge has remarked that to achieve change, one first changes the mental model.[25] Gary Hamel states that "to design business models, the existing mental models must first be exposed and challenged. Mental models form and reinforce the current business model."[26]

There are, of course, a great many patterns of mental models that have been applied to enterprises. Many are old, such as Fayol and Weber's view of the hierarchical organization. Many others have evolved—for example,

Ansoff's view of turbulence in the enterprise, Porter's competitive models, and so forth. Most if not all of these mental models apply to the business domain: its position in its industry, its competitive position, the role of the customer, the supply chain. Mental models for IT are developed as well; for example, see Weill's and Ross's view of the possible IT organizational forms (e.g., federal, centralized, etc.).[27] In all cases, the mental model gives a vocabulary and a visual image of the specifics introduced in the model, which is helpful in giving "meaning to our experience" per the earlier quote.[28]

Gary Hamel gives a strong argument that mental models applied to business are changing—and that they must change to deal with turbulence and uncertainty. He notes that the 20th century evolved a pretty clear business management model involving Standardization, Specialization of Tasks and Functions, Goal Alignment, Hierarchy, Planning and Control, and Extrinsic Rewards. He argues that while this has been valuable, particularly in conditions of relative stability, the current evolution of the management mental model has to embrace variety, flexibility, activism, meaning (for the actors in it), and serendipity.[29]

Thomas Davenport and his coauthors give a striking commentary on the changes in the business mental model, with words that characterize a *From* and *To* view. The *from* is the traditional model; the *to* is the expected changed model. The words are like Sales Push to Customer Pull, Production to Value Innovation focus, High Finished Good to Direct Delivery to Customer, Ownership of Production to Outsourcing.[30] These Davenport and Hamel discussions certainly fuel our discussion of turbulence in Chapters 3 and 5; here, they give important examples of what we mean by mental models. They are the ways managers, both business and IT, visualize, understand, and communicate the essence of the business in which they are engaged.

Our particular interest here is the mental model on which managers rely, which describes the relationships between business and IT. Much of this model is based on assumptions managers have about the kind of business they are, the role IT plays in the business, and the best way to govern, plan, and control IT. Our position is threefold:

- It is likely that business and IT, for a particular enterprise, in fact have different mental models about IT in the enterprise and the role that business and IT organizations have in planning and managing IT.[31]
- It is likely that the mental model about IT in the enterprise is inappropriate for the current business context for the enterprise.
- It is even more likely that increased turbulence will necessitate changes in the mental model and, accordingly, will drive even more differences in perspective between business and IT.

Our mental model addresses the assumptions managers have about six aspects of the business/IT relationship. Using a *From* and *To* perspective, the role of Strategic IT Management is to enable the enterprise to achieve a *To* endpoint in each of the six aspects of the relationship.

Of course this begs the critical question of whether the *From* position is bad and the *To* position is "good." We, of course, believe so, as you will note that the difference between our *From* and *To* is moving from a separate IT-centric technology organizational posture to a business-centric partnering relationship. Whether that is good on its merits remains to be seen; however, we believe it is critical. We also do not believe that one size fits all, and it may well be that for some enterprises, our *From* position is perfect. What comes to mind is an enterprise in a very unchanging business environment with little competition and stable demand for its products and services. These do exist. However, we also believe that our current climate of turbulence ultimately affects all and, more pertinently, that many of the traditional IT characteristics really do not serve the enterprise well. We will in subsequent chapters consider this one-size-fits-all issue.

Here, we describe these assumptions with two very district endpoints for each characteristic. At a high level, this model is shown in Exhibit 1.4, Changing Enterprise Characteristics. It describes one end of the endpoint as *traditional*; by this we mean viewing IT as it evolved from early data processing through MIS stages of development. As such, we observe that most, if not all, enterprises have been at the traditional end at some point in their history—and perhaps even today. We describe the other end as *not traditional*; by this we mean the evolution of the business–IT relationship into a more partnership-oriented, business turbulence–capable, and strategic destination. We do not attempt to specify the nature of this *To* destination; this is enterprise-specific. But the overall characteristics described here do apply.

Exhibit 1.4 shows a high-level comparison of the two endpoints, the *From* and the *To*. These are described in black/white terms; of course, no individual enterprise would be completely at one end or the other, and various parts of the enterprise and IT organizations would have different characteristics. But it is useful to consider where an enterprise is and where it needs to go.

(For self-assessment, pick the Enterprise Characteristics number that most closely reflects your enterprise. Choosing a 1 means the left-hand column is most descriptive; a 5 means the right is most descriptive. Exhibit 1.5 shows an example for two enterprises.)

The seven enterprise IT capabilities expect to cause change in the way information and IT are planned, managed, deployed, and provided to the enterprise, particularly in response to turbulence and uncertainty but also to

Exhibit 1.4   Changing Enterprise Characteristics

Enterprise Business and IT Characteristics	*From* **The Traditional View**	Enterprise Characteristic	*To* **The Transformational View—The evolution to partnership-oriented, turbulence-capable, strategic**
Business environmental context	The environment is stable, static. Changes come in relatively constant speed and are not transformational. The business and IT organizations focus on the enterprise level.	1 2 3 4 5	The environment is turbulent, dynamic. Change comes in unexpected ways and speeds. The business and IT organizations focus on the business unit and lines of business.
IT's primary focus	Cost reduction, cost management is key.	1 2 3 4 5	Strategic focus, optimal (not lowest) cost is key.
The values IT places on the business solutions delivered to the business	Stability, engineering, specifications, responsive to business requirements.	1 2 3 4 5	Flexibility, adaptability and responsiveness, modular, meet expectations.
The approach to governance	Hierarchical, orientation to control.	1 2 3 4 5	Network, participative, orientation to business problem solving.
IT's basic culture and values	Command the technology. Respond to the business. Service an arm's-length service client.	1 2 3 4 5	Know the business, proactive with solutions to business, partner.
How business views the relationship of IT and business organizations	Business is viewed as client, defines requirements. IT operates the technology, provides technical expertise. IT is a sole provider.	1 2 3 4 5	Business is viewed as partner, collaborative. IT as a transformative factor; IT functions as partner. Many sources of IT are possible and need management.
How IT views the relationship of IT and business organizations	IT is reactive to the business. Business is viewed as a client, defines requirements. IT operates the technology, provides technical expertise. IT is a sole provider.	1 2 3 4 5	IT is proactive, in collaboration with business partners. Focus on strategic use of IT. Need to manage the many sources of IT.

simply create more value from IT. In effect, we expect the seven capabilities to be a central factor in changing the mental model about the enterprise and how information and IT is used, planned, and managed.

Consider how the current enterprise mental model exists in the minds of senior business and IT executives. This model, as stated previously, is used to guide management actions about the use and development of IT. Three contexts are important. First is whether the mental model, in the minds of business management, is the same as in IT management minds . . . or even more so, whether the mental model is consistent throughout the enterprise and IT silos. Second is whether the current mental model is, in fact, good for the enterprise. Our point ultimately is that the endpoint we define here is the desired model and indeed the destination for the enterprise and its application of Strategic IT Management. Third is whether the current mental model(s) is consistent with changing environmental conditions. In short, does turbulence create change in the requirements reflected in the enterprise model, which may cause disruption in how managers on both sides think about governance and the role IT should play?

Consider an enterprise and where it stands. Again, we understand that this analysis may be quite different for separate business units and even separate providers of IT to the enterprise. Nevertheless it is interesting to consider where the enterprise stands. Using Exhibit 1.4, we can consider the situation for two different enterprises, answered by the senior IT executives, in Exhibit 1.5.[32]

Exhibit 1.5 Two Enterprise Examples

Enterprise Business and IT Characteristics	Enterprise 1 Characteristic	Enterprise 2 Characteristic
Business environmental context	1	5
IT's primary focus	2	5
The values IT places on the business solutions delivered to the business	2	4
The approach to governance	1	5
IT's basic culture and values	4	4
How business views the relationship of IT and business organizations	3	4
How IT views the relationship of IT and business organizations	1	5

Obviously, as Exhibit 1.5 shows, these are two different enterprises (or possibly two different lines of business within the same enterprise). Does this mean anything? Consider the three points we suggested earlier:

- Is the mental model the same in business and IT? Assume the answer is no; this offers some room for concern and possible action.
- Is the current mental model good for the enterprise? This of course depends, but our sense is that fundamentally, in the 21st century, the answer is no for enterprise 1.
- Is the current mental model consistent with the turbulence in the enterprise environment? This is the magic question, and we'd need to know more. But for enterprise 1, again, we would say no.

To Whom Are We Writing? Who Is Our Audience? Whose Mental Models Are We Changing?

We write for both IT and business executives/managers/professionals. The IT audience is easily seen as a prime focus, as so much of the gap with business is laid at their feet, based on things like culture, ignorance about the business, and excessive focus on technology. Given that the CIOs at most North American companies are viewed as responsible for closing the gap, consequently requiring the IT managers and professionals to master the concepts we describe, perhaps that focus is appropriate. Yet business management bears a considerable amount of responsibility for the current state of affairs and certainly has mental models that get in the way of partnership. In Europe, of course, business managers may be the key actors.

The bottom line is that Strategic IT Management applies to both domains, balancing the responsibilities and requirements for mastering the skills and capabilities to effectively apply IT in the enterprise. In turbulent times, this is of paramount importance.

In short, the systemic capabilities represented by the seven Enterprise IT Capabilities are required for coping with turbulence and change:

Strategic IT Management—The Business Outcomes

Deliver Superior Business Value. This consists of strategic effectiveness/ enlargement and operational effectiveness, which includes business and technical risk mitigation, and business and technical cost mitigation.

Deliver Superior Responses to Turbulence and Uncertainty. This consists of faster responses to conditions (as emphasized in Chapter 4), as well as adaptability and flexibility.

Strategic IT Management—The Systemic Capabilities for Producing the Outcomes

Build Trust and Partnership among Business(es) and IT(s). This consists of building the foundation for working together to achieve common goals, the essence of Strategic IT Management.

Provide Business and IT Leadership and Personal Responsibility. This includes individual accountability for results, as well as both business and IT leadership to overcome culture and trust barriers to the partnership.

Adapt to Enterprise and Leadership Characteristics and Culture. One size does not fit all, and Strategic IT Management approaches deal with the uniqueness of each enterprise.

Notes

1. Joseph A. Schumpeter, *Capitalism, Socialism and Democracy* (Routledge 1942), 8.
2. See Chapter 5's "Impact of Technology Turbulence" section for a description of the Hype Cycle.
3. The figure is adapted from the original "Square Wheel" in Robert J. Benson and Marilyn M. Parker, "Enterprise-Wide Information Management: An Introduction to the Concepts," LASC Report G320-2768 (May 1985).
4. See, for example, J. C. Henderson and N. Venkatraman, "Strategic Alignment: Leveraging Information Technology for Transformation Organizations," *IBM Systems Journal* 32, No. 1 (1993).
5. See, for example, Susan Cramm, *8 Things We Hate about IT* (Harvard Business Press, 2010).
6. See, for example, Robert J. Benson and Thomas L. Bugnitz, "Transformative IT: Creating Lean IT Portfolio Management . . . or Not," *Cutter IT Journal* 22, No. 1 (January 2009).
7. Recent developments in the "agile" community describe the barriers to adopting agile methods as people and culture. See, for example, Ken Collier, *Agile Analytics: A Value-Driven Approach to Business Intelligence and Data Warehousing* (Addison-Wesley, 2011) and Jim Highsmith, *Agile Project Management* (Addison-Wesley, 2004).
8. *Unlocking the Computer's Profit Potential* (New York: McKinsey and Company, 1968). See also John Dearden, "MIS Is a Mirage," *Harvard Business Review* (January–February 1972): 90–99.
9. See, for example, Paul Strassmann, *The Squandered Computer: Evaluating the Business Alignment of Information Technologies* (Information Economics Press, 1997) and *The Economics of Corporate Information Systems: Measuring Information Payoffs* (Information Economics Press, 2007).
10. Faisal Hoque et al., *The Power of Convergence: Linking Business Strategies and Technology Decisions to Create Sustainable Success* (Anacom, 2011).
11. See, for another discussion, Erik Brynjolfsson, *The Productivity Paradox* (CACM, 1993).
12. Nicholas G. Carr, "IT Does Not Matter," *Harvard Business Review* (May 2003): 5–12. See also Nicholas G. Carr, *Does IT Matter: Information Technology and the Corrosion of Competitive Advantage* (Harvard Business Review Press, 2004).
13. Michael Porter, quoted in Walter Kiechel, *The Lords of Strategy* (Harvard Business School Press, 2010): "To this day, I completely accept the premise that every company is different, that every company is unique . . . and there was a framework or structure for thinking about competition from which we can generalize."
14. Robert J. Benson, Thomas Bugnitz, and William Walton, *From Business Strategy to IT Action: Making Right Decisions for a Better Bottom Line* (Wiley, 2004).

15. See, for example, Igor Ansoff and Edward McDonnell, *Implanting Strategic Management*, 2nd ed. (Prentice Hall, 1990).

16. See Richard Hunter and George Westerman, *The Real Business of IT: How CIOs Create and Communicate Value* (Harvard Business Press, 2009), p. 8, which discusses avoiding the value trap of "The IT Customer." See also Cramm, *8 Things We Hate about IT*, who emphasizes that business is not an IT customer.

17. See John Ward and Joe Peppard, *Strategic Planning for Information Systems* (Wiley, 2004); Keri E. Pearlson and Carol Saunders, *Strategic Management of Information Systems*, 4th ed. (Wiley, 2009); and Lynda M. Applegate, F. Warren McFarlan, and James L. McKenney, *Corporate Information Systems Management*, 5th ed. (McGraw-Hill International Editions, 1999).

18. See, for the SIS era, "The Strategic Option Generator" chapter in Charles Wiseman, *Strategic Information Systems* (Irwin, 1988).

19. Ward and Peppard, *Strategic Planning for Information Systems*.

20. See Hunter and Westerman, *The Real Business of IT*. For example: "Effective CIOs do more than manage their units well; they help the rest of the company play their parts in producing and overseeing value generation" (p. xii).

21. In a McKinsey study about factors that most directly affect financial performance, flexibility ranked number one. Chris Bradley et al., "Putting Strategies to the Test: McKinsey Global Survey Results" *McKinsey Quarterly, the Online Journal of McKinsey*, www.mckinseyquarterly. com/arciles_aspx? L2=21ar=2011

22. Mark D. Lutchen, *Managing IT as a Business* (Wiley, 2004).

23. See, for example, Chapter 8: Strategic Alignment, in Lane Dean, *The Chief Information Officers' Body of Knowledge: People, Process, and Technology* (Wiley, 2011).

24. O'Conner (1997), quoted in "Mental Model," www.createadvantage.com/glossary/mentalmodel

25. Peter Senge, *The Fifth Discipline: The Art and Practice of the Learning Organization* (Doubleday, 2006).

26. Gary Hamel, *Leading the Revolution* (Harvard Business School Press, 2000), 136.

27. Peter Weill and Jeanne W. Ross, *IT Governance* (Boston: Harvard Press Business School Press, 2004).

28. Amy Edmondson uses the term "framing" to describe how leaders set the context for a cross-organizational or multiorganizational team: "A frame is a set of assumptions or beliefs about a situation." The orientation is to a problem or project, not an enterprise or business unit, but the concept and value is similar. Amy Edmondson, *Teaming: How Organizations Learn, Innovate, and Compete in the Knowledge Economy* (Jossey-Bass, 2012).

29. Gary Hamel, with Bill Breen, *The Future of Management* (Harvard Business Review Press, 2007), 151 and 176.

30. Thomas Davenport, Marius Leibold, and Sven Voelpel, *Strategic Management in the Innovation Economy: Strategy Approaches and Tools for Dynamic Innovation Capabilities* (Publicis and Wiley-VCH GmbH & Co., 2006), 65.

31. Davenport, Leibold, and Voelpel, *Strategic Management in the Innovation Economy*, 65.

32. See three case examples in Chapter 16 for other enterprise examples.

CHAPTER 2

The Barrier
Trust and Partnership

I want to apologise to our Ulster Bank customers for the significant inconvenience caused by these technology problems. I recognise that being sorry is not enough; we believe we have fixed the initial problem and are now making inroads in catching up with the knock-on effects to our customers in Ulster Bank. My colleagues and I are fully committed in support of our Board, management and staff in Ireland who have been tireless in their efforts to support our customers. We recognise that we are important to Ireland. And Ireland is important to us. We have been steadfast in supporting customers in Ulster Bank through the financial crisis, maintaining a full banking service as others have left the banking market. We will continue to meet our responsibilities and ensure we restore normal support to our customers.[1]

STEPHEN HESTER, RBS GROUP CHIEF EXECUTIVE
NATWEST, RBS, AND ULSTER BANKS

The relationship between IT and business is often characterized by a lack of trust and partnership. Yet it should be simple: trust flows from credibility, and partnership flows from trust combined with common goals. But why is such a simple thing so difficult? The answer lies in business and IT performance and culture, how they come together in IT governance, and the lack of understanding of the common goals to be pursued together. This chapter describes performance-based credibility, trust, a performance model, and leadership requirements, to understand the trust and partnership barriers business and IT face.

Trust and Performance Are Highly Correlated

One challenge in writing a book on Strategic IT Management is determining which elements to include and which to ignore. The field is target-rich, replete with juicy opportunities that can release the potential of information technology to improve and advance business value. With apologies to the Royal Bank of Scotland Group, as no one should be bayoneting the wounded, the events that unfolded from June 19, 2012, through July 18, 2012, forced a rewrite of the opening chapters to this book. Frankly, it is hard to think "big strategic thoughts" when the world's second largest bank cannot process payments for up to 13 million customers, as well as countless more who transact elsewhere but were nonetheless affected by the cascading failure of funds to flow through the RBS banking system and into external banking entities. But that is the rub—tactical and strategic thinking can be frequently one and the same or at least prerequisites for one another, as operational issues morph into massive strategic, financial, and reputational dilemmas. Initial reporting on the RBS IT failure suggested that the problem was created when systems maintenance activities caused an error in the scheduling of batch jobs responsible for processing approximately 20 million transactions. This failure is estimated to have cost RBS Group between £100 million and £200 million. Echoes of "for want of a nail" come to mind.

The most anticipated initial public offering (IPO) occurred on May 18, 2012, with the sale of Facebook shares to the public on the NASDAQ Exchange. There was much anticipation and fanfare in the media. To borrow a fishing term, there was lots of chum in the water, and demand was initially projected to be very high. The NASDAQ IT team had extensively tested its systems before the IPO. They took pains to simulate higher trading volumes than actually occurred. But they had not prepared for "increasing numbers of cancelled orders in the hours leading up to Facebook's debut." NASDAQ's chief executive, Robert Greifeld, explained that NASDAQ's ordering system had handled 480 IPOs in the prior five years without incident but was unprepared for the turbulence that Facebook's IPO presented. "Testing didn't account for the increasing volume at which cancellations can come in. . . . And NASDAQ executives relied too heavily on assurances from the exchange's technology group. There was not enough of a check and balance," he said. "We did not have enough business judgment in the process."[2]

These are not two isolated incidents on the shortfalls of routine operations, just two that are topical. Worse, if the focus is shifted to the performance of large IT-enabled projects, the trends are not particularly stirring. The Standish Group publishes a biennial report on IT project performance called the CHAOS Report, which is based on a worldwide survey of several thousand medium to large companies. The latest report, released in 2011, showed that important progress was being made, albeit not fast enough. It revealed that:

- 42 percent of business users believed that their IT projects were challenged (late, over budget, or missing required features/functions)

Exhibit 2.1 Summarized Data from Standish Group CHAOS Report (1994–2011)

	1994	1996	1998	2000	2002	2004	2006	2009	2011
Successful	16%	27%	26%	28%	34%	29%	35%	32%	37%
Challenged	53%	33%	46%	49%	51%	53%	46%	44%	42%
Failed	31%	40%	28%	23%	15%	18%	19%	24%	21%

- 21 percent of business users believed that their IT projects were outright failures
- 63 percent of business users believed that their IT projects were not successful

This last segment of respondents acknowledges that their projects may work technically but that overall business goals were not achieved.

One should not think that IT project success rates have suddenly and mysteriously declined. In fact, success rates in the latest report (37 percent successful) are at the highest point they have been since the Standish Group started their survey in 1994. Unfortunately, as described in Exhibit 2.1, project success rates (delivered on time, on budget, with desired scope, and with expected business results) have been uninspired since the Standish Group began surveying this topic in 1994.

When the data are graphed and trend lines added, the story becomes somewhat less painful (Exhibit 2.2).

In fact, the Standish analysis echoes what many "agilists" in the software development community have been arguing: Agile projects are more successful than non-agile projects. According to the 2011 CHAOS Report, "The agile process is the universal remedy for software development project failure. Software applications developed through the agile process have three times the success rate of the traditional waterfall method and a much lower percentage

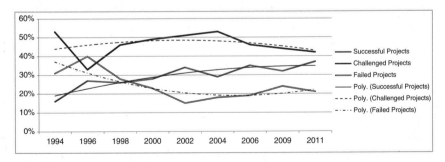

Exhibit 2.2 Summarized Data from Standish Chaos Report

of time and cost overruns." The increased adoption of agile methods and how they attack complexity and uncertainty in software development and project delivery has affected the trend line of project performance.[3]

It is worth noting that the cause of many software project failures can be found in exaggerated or overly optimistic business expectations of what technology can do and an equally simplistic view of what it takes to make software development projects successful. In fact, anyone reading this book should realize that vendor software rarely performs as advertised, and bespoke development is very hard to do without enormous clarity of vision and purpose—rare commodities, both. None of this bodes well for the building of trust.

Not to throw more cold water on the moment, but it is also worth noting that agile methods have been around, in one form or another, since before the Standish Group published its first report on project execution. Put another way, the availability of agile methods says little about IT's mastery of them or even acceptance of this powerful iterative approach by IT and business executives and managers. However, this book was not designed to explore the virtues enshrined in the Agile Manifesto.

In the parlance of organizational learning, failure is required to achieve progress and innovation. Indeed, failure is unavoidable. However, it is possible to fail well. To be clear, failing well is not about celebrating failure, repeating it endlessly and at great cost. Failing well means controlling failure, keeping the cost of failure low, and failing on paper or in a simulation, not after the bricks are set and the mortar has dried. Based on the success rates described in Exhibit 2.1, learning is occurring at a frustratingly slow pace and makes a mockery of the adage "fail fast, fail often, and fail cheap"—failing often represents only one-third of the art of failing well.

Despite weak-to-dispiriting operational and project performance, business leaders continue to spend extraordinary sums on IT-enabled projects and infrastructure. Perhaps they have been convinced that they have little choice; perhaps they believe that the IT profession will eventually discover how to get it right. Gartner Group, an IT advisory company, estimated that worldwide spending in 2011 on information technology was approximately $3.6 trillion. This figure includes all manner of hardware, software, services, and tele-communications. To put this in perspective, the amount of money spent on information technology in 2011 was slightly greater than the gross domestic product (GDP) of Germany, the world's fourth largest economy as measured by the World Bank and International Monetary Fund. Decision makers keep buying the dream, and for 2011, they invested approximately 5.1 percent of global gross world product (GWP) in the promise and potential of information technology to improve business outcomes.

Perhaps the Standish Group has it wrong; maybe project performance is not as bad as their data suggest. After all, the CHAOS Report measures failure as a percentage of projects attempted but does not measure the cost of failed projects or the opportunity cost associated with failure. It could be the case that many projects fail but the cost of failure is not unreasonable. Unfortunately, this argument does not seem to apply. In 2009, Roger Sessions, a leading systems architect, author, and the chief technology officer of ObjectWatch, published a white paper titled "The IT Complexity Crisis: Danger and Opportunity,"[4] which explored the global cost of IT failure and the role that complexity plays in the process. His analysis, which includes direct and indirect costs, concluded that the worldwide cost of IT failures was $6.2 trillion per year. This staggering sum handily exceeds the GDP of Japan, the world's third largest economy.

Perhaps a different methodology will demonstrate less damning data on failure and its concomitant costs. The Internet publishing group ZDnet published its own analysis of the worldwide direct cost of IT failures in 2012.[5] Using a very different methodology, they calculated that better management, operational excellence, and governance could save $3 trillion globally. Though the difference in magnitude is certainly substantial, it cannot be considered surprising given the variability in methodologies employed. The important message is not whether the correct number is $6.2 trillion or $3 trillion, as the true cost of IT failures cannot be precisely calculated in the first place. The point is that both figures boggle the mind and underscore that businesses, governments, nongovernmental organizations (NGOs), and intergovernmental organizations (IGOs) are losing exorbitant sums of money due to IT failures.

The picture is sobering at best. In this context, the notion of strategic IT management can sound high falutin' and pretentious, especially in the midst of crisis.

Trust and Partnership Are Highly Correlated

Technology in isolation has never created strategic value. More importantly, information technology is not a cure-all for systemic business challenges. What matters most is the tight alignment between IT and its organizational business partners. One can only wonder at the level of interaction between IT and its business partners at RBS Group, NASDAQ, or the respondents to the CHAOS Report survey. In the case of RBS Group: What is the role of the business in describing, defining, and validating use-cases for testing? For NASDAQ: Should technology teams really be expected to anticipate all risk variables on their own?

Sophisticated IT capabilities cannot, in a vacuum, lead the charge to faster cycles of innovation, lower defect rates, or higher productivity. The information technology organization can provide tools, capabilities, methodologies, and the like, but as a discipline IT is not a functional expert for sales, marketing, manufacturing, supply chain, and so on. Rather, effective leadership and demonstrated operational excellence are essential prerequisites—attributes that seem underdeveloped if a partnership is to be robust and vibrant. Only when a climate of trust exists can IT help enable businesses achieve their ambitions.

At present, the profile of IT performance is certainly not a recipe for partnership and trust. Since partnerships are built on trust, our focus must shift to improving our understanding of it, discovering its effect on organizations, and learning how to enhance it.

Trust is an elusive and mercurial entity. A precious commodity, it is also intangible, amorphous, fragile, and unquantifiable. Though dimensionless, it has a material effect on interpersonal and organizational relationships. The essence of trust is found in the tension one feels between depending upon someone else versus establishing measurements and controls to make sure that they perform. Anyone who has ever been in a meaningful relationship knows that when trust is low, friction is high. As trust is depleted, the fabric of relationships becomes frayed or worse.

This is true within a company as well. When trust is low, it is as if sand has been inserted into the organization's gears. Every interaction, transaction, strategy, and decision is affected by frictional losses. Enterprise velocity declines, transaction cost increases, and the overhead cost of getting anything done becomes maddening. By contrast, organizations that have learned to operate with high degrees of trust experience the opposite effect. Sand is replaced by a lubricant that removes friction from communications, interactions, and decisions, thus promoting momentum and lift.

D. M. Rousseau[6] suggests that there are three principle types of trust concepts. Importantly, these concepts are not only interconnected but each is the prerequisite for the one that follows. These are:

- *Trusting beliefs*: A secure conviction that the other party has sufficiently strong, favorable attributes (such as honesty, fairness, integrity, and competence) and that their intentions can be trusted
- *Trusting intentions*: A secure, committed willingness to embrace vulnerability and dependence on another party in ways that are strong enough to create trusting behaviors
- *Trusting behaviors*: Actions that demonstrate the reliance upon another party instead of on oneself or on controls; in short, the manifestation of the willingness to depend

President Ronald Reagan's paraphrase of a Russian proverb, "Доверяй, но проверяй," is an illustration of limited "trusting behaviors." Reagan's translation, "trust but verify," was used during negotiations on intermediate nuclear weapons with the former President of the Soviet Union, Mikhail Gorbachev. "Trust but verify" underscores the limits of trust, since "trusting behaviors" were not demonstrated clearly.

Studies suggest that societies with high trust may actually create more goods and services. In effect, economists are starting to believe that trust is partially responsible for the difference between the richest countries and the poorest. Steve Knack, a senior economist at the World Bank, posits, "If you take a broad enough definition of trust, then it would explain basically all the difference between the per capita income of the United States and Somalia."[7]

In his book *The Speed of Trust*, Stephen R. Covey suggests that trust has a significant effect on speed and cost: the greater the trust, the faster the speed; the lower the trust, the higher the costs. In effect, the absence of trust behaves like a tax on transactions, while the presence of trust performs like a dividend. Covey argues that for organizations, trust is a performance multiplier that can be seen in all undertakings from the relationships with suppliers to deployment of new strategies. He states, "You could have good strategy and good execution (10 on a 1–10 scale), but still get derailed by low trust. Or high trust could serve as a performance multiplier, creating synergy where the whole is more than the sum of its parts."[9] This is represented in Exhibit 2.3.

Was there ever a time when IT was not in a deficit position regarding trust? Societal views on any number of subjects are often well represented or shaped by how they are depicted in films. Using cinema as a lens, one sees that film makers have generally viewed computers with suspicion. One need not consider obvious entries like *Dr. Strangelove* (1964), *2001: A Space Odyssey* (1968), *The Terminator* (1984), or *The Matrix* (1999) to find stirring examples of this view. Movies such as Franz Lang's *Metropolis* (1927) or even a playful romp starring Spencer Tracy and Katherine Hepburn called *Desk Set* (1957) make the point quite aptly. Computing in movies is generally seen as something to be feared. Computers led to the subordination of mankind and/or the destruction of the world, become sources of surveillance and control, become the source of job losses, or serve as the wellspring of a maddening bureaucracy.

Part of the challenge of achieving trust flows from how relationships are fashioned and described. The language used to depict the interaction between

Exhibit 2.3   Speed of Trust: Trust as a Performance Multiplier

Strategy	×	Execution	=	Result	Trust Coefficient	=	Net Result
10	×	10	=	100	.6	=	60
10	×	10	=	100	.9	=	90
10	×	10	=	100	1.2	=	120

business and IT is a foundational element of the problem. For most organizations, the relationship is burdened with the baggage of a customer/supplier connection. This is folly. Internal consumers of IT services are not "customers." A company's internal consumption is not and should never be confused with the people who pay real money for the products and services offered by the business.

The notion of internal consumer as customer creates all sorts of relationship problems from the onset. Our culture is replete with invocations on the supremacy of customers: "the customer is king" and "the customer is always right" are merely two that quickly spring to mind. However, internal consumers of internal services (IT or any other) are *not* always right. More importantly, the work profile executed by IT is not designed to make any one line of business or functional area happy; it is designed by executive leadership to maximize business value to the enterprise. IT is cross-organizational, and its impact transcends the need of any single locality, function, or business unit.

A small but vital first step in creating the rapport that promotes trust is to avoid terms with baggage and call internal consumers what they truly are: business partners. Business partners are engaged in the challenge of growing the value of the overall partnership (the business). Along the way, business partners argue and disagree, but they keep coming back to the table because there is respect and agreement about the need for and/or the value of the partnership.

Given their uneven performance, it should come as no surprise that information technology organizations are regularly in the crosshairs for budget cuts, suffer from lack of enterprise status, and must counter and deflect negative perceptions. Until information technology organizations take real and committed actions to address weak project execution and delivery, IT's brand reputation and trustworthiness are unlikely to improve.

However, the challenge of trust for IT organizations is not limited to relationships with business partners. The fact is that for most IT organizations of scale, intrafunctional trust is also very low. Applications and infrastructure operations frequently live in conflict, security operations clashes with operations and development teams, service desk personnel quarrel with technical support . . . the constellation of alignment challenges becomes almost fractal. The irony is that business partners see IT as monolithic and have little interest the internecine disputes that may exist. Regardless, it is difficult to create trust with business partners when an organization cannot stay on message and its members do not rigorously support one another.

Growing trust across an enterprise can seem to be akin to boiling the ocean. It appears to be something so ambitious and so complicated that it is impossible to know where or how to begin. The fact is that growing trust happens in stages or steps. One cannot progress from unreliable resource to trusted counsel and advisor overnight. Trust is not some magnetic field to be reversed or switch that can be thrown. The steps required to build trust in a department or division are similar to the efforts required interpersonally. The question is how frayed is the fabric of trust between IT and the business? Where does the level of trust stand today?

FranklinCovey[10] offers a Speed of Trust Team/Organizational Diagnostic[11] to describe where trust lives today. The diagnostic has been converted into Exhibit 2.4 to provide readers with a means of quickly calibrating where trust lives within IT's many functions and with IT's many business partners.

Exhibit 2.4   Our Adaptation of FranklinCovey Trust Diagnostic

Level	In Organizations	Interpersonally
No Trust	• Dysfunctional environment and toxic culture • Militant stakeholders • Intense micromanagement • Redundant hierarchy • Punishing systems and structures	• Dysfunctional relationships • Hot, angry confrontations or cold, bitter withdrawal • Defensive posturing and legal positioning • Labeling others as enemies or allies • Verbal, emotional, and/or physical abuse
Very Low Trust	• Unhealthy working environment • Unhappy employees • Intense political atmosphere with clear camps and parties • Excessive time wasted defending positions and decisions • Painful micromanagement and bureaucracy	• Hostile behaviors (blaming, accusing, name calling) followed by periods of brief contrition • Guarded communication • Constant worrying and suspicion • Mistakes remembered and used as weapons • Real issues not surfaced or dealt with effectively
Low Trust	• Common cover-your-ass behavior • Hidden agendas • Political camps with allies and enemies • Many dissatisfied employees • Bureaucracy and redundancy in systems and structures	• Energy-draining and joyless interactions • Evidence gathering of other parties' weaknesses and mistakes • Doubt about others' reliability or commitment • Hidden agendas • Guarded (often grudging) dispersing of information
Some Trust Issues Exist	• Some bureaucratic rules and procedures • Unnecessary hierarchy • Slow approvals • Misaligned systems and structures • Some dissatisfied employees	• Regular misunderstandings • Concerns about intent and motive • Interactions characterized by tension • Communications colored by fear, uncertainty, doubt, and worry • Energy spent maintaining (instead of growing) relationships

(continued)

Exhibit 2.4 (*continued*)

Level	In Organizations	Interpersonally
Trust Is Not an Issue	• Healthy workplace • Good communication • Aligned systems and structures • Few office politics	• Polite, cordial, healthy communications • A focus on working together smoothly and efficiently • Mutual tolerance and acceptance • No worries
Trust Is a Visible Asset	• The focus is on work • Effective collaboration and execution • Positive partnering relationships with employees and other stakeholders • Helpful systems and structures • Strong creativity and innovation	• Cooperative, close, vibrant relationships • A focus on looking for and leveraging one another's strengths • Uplifting and positive communication • Mistakes seen as learning opportunities • Positive energy and positive people
World-Class Trust	• High collaboration and partnering • Effortless communication • Positive, transparent relationships with employees and all stakeholders • Fully aligned systems and structures • Strong innovation, engagement, confidence, and loyalty	• True joy in family and friendships characterized by genuine caring • Free, effortless communication • Inspiring work done together and characterized by purpose, creativity, and excitement • Completely open, transparent relationships • Amazing energy created by relationships

Context and Performance Affect Trust and Ability to Partner

Organizations replace CIOs for many reasons. In some cases, a CIO becomes redundant as the result of a merger. In other cases, there may be insufficient bench strength to promote from within when the incumbent CIO chooses to leave the enterprise. Alternatively, business leadership may believe that new perspectives or capabilities are required beyond the level that the incumbent CIO can deliver. In many instances, the inability to forge productive relationships is the underlying driver for a change in IT leadership. As mentors to many CIOs and barring situations where a CIO leaves to pursue more attractive career alternatives, we observe that CIOs are frequently replaced because trust is not manifest in the relationship across the executive team.

Business leaders frequently describe this by saying that "the organization needed a change" or that they do not believe that the CIO "has what we need." Unfortunately, they are rarely able to enumerate their "special" needs in any meaningful detail.

It is not unusual for organizations to employ psychological tests and assessments when hiring to improve the odds against hiring someone that may not be a good cultural fit. Tools like the Personality and Preference Inventory, EQSQ, Enneagram, and the Myers-Briggs Inventory, as well as an array of other psychometric tests, all attempt to assess knowledge, skills, abilities, attitudes, interests, or personality types.

Missing from these tools is an understanding of the key traits that are required of someone who must fill the specific leadership role *at this moment* in the organization's development. In professional sports, teams hire coaches who range from disciplinarians to "a player's coach." Team owners make an assessment of the traits they wish to emphasize given the team's roster and then hire accordingly. A team that is young and talented is likely to choose a coach who highlights discipline and fundamentals. A team comprised of accomplished veterans is likely to emphasize other managerial traits. The key message is that a shared view of the job the coach must perform is understood, beyond just winning games. The disciplinarian coach model is seldom seen on teams comprised of all-star players. That said, misaligned expectations do occur.

The world of IT leadership is even fuzzier and less defined regarding an organization's life cycle needs for its "IT coach." The enterprise may be attempting to respond to compelling shortfalls in operational excellence and cannot conceive of higher-order statements of value or discover new operating paradigms and markets. Prospective CIOs would like to imagine that operational excellence is at least at an acceptable level so they can pursue more interesting, exciting, and valuable pursuits. Unless these views are reasonably aligned, the mismatch that results will rarely set the stage for relationships defined by trust.

This becomes especially true when thinking about the forces that drive someone to become a CIO. Beyond issues of remuneration, many prospective CIOs want the role because they have a vision for how IT can create business value and improve business outcomes, are comfortable with making information technology decisions, and want to responsibly exploit those potentials. It is important to recognize that industry sectors with a low velocity of change will invariably require less dynamic IT capabilities.

When technologies, competitors, products, or customers have long, stable life spans, IT is recognized as an operating cost and is typically focused on cost reduction that can make customer transactions easier. The opposite is true for industry sectors that have a high velocity of change. When technologies, competitors, products, or customers have short, volatile life spans, IT can become a means of competitive differentiation. In this case, businesses require IT capabilities that are more dynamic. IT will tend to focus on creating new sources of revenue, organization transformation, and new forms of value, as well as improved operating margins. Can a transformation-minded CIO be happy and successful in an organization/industry that is characterized by a low velocity of change? We think not; when IT-based transformational energy meets organizational inertia, mass wins. Expectation mismatches at the onset of a CIO's tenure may help describe why building trust can be so elusive.

Trust and the Total Value Performance Model

There are many models that describe how IT must earn the right to contribute to business performance. The version shown in Exhibit 2.5 is based on a staircase metaphor and serves to demonstrate several messages. The over-arching message is the staircase itself, which reflects the journey that IT organizations must travel to achieve the role of trusted business partner. As an IT organization climbs the staircase, the degree of business value enabled by information technology increases as well. You will see several "builds" on this basic model as the book unfolds.

Each step on the staircase represents a level of achievement and perform-ance that must be demonstrated. The right to climb the next stair is not

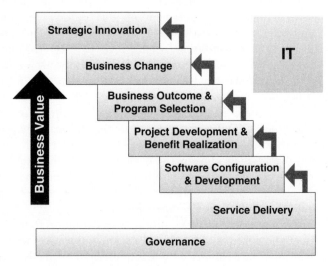

Exhibit 2.5   Total Value Performance Model (IT)

necessarily determined by an external measure of "excellence" or top-quartile performance. CMMI level 5 performance may not be especially meaningful to your business partners. As such, this should not be seen as a maturity model.

The right to ascend is determined by meeting or exceeding the expect-ations of your business partners at each step along the staircase. As IT leadership climbs the staircase, it builds goodwill and trust with its business partners. However, if IT leadership attempts reach beyond its demonstrated level of mastery—say, to influence project selection or strategic alternatives before it has delivered against expectations of operational excellence—it will be rebuffed.

Our staircase model has six steps of mastery. Step 1 is Service Delivery. In short, this means that "the trains run on time": service is reliable and dependable. Once this is achieved, IT leadership can better attend to the challenges on the next stage, Software Configuration and Development. This second stage is focused on the speed to market and level of quality that is associated with IT's delivery of new software or third-party software configu-rations used by the enterprise. Mastery on step 2 delivers software that is functionally complete, easy to use, well architected, well integrated, easy to modify, and absent paralytic levels of technical debt. Step 3, Project Deploy-ment and Benefits Realization, addresses the quality, predictability, and timeliness associated with the deployment of projects.

The first three stages should be considered table stakes; they are basic performance levels and are measured by business expectations. If step 1 mastery is not achieved, performance in stages two and three will be com-promised. The same holds true for the effect of low performance at step 2 and the consequences incurred in step 3. If this were a game of Monopoly, you would not "pass go" and you would not collect $200. You do not get to truly influence how your business operates. Instead, IT is relegated to reacting to the agenda of each line of business. Steps 1, 2, and 3 are basic performance levels that IT must master to create and grow trust.

Again, it is important to remember that for organizations marked by a low velocity of change, the top step of the staircase is likely to be Project Delivery, at least until the industry is under threat and the need for change becomes tantamount with survival.

If the first three steps are basic performance levels, steps 4 through 6 represent more advanced performance levels. Step 4, Planning and Program Selection, is found when IT leaders are trusted to be active participants, influencers, and decision makers in the planning and selection of projects or programs. The emphasis is on trust. At this stage, IT leaders have demon-strated that "the basics" are managed well. When the IT function reliably delivers against its commitments, it can be trusted to reach the next level on the staircase.

Trust and Governance

Interestingly, some two months following the systems failure that compromised the flow of funds throughout the RBS Group and beyond, its chief executive, Stephen Hester, explained that the banking group might have been able to avoid the major IT glitch if it had focused more on keeping its existing systems up-to-date rather than developing new systems. As reported in *The Guardian*:

> RBS has seen a big mushrooming in spending on technology. With hindsight maybe a bit more of that increase in spend should have been in the core, taken-for-granted systems that work every day.[11]

Hester's comments are quite revealing and provide a useful illustration of the foundational layer for business value ascendancy depicted in our stair-step model, which is governance. The concept of IT governance can be a squishy term because it is broad and ill-defined. Let it suffice to say that IT governance is a process that invariably ensures you reap what you sow. Governance must be a holistic balancing act and not a headlong pursuit across one dimension of IT governance.

As suggested by the global IT advisory service Cutter Consortium, the scope of IT governance should include the following components:

- Business Alignment
- Project/Program Selection and Sequencing
- Technology Selection
- Financial Constraints
- Organization Structure
- Risk Management
- Performance Requirements and Measurement

As shown in Exhibit 2.6, governance forms the connective tissue that balances unbridled demand with unfettered supply.

When done well, the role of IT is easy to explain. IT serves the business by enabling its current goals and strategic ambitions while enlarging its plate of future opportunities. In effect, business and IT are an ecosystem, where governance acts as the laws of nature. Overemphasize one area, and like balloon hydraulics, problems will surface in the domains that have been underserved or ignored. For RBS, Hester's comments suggest that basic services across the legacy portfolio did not receive the appropriate level of attention by the group of IT and business executives that constitute the governance process. This is not the same as an IT failure; this is a partnership failure. It comes as no surprise that countless surveys and assessments describe the state of IT governance for many companies as uninspiring and frustrating to the very aims it should seek to achieve.

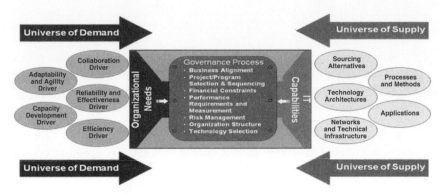

Exhibit 2.6   Governance Processes

In many organizations, protocols and practices are not being done well, if they are being done at all. In some cases, the approaches may be followed religiously but are not suited to the task. When done well, IT governance becomes the vehicle to knit together a more robust fabric of accountability, capability, value, and confidence. It is by matching current practices and accountabilities to the problems and opportunities facing the enterprise, surmounting and surpassing these elements, that trust is built.

When RBS chief executive Stephen Hester speaks of inadequate balance between support for daily operations and innovation, he is describing deficiencies in governance. Similarly, when NASDAQ's chief executive Robert Greifeld says that they did not have enough business judgment in the process of determining the level of testing that would be performed in advance of the Facebook IPO, he too is describing a governance shortfall.

A Case of Broken Trust

A client asked us about methods to increase the trust between IT and business executives and staff. It seemed the relationship was broken: business executives didn't trust IT and vice versa. How did this happen? Why are key business leaders and functional heads squabbling like children?

In our experience with clients, lack of trust between IT and business is not one dimensional, but rather based on several interrelated factors that affect the ability to perform.

1. *Strategic Plan/Roadmaps.* The lack of an agreed-upon strategic plan for investment and support of the business's strategic intentions sows the seeds of confusion and mistrust.

2. *Project Prioritization.* Like IT, the business is also not monolithic; it too has factions. If the process for evaluating and selecting projects results in projects being accepted that are not critical to the enterprise, trust is lost for all parties. When the stack ranking of investment projects appears arbitrary, business leaders will quietly fund their "key" project some other way. This leaves IT unable to respond or support, since this quietly funded initiative is not on their roadmap or radar.

3. *Project Ownership.* In many organizations, IT does not feel co-responsible to ensure the delivery of the business case and its outcomes. The refrain is something like "They run the business, I deliver the technologies and tools." This fuels distrust.

4. *Project Estimates.* When projects are not completed on scope, on budget, and on time, it breeds mistrust for all project estimates. The refrain sounds something like "Whatever cost estimate 'they' developed, just double it."

5. *Business Requirements.* When dynamic businesses operate under turbulence, their ability to offer crisp and complete requirements is compromised. To IT, the business is seen as mercurial and indecisive. To the business, IT is seen as plodding, bureaucratic, and the last place they should go to get problems solved.

6. *(Weak) Project Outcomes.* There may be tendencies to point fingers, which is a behavior that good partners would not demonstrate. Why did our project not achieve the goals stated in its business case? IT will complain that the business didn't know what it wanted, or didn't understand its own processes, or didn't make key resources available or didn't make timely decisions, or any number of other complaints. The business will complain that IT didn't understand the problem, or the technology, or diverted key resources to address something else, or didn't understand the change management plan, or any number of other complaints.

7. *Overall IT Costs.* When IT costs are not transparent (both project costs and ongoing "lights-on" costs), business executives can come to believe that IT is spending money on things that don't benefit the business. When IT is perceived to be spending scarce resources on new technology toys that business executives do not see as enhancing their business goals, suspicions rise and trust is degraded.

The Role of Executive Leadership

Anyone who has led an organization will recognize that the development of a parent–child dynamic within an organization is not unusual. Individual contributors seek approval from their supervisors, sibling rivalry emerges among peers, and bullying will occur unless leaders set the right tone. This makes the discussion on governance and various items described earlier in this chapter all the more frustrating. When children squabble, it is the parent who restores order and sets priorities for the work to be done. Who is the leader that steps up when business units follow their own path? Can the CIO really be expected to take on revenue-producing executives without formidable air cover? The answer to the latter is "not if they expect to keep their jobs" and the answer to the former is "the CEO."

At this point, readers of this book are either cheering or about to close the cover. All we ask it that you hang in there and allow us to develop this thesis. Your shareholders are counting on you.

It turns out that there may be a strong business reason for the "children" to get along and play nicely. PwC, the global audit and advisory company, conducts an annual survey to assess how well companies understand the value of technology and how well they integrate information technology into their organizational business strategies. Administered by PwC's International Survey Unit, the Digital IQ Survey has been conducted for five years.[12] The 2013 Survey reflects responses across a variety of industries, from more than 1,100 people in 12 countries (Australia, Brazil, China, France, Germany, India, Japan, Netherlands, Russia, Sweden, the United Kingdom, and the United States). PwC describes the respondents as "evenly divided between IT and business leaders" and noted that "more than 75% of respondents work in organizations with revenues of $1 billion+."

The survey's findings are very revealing and encouraging. "Within top-performing companies, IT and business leaders are more likely to share the same understanding of the corporate strategy and the costs needed to implement the strategic roadmap." Importantly, they tend to view their CEO as "a champion of IT." By setting the tone for collaboration and inclusion, these chief executives ensure that enterprise leaders act as one. The survey found that top performers tend to have "explicit processes in place to link the IT roadmap to the corporate strategy." As a consequence, these top performers, "strong collaborators" all, achieve superior business results.

Chris Curran, principal and chief technologist at PwC, commented, "These companies clearly have a higher Digital IQ—they understand the value of technology and weave it into every aspect of their organization." The survey's top performers:

> . . . reported revenue growth that was greater than 5% and described their companies as being in the top quartile for revenue, profitability and innovation. Moreover, of top performers, 82% viewed their CEO as a champion of information technology who is "actively involved in driving information technology's inclusion in the strategic and operational dialog."[13]

There is a strong message for ramping up inclusion and collaboration among enterprise executives, including the relationship between the CIO and the rest of the C-suite. It is the CEO who must set the tone for this behavior, or the "children" will get restless. At the same time, we contend that IT must simultaneously take actions to ascend the business value staircase or the CEO will not take IT seriously.

The next chapters describe the issues underlying trust (or lack of it.)

Notes

1. Stephen Hester, "RBS Group Updates on Technology Issues Affecting Its Ulster Bank Customers," RBS Group website. www.rbs.com; www.rbs.com/news/2012/07/rbs-group-updates-on-technology-issues-affecting-its-ulster-bank.html
2. Scott Thurum, *Wall Street Journal*, June 25, 2012.
3. Standish Group, Boston MA, www.standishgroup.com
4. ObjectWatch, Inc., Houston, Texas. http://ww.objectwatch.com/whitepapers/ITComplexity WhitePaper.pdf
5. Michael Krigsman, "Who's Accountable for IT Failure? (part one)," ZDNet, April 16, 2012, www.zdnet.com/blog/projectfailures/whos-accountable-for-it-failure-part-one/15451
6. D. M. Rousseau, S. B. Sitkin, R. S. Burt, and C. Camerer, "Not So Different After All: A Cross-Discipline View of Trust," *Academy of Management Review* 23, No. 3 (1998): 393–404.
7. http://www.forbes.com/2006/09/22/trust-economy-markets-tech_cx_th_06trust_0925harford .html
8. Stephen M. R. Covey, with Rebecca R. Morrow, *The Speed of Trust: The One Thing That Changes Everything* (Free Press, 2008): 3.
9. Covey, *The Speed of Trust.*
10. FranklinCovey, "Speed of Trust Practice." Available at: www.speedoftrust.com/survey/SOT-Diagnostic.php
11. Charles Arthur, "How NatWest's IT Meltdown Developed," *The Guardian*, June 25, 2012, www.theguardian.com/technology/2012/jun/25/how-natwest-it-meltdown
12. PwC's *2013 Digital IQ Survey: Digital Conversations and the C-Suite*, www.pwc.com/us/digitaliq (download report on lower right)
13. www.pwc.com/us/digitaliq

CHAPTER 3

A Staircase to Trust

I n this chapter, we focus on trust as a key condition for effective business–IT collaboration. In the first section, the discussion starts by defining trust and continues with an analysis of the different dimensions of trust and how trust affects business performance. An important question for business–IT collaboration is whether trust can be built intentionally and, if not, how the creation of trust can be supported actively. Trust between business functions and IT constitutes organizational trust. The discussion in Chapters 1 and 2 begets the question: To what extent does personal trust interact with organizational trust?

A compelling basis for trust is competent past performance. Inspired by the work of Abraham Maslow and his hierarchy of needs, in Part II we expand on the staircase model of IT performance and needed capabilities. Each stair represents a level of IT business needs that have to be met, ranging from operational support to strategic innovation. Each level also represents a different *intensity* of business–IT collaboration. Higher levels of collaboration depend on increasing levels of trust created in previous stair steps.

What Is Trust?

The saying "No trade without trust" indicates, in a concise way, the crucial role trust plays in business. And, of course, this occurs not only in business: No sustainable interpersonal relationship can develop in the absence of mutual trust. Trust is a key factor in any situation where people and/or organizations depend on each other. The higher the interdependence, the more important trust becomes. With regard to organizations, mutual trust is a precondition for interorganizational cooperation. Collaboration in the primary activities of the value chain, which aims at a highly efficient supply chain (e.g., through reductions in safety stocks), requires sharing confidential planning information, which will not happen without trust. Collaboration between two firms in product development constitutes a key strategic activity and is unthinkable without the existence of mutual trust. Trust also occurs on an intraorganizational level and is a precondition for superior performance. Without vertical trust between different hierarchical levels and horizontal trust between different groups in the organization, the organization is paralyzed. In the absence of trust, any collaboration is characterized by shielding important information and setting up controls and procedures to protect one's interests. In essence, trust is a critical coordination mechanism.[1]

Trust in a business setting can be defined as the expectation that the other (person or organization) will behave in a mutually acceptable manner; this includes the expectation that neither party will take advantage of the other's vulnerabilities.[2] In the new business environment,[3] characterized by turbulence and complexity, sustainable competitive success is widely perceived as being dependent on the existence of trust between the parties commonly engaged in a business venture. Handling turbulence requires swift actions, which only can be developed if the parties have strong faith in each other. Equally, when facing complex managerial problems (e.g., business and IT), no one has, nor can have, a full view on the situation at hand. As a result, the views and opinions of those implicated in the problem situation should be trusted. Simon and March labeled the situation that occurs under these circumstances *uncertainty absorption*:[4] "Uncertainty absorption takes place when inferences are drawn from a body of evidence and the inferences, instead of the evidence itself, are then communicated." The decision maker, who has to rely on this information, is very limited in his/her ability to judge its correctness, and so must rely on the confidence s/he has on the information provider. Developing trust within business–IT relationships is inherently difficult. Creating business value requires synchrony and symmetry between the parties involved—trust. Generally speaking, more value can be created only as trust grows. However, achieving this harmony requires that all parties recognize their differences in backgrounds, knowledge, and culture as a strength and a unique source of value.

Dimensions of Trust

Trust is a concept with different dimensions. Trust is based on the expectation that the party concerned is competent, open, caring, and reliable.[5] In case of interorganizational trust (e.g., between a supplier and a client), trust encompasses also contractual trust.[6] Competence-based trust refers to the skills and capabilities of the other person or organization in a specific domain. Is the other capable of doing what s/he says s/he will do? It requires a common view on professional conduct and standards in order to assess the activity. It is based on the perception that one can rely on processes and activities performed by the other. The credibility of the other, in this respect, improves with competent behavior through the course of time; it will be built by demonstrated capability in the past to solve problems, by interpersonal skills, and by consistent professionalism.[7]

Openness-based trust is founded on perceived honest, morally sound behavior; open communication contributes to openness-based trust. Openness impacts the willingness to share information and knowledge. *Caring-based trust* refers to the belief that the other party will support my and my organization's interests. This goes beyond the basic expectation that the other will refrain from opportunistic behavior by taking unfair advantage; the other party is also expected to be concerned that my interests will not be damaged.[8]

Reliability-based trust refers to the expected consistency in behavior based on experience with and promises made by the business partner. Personal, not just organizational, integrity and reliability are foundations for reliability-based trust within and between organizations.[9] Finally, *contractual trust* refers to the question of whether the other party will carry out the contractual agreements.[10]

These dimensions also suggest a hierarchy of trust.[11] First, higher levels of trust depend on the existence of competence-based trust or, in interorganizational settings, on contractual trust. If one proves not to be able to do and deliver what was promised or does not live up to one's contractual obligations, there is no basis for higher levels of trust. However, next to competence, openness (showing moral responsibility and positive intentions) is necessary for the other party to accept a potentially vulnerable position.[12]

Trust Improves Business Performance

There is a wide belief that trust improves business performance—the question is, how? First, trust causes a reduction in coordination costs; it is a coordination mechanism in and of itself. Through trust, there is a reduced need for extensive procedures and protocols, for intensive communication and negotiation to reach a mutually supported solution for a specific problem as well as a reduced need to strictly monitor behavior and its outcomes. Further, the presence of trust acts as an antiseptic to CYA (cover your ass) behavior and e-mails. Importantly, under conditions of change, all possible future contingencies need not be anticipated, because one can rely on adequate adjustments (and judgment) when necessary. Second, trust is expected to contribute to innovation and learning. Under conditions of trust, free information and knowledge sharing are possible, as the other(s) are not expected to use these for their own benefit at the expense of the one from whom this information was received. In other words, the other is not expected to behave opportunistically.

Can Trust between Business and IT Be Built?

According to an adage, trust comes by foot and leaves by horse. Establishing trust takes time and is based on past experience of trustworthy behavior; losing trust goes faster. There is considerable disagreement among theorists on whether trust can be built actively. However, it is believed that an organization can adopt and manage practices that promote trust.

Trust between the business functions and the IT function is hampered by a high degree of differentiation between the two domains. Differentiation refers to the degree of segmentation within an organization as a whole. Highly differentiated units are characterized by strong disparities in their goal orientation, values, culture, and knowledge and skill base. Differentiation is a necessary condition for an organization to function, as it provides the specialization in different functions needed to realize the overall organizational goals. However, differentiation also has a downside: It builds mental fences between functional domains. Differentiated units develop their own view—a mental model—of reality and, thus, of the enterprise to which they belong.

Mental models are based on ideas and beliefs that develop from educational backgrounds, structures and environments in which we work, reward and incentive schemes that affect how we operate, and so on. They function like a filter, which allows certain information to flow through while blocking other information that does not fit our mental model. Psychologists refer to the filtering process as *confirmation bias*—seeking information that reinforces our world view and rejecting information that does not. It is worth noting that the confirmation bias grows stronger when confronting dissonance with deeply entrenched beliefs.[13] Our world view or mental models guide our thinking and actions. In our perceived reality, they provide us with a swiftly developed cause-and-effect explanation that helps us to understand the environment in which we work and live. Psychologists refer to the natural creation of perceived reality as our *cognition*.

While mental models provide us with a stable basis for understanding the world around us, they also narrow our perception of this world and blind us to facts that may challenge our deeply held beliefs.[14] When people share a mental model, communication is easy, as everyone attaches the same explanation and meaning to the information exchanged; probably nobody will even challenge that information (which actually is a problem and leads to group-think). When mental models differ strongly, communication becomes more difficult. The different models explain the same reality but in different ways, using different terms, emphasis, aspects, and cause-and-effect relations embedded in them. As a result, shared understanding and shared meaning become very difficult, if not impossible, to achieve.

The theory of cognitive dissonance in psychology proposes that people have a motivational drive to reduce dissonance in their world view and will employ three principle strategies to restore balance to their mental models. They may alter their existing cognitions, add new ones to create a consistent belief system, or reduce the importance of any one of the dissonant elements.[15] A key theoretical assumption is that people want their expectations to meet reality, creating a sense of equilibrium.[16] Likewise, another assumption is that a person will avoid situations or information sources that give rise to feelings of uneasiness or dissonance.[17]

A high degree of differentiation implies the need for barriers for cooperation to evolve.[18] Although there is disagreement as to whether trust can be intentionally created, organizations should act "in a trust-sensitive way when building and sustaining . . . relations or networks."[19,20] Work on trusting relationships should target the different dimensions of trust that we discussed earlier and should aim at creating organizational conditions to overcome the consequences of high differentiation.

The value of overcoming dissimilar mental models should be obvious; the achievement of major initiatives and the advancement of knowledge invariably occurs at the intersection of cross-disciplinary thinking. One need only reflect on such notable projects as the Manhattan Project, the Human Genome Project, or the epidemiology of AIDS as examples.

The different dimensions of trust can be improved by a set of interdependent and mutually reinforcing policies. First, proven competency through past performance is a key condition for business and IT functions to gradually develop and establish reciprocal trust. Performance not only relates to competent execution of responsibilities but also to the ability for partnering in open, caring, and reliable ways. This implies that, on one hand, both IT and business functions should be able to apply the right tools and techniques to ensure the business gets the systems and system support that it needs. On the other hand, applying the right tools and techniques is not enough on its own. A good functioning of the informal organization, through socializing and team development, has proven to be a prerequisite for a sound collaboration.[21]

Related to the latter is a second policy. Open communication about goals, commitments, and intentions has always been an important factor in establishing trust. Communication on each organizational level has to take place regularly and must be embedded in organizational processes and procedures.

Third, various organizational measures can help overcome the barriers of differentiation and different mental models. They include promoting team-based work, encouraging joint training and learning experiences, job rotation, co-location, and the like. In developing information systems, strategy teams can work on themes.[22] IT personnel should develop a competent under-standing of the business it serves, while business managers should understand how IT brings value to the business. Through job rotation, managers can develop a more holistic understanding of the business; IT managers can assume responsibility for a business activity, while business managers may become responsible for an IT activity.[23] The organizational effects of physical prox-imity (or its absence) should be well understood. For instance, taking systems understanding out of business functions and concentrating it in a shared service only makes the consequences of differentiation worse. These types of actions are frequently an impediment to effective communication. At best, they make development of trusting relationships harder to achieve. At worst, trust is not established.

Finally, one must keep in mind that what you cannot measure, you cannot manage. Organizations promoting trust should actively measure and monitor the level of existing trust. To measure trust, objective instruments should be used. Several consulting companies such as FranklinCovey offer tools to facilitate such measurements. These tools generally resemble balanced scorecards.

A good example of one such formal tool is the Organizational Trust Index (OTI) developed by researchers at the University of Colorado.[24] It is based on the trust dimensions discussed previously and assists managers in determining the level of existing trust in their organizations. It provides information on where best to build on a strong foundation of trust and where special attention is needed to enhance existing levels of trust. Once the degree of trust between partners has been measured, the results must be used to increase it further. To this end, boot camp sessions can be effective, but it may also be necessary to replace some of the staff operating at the interface level between business and IT.

Although differentiation has its downside, it is simultaneously necessary for an organization to achieve its overall goals. To overcome the barriers resulting from disparities in knowledge, culture, and the like, organizations introduce boundary-spanning roles. Boundary spanners build bridges between highly differentiated organizational domains. They are able to cope with the different worlds because they understand their culture and their technical content. Their role is to facilitate communication and help to ensure decisions that require the contribution of different domains are reached in a way that satisfies the overall objectives of the firm, rather than the suboptimal objectives of a single domain at the expense of the whole. Referring to the concept of *uncertainty absorption* discussed earlier, boundary spanners are able to overcome the negative consequences, because domain specialists know that expertise is available to assess their statements, which increases overall trust.

For aligning business and IT, there is an intense need for boundary spanners: people who understand both the worlds of business and of IT. These types of professionals have been labeled with different names, such as hybrid managers, or T-shaped managers. They have a competency in both technology and business; they are neither software developers nor installers of infrastructure. They understand how IT functionality can be translated into business benefits.

Personal Trust versus Organizational Trust

Trust between business functions and the IT function works at the level of organizational trust. However, for collaboration efforts to work, personal trust is needed as well.[25] Organizational trust concerns the expectation that the other organization will act in a competent, open, caring, and reliable way. This expectation is based on past performance, reputation, certifications, and other similar requisites. For instance, audits may certify that adequate structures, procedures, and processes have been put in place and are adequately executed, so that a predictable and trustworthy behavior may be expected.

From research on business–IT alignment, we know that having the right tools, models, and techniques in place and being able to apply them correctly is a necessary precondition for effective collaboration between business functions and IT. However, this is not a sufficient condition. From the same research, we know that having good working relations, primarily based on personal trust, is equally important. For example, just having the right data models, process modeling techniques, and formal investment justification methods in place does not result in business and IT working well together if these are not complemented with mutual respect and trust on a personal level. In cases where a high level of differentiation exists, such as between business functions and IT, working on the development of good and respectful working relationships (i.e., personal trust) may be considered a prerequisite to promote organizational trust.[26]

Maslow's Hierarchy of Needs and IT

In the 1940s, Abraham Maslow, a clinical psychologist, developed a world-renowned theory of motivation.[27] The basic assumption of this theory is that people are motivated by their own different needs. These needs are structured in a hierarchy, the so-called *pyramid of needs*. At the foundation of the pyramid are basic physiological requirements for survival, such as food, water, and warmth. Once these basic needs are met, people will progressively move to higher-level needs to achieve personal safety, for a sense of belonging, esteem, and eventually self-actualization. If, however, a basic need is not met fully and satisfactorily, attention moves immediately back from the higher level to the lower level as the most important priority.

These needs are arranged in two categories. The physiological needs, the need for safety, and the need to belong are *deficiency needs*. Deficiency needs are needs that must be satisfied for someone to feel healthy and secure. If deficiency needs are not met, the individual will not develop a healthy personality and will not have the foundation for personal stability necessary to move forward in the needs hierarchy. The second category of needs is called *growth needs*. These are the needs of esteem and self-actualization. After the basic levels of needs have been met, individuals will strive to achieve a comfortable level of self-confidence and respect within groups with which they identify. At the next level, self-actualization, individuals will eventually aim to attain all of which they are capable: their full potential.

Maslow's hierarchy of needs has been popularly applied to management theory and practice as well. It is easy to understand and appealing. Although there is little empirical evidence to support it, Maslow's hierarchy of needs has proven to be a useful metaphor in thinking about various growth models in organization and management. For IT, the model provides an interesting perspective when considering how IT relates to the rest of the business.[28] Having a foundation of reliable IT infrastructure is, for any business, a necessary requirement to survive and function well. After having achieved acceptable levels of stability and basic services, the focus turns to higher levels of need. The business then expects interoperable systems to support efficient execution of business processes and provide reliable information for business decision making. Next, IT may be used to achieve a competitive impact. However, the latter will probably not be on the management agenda if the basic infrastructure needs of available and reliable IT services are not met or are met insufficiently.

Based on existing research[29] and our own experiences, we propose a staircase model of IT performance in Exhibit 3.1 to explain the evolving value of IT to the organization and the consequential interactions between business functions and IT. The Total Value Performance Model (TVPM)[30] is a staircase that applies to both business functions and the IT function, but with a different emphasis: Each stair of competencies mirrors IT-centric performance as well as business-centric performance—in effect, codependent performance. The building blocks of the staircase model resemble Maslow's hierarchy of needs. Instead of focusing on the needs themselves, we address the IS capabilities needed to satisfy each step of the business's need for IT. Each level is described in some detail below, starting from the bottom of the hierarchy.

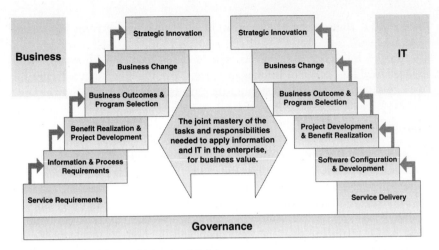

Exhibit 3.1   Total Value Performance Model

This is not the first staircase performance model.[31] Organizational models describing how organizations develop through levels of growth or maturity have been popular in the management literature for a long time. A well-known model is the one from Greiner, which describes phases that organizations go through as they grow.[32] In other management areas, growth models have been developed as well—for example, in knowledge management[33] and more recently in e-government.[34]

Also the field of IT management has its models of growth in IT utilization and management. Two interesting papers that review the various existing models are Galliers and Sutherland's article on information system management and strategy formulation[35] and Poeppelbuss and colleagues' article on maturity models in information systems research.[36]

Governance

The business relevant deployment of the competences needs to be founded on adequate governance. As defined by ISACA, "IT governance consists of the leadership and organizational structures and processes that ensure that the organization's IT sustains and extends the organization's strategies and objectives."[37] In 2009, Van Grembergen and De Haes focused on enterprise governance of IT and defined this as "an integral part of corporate governance", something which "addresses the definition and implementation of processes, structures and relational mechanisms in the organization that enable both business and IT people to execute their responsibilities in support of business/IT alignment and the creation of business value from IT enabled investments."[38]

In the following, we first describe, stair-by-stair, the IT competencies needed for IT to be a true business partner. Next, the discussion will continue with the business competencies and the necessary business–IT interactions.

Service Delivery

At this level, the focus is on IT infrastructure and operations. The IT organization must ensure that basic IT services are delivered against agreed-upon service levels and at an acceptable cost. In addition, the right technologies and organizational capabilities must be in place or must be sourced, and appropriate standards, methods, and procedures for the utilization of IT resources must be developed and applied. Available staff must possess the skills to answer the organization's needs. At this level of the TVPM, the business views the contribution of the IT function as one that provides acceptable support for the technology infrastructure that has been deployed.

Software Configuration and Development

Here, the IT organization must demonstrate the ability to develop, acquire, and implement technology solutions that satisfy the business's transactional and informational needs. As suggested by Maslow's second level, which focuses on safety-related needs, the TVPM assumes that the IT organization already will have technical and organizational measures in place to ensure a secure operation that guarantees confidentiality, integrity, and availability (CIA). It is not a surprise that at this level, management typically recognizes the critical nature of IT in providing and contributing to successful business operations.

Project Development and Benefit Realization

The third step is marked by an IT function that has expanded its impact and value and now has the ability to optimize business benefits from investments that have high information technology content. Benefits will be identified, planned, delivered, measured, and monitored. The IT organization will contribute to delivering the required organizational changes that will maximize the contribution of the planned business system.

Business Outcome and Program Selection

At this level on the staircase, the IT organization must demonstrate its ability to collaborate closely with its business partners so that business strategy and intentions can be translated into strategic IT intentions and solutions. It is here that IT technology trends are not only actively monitored by the IT organization but form an input for business strategic planning, including decisions concerning the strategic sourcing of IT.

Business Change

This level refers to the ability to implement business strategy by investing in programs with high levels of IT content. These business investments invariably require significant change plans because of their effects on markets, products, structures, processes and procedures, and IT. Plans are thoroughly integrated– business and IT change plans. This stair step includes the ability to prioritize technology-enabled investments across the organization according to business objectives.

Strategic Innovation

At this level, an organization develops unique uses of IT that form the basis for a radical change in its business model: IT becomes a key driver of innovation. Business strategy development is the result of co-creation. The business vision affects the IT solutions to be applied, and new IT solutions affect the business's vision.

Analogous to the Maslow hierarchy of needs, embedded in this staircase are the three basic stairs of Service Delivery, Software Configuration and Development, and Project Development and Benefit Realization, which may be viewed as *foundational needs*, as described earlier.[39] If these are not met, the business cannot develop, or at least will be hampered in its development. Thus, having the ability to act successfully within each of these three stair levels is important for any organization, even when IT functions in a supporting role. The growth needs, comprising the stair steps of Business Outcome and Program Selection, Business Change, and Strategic Innovation, however, need not be addressed to the same extent by every organization. It will depend on the role information technology plays in the industry and within the particular firm. If the role is already a strategic one, then indeed, these growth needs are present and will need to be fulfilled. If the role of information technology within the industry is limited to a back-office, factory-type function, it is less probable that growth needs will be actively pursued. Consequently, it is not necessary for every organization to progress on the staircase in the same way.

Growth needs are unlikely to be addressed when the enterprise must contend with a faulty and unstable infrastructure or is not able to identify and effectively develop new applications that may benefit the organization.

Management's attention and priorities automatically shift to solving these operational problems. As discussed earlier, past performance (in this case, of the IT function) is an important basis for trust. Under these conditions, it is highly unlikely the IT function will be invited into the boardroom to discuss business strategy.

Business Requirements for Total Value Performance

The relationship with business functions changes within the staircase framework (see Exhibit 3.1, Total Value Performance Model, and the subsequent discussion). From the basic stairs upward, the IT function moves gradually from a support function to a business partner, critical to the organization's future. For the first two stairs, interactions between business and IT are tactical, concerned with service delivery to users. At the lowest level, business functions are expected to define their *Service Requirements*. These have to be met by the IT function's Service Delivery apparatus. At the next level, business functions need to define their *Information and Process Requirements*, which are the input for *Software Configuration and Development*. For the next level, closer collaboration with the business is necessary to establish how best to optimize IT's contribution to the business as a whole. Here, business-side IT capabilities resemble the IT-side IT capabilities. The important distinction is one of emphasis—where IT is oriented on *Project Delivery* in the first place, the focus of business functions is on *Benefit Realization*. At this level, it is a primary business responsibility to ensure adequate conditions (like sufficient training) for optimal utilization of installed systems. As prior research has indicated,[40] the capabilities of being successful with IS, particularly on the higher growth stairs, are not located within the IT function alone. Business functions have a responsibility, too. The capabilities to identify, select, deploy, and implement new IT-based solutions, which are in line with the business strategy, need to exist in the business functions themselves. Business managers need to:

- Understand how IT can affect their organizations and processes
- Identify strategic business opportunities with IT
- Assess technological innovations on their applicability in the business
- Understand the potential impact on their business model as well as the industries in which they operate
- Prioritize investment opportunities
- Manage IT-enabled change, vendors, and the like[41]

The next stairs concern *Business Outcomes & Program Selection*, *Business Change*, and eventually *Strategic Innovation*. From here on, the higher one goes on the staircase, the more intense the business–IT collaboration will be and the more important all dimensions of trust become. Our prior discussion on the effects of trust is very relevant at this level, with the remark that for trust to exist at growth levels, it first has to be earned at foundational levels. If the company is unhappy with IT's performance and contribution, there will be no room for IT to participate in strategic discussions in the boardroom. However, this situation also applies the other way around. If business functions are not able to show a competent performance in these matters, it is the IT function that loses trust, regardless of where the deficiencies actually lie. Besides the negative impact this will have on the business–IT relationship (and thus on the overall long-term company performance), valuable IT professionals may lose interest and leave the company as a result.

How Does Trust Affect IT Strategy in Turbulent Times?

Change and turbulence force the organization to adapt. Business and technology factors compel companies to continuously monitor and reconsider their position in their competitive environments. Business models and business processes are adapted to respond to change. To an increasing extent, these reactions are based on a fusion of business knowledge and IT knowledge. New governance and business models are not feasible without adequate IT support; even defining those models requires knowledge of IT trends and possibilities. In short, defining the strategy, and thus the future of the company, is a matter of co-creation and close collaboration between business functions and IT.

The new governance structures, business models, and business processes have to be implemented. These implementations touch the heart of the organization. Besides IT change, they encompass business changes. Changes in reporting relationships (i.e., governance structure), in business models, and in business processes fundamentally affect the ways of thinking and the ways of working for everyone involved. Cultures that developed within departments frequently need to change. Achieving alignment when designing the appropriate strategy is hard; achieving alignment when implementing the new strategy is even harder, as it potentially affects everyone in the organization. Close partnership between IT and business at all levels is a critical success factor to make this happen;[42] without it, those efforts will not succeed.

While preparing for the future, current operations must go on and service levels have to be maintained: "performing while transforming," as Marilyn Parker characterized it in an earlier publication.[43] Adequate service delivery also requires good working relationships between IT and business functions.

In short, co-creation of new strategies and implementing them, while maintaining an effective operational performance, requires a close partnership between business and IT at all levels, not only in formal processes, but also in informal working relationships.[44] Trust is a key ingredient to make this happen. We defined trust as "the expectation that the other (person or organization) will behave in a mutually acceptable manner, and in particular, will be competent, open, caring, and reliable." Past good performance in each of these dimensions, complemented by various organizational policies, contributes to trusting relations. Given the high degree of differentiation between business functions and the IT function in terms of knowledge base, values, and culture, an active policy on creating conditions for trust should be pursued.

Based on Maslow's hierarchy of needs, we designed a staircase of IT performance characterized by different performance requirements and capabilities per level. The lower-level capabilities, addressing certain foundational needs, ensure the company functions operationally in an effective way. Here, business trust in IT is built through reliable IT services and support. However, at this level, the interaction between business and IT is limited. The higher-level capabilities, addressing the growth needs, prepare the company for the future; they require a much closer integration of business and IT. Although not all organizations necessarily operate on these stairs, we expect that only a few of them can afford not to do so. Still, the trust that is necessary at these levels of collaboration is built on the way that lower foundational needs are met.

Trust must be reciprocal; IT must trust the business, also. Business must be engaged in tough IT decisions; this is not a spectator sport. Consequently it needs (to develop) the required competencies and capabilities for it. If not, IT will lose trust in the business.

Producing Business Outcomes—An Assessment

The TVPM describes six levels of performance that build the credibility basis for trust for both business and IT. While it is straightforward to look at the underlying methods in use (e.g., strategic planning or service management), credibility and trust come from the business outcomes actually produced. That is, processes and methodologies are good, but actual outcomes are better.

Exhibit 3.2 offers example (business) outcomes for each staircase level from the business perspective. This is not an exhaustive list, but does suggest what does actually create credible (and valuable) outcomes. The figures show example outcomes in two contexts: those that relate to "superior business value" and those that relate to "superior response to turbulence and uncertainty." And, perhaps most importantly, these outcomes apply both to business and IT performance, according to the staircase model Exhibit 3.1.

Exhibit 3.2   Business Outcomes: Superior Value from IT

Total Value Performance Model (Combined IT and Business Perspective)	Examples of Business Outcomes: Execution & Performance for "Superior Business Value"	Current Status— Assessment
Strategic Innovation	• Business strategic effectiveness, direct support for strategic intentions • Transformative changes to the business model • Transformative changes in relationships to market and customer	2
Business Change	• Improvements in business's operational effectiveness • Changes to the business organization and processes • Changes to relationships in the supply chain	1
Business Outcomes & Program Selection	• Effective business change management • Priorities based on business strategies and requirements	2
Benefits Realization/ Project Development	• Business requirements across the enterprise are defined and met • Successfully implemented and business-operationalized projects	3
Requirements & Development	• Projects meet business requirements • Successfully developed/completed projects • Successfully acquired software and solutions	4
Service Requirements & Delivery	• Cost and risk mitigation are supported • IT services meet business requirements • IT services support and do not disrupt business processes	5

Scale:
5. These business outcomes are often produced through the use of information and IT.
4. These business outcomes are occasionally produced through the use of information and IT.
3. Don't know, or this does not apply to my enterprise.
2. These business outcomes are made more difficult by issues with information and IT performance.
1. These business outcomes are inhibited by issues with information and IT performance.

Exhibit 3.2 does not deal with turbulence and uncertainty, something we'll introduce in Chapters 4 and 7. The outcomes described here form the basic expectations for delivering superior value from IT. This is the starting point for credibility and trust.

Exhibit 3.2 shows the current assessment for a typical enterprise named Angus International. See the Introduction to Part IV for a description of this enterprise.

The reader is encouraged to apply Exhibit 3.2 to the current situation in his/her enterprise. While the exhibit is not intended as an exhaustive set of characteristic business outcomes for each stair-step stage, it provides enough information to allow the reader to make an assessment of the current situation. As it is not a complete picture, the result should show current level of performance; we would expect 5s for the lowest stair steps, and where they become less than that, the stair-step status is defined. Note in particular that we do *not* use the process/methodology tests here. In effect, it does not matter how well the business–IT organizations perform the methodologies at stair-step level; what matters is the business outcomes actually produced.

We will add the business outcomes pertaining to turbulence and uncertainty in Chapters 4 and 7. We will connect these example outcomes to the Strategic IT Management descriptions in Parts II and III, to show how enterprise IT competencies and capabilities can be built and used to produce business outcomes like these.

References

Bytheway, A. *Exploring Information Management.* Downloaded from: www.imbok.org/docs/ExploringIM.pdf, on October 2012.

Lawrence, P., and J. Lorsch. "Differentiation and Integration in Complex Organizations." *Administrative Science Quarterly* 12 (1967).

Swan, J. E., and J. J. Nolan. "Gaining Customer Trust: A Conceptual Guide for the Salesperson." *Journal of Personal Selling and Sales Management* (1985).

Notes

1. C. Lane, "Introduction: Theories and Issues in the Study of Trust," in *Trust within and between Organizations*, ed. C. Lane and R. Bachman (Oxford University Press, 1998).
2. M. Sako, "Does Trust Improve Business Performance?" in *Trust within and between Organizations*, ed. C. Lane and R. Bachman (Oxford University Press, 1998).
3. See Stacey Hamaker, "Spotlight on Governance," *ISACA Journal* 1 (2003), www.isaca.org/Journal/Past-Issues/2003/Volume-1/Pages/Spotlight-on-Governance.aspx
4. J. G. March and H. A. Simon, *Organizations* (Wiley USA, 1958).

5. A. K. Mishra, "Organizational Responses to Crises: The Centrality of Trust," in *Trust in Organizations*, ed. R. M. Kramer and T. Tyler (Beverly Hills: Sage, 1996).
6. Sako, "Does Trust Improve Business Performance?"
7. K. Blomqvist and P. Stahle, "Building Organizational Trust," in the Proceedings of 16th Annual IMP Conference, 2000.
8. Mishra, "Organizational Responses to Crises."
9. Blomqvist and Stahle, "Building Organizational Trust."
10. M. Sako, "Does Trust Improve Business Performance?"
11. M. Sako, "Does Trust Improve Business Performance?"
12. Blomqvist and Stahle, "Building Organizational Trust."
13. Scott Plous, *The Psychology of Judgment and Decision Making* (McGraw-Hill, 1993).
14. P. Senge, *The Fifth Discipline: The Art and Practice of the Learning Organization* (Doubleday, 2000).
15. L. Festinger, *A Theory of Cognitive Dissonance* (Stanford University Press, 1985, first published 1957).
16. Michael Ryan, ed., *Introducing Communication Theory: Analysis and Application* (McGraw-Hill, 2010), 113–116.
17. Ryan, *Introducing Communication Theory*.
18. Lane, "Introduction."
19. J. Sydow, "Understanding the Constitution of Interorganizational Trust," in *Trust within and between Organizations*, ed. C. Lane and R. Bachman (Oxford University Press, 1998).
20. Blomqvist and Stahle, "Building Organizational Trust."
21. P. M. Doney and J. P. Cannon, "An Examination of the Nature of Trust in Buyer–Seller Relationships," *Journal of Marketing*, 61, No. 2 (1997): 35–51.
22. J. Ward and J. Peppard, *Strategic Planning for Information Systems* (Wiley, 2002).
23. M. M. Parker, *Strategic Transformation and Information Technology: Paradigms for Transforming While Performing* (Prentice Hall, 1995).
24. P. Shockley-Zalabak and K. Ellis, *Measuring Organizational Trust—Trust and District across Cultures* (IABC Research Foundation, 1999).
25. F. Fukuyama, *Trust* (Hamish Hamilton, 1995).
26. Blomqvist and Stahle, "Building Organizational Trust."
27. R. A. Baron, *Behavior in Organizations* (Pearson, 1999).
28. R. N. Urwiler and M. N. Frolick, *The IT Value Hierarchy: Using Maslow's Hierarchy of Needs as a Metaphor for Gauging the Maturity Level of Information Technology Use within Competitive Organizations* (Information Systems Management, 2008).
29. J. Peppard and J. Ward, *Beyond Strategic Information Systems: Toward an IS Capability* (Strategic Information Systems, 2004).
30. See Chapter 2 for an introduction of the TVPM to IT.
31. See R. J. Benson et al., *From Business Strategy to IT Action* (Wiley, 2004), 255. There, Bill Walton established the Five Performance Stages Model.
32. See Larry Greiner, "Evolution and Revolution as Organizations Grow," *Harvard Business Review* (May–June 1998).
33. See Petter Gottschalk, "Toward a Model of Growth Stages for Knowledge Management Technology in Law Firms," *Informing Science* 5, No. 2 (2002).
34. Kim Viborg Andersen and Helle Zinner Henriksen, "E-Government Maturity Models: Extension of the Layne and Lee Model," *Government Information Quarterly* 23 (2006).
35. R. D. Galliers and A. R. Sutherland, "Information Systems Management and Strategy Formulation: The Stages of Growth Model Revisited," *Journal of Information Systems*, No. 1 (1999).
36. Jens Poeppelbuss, Björn Niehaves, Alexander Simons, and Jörg Becker, "Maturity Models in Information Systems Research: Literature Search and Analysis," *Communications of the Association for Information Systems* 29, Article 27 (2011). Available at: http://aisel.aisnet.org/cais/vol29/iss1/27

37. ISACA, See Office of Government Commerce. Service Delivery. IT Infrastructure Library. (The Stationery Office, 2001).
38. W. Van Grembergen and S. De Haes, *Enterprise Governance of IT: Achieving Strategic Alignment and Value* (Springer, 2009).
39. The Maslow Hierarchy of Needs model uses the term "deficiency needs." In our context, we prefer to use the term "foundational needs."
40. Peppard and Ward, *Beyond Strategic Information Systems*.
41. Peppard and Ward, *Beyond Strategic Information Systems*.
42. March and Simon, *Organizations*.
43. Parker, *Strategic Transformation and Information Technology*.
44. Peppard and Ward, *Beyond Strategic Information Systems*.

CHAPTER 4

IT Strategy in Turbulent Environments

A key theme of this book is how turbulence and change impact the formation of IT strategy and IT strategy itself. In this chapter, we define *change*, distinguish levels of change, and finally delineate the meaning of *turbulence*. Next, we discuss how organizations in general may deal with change and turbulence in order to remain effective. In particular, we will discuss the impact of environmental turbulence on necessary organization capabilities. This will take us to the discussion of how IT and IT strategy are affected by change and turbulence, and eventually, how IT and management may cope with change and turbulence.

Change and Turbulence Defined

Since the 1960s, the notion that the context in which organizational activities take place affects the way they are managed is well developed in management theory. In their seminal work, two Harvard professors, Lawrence and Lorsch,[1] analyzed how environmental uncertainty and complexity under which an organization operates determine how it will be managed. Their analysis was supported by many case examples. "Environment" refers to factors outside the control of the organization's management. Environmental factors may be both internal and external to the organization. Market developments are one example of an external environmental factor; the potential for unpredictable decision making by the sales department is an example of an internal environmental factor for the manufacturing department. Different functional domains have their own environment; different management levels deal with their own environments as well. These (sub)environments may differ in uncertainty and complexity, which results in different management and organization challenges per functional domain or organizational level. Managing these differences, while assuring integration of the company's organizational structure and delivering acceptable to superior enterprise performance, is one of the more challenging demands on management, according to Lawrence and Lorsch.[2]

To understand the impact of uncertainty on management, we have to distinguish factors that management can control and those they cannot. This is, of course, a quite binary approach; in reality, the situation is mostly gray, with factors that are partially controllable or not. However, for the sake of analysis, this distinction is useful. For those factors that are controlled, management may make their decisions—that is what control is about, after all—by choosing one course of action out of a set of possible courses of action in the pursuit of expected results. For those factors that are not controllable, however, there is nothing to decide. For example, one can decide yes or no to swimming in the North Sea; one cannot decide the tides. For any organization, profit or nonprofit, these are just factors it must take into account and that will affect its decisions. Similarly, one can decide not to swim when the sea is retreating. These factors affect the results of activities in which the organization is involved. The bottom line is they may increase or decrease costs and revenues and, thus, the financial health of the organization.

Companies are confronted with these "environmental factors" when making plans. Planning has been defined as "anticipatory decision making":[3] A plan contains decisions that will be executed and have an impact in the future. This future may be quite soon (short-term planning, e.g., operational planning) or may be in a more distant future (long-term planning, e.g., strategic planning). Management makes plans about factors they can control; making a plan about something one cannot control is useless. Accounting for the future impact of noncontrollable factors requires forecasts. These forecasts relate to which factors have to be taken into account and to what extent their impact will have. If the future state is near (e.g., tomorrow), the forecast will be more reliable than if the future state is further away. When making decisions, one needs to rely on forecasts, and their accuracy affects the reliability of human decisions.

Under conditions of relative certainty in major parts of its environment, an enterprise can, for the most part, initiate its own agenda of change.[4] Under stable conditions, when launching a new product line or entering a new market, an enterprise would make incremental, planned modifications to its organization, strategy, and technology support. Strategies and operational planning methodologies would focus on change management, based upon those assumptions that the enterprise could anticipate, plan for, and methodically integrate any change into its existing structure. Businesses used to have yearly strategic planning sessions to plan for incremental changes for the next year, and every two to five years they developed (or updated) a long-range plan. This was an effective approach in a relatively stable economic environment. But for IT strategy development, many business managers did not include the IT organization in its strategic sessions. They were advised by managers on a need-to-know basis, and only after completion of the strategic business plan.

How different a dynamic environment is. A dynamic environment is the opposite of a stable environment, with regard to both how the environment looks and how the organization has to deal with it. It changes frequently, if not constantly, in an unpredictable way. The turn of this century coincided with an increasingly turbulent and competitive business landscape, in which the intensity, unpredictability, and diversity of change accelerated to create a condition of constant flux.[5,6] D'Aveni describes this business environment as "hypercompetitive," characterized by:[7]

- Time and cost compression in product-life and design cycles
- Accelerating technological advancements
- Fickle customer loyalty
- Unexpected entry by new competitors and repositioning of incumbents
- Redefinition of industry and organizational boundaries
- Lethargic economic growth

The combination of these developments creates a new contextual environment for most businesses, involving reassessment of potential markets, customers, and competitors. The problem is how much time is available for making these reassessments and for developing new plans. Under conditions of relative certainty, changes can be predicted relatively far in advance, leaving ample time for the organization to make adjustments. However, under highly unpredictable and ambiguous conditions, there is no time to reassess and plan; unexpected changes occur almost immediately. In this context, elongated strategic planning processes and cycles have all the benefit of a séance. The organization must be able to adapt flexibly to changing conditions.

From this follows that change per se does not cause many problems, provided that organizations have time to prepare for it. Problems arise when they don't, or when, to put it more precisely, the available time to react to change is shorter than the time needed for preparing and implementing a response. This happens when changes are difficult to predict and the time to adapt (reaction time) is long. In line with Ansoff,[8] we shall refer to the degree of changeability of environmental challenges as the "level of environmental turbulence." The level of turbulence is determined by a combination of numerous factors, as listed earlier. High levels of turbulence are characterized by highly uncertain and unexpected events.

Exhibit 4.1 depicts the effect of uncertainty on planning. The figure applies to any (functional) area for which planning takes place and to each of the planning levels we distinguished. So it may represent a situation, for example in supply chain management, in marketing as in IT. It also applies to

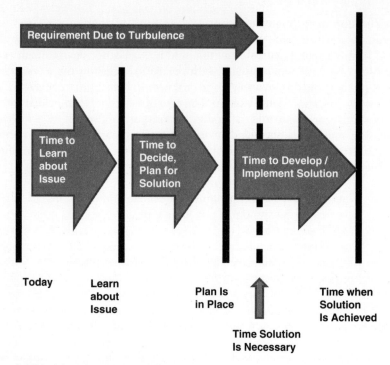

Exhibit 4.1   Uncertainty and Planning

planning on a strategic, tactical planning, and operational level. The figure shows a decision maker who finds out "today" that in the foreseeable future, the current activities of the firm, a department, or the like will be affected by a change in environmental conditions. The decision maker may be the corporate management team, a chief experience officer (CXO), or a departmental manager. The change in conditions may be an important client who will discontinue a contract; a supplier of a critical raw material who will be out of business; a sudden turndown of the economy; the IT services supplier who stops supporting one of the key systems; and the like. As a consequence, existing plans need to be adapted or reconsidered in order to create a solution for the new situation at hand. The dotted line shows when the solution will be needed. In this example, the solution is achieved much later than when it is actually needed.

The actual time available for developing a solution comprises the time that elapses between when management learns about the issue and the moment that a solution has to be implemented and available. We call this the available "reaction time." The important management question here is how the available reaction time relates to the necessary reaction time.

The reaction time consists of a few stages. First the organization has to "learn about the issue." Available forecasts, business intelligence, and the like indicate a change in an external condition is likely to happen in the near future. It depends on the predictability of the environment how "near" this actually is: is it within five years or five months? Next, having learned about and having assessed the situation, the organization needs to develop a response: In other words, it needs to come up with a solution for the new problem. This second step takes time, which is dependent on the seriousness of the problem and the number as well as level of stakeholders involved in the decision-making process. Finally, the solution has to be developed and implemented. The three stages also make clear that when dealing with environmental change, management is confronted with different types of uncertainty, which are inherent to the stages. First, there is uncertainty about whether or not an issue will happen. Second, leaders must assess the environment change on a temporal plane. Third, if there is agreement that it is likely to happen and that a response is required and can be developed, management must posit the likely consequences that will unfold. Next, there is the uncertainty about how to respond to the issue and what the likely implications will be for the range of responses that are available to select. Finally, there is uncertainty about the success of the implementation of the new plan.

The organization is in trouble if more time is needed than is available to react. Compare the situation of a driver on the highway who sees a traffic jam far enough in advance to stop his car before reaching the point of congestion. If, however, the available time to react is shorter than the time needed, then both the driver and the manager are in trouble. For the manager this means that a workable solution for the problem is not (yet) available and/or implemented when the change hits the company (and for the driver that he will probably crash his car). The latter situation characterizes management under turbulence. Due to high levels of uncertainty, it is almost impossible to foresee changes in timely way and be prepared for the arrival of the new uncertainty.

How to deal with change has always been an important issue for organizations. Change requires an organization to be adaptable and responsive. Conditions of stability do not impose an acute level of responsiveness on an organization; even a blind squirrel can find an acorn if given enough time and an absence of predators. Enterprises that principally operate in stable conditions (i.e., markets, products, customers, etc.) are typically designed to promote efficiency, control, and predictability of behavior/outcomes. However, different levels of change require different levels of responsiveness. When change is reasonably predictable, the organization must have the capabilities to adjust, on a timely basis, its structures, processes, and systems. However, when confronted with change that is unfamiliar (i.e., scale, range, depth, speed, etc.), this type of flexibility may not be sufficient. Under these conditions, organizations need the capability to "sense and respond":[9] to detect potentially important developments and respond to them by adjusting their ways of working beyond its normal level of flexibility. This is called business agility. In the next section, we discuss the impact of high levels of turbulence on organizations.

How Do Organizations Cope with Change and Turbulence?

In this section, we discuss how environmental change and turbulence affect the functioning of organizations. Basically, under these conditions, organizations have to deal with two challenges: to be informed in as timely a manner as possible about developments that will affect them, and to be able to adapt fast enough to changing conditions. These challenges require new competencies, structures, and processes. They also require a different support from IT itself. The business and enterprise architecture have a key role in creating business flexibility and agility, while maintaining necessary levels of efficiency.

Impact of Turbulence on Structure and Processes

Organizations facing environmental turbulence are confronted with two fundamental problems: the inability to make reliable forecasts over a period that is long enough, and the inability to react fast enough. Under high turbulence, the assumptions that underlie an organization's current plans (e.g., marketing, supply chain, IT, etc.) will change, which will force changes to these plans. If not, the organization's performance (financial, operational) will deteriorate. The challenge is to be aware of potentially disruptive environmental events as early as possible, despite unreliable forecasts. Moreover, regardless of how early the organization may be informed in advance of disruptive events, it will need to react as quickly as possible by swiftly formulating and implementing new plans. As Steve Haeckel states, the organization needs to sense and respond.[10]

To be better informed and so design plans that better fit environmental conditions, the organization needs to develop specific competencies:

- Perform environmental scanning: surveying the organization's environment, including subenvironments, for each functional activity, such as marketing, manufacturing, IT, and so on in order to have early visibility of upcoming developments.

- Develop early warning signals that have to be watched closely in environmental scanning activities.
- Develop approaches and models to improve statistical analyses and forecasts (business analytics).
- Develop an (internal) organization based on open and transparent communication, instead of one based on command and control. Open and transparent communication crossing functional and other silos is a prerequisite for fast decision making.
- Engage in partnership relations with key stakeholders who control important environmental factors, like suppliers, clients, and so on. Through collaboration with key stakeholders, the organization may exert some influence on key environmental developments.
- Engage in scenario planning; scenarios offer a view on possible futures. They are not statistical extrapolations but present likely futures under assumptions associated with key environmental conditions.[11] Importantly, to be useful to the enterprise, scenarios need not unfold as envisioned. The process of scenario planning, if done well, should reveal useful responses to scenarios that are directionally similar to those that were developed. Borrowing from the former president of the United States, Dwight D. Eisenhower, "In preparing for battle I have always found that plans are useless, but planning is indispensable."

This strategy of trying to be better informed ("knowing earlier"[12]) about future conditions under which the firm will operate basically aims at giving the organization more time to react and be better prepared for what is coming.

A second and different approach is to improve the speed of the organization and so its ability to react faster. This helps the organization by quickly creating intelligent responses and implementing them before change hits. This strategy directly affects organizational design, as the ability to react swiftly requires a change in structure, processes, and culture.

Conditions of certainty and stability underline the necessity of efficiency and economies of scale as well as predictable and controllable behavior. The organizational structure is characterized by high functional (task) specialization, centralized control and decision making, many rules and procedures (as most decisions relate to recurring situations), an emphasis on consistency versus invention, strict hierarchy, and vertical communication. Coordination is mainly achieved through vertical linkages.[13] The most important of these is hierarchical referral, especially for problems that involve two or more departments. For decisions that have a recurrent character, rules and procedures exist. When applying them, employees can respond without needing to communicate with each other. Vertical information systems support communication up and down the hierarchy and include reports, exception reporting, and computer-based communication between managers and subordinates. If there is an increase in the number of nonrecurring decisions for which established procedures do not apply, the hierarchy becomes overloaded. The classic bureaucratic reaction to such a situation is to add positions to the hierarchy and/or increase the capacity of vertical information systems.[14]

This traditional machine type of functioning does not work under conditions of environmental turbulence. The top level would be overloaded; planning and decision making would consequently be too late to have real utility; and as a result, organizational performance would be severely degraded. Moreover, increased environmental turbulence is often associated with increased complexity, for which the expertise cannot consist of just a few centrally located individuals. This situation requires a new organizational form, also known as organic organizations or adhocracies.[15] Organic organizations are based on delegation, empowerment, and mutual adjustment supported by cross-organizational (lateral, horizontal) communication that enables people in different positions and departments to exchange information and collaboratively make decisions. A network organization emerges. Horizontal linking mechanisms to support this type of communication include direct contact; liaison roles created for communication and achieving coordination with other departments, positions, or departments that act as full-time integrators; and information systems that support cross-organizational communication. Adaptive organizations rely on open collaboration.

As mentioned before, there are different levels of change. Incremental changes are made within the mission, objectives, and thrust of the current organization. Discontinuous change is a fundamental departure from the current organization. It involves a significant renunciation of the current markets, the technologies applied, the products, and the ways of working. It requires a revision of culture, and affect the organizational structure and reward systems.[16] In most situations, change will have characteristics of both types, but under conditions of environmental turbulence, the characteristics of discontinuous change will dominate. Managing incremental change follows a pattern of change management; the changes do not represent fundamental modifications of the character, strategy, or identity of the organization. When managing discontinuous change, however, the capability for incremental organizational change is not enough, and more radical interventions are required. The organization faces threatening external conditions and possibly a fundamental crisis. Actions must be swift, decisive, and all-encompassing. The consequences of resisting change, or even managing it badly, become more serious. Where traditional organizations were designed around the concepts of stability and repeatability, radical or disruptive change in technological and competitive forces requires the opposite—speed, innovation, and flexibility.[17]

Before proceeding to the next section, a final remark needs to be made. It is customary in management literature to speak about the organizational environment in general terms, as in "the competitive environment," "the uncertainty of the environment," and the like. However, organizations operate in a variety of environments, confronted with different challenges and opportunities when they interact with one or another. Each may differ in stability, level of turbulence, and complexity. Different product–market combinations, possibly organized in different business units or different functional departments, have their own subenvironments. The environment of the sales department may be quite volatile, while the environment of the accounting department is likely to be comparatively stable. The reality is that every organization of scale must deal with multiple environments with different characteristics simultaneously, even as an organizational unit deals with more narrowly defined environments with its own set of unique characteristics.

To deal with its subenvironment effectively, each organizational unit will develop structures, processes, and mechanisms that fit its respective goals and environments. Picking up the prior example of the sales and accounting department, these departments may differ considerably in their way of working, their processes and structures, and their use of information systems due to differences in the environmental turbulence that they must confront. Managing this diversity while ensuring coherent operations is a key management challenge.

The Impact of Turbulence on IT

The relationship between business agility and IT is at least problematic.[18] In many cases the installed IT is a hindrance for flexibility and agility and requires a major redesign. Functional silo architectures, often from a variety of vendors, and hardcoded business rules embedded in information systems can make even the smallest adaptation difficult. Enterprise resource planning (ERP) systems that are have been implemented as a reaction to this situation are often overly complex and create process silos as a replacement for functional silos. Their implementation often requires complex organizational changes. As a result, they can take relatively long to implement and longer still to master. In that case, there is little IT resource left to support business flexibility and agility.

New technologies and better application of existing technology do, however, have the potential to play a strategic role in creating business agility. Developments like end-to-end business process automation within and across the enterprise, real-time monitoring of events through portals and dashboards, rapid and agile application development (e.g., scrum), anywhere and anytime access to applications and data, and infrastructure on demand make agility more attainable. These developments are enabled by (for example) workflow and business process design and management tools, integration technologies and standards (e.g., XML, Web services), mobile technologies, and cloud computing.[19] In this way, IT may support sensing: the capture of structured and unstructured data that help to form the view on the environment in which the business operates. Information acquired from social media, virtual communities, and blogs supports product development and helps insurance companies, for example, to better assess the risks they run. IT may also support responding by integrating inter- and intraorganizational business processes and by enabling information flows that cross functional, departmental, and organizational boundaries.

The Key Role of Enterprise Architecture

As defined by Ross, Weill, and Robertson,[20] the enterprise architecture represents the organizing logic for business processes, IT applications, and infrastructure. The enterprise architecture is composed of a number of layers, each with its own architecture, which are interdependent. A common classification distinguishes the business layer, the application layer, the data layer, and the infrastructure layer. In the past decades each layer underwent architectural changes:[21]

- The business layer evolved from a strictly vertical hierarchical functional structure, to a horizontal business process orientation, to a focus on supply chains, and eventually to a focus on flexible global business networks.
- The application layer developed from a silo structure offering support to individual business functions, to enterprise-wide applications like ERP and customer relationship management (CRM), to (more recently) a services orientation.
- The information layer evolved from centralized data per function, to shared data, to distributed data today.
- The infrastructure layer developed from mainframe architecture, to client–server, to ubiquitous computing. Architectural choices on this level today are challenged by developments like mobile computing, bring your own device (BYOD), and cloud computing.

The common misperception regarding architecture is that it is merely a(n) (IT-) technical construct that belongs to the domain of the IT function and its staff. Under this assumption, the business functions remain at a distance when it comes to discussions about architectural choices. However, from the layered model, it is clear that IT architectural choices are not and must not be independent from business-focused architectural choices. When, for example, a business changes its functional or regional orientation to a corporate (enterprise-wide) orientation, this will directly affect the IT architecture. A move to an enterprise-wide orientation makes possible the standardization of business processes and common use of company data, like customer and supplier data. This is a choice that may be driven by the business objective to reduce cost and enable cross-selling. On the other hand, a change in the IT architecture to a single instance of one enterprise system (to reduce IT costs) may be very detrimental to the business results of a highly diversified company. This example also shows that if, for some reason or another (strategic or regulatory), a company has to change its business model, this change can be heavily constrained by earlier architectural choices in their IT systems.

This example takes us back to the question of how IT can contribute to business flexibility and agility. From current practice and literature, some principles emerge:

- Use of modular structures, instead of monolithic silos, for both business processes and systems. Modularity allows reconfiguring easily in multiple combinations and facilitates changes and scalability.
- Ensure that interfacing between modules is based on open standards to enable interoperability.
- Accelerate the software development process by applying rapid and agile software application development methodologies.
- Embed options in software functionality based on plausible scenarios and supported by clear business cases.
- Promote shareability of data; for structured data this requires a policy of semantic standardization.
- Recognize that the basic infrastructure is probably the least affected by turbulence, provided it is easily scalable and does not stand in the way of compatibility.

Concluding Remarks

Creating an agile IT support for business necessitates that all IT activities are managed and synchronized from the perspective of making the business increasingly more flexible. This vision drives the design of the enterprise architecture in all its layers, directly affects the way business processes are organized and managed, has implications for software architecture and the accessibility of data, and forces a high level of connectivity and scalability on the infrastructure level. Realizing this vision is a shared responsibility of business and IT management. They must have a clear and shared vision on which processes and business units should be most focused to enhance flexibility and agility. The role of IT in this partnership is to select and implement those technologies that best support the required agility. The success of this relationship depends on close and trusting collaboration between IT and business functions at all levels, a key theme of this book.

Assessing Turbulence in the Enterprise

While we believe turbulence is endemic and likely applies to all businesses, perhaps not every reader believes it applies to his/her industry and enterprise. In our academic and professional programs, we use a simple questionnaire to allow individuals to determine the level and impact of turbulence being faced by their enterprise (Exhibit 4.2). To make a rough estimate of the degree of turbulence, we suggest applying a 6-point scale; the scoring alternatives are listed in Exhibit 4.3 and range from 0 to 5.

Exhibit 4.2   Impact of Turbulence

Turbulence	A Simple Description of the Expression and Impact of Turbulence on the Enterprise	Applies to the Enterprise	Affects the Use of IT in the Enterprise
External Turbulence: Society, Economy, Government, Competition	Increased regulation and compliance		
	Increased competitive cost pressures		
	Increased dynamics in the global supply chain		
	Increased global competition		
	Increased focus on "green" and sustainability		
	Decreased availability of skilled staff		
	Significant entrance of new competitors		
	Increased political disruption affecting the enterprise		
	Increased societal disruption (e.g., haves and have-nots).		
	Loss of price control: industry prices going lower		
	Highest Score for External Turbulence in Business and Use of IT Impact		

(continued)

Internal Turbulence in the Enterprise or Business Unit, or Management and Customer Expectations	Increased dynamics in customer expectations		
	Increased impact of flat, mature growth		
	Increased need for customer intimacy/ integrated 360-degree view of customer		
	Increased requirements to solve customer problem, not sell product or service		
	Transformation of internal supply chain		
	Increased requirement to individualize products and services		
	Increased use of technology, reducing workforce		
	Increased shift from corporate to business unit		
	Increased shift from back office to front office		
	Highest Score for Internal Turbulence in Business and Use of IT Impact		

Exhibit 4.3   Scales for Impact of Turbulence Self-Assessment

Scoring Scale			
Business Impact: Effects on the Enterprise		**IT Impact: Affects the Use of IT in the Enterprise**	
5	Threatens the ability of the enterprise to perform	5	This is a critical factor in new IT investments
4	Adds to cost or decreases revenue	4	This is significant factor in new IT investments
3	Is a factor in management planning and discussion	3	No effect or impact on IT
2	Is not a major factor	2	Is a negative factor in the ability of IT to perform
1	Is not a factor, not applicable to the enterprise	1	Significantly disrupts the use of IT in the enterprise
0	Don't know	0	Don't know

While this is an imprecise assessment, it does point the direction in terms of the highest impact on business and IT, and consequently for management concern. On the business side, any 4 or 5 is of course a concern. But more importantly, the differences in results for the business and IT impact would be an issue: For example, any "5" on the business side should probably have some bearing on the use of IT, and if it does not, or if "Don't Know" is the answer, some concern would be appropriate.

Organizational Capabilities and Environmental Turbulence

To be able to achieve its goals, an organization must have a set of functional and managerial capabilities. The set of needed capabilities depends on the purpose of the organization, its activities, and external market and regulatory requirements and the like; consequently, it is dependent on the organization. Whether an organization actually possesses the required capabilities depends on its internal culture and structures, processes, available technology, and specific skills of people. Environmental change and uncertainty have a specific impact on the required capability set. They require dynamic capabilities.

A Static View on Organizational Capabilities

Organizational capability is the firm's ability to achieve its goals. Organizational capabilities depend on the internal culture and structures, processes, and specific skills of people. Developing and maintaining organizational capabilities requires ongoing purposeful management and action. Well-developed capabilities enable an organization to meet customer demands, acquire and maintain a competitive position, act in a specific environmental setting, and so forth. Capabilities are, in essence, collections of routines, where the essential question is how well they are executed compared to the competition.[22] They encompass (general) management capabilities and (technical) functional capabilities. More formally defined, an organizational capability refers to "an organization's capacity to deploy resources, usually in combination, using organizational processes, to effect a desired end," whereas resources are "stocks of available factors that are owned or controlled by the firm."[23] Resources are thus the basic building blocks of capabilities. When applied to IT, capability describes the systemic ability of the enterprise as a whole to perform the partnership efforts and tasks necessary to 1) create superior business value from investments that exploit IT and 2) produce superior response to turbulence and uncertainty.[24]

The concept of organizational capability has an economic foundation in the resource-based view of organizations. The resource-based view focuses on internal characteristics of firms as factors for their competitive success. Enterprises are considered collections of resources and capabilities that must be maintained and developed.[25] Only their core and unique, difficult-to-imitate resources contribute significantly, as they are the foundation of the company's competitive position in their business environment. These resources cannot deliver on their own; one has to select the right ones and combine them in the right way for the company to be successful. The central idea of the resource-based view is, then, that combining a set of complementary and specialized resources in a unique way may enable a company to generate value from them—if these resources reduce its cost and raise its revenues in comparison with a situation without them.[26] The resources are of many kinds: capital, equipment, patents, experience, knowledge, skills, and the like. Some are tangible; others are not. Some are easily bought and sold, but management skills, for example, are not. Consequently, not all resources are equally important. To become the basis of a sustainable competitive advantage, resources must be difficult to buy, difficult to imitate, and difficult to substitute—or else your competitor will simply do the same as you and devour your profit. Additionally, such resources must have been acquired against reasonable costs, or they will be a burden rather than an asset. Generally, intangible assets such as knowledge, skills, and experience are more difficult to acquire, imitate, or substitute than tangibles like equipment or real estate.

In the IT literature, the notion is well accepted that competitive performance and differences in competitive performance are not so much a result of hardware and software resources alone, but more of how well they are combined with non-IT resources, such as tacit knowledge capabilities in specific business processes that support a company's strategic intentions.[27] In the field of intangible assets, the concept of core competence has come to play an important role. Core competencies are considered the root of the enterprise: its collective knowledge base, skill sets and activities, upon which its competitive position is built.[28] This concept plays an important role in analyzing the viability of business models. Regrettably, many organizations, especially those that are long tenured, frequently find it difficult to identify the wellspring of their competitive position and mistake capabilities for competencies. These enterprises have ossified and will find it difficult to respond to changing conditions or even discover available "the white spaces" for growth.

The capabilities that allow a company to realize its goals are assumed to be dependent on the changeability of the environment.[29] This assumption is rooted in the link between strategic choices, organizational structures, and environmental conditions. Strategic choices determine the environmental context in which companies operate; in turn, the environmental conditions—in terms of uncertainty and complexity—affect the organizational design needed for effective and efficient operations. The organizational way of working will vary from the stable mode that is typical for most bureaucratic organizations to the proactive mode that characterizes firms responding to significant levels of uncertainty and change.

A key characteristic of management capability is the management culture.[30] Important attributes of the management culture are the focus of behavior, the trigger for change, risk preference, the goals of the intended response, and so forth. Under stability, the focus of behavior is on efficiency and repetitive operations. Unsatisfactory performance is the major trigger for change; typically, the reaction to change is negative or, at best, to adapt. Past practice is the major source of alternatives for how to react. In general, there is risk avoidance; the thrust of the response to the problem is to minimize disturbance of organizational efficiency. How different is the management culture under conditions of change and turbulence? The focus of behavior here is (global) effectiveness. There is a continuous search (scanning) for developments that may affect the organization. The attitude to change is proactive; there is an open mind for future opportunities, including those unrelated to past experience. Risk is not avoided but weighed against potential gains. The overall goal is to create a best possible performance potential.

Competencies are another key characteristic of the management capability. They comprise attributes like problem solving, the management system applied, and environmental surveillance. Under conditions of stability, management is triggered by occurring problems, which are deviations from plans, brought to their attention by exception reporting. Policies and procedures determine the reactive way of working. There is no environmental surveillance whatsoever. Under higher levels of turbulence, management is triggered by perceived opportunities, which will create ill-structured problems. The management style is based on anticipation and strategic planning. There will strong activity in environmental scanning and scenario analysis.

Next to (general) management capabilities, organizations also need technical or functional capabilities: skills, knowledge, and facilities in the various functional domains.[31] The profile of these capabilities is primarily determined by what is required in the marketplace. Organization theory developed functional capabilities for different functional areas in the period in which they became important. It started with the production function in the beginning of the 20th century. Dividing work, plant layout, and production scheduling are all examples of know-how to build efficient production organizations. The focus on production was followed by attention toward sales and marketing. New capabilities included sales analysis, sales strategies, and advertising, all geared toward building an effective marketing organization. After World War II, research and development (R&D) came into the picture as a driver of innovation and a key factor to success. It is obvious that from today's perspective, certain functional domains that have become important are missing, such as human resources (HR) and IT. To complement Ansoff's list, a question that we will address in a later chapter is: What is the required functional capability profile of the IT department, acting under higher levels of turbulence?

A Dynamic View on Organizational Capabilities

Teece et al. made a recent contribution to the organizational capabilities discussion.[32] In an attempt to understand the nature of a firm's sustainable competitive position in a changing environment, they developed the concept of "dynamic capabilities." In this section, we do not intend to provide a full discussion on the subject of dynamic capabilities; instead, we highlight those aspects that are relevant for understanding the capabilities for the IT function. A definition of dynamic capabilities is "the ability to sense and then seize new opportunities, and to reconfigure and protect knowledge assets, competencies and complementary assets so as to achieve sustained competitive advantage."[33] Key concepts in the definition are "change" and the ability to function effectively—to survive if not thrive—under changing conditions.

Dynamic capabilities have to be distinguished from static or operational capabilities. The latter refer to the ability to run an organization that functions effectively under specific conditions and context; in other words, they correspond to the efficient exploitation of existing resources. These capabilities, however, have to change when conditions change. Under high levels of turbulence, there will be a discrepancy between the required and the present operational capabilities. The presence of dynamic capabilities ensures the possibility of changing the operational capabilities. Without dynamic capabilities, the organization would stick rigidly to its known pattern of behavior and would, in the end, lose its relevance and die. So, in this view, dynamic capabilities do not come instead of operational capabilities; they complement them.

Examples of dynamic capabilities include:[34] sensing and shaping opportunities and threats, seizing opportunities, and maintaining competitiveness by adjusting or reconfiguring business resources. In fast-changing environments, firms need to invest in scanning and surveying external developments and learn how to interpret them. The sensing capability may be defined as "the ability to spot, interpret, and pursue opportunities in the environment."[35] Once the organization has become aware of a new opportunity or risk, it must have the bias for action to take appropriate measures to develop new products, services, or market approaches. Finally, when the enterprise is successful in its reaction to the identified market and other opportunities, it will have to remain alert to changes and be willing and able to adapt accordingly. The essence of an organization's dynamic capabilities resides in its organizational processes and the leadership skills of its management. Organizations with strong dynamic capabilities have the ability to adjust.

A final question to be addressed is whether dynamic capabilities are only connected to dynamic environments. There has been quite some debate in the literature as to whether the relevant context for dynamic capabilities is limited to rapidly changing environments. Research is inconclusive at this point.[36] Taking an economic stance in this matter, one may conclude that in turbulent environments, there is an urgent need for the ability to reconfigure operational capabilities. The value of dynamic capabilities in such a setting is expressed to a greater extent than under more stable conditions.[37]

How Do IT and IT Management Cope with Turbulence and Change?

Environmental turbulence and change affect the applied IT in companies in two ways. First, it will affect IT in its role to support or enable strategies and business models. Businesses are confronted with a variety of changes, for example, in their markets, products, supply chains, and in regulatory and legal requirements. These changes have a direct impact on business process and information requirements. As a result, the information services delivered by IT will have to change accordingly, which may in turn affect the underlying technology, like software, databases, and possibly technical infrastructure. To continuously fulfill its supporting and enabling role, IT will have to adapt to the changes imposed by the business environment. Second, the applied IT in the organization is affected by technology changes that directly affect the way information services can be delivered. These technology changes may affect both the effectiveness and efficiency of current information delivery. An example of the former is the introduction of mobile business intelligence to better support decision makers; an example of the latter is a change in software architecture that makes a more efficient maintenance possible. They also may, and probably will, impact the business models and strategies that can be supported. This is the enabling power of technology that translates directly into ways of working and the objectives of the organization.

To summarize, the level of environmental turbulence that has an impact on IT is determined by:

- Market change that indicates the pace of change in customer needs. Turbulent markets are characterized by rapid product obsolescence, short product cycles, product substitutions, high customer turnover, the presence of new competitors, and price volatility[38]
- Organizational change that reflects the changes in business models and business processes
- Legal and regulatory changes with which the business must comply and to which IT and its organization must be adapted

■ Technological change with a dual impact: First, it has direct implications for the efficiency and effectiveness of the current information provisioning with no noticeable impact on current business; it may also impact the efficiency and effectiveness of organizational processes and strategies

Managing IT requires specific management and technical capabilities. In general, IT capabilities may be defined as "the ability to mobilize and deploy IT-based resources in combination or co-present with other resources and capabilities."[39] They include a variety of interrelated technical and managerial capabilities. As discussed before, the required capabilities per functional domain will vary with the level of turbulence under which an organization operates. In a stable environment, the characteristics of the IT systems, the application landscape, the databases, and also the practice of IT planning will reflect the stable situation under which the business operates. Systems and specifications may remain unchanged for a long period; the system architecture is designed to fit stable business requirements and is not designed to adapt easily to frequent changes. For organizations facing turbulence and change, legacy systems then become the rigidity trap. Business and IT plans can and, more probably than not, will be made in relative isolation. Alignment as an issue only pops up at the moment of new implementations and required system changes, but these are limited in number and in scope. As a result, business and IT can operate in silos.

How different the situation is under highly dynamic conditions. Systems specifications will have to change on a regular basis and applications have to be adapted, added, or put aside. The system architecture necessarily reflects the volatility of the environment under penalty of being obsolete. Instead of (full) integration, the IS landscape is based on modular design, middleware technology, and loose coupling. These conditions require frequent and close collaboration between business and IT at all organizational levels. At the strategic level, the views in the board of how IT and the business need to fit together in order to cocreate the business strategy need to be aligned well. But also at lower organizational levels, close working relationships between business and IT must be developed. At tactical management levels, the volumes, type, and quality of IS/IT services required should be carefully planned; for the IT organization to avoid interruptions in business operations, business demands should not come unexpectedly. At an operational level, the actual service delivery needs to be aligned with the strategic thrust of the organization and may be confronted with unexpected requests that need to be fulfilled quickly. For example, whether a company focuses on customer intimacy or on a positioning as a low-cost market player directly affects the types and quality of services expected from the IT organization.

Under conditions of high turbulence, the IT function must be able to adapt its skills and resources to changing environmental requirements. In terms of the former section, it must possess dynamic capabilities. These will allow the firm to sense changes, respond and adapt to them, and maintain its competitive position. In other words, these will allow the firm to develop a strategic behavior and strategic flexibility with IT. Required dynamic capabilities for IT are, among others, environmental scanning and scenario planning, ability to design an adaptive system architecture to enable fast IT response to change, building close business–IT partnerships to create the organizational ability to respond in a timely manner to the environmental challenges, and creating a learning organization that fosters use of best practices to create optimal business value out of IT.

We may conclude that under volatile business conditions, managerial attitudes toward IT and effective models of IT governance are essential for delivering superior agility. Among those, building a close business–IT partnership is key. Creating close cross-functional relationships between IT and other business functions serves two purposes. First, it abolishes the silo culture and contributes to the organizational ability of fast and timely responses to challenges posed. Second, it will foster trust between business and IT groups, helping IT to become a facilitator rather than an inhibitor of agility.[40]

Producing Business Outcomes Despite Turbulence and Uncertainty: An Assessment

At the end of Chapter 3 we included an assessment template (Exhibit 3.2, "Examples of Business Outcome") that evaluates the relative success of the enterprise to produce business outcomes through the value of IT. At that point we acknowledged that turbulence and uncertainty were not considerations. Here we provide for that assessment, identifying possible business outcomes as an indicator of the stair step in the Total Value Performance Model (TVPM; see Chapter 3, Exhibit 3.1) that describes a particular enterprise.

We encourage the reader to use Exhibit 4.4 to self-assess the current enterprise status. We include the "Superior Business Value" section from the Chapter 3 template referenced earlier, because the primary outcomes of turbulence and uncertainty are the same, but are required to be faster, more adaptable, and more built for change.

As we suggested in Chapter 3, the reader is encouraged to apply Exhibit 4.4 to the current situation in his/her enterprise. While the exhibit is not intended as an exhaustive set of characteristic business outcomes for each stair-step stage, the figure provides enough to allow the reader to make and assessment of

Exhibit 4.4 Business Outcomes: Superior Value from IT Despite Turbulence and Uncertainty

TVPM (Combined IT and Business and Business Perspective)	FROM CHAPTER 3 Examples of Business Outcomes: Execution and Performance for "Superior Business Value"	Examples of Business Outcomes: Execution and Performance for "Superior Response to Turbulence"	Current Status
Strategic Innovation	• Business strategic effectiveness, direct support for strategic intentions • Transformative changes to the business model • Transformative changes in relationships to market and customer	Strategic innovation done faster Flexible, adaptable, integratable business and IT platforms Enterprise-wide applicability	
Business Change	• Improvements in business operational effectiveness • Changes to the business organization and processes • Changes to relationships in the supply chain	Requirements and changes done faster Flexible, adaptable results	
Business Outcomes & Program Selection	• Effective business change management • Priorities based on business strategies and requirements	Establish platforms for change Adaptability beyond individual business units Enterprise-wide applicability	
Benefits Realization/ Project Development	• Business requirements across the enterprise are defined and met • Successfully implemented and business-operationalized projects	Adaptable solutions Integratable solutions Dynamic capabilities	
Requirements & Development	• Projects meet business requirements • Successfully developed/completed projects • Successfully acquired software and solutions	Adaptable business solutions Dynamic business capabilities	
Service Requirements & Delivery	• Cost and risk mitigation are supported • IT services meet business requirements • IT services support and do not disrupt business processes.	Services are flexible and adaptable	

Scale:

5. These business outcomes are often produced through the use of information and IT
4. These business outcomes are occasionally produced through the use of information and IT
3. Don't know, or this does not apply to my enterprise
2. These business outcomes are made more difficult by issues with information and IT performance
1. These business outcomes are inhibited by issues with information and IT performance

the current situation. As it is not a complete picture, the result should show current level of performance; we would expect 5s for the lowest stair steps, and where they become less than that, the stair-step status is defined. Note in particular that we do *not* use the process/methodology tests here. In effect, it does not matter how well the business/IT organizations perform the methodologies at stair-step level; what matters is the business outcomes actually produced.

References

Ansoff, Igor, and Edward Mc Donell. *Implanting Strategic Management*, 2nd ed. Wiley, 1990.
Haeckel, S., and R. L. Nolan. *Managing by Wire*. Harvard Business Review, 1993.
Prahalad, C. K., and G. Hamel. "The Core Competence of the Corporation." In *Seeking and Securing Competitive Advantage*, ed. Cynthia A. Montgomery and Michael E. Porter. Harvard Business School Press, 1991.

Notes

1. P. R. Lawrence and J. W. Lorsch, *Organization and Environment: Managing Differentiation and Integration* (Irwin, 1973).
2. Lawrence and Lorsch, *Organization and Environment*.
3. Russel L. Ackoff, *A Concept of Corporate Planning* (Wiley, 1970).
4. Marilyn Jane Parker-Priebe, *Theory and Practice of Business/IT Organizational Interdependences*, Ph.D. dissertation, Tilburg University, 1999.
5. R. A. D'Aveni and R. Gunther, *Hypercompetition: Managing the Dynamics of Strategic Maneuvering* (The Free Press, 1994).
6. Peter Schwartz, *The Art of the Long View* (Currency Doubleday, 1996).
7. Ryan R. Peterson, *Information Governance*, Ph.D. dissertation, Tilburg University, 2001.
8. Igor Ansoff, *Corporate Strategy* (Penguin Business Books, 1987).
9. S. Haeckel, *Adaptive Enterprise—Creating and Leading Sense-and-Respond Organizations* (Harvard Business School Press, 1999).
10. Haeckel, *Adaptive Enterprise*.
11. Schwartz, *The Art of the Long View*.
12. Haeckel, *Adaptive Enterprise*.
13. J. R. Galbraith, *Organization Design* (Addison-Wesley, 1974).
14. Galbraith, *Organization Design*.
15. Henry Mintzberg, *The Rise and Fall of Strategic Planning* (Prentice Hall, 1994).
16. Ansoff, *Corporate Strategy*.
17. David A. Nadler, Robert B. Shaw, A. Elise Walton, and associates, *Discontinuous Change—Leading Organizational Transformation* (Jossey-Bass, 1995).
18. Marcel van Oosterhout, *Business Agility and Information Technology in Service Organizations* (Erasmus Research Institute of Management, 2010).
19. A. Melarkode, M. From-Poulsen, and S. Warnakulasuriya, "Delivering Agility through IT," *Business Strategy Review* 15, No. 3 (2004): 45–50.
20. Jeanne W. Ross, Peter Weill, and David C. Robertson, *Enterprise Architecture as Strategy—Creating a Foundation for Execution* (Harvard Business School Press, 2006).

21. A. T. M. Aerts, J. B. M. Goossenaerts, D. K. Hammera, and J. C. Wortmann, "Architectures in Context: On the Evolution of Business, Application Software, and ICT Platform Architectures," *Information & Management* 41, No. 6 (July 2004): 781–794.
22. S. Winter, "Understanding Dynamic Capabilities," *Strategic Management Journal* 24 No. 10 (2003).
23. Ackoff, *A Concept of Corporate Planning.*
24. See Preface for more information.
25. J. B. Barney, *Gaining and Sustaining Competitive Advantage* (Addison-Wesley, 1997).
26. Barney, *Gaining and Sustaining Competitive Advantage.*
27. Paul Patrick Tallon, "Inside the Adaptive Enterprise: An Information Technology Capabilities Perspective on Business Process Agility," *Information Technology Management* 9 (2008).
28. David J. Teece, *Dynamic Capabilities & Strategic Management* (Oxford University Press, 2011).
29. R. Amit and P. Schoemaker, "Strategic Assets and Organizational Rents," *Strategic Management Journal* 14, No. 1 (1993).
30. Amit and Schoemaker, "Strategic Assets and Organizational Rents."
31. Amit and Schoemaker, "Strategic Assets and Organizational Rents."
32. Teece, *Dynamic Capabilities & Strategic Management.*
33. Teece, *Dynamic Capabilities & Strategic Management.*
34. Teece, *Dynamic Capabilities & Strategic Management.*
35. Paul A. Pavlou and Omar A. El Sway, "Understanding the Elusive Black Box of Dynamic Capabilities," *Decision Sciences* 42, No. 1 (February 2011).
36. Ilido Barreto, "Dynamic Capabilities: A Review of Past Research and an Agenda for the Future," *Journal of Management* 36, No. 1 (January 2010).
37. Pavlou and El Sway, "Understanding the Elusive Black Box of Dynamic Capabilities."
38. Pavlou and El Sway, "Understanding the Elusive Black Box of Dynamic Capabilities."
39. Paul A. Pavlou and Omar A. El Sway, "From IT Leveraging Competence to Competitive Advantage in Turbulent Environments. The Case of New Product Development," *Information Systems Research* 17, No. 3 (September 2006).
40. Tallon, "Inside the Adaptive Enterprise."

CHAPTER 5

Turbulence in Information Technology

The movement from static to dynamic, from changeless perfection to continual change . . . shows up as the crux of scientific thinking about complex systems, poised on the edge of chaos.

RICHARD LANHAM, *THE ELECTRONIC WORD*
(THE UNIVERSITY OF CHICAGO PRESS, 1993)

S tated most broadly, information technology (IT) is the application of abstractions that are designed to enhance the ability of people and organizations to solve problems. By applying a variety of mechanisms, IT enhances the utility of information in the performance of operational, tactical, or strategic tasks. This outcome is achieved by analyzing the information needs of people as they grapple with problem-solving tasks and translating this analysis into an array of computational aids. IT serves the business by enabling its current goals and strategic ambitions while enlarging its plate of future opportunities.

As practitioners, consultants, researchers, and educators, the authors have been struck by the turbulence ripping through the fabric of contemporary information technology. We consider turbulence to be a state of sudden disorder. It suggests unanticipated and abrupt changes in the status quo. One expects some degree of turbulence before boarding an aircraft. However, once airborne, the moment-to-moment changes in flight stability remain unexpected and frequently catch us by surprise regardless of our frequent flier status.

In this regard, IT turbulence is analogous to airborne turbulence—we know there will be some, and yet we still manage to spill our coffee when it arrives. You would think that we could be better prepared. Similarly, IT or computational turbulence is not a new phenomenon.

89

Humankind has been developing IT tools in one form or another for at least 35,000 years. So the question one might ask is, "What is different now?" It is one thing to say blithely that the rate of change has increased substantially. Alvin Toffler made that observation in 1970 in his book titled *Future Shock*. He argued that the rate of change was going to accelerate and that the speed of change could induce disorientation for many people. We would suggest that even Toffler's view understates the speed with which meaningful computational innovations are affecting society.

To gain some perspective, we provide a high-speed and cursory review of humanity's achievements in computational/information technology. Our journey will reveal that humankind has done a remarkable job with resources of land, labor, and capital but that knowledge absorption, exploitation, and transfer proceed at a slower and more uncertain rate. Moreover, as will be discussed later in this chapter, the march of computing technology has progressively removed the aspects of the "specialist technician" from the business equation. The impact of this on reaction time as well as complexity is very real but not expressed in ways that are necessarily desirable. In fact, the disintermediation of certain IT specialties has not improved time to market for solutions or innovations for the business, but may have created more work and consternation for the enterprise.

The authors acknowledge that any effort to describe major accomplishments in any domain is inherently subjective. Though we have endeavored to be reasonably complete, some inventions may have been overlooked; should that be the case, we request clemency. Many sources were used to compile this journey. Interestingly, we found that the use of multiple "authorative sources" created date controversy. When this occurred, we chose dates that were cited most frequently.

History of Technology Turbulence

Early Man (200,000–35,000 BCE)

We will skip most of the Early and Middle Paleolithic era but will point out that early man discovered fire, created stone tools, sewed clothing, and developed composite spears. Our first stop in the annals of computation is a rock shelter situated almost 500 miles south of Kruger National Park. Here, near the crest of the Lebombo Mountains, was found one the earlest examples of computing technology. Sitting approximately 2,000 feet above sea level, Border Cave is tucked between South Africa and Swaziland. Just beyond its entrance is a sheer drop of almost 1,700 feet onto the Swaziland plains and the home of the Zulu nation. Border Cave is considered a Middle Stone Age site and was used by early *Homo sapiens* dating back almost 200,000 years. It is also home to more than 69,000 artifacts of early human history. One artifact is a small fibula from a baboon.

Dating from approximately 35,000 BCE, this bone is marked with 29 clearly defined notches, which suggest that it may have been used to calculate and monitor lunar cycles. Insofar as the development of protofarming or agrarian societies did not emerge until some 20,000 years later, one wonders to what use a counting stick with 29 hash marks was applied. It is speculated that humanity's earliest mathematicians may have been women who needed to track fertility cycles.[1]

Late Paleolithic to Mesolithic Era (35,000–10,000 BCE)

Throughout this period, humans grouped together in small societies and subsisted by gathering plants and hunting wild animals. Humanity continued to improve its tool-making skills but remained nomads and hunter-gatherers. Early man develops the principle of the bow and arrow, creates rudimentary ceramics as well as figurines, and creates cave paintings. No obvious computational breakthroughs occur.

Antiquity (10,000 BCE–1 BCE)

The Neolithic Era witnessed major changes in social systems and techniques as permanent settlements emerged. Counting sticks or tally sticks of diverse forms emerged in various parts of the world. Humanity domesticated wheat and some animals as early as 8,000 BCE. Sun-dried bricks were used in the construction of buildings in Jericho. Hammered copper tools were created, the grain barley was domesticated, and beer was brewed. Grapes and olives were also cultivated, and oxen were used as draft animals to pull plows. Wine was produced. Writing was developed as Sumerian cuneiform script as well as Egyptian hieroglyphics on clay tablets. Trade between settlements developed. Commercial transactions were recorded. Wind-powered boats were developed.

Much change occurred in this 10,000-year span. However, the counting or tally stick would reign as the preeminent computational tool. In fact, the tally stick remained a significant tool well into the 1820s. It would take approximately 32,000 years from the creation of the first known counting stick before the next great development in computing—the invention of the decimal system. This was offered by the great Egyptian culture, which invented the use of fractions in 5500 BCE and the base 10 decimal system in 3000 BCE. The pace of change moved smartly at that point. By approximately 2700 BCE, the Sumerians offered mankind the first known example of the abacus, albeit not using base 10. Mesopotamians recognized that the ratio of a circle's circumference to its diameter is constant, which leads to the calculation of π (at one decimal place). Egyptians offered the first-known means of counting small units of time, the water clock, at approximately 1500 BCE. Socrates, Aristotle, and Plato established the basis of rational thought and mathematical logic, while Diophantus of Alexandria offered the equal sign and introduced the symbolic language of algebra. Euclid provided the definitive text on geometry circa 300 BCE. The Greek mathematician Archytas created the first known robot, a steam-powered pigeon. Counting boards emerged as another computing tool. Chinese philosophers from the Han Dynasty offered the ability to conceptualize and manipulate negative numbers by roughly 200 BCE. Chinese artisans created the first mechanical orchestra. Also in this time frame, the Greeks offered humanity the Antikythera mechanism and the astrolabe, a loose equivalent of analog computers used to calculate astronomical positions.

Darkness in Europe but Sunshine in the East (1 CE–1200 CE)

This period witnessed continued development of important conceptual advances as well as the invention of mechanical timekeeping devices—but less in Europe. In 60 BCE, Heron of Alexandria offered the first string-based programming language to control the movement of a self-powered robot. By 100 BCE, Zhang Heng invented the seismograph. In 264 CE, Liu Hui, a Chinese mathematician, successfully calculated the value of π at five digits past the decimal (3.14159). Eratosthenes calculated the circumference of the Earth and the angle of the Earth's axis, and invented a system of longitude and latitude. He also proposed a method of finding prime numbers, the Sieve of Eratosthenes, in 276 CE. Almost 650 years after the Han Dynasty developed negative numbers, a Jain text from India reveals the first written use of the zero. Brahmagupta, from India, was the first to use zero as a number, and used negative numbers and zero for computing in 618 CE. Also in that time frame, block printing was introduced during the T'ang Dynasty in China. Chinese mathematicians created the first fully mechanical clock, which made its appearance in 723 CE. Early computers and other counting devices later exploited the gear-and-spring technology from these early devices. By 1202 CE, the concepts of algorithms and algebra were recognized in Europe, building on the work of Muhammad ibn Musa al-Khwarizmi, who 400 years earlier had described a method to achieve calculations.

The Renaissance (1300–1600 CE)

From a computational perspective, the European Renaissance ushered in key computational advances, including mechanical calculation and invention of the logarithm. Mechanical clocks appeared in Europe in the 1300s. As the 1400s concluded, Leonardo da Vinci drew the first clock powered by a pendulum, as well as sketched the first mechanical calculating device. Da Vinci also created the first humanoid robot, which could sit up, wave its arms, and flex its neck/head while opening and closing its jaw. Miniaturization technology appeared in the development of the first watch, which occurred in 1502. By 1543, Copernicus described, with reasonable accuracy, the movement of planets around the sun. Switzerland's Joost Buerghi brought us the development of the logarithm table in 1588. The logarithm table was also developed independently by John Napier, who additionally developed a mechanical calculator that greatly accelerated multiplication, division, and square root computations.

Pre-Industrial Age (1600–1750 CE)

The early 1600s witnessed Galileo Galilei's invention of the thermometer and a geometrical/military compass, which also served as a "pocket calculator." Galileo successfully confirmed Copernicus's theory that the planets revolve around the sun and also recognized the principle governing the movement of pendulums and the "law of falling bodies," establishing mathematics as the language of scientific discovery. Johannes Keppler expanded humankind's body of knowledge with the publication of *Astronomica Nova* in 1609, which describes, among other things, how planets move around the sun. William Oughtred successfully improved calculation processes with the development of the slide rule and the logarithmic calculating disk. In the 1630s, Rene Descartes contributed analytical geometry and his theory of vortices to the stew. Along the way, Blaise Pascal contributed principles of hydraulic fluids, as well as his treatise on the arithmetical triangle, which describes a tabular presentation for binomial coefficients (aka the Pascal Triangle). Pascal collaborated with Pierre de Fermat on the development of a theory of probabilities. By 1679, reasonably accurate measurements of the speed of light were made by the Danish astronomer Ole Rømer. In 1694, Gottfried Leibnitz built the first mechanical calculator that employs an accumulator, which is akin to machine memory, and also advanced humanity's understanding of binary numeral system or base 2. Sir Isaac Newton published his laws of kinetics and gravity.

First Industrial Age (1750–1850 CE)

The first industrial revolution was centered on iron, steam technologies, and textile production.

By 1728, Jean Falcon invented the first machine using punch cards—a programmable loom based on wooden punch cards. In 1750, Benjamin Franklin discovered that lightning is a form of electricity. James Watt invented the steam engine in 1765. Pierre and Henry Louis Jaquet-Droz invented the first automaton (robot) that could write in 1773. The telegraph arrived on the scene in 1774, followed shortly thereafter by the invention of the first battery in the late 1790s by Alessandro Volta. In 1801, building on Falcon's work, Joseph Marie Jacquard introduced the first commercially successful mechanical loom that used punch cards as stored programs, where each row corresponded to one row of the fabric's design. In 1815, Giuseppe Zamboni of Verona invented an electrostatic clock that was so energy efficient that it could operate on one battery for more than 50 years. In 1820, the prototype of the first commercially successful machine that performed addition, subtraction, multiplication, and division calculations was produced (approximately 1,000 devices were produced). In 1821, Michael Faraday established the concept of the electromagnetic field and developed the electric motor. Charles Babbage offered the Difference Engine in 1822 and the Analytical Engine in 1837. The latter device presaged the basic architecture of modern computing; data and program memory were separated, its operation was instruction-based, the control unit could make conditional jumps, and the machine had a separate input/output unit. Building on Jacquard's work with punch cards, Babbage also designed the first calculator that printed its output on paper. In 1827, George Simon Ohm introduced Ohm's Law, which describes the relationship between electric voltage, current, and resistance. William Burt invented the first typewriter constructed in America in 1829. In 1835, Joseph Henry invented the relay, which allowed electrical pulses to be transmitted over a distance. In 1843, Ada Lovelace developed the first computer program, an algorithm encoded for processing by a machine to create Bernoulli numbers. At that same time, and based on Babbage's work, Pehr Georg Scheutz and Edvard Scheutz created the first machine that could print tables that were mechanically calculated. In 1844, Samuel Morse demonstrated the telegraph by sending a message between Baltimore, Maryland, and Washington, D.C. Two years later, Alexander Bain used perforated tape to transmit a telegram. Bain also received a patent for the concept of a facsimile machine. In 1847, George Boole introduced his algebra of logic (Boolean algebra), which made it possible to treat a number of logical problems as algebraic operations.

Second Industrial Age (1850–1900)

The second industrial revolution revolved around steel, railroads, electricity, and chemicals. Progress across diverse industrial sectors such as transportation, manufacturing, and construction is evident. In this era, great achievements are built on the use of numbers. Companies will take mechanical calculators and electrify them. Storage features will be incorporated, as will the ability to manipulate stored results. The capability of printing results to paper emerges. Scientists, inventors, and entrepreneurs like Scheutz, Geissler, Bell, Westinghouse, Burroughs, Tesla, Wheatstone, Casselli, Felt, Hollerith,

Philips, Marconi, Smith, Poulsen, Boltzmann, Braun, and Thompson made their mark.

Pehr Georg Scheutz and Edvard Scheutz completed the first full-scale difference engine, which they call a Tabulating Machine, in 1853. Based on principles described by Charles Babbage, the machine operated on 15-digit numbers and fourth-order differences and produced printed output. In 1855, Heinrich Geissler developed a vacuum pump that was almost capable of producing an absolute vacuum. This device enabled the subsequent development of the cathode-ray tube in 1897. In 1857, Charles Wheatstone introduced paper tapes as a medium for the preparation, storage, and transmission of data. Outgoing messages could be prepared offline on paper tape and transmitted later. The first communications across a transatlantic cable occurred in 1858, which reduced the communication time between North America and Europe from ten days to a matter of minutes. In 1856, the world's first operating facsimile machine prototype was demonstrated by its inventor, Giovanni Casselli. In 1868, the first QWERTY keyboard was developed, which ushered in the production of the first commercially successful typewriter in 1873. The first successful bidirectional transmission of clear speech by Alexander Bell and John Watson occurred in 1876, which enabled the commercialization of the telephone. At the same time, the Tachylemme calculator, a specialized device showing the daily interest on sums of money at various interest rates, was invented. In 1878, Ramon Verea invented a calculator with an internal multiplication table. In 1879, Gottlob Frege wrote *Concept-Script: A Formal Language for Pure Thought Modeled on that of Arithmetic*, which marked a turning point in the history of logic by breaking new ground in functions and variables. In that same year, Thomas Edison invented the first commercially viable incandescent light bulb, as well as discovered the basis of the vacuum tube. In 1883, Dorr Felt made his Comptometer, which was the first calculator for which the operands were entered simply by pressing keys. In 1885, William Burroughs patented an adding machine that printed lists of added numbers. Alexander Graham Bell utilized Edison's phonograph design and created a wax recording of the children's rhyme "Mary Had a Little Lamb" in 1886. Also in that year, Westinghouse Manufacturing Company installed the first alternating-current (AC) electrical power system. On the theoretical front, Charles Pierce recognized the connection between the concepts of Boolean algebra and circuits based on switches. In 1888, Heinrich Hertz performed experiments with electromagnetic waves that would become known as radio waves. Also that year, Obeline Smith made the basic suggestion for magnetic storage of data. The 1890 census of the United States was performed using designs inspired by Charles Babbage and punch card technology refined by Herman Hollerith. In 1892,William Burroughs produced a commercially successful calculating machine, launching the mechanical office calculator industry. Gerard Philips founded Philips & Co. in 1891. Guglielmo Marconi built the first radio transmitter in 1894. In 1897, Sir John Joseph Thomson discovered the electron and Karl Braun invented the cathode-ray oscilloscope. The following year, Valdemar Poulsen invented the magnetic recorder. In 1899, NEC Corporation was founded in Japan.

Machine Age (1900–1945)

Beyond epic wars, this era witnessed several key advances in computing. Calculating machines began to contain built-in logic and transitioned from scientific applications to business challenges. Many well-known computing companies were founded as computers entered the battlefield.

The introduction of an automatic punch card feeder by Herman Hollerith increased the speed with which the 1900 census of the United States was processed. The year 1901 saw Clarence Locke receive a patent for his multi-slide calculator. The Dalton adding-listing machine, introduced in 1902, was the first of its type to use only ten keys. Also in 1902, Guglielmo Marconi successfully transmitted the first radio message across the Atlantic Ocean. Orville and Wilbur Wright used a mechanical airplane to achieve flight in 1903. Also that year, Nikola Telsa patented electrical logic circuits called switches or gates. John Fleming filed a patent in 1904 for the first vacuum tube, which was a diode. In 1905, Albert Einstein offered his theory of relativity. At the same time, aluminum made its appearance in lightweight "pocket" calculators. In 1906, Lee DeForest added a third electrode to the vacuum tube to create the triode, which served as an electronic switch and ultimately replaced electromechanical relays; and Herman Hollerith added the plugboard to a tabulator, which allowed the device to be adapted for different applications. The Haloid Company, which would later become Xerox Corporation, was founded in 1906 as well. In 1907, Austrian physicist Robert von Lieben patented a cathode-beam relay. Alan Archibald Campbell Swinton proposed, in 1908, an electronic system of photography that presaged television's use of the cathode-ray tube by describing an electronic scanning method.

In 1910, the first installation of the telegraph occurred on postal lines between New York City and Boston, and Hitachi was founded in Japan. In 1911, Henry Prevost Babbage, son of Charles Babbage, completed a calculator based on his father's analytical engine. Superconductivity was discovered by Professor Heike Kamerlingh Onnes and his collaborators, Cornelis Dorsman, Gerrit Jan Flim, and Gilles Holst, in 1911 at the University of Leiden in the Netherlands. Also in 1911, the Tabulating Machine Company, the International Time Recording Company, the Computing Scale Company, and the Bundy Manufacturing Company merged to form the Computing Tabulating Recording Company, which became the International Business Machine

(IBM) Company in 1924. In 1912, the Institute of Radio Engineers, the precursor to the Institute of Electrical and Electronics Engineers (IEEE), was formed. *Principia Mathematica*, the landmark work in formal logic written by Alfred North Whitehead and Bertrand Russell, was first published in three volumes in 1910, 1912, and 1913; it offers a defense of "logicism" and was instrumental in developing modern mathematical logic. In 1915, Albert Einstein completed his general theory of relativity. Also that year, physicist Manson Benedicks discovered that the germanium crystal could be used to convert alternating current to direct current, foreshadowing the use of microchips. Max Planck was awarded the Nobel Prize in Physics in 1918 for his work describing energy quanta. This work provided the foundation for quantum mechanics and was an important theoretical input in the development of microprocessors. That same year, German engineer Arthur Scherbius applied for a patent for a cipher machine that would become known as the Enigma Machine. The year 1918 also witnessed the discovery of the proton by Ernest Rutherford. In 1919, U.S. physicists William Eccles and F. W. Jordan invented the flip-flop electronic switching circuit, which is critical to high-speed electronic counting systems and the forebear of the ability to store binary information. Also that year, Norton Hinckley and Dave Tandy founded the Hinckley–Tandy Leather Company, the precursor of the Tandy Corporation.

In 1920, the first cash register that prints numbers was introduced on the market by C-T-R (later IBM). Also that year, Leonardo Torres y Quevedo demonstrated a calculator that used a typewriter for input and output. Polish notation (the precursor to reverse Polish notation) was invented by Jan Łukasiewicz as a way to write mathematical expressions without using parentheses or brackets, which had the benefit of reducing computer memory access and utilizing the stack to evaluate expressions. This notation, beloved by at least one of the authors, found its way into the HP series of handheld calculators in 1968 with the HP10c. The year 1923 witnessed the first demonstration of an electronic television camera tube by Westinghouse engineer Vladimir Kosma Zworykin. In 1924, IBM was formed; and Bell Telephone Laboratories was founded in 1925. The first television receiver based on the principle of Braun's tube was demonstrated in Germany. Also that year, Julius Lilienfeld filed a patent in Canada for a "Method and apparatus for controlling electric current" through the use of a metal–semiconductor field effect transistor. In 1927, Remington Typewriter and Rand Kardex merged into Remington Rand, and that same year, Philo Farnsworth demonstrated the first working television. The first videophone conversation in the United States was held between Herbert Hoover, then American Secretary of Commerce, and Walter Sherman Gifford, then president of AT&T; the accompanying voice segment was transmitted using telephone wires. In 1928, Fritz Pleumer of Germany patented his invention of magnetic tape, which allowed data to be recorded and read back. The hole count for punched cards increased from 45 to 80 and became the standard for the industry until the technology was retired. Also that year, Warren Marrison, a telecommunications engineer at Bell Telephone Laboratories, developed a highly accurate clock based on the regular vibrations of a quartz crystal in an electrical circuit. The quartz crystal clock made possible new levels of accuracy in timekeeping. John von Neumann's minimax theory was published and became a foundational element in game-playing programs. In 1929, the German engineer Rudolf Hell patented the first form of fax machine. In 1930, while at the Massachusetts Institute of Technology (MIT), Vannevar Bush constructed a differential analyzer that could solve differential equations with as many as 18 independent variables. This work was extended, with the assistance of Harold Hazen, to handle second-order differential equations. That same year, John Bernard Gudden discovered that silicon in pure form worked as an insulator, but if it were impure, the material behaved as a metallic conductor.

In 1931, Alan Blumlein applied for a patent concerning "Binaural Sound," or stereo sound. That same year, a Michigan high school teacher, Reynold B. Johnson, developed a way to score multiple-choice tests by sensing conductive pencil marks on a coded answer sheet. IBM later bought the technology and adapted it to read data mechanically. The magnetic drum was invented by G. Taushek in 1932 in Austria, based on principles discovered by Pfleumer. Also that year, while working at Werner Heisenberg's institute in Leipzig, Germany, Felix Bloch and Rudolf Peierls developed the quantum theory of solids. EMI engineers W. F. Tedham and J. D. McGee produced the first electronic picture pickup tube by displaying their images on a cathode-ray tube. The year 1933 witnessed the founding of Canon Corporation. In 1934, Tommy Flowers, a researcher working in London at the British Post Office Research Station, designed electronic digital equipment for controlling the connections between telephone exchanges. This was the enabling technology for vacuum tubes switching that later would be used by computers. Flowers's first prototype went online in 1939. In 1935, the first fax transmission via a telephone line took place, taking approximately 30 minutes. That same year, IBM introduced the "IBM 601," a punch card machine with an arithmetic unit based on relays. Also that year, Alan Turing, at Cambridge University, invented the principle of the modern computer by describing an abstract digital computing machine that consisted of a limitless memory and a scanner that moved back and forth through the memory, symbol by symbol, reading what it found and writing further symbols. In turn, the scanner's actions were dictated by a program of instructions that were stored using symbols in memory. In1936, Konrad Zuse (Germany) started the construction of the Z1, world's first programmable computer, which would take three years to complete. Alan Turing also published his paper "On Computable Numbers," which described a machine that could make any calculation or logical operation. Also in 1936, IBM sold its first electric typewriter. In 1937, Claude Shannon wrote his master's thesis on machine logic, which explained that an electric circuit used the same concept as Boolean algebra. Howard Aiken developed plans for a machine that executed commands step by step; this would ultimately become the basis for the Harvard Mark-1 computer. George Stibitz, a researcher at the Bell Telephone Laboratories, constructed a demonstration one-bit binary adder using relays. In 1938, Konrad Zuse completed construction of the world's first binary digital computer, the Z1. Samsung was set up by Byung-Chull Lee in Taegu, Korea. The year 1939 saw the founding of Hewlett-Packard, as well as Luther George Simjian's invention of the automatic teller machine (ATM), which was rejected by the City Bank of New York (now Citibank). Also that year, the Atanasoff–Berry Computer (ABC) was successfully demonstrated. The full-scale machine was completed in 1940.

In 1940, the Complex Number Calculator (CNC) was completed; its designer, George Stibitz, demonstrated it by performing calculations remotely on the CNC (located in New York City) using a teletype connected via special telephone lines. This is considered to be the first demonstration of remote access computing. Also that year, the first color television broadcast occurred, and Russell Ohl discovered the P-N junction, by accident, while refining silicon. Konrad Zuse completed the Z2 computer, which used telephone relays instead of mechanical logical circuits. In 1941, Zuse finished the Z3 computer, which used 2,300 relays. The Z3 used floating-point binary arithmetic and had a 22-bit word length. Also that year, the first Bombe was completed, which provided a mechanical means of decrypting Nazi military communications during WWII. The British Bombe design was greatly influenced by the work of Alan Turing, among others. C. Marcus Olson, a Du Pont researcher, discovered the process to make silicon with a high degree of purity. The year 1942 saw Konrad Zuse deliver an improved version of the Z4, still mechanical, to calculate the aerodynamic characteristics of wings and rudders. The U.S. Army commissioned Dr. John Mauchly and J. Presper Eckert to design an electronic machine that could compute trajectory tables quickly; this would become ENIAC. IBM developed a multiplier based on vacuum-tube technology, which delivered substantial improvements in speed. Paul Eisler, an Austrian inventor, created the printed circuit board. In 1943, a request by the U.S. Navy to MIT became known as Project Whirlwind, which attempted to build an analog computer-based flight simulator to train bomber crews. Also that year, George Stibitz of Bell Laboratories designed the Relay Interpolator to assist in testing the military's M-9 Gun Director. The Relay Interpolator used 440 relays, and since it was programmable by paper tape, it was used for other applications following the war. In 1944, Harvard Mark-1, a room-sized, relay-based calculator conceived by Harvard professor Howard Aiken and designed and built by

IBM, was completed. The machine had a 50-foot-long camshaft that synchronized the machine's thousands of component parts. That year also witnessed the first Colossus, which became operational at Bletchley Park in the United Kingdom. Colossus was designed by British engineer Tommy Flowers to break the complex Lorenz ciphers used by the Nazis during WWII.

Post–World War (1945–1957)

In 1945, John von Neumann wrote "First Draft of a Report on the EDVAC," in which he outlined the architecture of a stored-program computer. In September of that year, the first actual computer "bug" was reported by Grace Hopper (a programming pioneer), as a moth became stuck between the relays on the Harvard Mark II. Hopper, a rear admiral in the U.S. Navy, helped program the Harvard Mark I and II and developed the first compiler, A-0. Her subsequent work on programming languages led to COBOL, a language specified to operate on machines of different manufacturers. Konrad Zuse began work on Plan Calculus, the first algorithmic programming language. After three years of effort, ENIAC was completed in 1946 by John Mauchly and J. Presper Eckert; ENIAC delivered 5,000 operations per second, which was 1,000 operations faster than its contemporaries. Also that year, Masaru Ibuka and Akio Morita established Sony in Tokyo.

The year 1947 saw the Williams tube win the race for a practical random-access memory. Sir Frederick Williams of Manchester University modified a cathode-ray tube to paint dots and dashes of phosphorescent electrical charge on the screen, representing binary ones and zeros. That year also witnessed the invention of the transistor at Bell Telephone Laboratories by William Shockley, John Bardeen, and Walter Brattain. Eckert–Mauchly Computer Corporation chooses the name "UNIVAC" (Universal Automatic Computer) for its company's product.

In 1948, IBM's Selective Sequence Electronic Calculator computed scientific data in a public display near the company's Manhattan headquarters. Norbert Wiener published *Cybernetics*, which had a major influence on later research into artificial intelligence. Claude Shannon's "Mathematical Theory of Communication" showed engineers how to code data so they could check for accuracy after transmission between computers. Shannon identified the *bit* as the fundamental unit of data and, coincidentally, the basic unit of computation.

In 1949, Maurice Wilkes assembled the EDSAC, the first practical stored-program computer, at Cambridge University. Also that year, the Manchester Mark I computer functioned as a complete system using the Williams tube for memory.

In 1950, Engineering Research Associates built the ERA 1101, the first commercially produced computer; the company's first customer was the U.S. Navy. It held 1 million bits on its magnetic drum, the earliest magnetic storage device. The National Bureau of Standards constructed the SEAC (Standards Eastern Automatic Computer) in Washington as a laboratory for testing components and systems for setting computer standards. The SEAC was the first computer to use all-diode logic, a technology more reliable than vacuum tubes, and was the first stored-program computer completed in the United States. The National Bureau of Standards completed its SWAC (Standards Western Automatic Computer) at the Institute for Numerical Analysis in Los Angeles. Rather than testing components like its companion, the SEAC, the SWAC had an objective of computing using already-developed technology. Alan Turing's philosophy directed the design of Britain's Pilot ACE at the National Physical Laboratory.

In 1951, MIT's Whirlwind was completed. England's first commercial computer, the Lyons Electronic Office, solved clerical problems. The president of J. Lyons & Co. had the computer, modeled after the EDSAC, built to solve the problem of daily scheduling production and delivery of cakes to Lyons' tea shops. The UNIVAC I delivered to the U.S. Census Bureau was the first commercial computer to attract widespread public attention. Although manufactured by Remington Rand, the machine often was mistakenly referred to as the "IBM UNIVAC."

In 1952, Heinz Nixdorf founded Nixdorf Computer in Germany. John von Neumann's IAS computer became operational at the Institute for Advanced Studies in Princeton, N.J. Its design spawned clones such as the MANIAC at Los Alamos Scientific Laboratory, the ILLIAC at the University of Illinois, the Johnniac at Rand Corp., and the SILLIAC in Australia. On election night, November 4, CBS News borrowed a UNIVAC to make a scientific prediction of the outcome of the race for the presidency between Dwight D. Eisenhower and Adlai Stevenson. The opinion polls predicted a landslide in favor of Stevenson, but the UNIVAC's analysis of early returns showed a clear victory for Eisenhower. That same year, mathematician Grace Hopper completed what is considered to be the first compiler. The IBM 726 was one of the first practical high-speed magnetic tape systems for electronic digital computers.

At MIT, in 1953, Jay Forrester installed magnetic core memory on the Whirlwind computer. Core memory made computers more reliable, faster, and easier to make. IBM shipped its first electronic computer, the 701. John Backus completed speedcoding for IBM's 701 computer. Although speedcoding demanded more memory and computing time, it trimmed weeks off of the programming schedule.

In 1954, a silicon-based junction transistor, perfected by Gordon Teal of Texas Instruments, Inc., became the first commercial production of silicon transistor substitutes for vacuum tubes. At the same time, the IBM 650 magnetic drum calculator established itself as the first mass-produced computer.

In 1955, AT&T Bell Laboratories announced the first fully transistorized computer, TRADIC, designed by researchers Felker and Harris. Transistors enabled the machine to operate on fewer than 100 watts, or one-twentieth the power required by comparable vacuum tube computers. That year also witnessed the first meeting of SHARE, the IBM user group. User groups became a significant educational force, allowing companies to communicate innovations and users to trade information. Herbert Simon and Allen Newell unveiled Logic Theorist software, which supplied rules of reasoning and proved symbolic logic theorems. The release of Logic Theorist marked a milestone in establishing the field of artificial intelligence.

In 1956, calculator manufacturer Burroughs gained entry to the computer industry by purchasing the southern California company Electrodata Corporation. The combined firm became a giant in the calculating machine business and expanded into electronics and digital computers when these technologies developed. Burroughs would go on to create many computer systems in the 1960s and 1970s and eventually merged with Sperry Rand (maker of UNIVAC computers) to form Unisys. MIT researchers built the TX-0, the first general-purpose programmable computer built with transistors. The first operating system for the IBM 704 reflected the cooperation of Bob Patrick of General Motors Research and Owen Mock of North American Aviation. Called the GM-NAA I/O System, it provided batch processing and increased the number of completed jobs per shift with no increase in cost. The era of magnetic disk storage dawned with IBM's shipment of a 305 RAMAC to Zellerbach Paper in San Francisco. The IBM 350 disk file served as the storage component for the random access method of accounting and control. At MIT, researchers began experimentation on direct keyboard input on computers, a precursor to today's normal mode of operation.

Space Age (1957–1970)

In 1957, a group of engineers led by Ken Olsen left MIT's Lincoln Laboratory and founded a company based on the new transistor technology called Digital Equipment Corporation (DEC). In Minneapolis, the original Engineering Research Associates group led by Bill Norris left Sperry Rand to form a new company, Control Data Corp., which soon released its model 1604 computer. Sperry Rand released a commercial compiler for its UNIVAC. Called MATH-MATIC, it was developed by Grace Hopper as a refinement of her earlier innovation. Development of the first English-language business data processing compiler, B-0 (FLOW-MATIC), was also completed in 1957. A new language, FORTRAN (short for FORmula TRANslator), enabled a computer to perform a repetitive task from a single set of instructions by using loops. The first commercial FORTRAN program ran at Westinghouse.

In 1958, Texas Instruments engineer Jack Kilby created the first integrated circuit, proving that resistors and capacitors could exist on the same piece of semiconductor material. That year also saw Semi-Automatic Ground Environment (SAGE), which linked hundreds of radar stations in the United States and Canada in the first large-scale computer communications network. The air defense system operated on the AN/FSQ-7 computer, which was also known as Whirlwind II during its development at MIT. Japan's NEC built that country's first electronic computer, the NEAC 1101.

In 1959, Jean Hoerni's planar process, invented at Fairchild Camera and Instrument Corp., protected transistor junctions with a layer of oxide to improve reliability and allow conducting channels to be printed directly on the silicon surface. IBM's 7000 series mainframes were the company's first transistorized computers. MIT's Servomechanisms Laboratory demonstrated computer-assisted manufacturing. The school's Automatically Programmed Tools project created a language, APT, used to instruct milling machine operations. ERMA (Electronic Recording Machine, Accounting), provided digitized checking for the Bank of America by creating a computer-readable font.

In the 1960s, computers became cost effective for private companies and provided increased storage capability. Two main data models were developed: network model (CODASYL) and hierarchical (IMS). Access to the database was through low-level pointer operations linking records. Storage details depended on the type of data to be stored. Thus, adding an extra field to a database required rewriting the underlying access/modification scheme. Emphasis was on records to be processed, not overall structure of the system. A user would need to know the physical structure of the database in order to query for information.

Working at Rand Corporation in 1960, Paul Baran developed the principles of packet switching for data communications. Standards for Algol 60, the first structured, procedural programming language, were established jointly by American and European computer scientists. DEC's PDP-1 was introduced; the average PDP-1 included with a cathode-ray tube graphic display needed no air conditioning and required only one operator. AT&T designed its Dataphone, the first commercial modem, specifically for converting digital computer data to analog signals for transmission across its long-distance network. Also that year, the Livermore Advance Research Computer (LARC) by Remington Rand was designed for scientific work and used 60,000 transistors. Meanwhile, at Cornell University, Frank Rosenblatt built a computer known as the Perceptron, which could learn by trial and error through a neural network. A team drawn from several computer manufacturers and the Pentagon developed COBOL, Common Business-Oriented Language. Designed for business use, COBOL promoted a significant level of machine independence. The LISP programming language, created by John McCarthy, made its debut as the first computer language designed for writing artificial intelligence programs. Quicksort was developed by C. A. R. Hoare while working for the British computer company Elliott Brothers. Quicksort is an algorithm that would go on to become the most used sorting method in the world.

In 1961, Fairchild Camera and Instrument Corp. invented the resistor-transistor logic (RTL) product, a set/reset flip-flop and the first integrated circuit available as a monolithic chip. The IBM 1401 mainframe, the first in the series, replaced the vacuum tube with smaller, more reliable transistors and used a magnetic core memory. UNIMATE, the first industrial robot, began work at General Motors. Obeying step-by-step commands stored on a magnetic drum, the 4,000-pound arm sequenced and stacked hot pieces of die-cast metal. That same year, IBM's 1301 Disk Storage Unit was released.

In 1962, Fairchild Camera and Instrument Corp. produced the first widely accepted epitaxial gold-doped NPN transistor. The NPN transistor served as the industry workhouse for discrete logic. The LINC (Laboratory Instrumentation Computer) offered the first real-time laboratory data processing solution. Designed by Wesley Clark at Lincoln Laboratories, Digital Equipment Corp. later commercialized it as the LINC-8. That same year, MIT students Slug Russell, Shag Graetz, and Alan Kotok wrote SpaceWar!, which is considered the first interactive computer game and was played on a DEC PDP-1. APL evolved into a practical programming language and was widely used in scientific, financial, and especially actuarial applications. Virtual memory emerged from a team under the direction of Tom Kilburn at the University of Manchester on its Atlas computer. Atlas introduced many other modern architectural concepts, such as spooling, interrupts, pipelining, interleaved memory, and paging. It was the most powerful machine in the world at the time of release. That same year, IBM announced its 1311 Disk Storage Drive, the first disk drive IBM made with a removable disk pack.

In 1963, Tandy Radio Shack (TRS) was formed by the merger of Tandy Leather Company and Radio Shack. DAC-1 (Design Augmented by Computer) systems, was developed by General Motors with support from IBM, and was one of the earliest graphical computer-aided design programs. That project spawned the IBM 2250 display terminal as well as advances in computer time-sharing and the use of a single processor by two or more terminals. In Downey, California, researchers at Rancho Los Amigos Hospital designed the Rancho Arm, which had six joints to approach the flexibility of a human arm. Acquired by Stanford University, it holds a place among the first artificial robotic arms to be controlled by a computer. Ivan Sutherland published

Sketchpad, an interactive, real-time computer drawing system, as his MIT doctoral thesis. Using a light pen and Sketchpad, a designer could draw and manipulate geometric figures on the screen.

In 1964, IBM announced the System/360, a family of six mutually compatible computers and 40 peripherals that could work together. CDC's 6600 supercomputer, designed by Seymour Cray, performed up to 3 million instructions per second, a processing speed three times faster than that of its closest competitor, the IBM Stretch. Online transaction processing made its debut in IBM's SABRE reservation system, set up for American Airlines. Using telephone lines, SABRE linked 2,000 terminals in 65 cities to a pair of IBM 7090 computers, delivering data on any flight in less than three seconds. The JOSS (Johnniac Open Shop System) conversational time-sharing service began on Rand's Johnniac. Thomas Kurtz and John Kemeny created BASIC, an easy-to-learn programming language, for their students at Dartmouth College.

In 1965, Commodore Business Machines (CBM) was founded. Digital Equipment Corporation introduced the PDP-8, the first commercially successful minicomputer. The speed, small size, and reasonable cost enabled the PDP-8 to go into thousands of manufacturing plants, small businesses, and scientific laboratories. Led by Ed Feigenbaum, a team at Stanford University created DENDRAL, the first expert system. DENDRAL applied a battery of "if-then" rules in chemistry and physics to identify the molecular structure of organic compounds. Object-oriented languages got an early boost with Simula, written by Kristen Nygaard and Ole-Johan Dahl. Simula grouped data and instructions into blocks called objects, each representing one facet of a system intended for simulation. That year also saw the introduction of Multics (Multiplexed Information and Computing Service), which was a mainframe time-sharing operating system in use until 2000. Multics began as a research project and was an important influence on operating system development.

In 1966, the Department of Defense Advanced Research Projects Agency (DARPA) contracted with the University of Illinois to build a large parallel processing computer, the ILLIAC IV, which did not operate until 1972 at NASA's Ames Research Center. The first large-scale array computer, the ILLIAC IV achieved a computation speed of 200 million instructions per second and 1 billion bits per second of input/output transfer via a unique combination of parallel architecture and the overlapping or "pipelining" structure of its 64 processing elements. Hewlett-Packard entered the general-purpose computer business with its HP-2115, which offered a computational power formerly found only in much larger computers. It supported a wide variety of languages, among them BASIC, ALGOL, and FORTRAN. John van Geen of the Stanford Research Institute improved the acoustically coupled modem's ability to reliably detect bits of data through a standard telephone handset (landline), in the presence of background noise, transmitted over long-distance phone lines. Ralph Baer designed a ping-pong game for his Odyssey gaming console.

In 1967, Fairchild Camera and Instrument Corp. built the first standard metal oxide semiconductor (MOS) product for data-processing applications, an eight-bit arithmetic unit and accumulator. Using integrated circuits, Medtronics constructed the first internal pacemaker. Seymour Papert designed LOGO as a computer language for children. Initially a drawing program, LOGO controlled the actions of a mechanical "turtle," which traced its path with pen on paper, while electronic turtles made their designs on a video display monitor. That same year the IBM 1360 Photo-Digital Storage System was delivered to Lawrence Livermore National Laboratory. The system could read and write up to a trillion bits of information.

In 1968, Professor David Evans and Professor Ivan Sutherland founded the eponymously named company, Evans & Sutherland to develop a special graphics computer known as a frame buffer. This device was a special high-speed memory used for capturing video. Data General Corporation, started by a group of engineers led by Ed deCastro, left Digital Equipment Corp. and introduced the Nova, with 32 kilobytes of memory. The Apollo Guidance Computer made its debut orbiting the Earth on Apollo 7. A year later, it steered Apollo 11 to the lunar surface. That same year, Marvin Minsky developed the Tentacle Arm, which moved like an octopus. It had 12 joints designed to reach around obstacles and could lift the weight of a person. A DEC PDP-6 computer controlled the arm, powered by hydraulic fluids.

In 1969, Xerox Corporation bought Scientific Data Systems for nearly $1 billion. The SDS series of minicomputers in the early 1960s logged more sales than did Digital Equipment Corp. Victor Scheinman's Stanford Arm made a breakthrough as the first successful electrically powered, computer-controlled robot arm. By 1974, the Stanford Arm could assemble a Ford Model T water pump, guiding itself with optical and contact sensors. The RS-232-C became the standard for communication and permitted computers and peripheral devices to transmit information serially via a serial plug's 25 connector pins. AT&T Bell Laboratories programmers Kenneth Thompson and Dennis Ritchie developed the UNIX operating system on a spare DEC minicomputer. UNIX combined many of the time-sharing and file management features offered by Multics, from which it took its name.

The Information Age (1970–Present)

In the 1970s, E. F. Codd proposed a relational model for databases in a landmark paper on how to think about databases. He disconnected the schema (logical organization) of a database from the physical storage methods. Several camps of proponents argued about merits of these competing systems while the theory of databases led to mainstream research projects. Two main prototypes for relational systems were developed between 1974 and 1977. The first was Ingres, which used QUEL as query language and was developed at the University of California Berkeley. This ultimately led to Ingres Corp., Sybase, MS SQL Server, Britton-Lee, and Wang's PACE. The second was System R, which was developed at IBM San Jose and led to IBM's SQL/DS & DB2, Oracle, HP's Allbase, and Tandem's Non-Stop SQL. This system used SEQUEL as query language. The term "relational database management system" (RDBMS) was coined during this period, and Peter Chen proposed the entity–relationship (ER) model for database design, giving yet another important insight into conceptual data models. Such higher-level modeling enabled the designer to concentrate on the use of data instead of logical table structure.

In1970, Xerox Corporation opened Palo Alto Research Center (PARC), which produced many groundbreaking inventions that transformed computing. Some of these included the personal computer graphical user interface, Ethernet, the laser printer, and object-oriented programming. Xerox was unable to market the inventions from PARC, but others did, including Steve Jobs (Apple), Bob Metcalfe (3Com), as well as Charles Geschke and John Warnock (Adobe). Citizens and Southern National Bank in Valdosta, Georgia, installed the country's first ATM. Computer-to-computer communication expanded when the Department of Defense established four nodes on the ARPANET: the University of California Santa Barbara, University of California Los Angeles, SRI International, and the University of Utah.

In 1971, *The Electronic News* ran the first advertisement for a microprocessor, the Intel 4004, which had 2,250 transistors and could perform up to 90,000 operations per second in four-bit chunks. The Intel 4004 development was led by Federico Faggin (design) and Ted Hoff (architecture). RCA sold its computer division to Sperry-Rand. The Kenbak-1 made its debut as the first personal computer. Designed by John V. Blankenbaker using standard medium-scale and small-scale integrated circuits, the Kenbak-1 relied on switches for input and lights for output from its 256-byte memory. The first e-mail was sent by Ray Tomlinson of the research firm Bolt, Beranek, and Newman over the ARPANET. An IBM team, originally led by David Noble, invented the 8-inch floppy diskette, which allowed users to easily transfer a floppy in its protective jacket from one drive to another. SRI International's Shakey became the first mobile robot controlled by artificial intelligence. Equipped with sensing devices and driven by a problem-solving program called STRIPS, the robot found its way around the halls of SRI by applying information about its environment to a route. Shakey used a TV camera, laser range finder, and bump sensors to collect data, which it then transmitted to a DEC PDP-10 and PDP-15. The computer radioed back commands to Shakey, which then moved at a speed of 2 meters per hour.

In 1972, Intel's 8008 microprocessor made its debut and allowed a microprocessor to handle, for the first time, both uppercase and lowercase letters, all 10 numerals, punctuation marks, and a host of other symbols. Hewlett-Packard announced the HP-35 as "a fast, extremely accurate electronic slide rule" with a solid-state memory similar to that of a computer. Pong, the video game, was tested in bars in Grass Valley and Sunnyvale, California, and would go on to revolutionize the arcade industry and launch the modern video game era. SuperPaint, developed by Richard Shoup and others at the Xerox Palo Alto Research Center (PARC), was completed. SuperPaint was the first digital computer drawing system to use a frame buffer and is considered the progenitor of all modern paint programs. That same year, Steve Wozniak built a tone generator, his "blue box," to make "free" phone calls. Wozniak sold the boxes in dormitories at the University of California Berkeley, where he studied as an undergraduate. Nolan Bushnell introduced Pong and his new company, Atari video games.

In 1973, Bill Millard left his regular job in management to found the consulting firm Information Management Services or IMS. The following year, he developed a small computing system using the then-new Intel 8080 microprocessor and offered it in kit form as the IMSAI 8080. The TV Typewriter, designed by Don Lancaster, provided the first display of alphanumeric information on an ordinary television set. The Micral was the earliest commercial, non-kit personal computer based on a microprocessor, the Intel 8008; Thi Truong developed the computer and Philippe Kahn the software. Truong was the founder and president of the French company R2E, and he created the Micral as a replacement for minicomputers in situations that didn't require high performance. Robert Metcalfe devised the Ethernet method of network connection at the Xerox Palo Alto Research Center.

In 1974, researchers at the Xerox Palo Alto Research Center designed the Alto, the first workstation with a built-in mouse for input. The Alto stored several files simultaneously in windows, offered menus and icons, and could link to a local area network. Scelbi produced the 8H computer, which was the first commercially advertised U.S. computer based on a microprocessor, Intel's 8008. David Silver at MIT designed the Silver Arm, a robotic arm to do small-parts assembly using feedback from delicate touch and pressure sensors. The arm's fine movements corresponded to those of human fingers.

In 1975, after acquiring computer maker Scientific Data Systems (SDS) in 1969 and redesigning SDS's well-known Sigma line of computers, Xerox closed its computer division; most of the rights to the machines were sold to Honeywell. The January edition of *Popular Electronics* featured the Altair 8800 computer kit, invented by Ed Roberts and based on Intel's 8080 microprocessor. Within weeks of the computer's debut, customers inundated the manufacturing company, MITS, with orders. Bill Gates and Paul Allen, who had founded Microsoft that same year, licensed BASIC as the software language for the Altair. The visual display module (VDM) prototype, by Lee Felsenstein, marked the first implementation of a memory-mapped alphanumeric video display for personal computers. The visual display module allowed use of personal computers for interactive games.

In 1976, Intel and Zilog introduced new microprocessors the 8080 and the Z-80, respectively. Steve Wozniak designed the Apple-1, a single-board computer for hobbyists. Wozniak and best friend Steve Jobs then started a new company, naming it Apple Computer, Inc. The Cray I made its name as the first commercially successful vector processor. The fastest machine of its day, its speed came partly from its shape, a C, which reduced the length of wires and thus the time signals needed to travel across them. That same year, Queen Elizabeth II of England sent her first e-mail as a part of a demonstration of networking technology. Shigeo Hirose's Soft Gripper could conform to the shape of a grasped object, such as a wine glass filled with flowers. The design Hirose created at the Tokyo Institute of Technology grew from his studies of flexible structures in nature, such as elephant trunks and snake spinal cords. Gary Kildall developed CP/M, an operating system for personal computers. Widely adopted, CP/M made it possible for one version of a program to run on a variety of computers built around eight-bit microprocessors. Tandem Computers tailored its Tandem-16, the first fault-tolerant computer, for online transaction processing. The banking industry rushed to adopt the machine, which was built to run during repair or expansion. Telenet, the first commercial packet-switching network and civilian equivalent of ARPANET, was born. The brainchild of Larry Roberts, Telenet linked customers in seven cities and represented the first value-added network. The 5¼-inch flexible disk drive and diskette were introduced by Shugart Associates in 1976. This was the result of a request by Wang Laboratories to produce a disk drive small enough to use with a desktop computer, since 8-inch floppy drives were considered too large for that purpose. By 1978, more than 10 manufacturers were producing 5¼-inch floppy drives.

Tandy's TRS-80 Model I computer, introduced in 1977, was a major step in introducing home computers to the public. Like the Commodore PET and the Apple II, which were introduced within months of the TRS-80, the computer came assembled and ready to run. Also that year, Commodore released the Commodore PET computer. Atari launched the Video Computer System game console, the Atari 2600. The VCS was the first widely successful video game system, selling more than 20 million units throughout the 1980s. The U.S. government adopted IBM's data encryption standard to protect confidentiality within its agencies. Available to the general public as well, the standard required an eight-number key for scrambling and unscrambling data. The 70 quadrillion possible combinations made breaking the code by trial and error unlikely.

In 1978, the VAX 11/780 from DEC featured the ability to address up to 4.3 gigabytes of virtual memory, providing hundreds of times the capacity of most minicomputers. Texas Instruments Inc. introduced Speak & Spell, a talking learning aid for ages 7 and up. Its debut marked the first electronic duplication of the human vocal tract on a single chip of silicon. Speak & Spell utilized linear predictive coding to formulate a mathematical model of the human vocal tract and predict a speech sample based on previous input. The key developers of the Speak & Spell program included Gene Frantz, Richard Wiggins, Paul Breedlove, and George Brantingham.

In 1979, Motorola introduced the 68000 microprocessor. This high-performance processor found its place in powerful workstations intended for graphics-intensive programs common in engineering. California Institute of Technology professor Carver Mead and Xerox Corp. computer scientist Lynn Conway wrote a manual of chip design, *Introduction to VLSI Systems*. Demystifying the planning of very large scale integrated (VLSI) systems, the text expanded the ranks of engineers capable of creating such chips. Atari introduced the Model 400 and 800 computers. The two machines were built with the idea that the 400 would serve primarily as a game console while the 800 would be more of a home computer. John Shoch and Jon Hupp at the Xerox Palo Alto Research Center discovered the computer "worm." Initially designed to provide more efficient use of computers and for testing, the worm had the unintended effect of invading networked computers, creating a security threat. Also that year, USENET was invented as a joint project by Duke University and the University of North Carolina at Chapel Hill by graduate students Tom Truscott, Jim Ellis, and Steve Bellovin. It provided a means for providing mail and file transfers using a communications standard known as UUCP. The first Multi-User Domain (or Dungeon), MUD1, went online thanks to two students at the University of Essex, Richard Bartle and Roy Trubshaw, who wrote a program that enabled many people to play against each other online. The Stanford Cart, in development since 1967, successfully crossed a chair-filled room without human intervention in 1979. Harvard MBA candidate Daniel Bricklin and programmer Robert Frankston developed VisiCalc, the program that made a business machine of the personal computer, for the Apple II.

During the 1980s, SQL (Structured Query Language) became a de facto standard, and DB2 became IBM's flagship product. Network and hierarchical models faded into the background; there is essentially no development of these systems today, but legacy systems are still in use. Development of the IBM PC gave rise to many DB companies and products, such as RIM, RBASE 5000, PARADOX, OS/2 Database Manager, Dbase III, IV (later Foxbase, even later Visual FoxPro), and Watcom SQL.

In 1980, Doug and Gary Carlston found Broderbund to market the games Doug had created. Their first games were *Galactic Empire*, *Galactic Trader*, and

Galactic Revolution. They continued to have success with popular games such as *Myst* (1993) and *Riven* (1997) and a wide range of home products, such as Print Shop, language tutors, and so on. In 1998, Broderbund was acquired by The Learning Company, which, a year later, was itself acquired by Mattel, Inc. Seagate Technology created the first hard disk drive for microcomputers, the ST506, which held 5 megabytes of data, or five times as much as a standard floppy disk. IBM announced its most successful mainframe hard disk, the Direct Access Storage Device (DASD).

In 1981, IBM introduced its PC, which sparked fast growth of the personal computer market. The first PC ran on a 4.77 MHz Intel 8088 microprocessor and used Microsoft's MS-DOS operating system. It established a long partnership between IBM and Microsoft. Adam Osborne completed the first portable computer, the Osborne I, which weighed 24 pounds and cost $1,795. Apollo Computer unveiled the first work station, its DN100, offering more power than some minicomputers at a fraction of the price. Sony introduced and shipped the first 3½-inch floppy drives and diskettes.

In 1982, Hewlett-Packard adopted Sony's 3½-inch floppy standard for general use, which established momentum for the format over other contenders for the microfloppy standard. The Cray XMP almost doubled the operating speed of competing machines with a parallel processing system that ran at 420 million floating-point operations per second. Commodore introduced the Commodore 64. The use of computer-generated graphics in movies took a step forward with Disney's release of *Tron*. Mitch Kapor founded Lotus Development Corporation to market the spreadsheet program he developed called Lotus 1-2-3.

In 1983, Thinking Machines was founded by MIT graduate student Danny Hillis and others to develop a new type of supercomputer. Their idea was to use many individual processors of moderate power rather than one extremely powerful processor. Their first machine, called the Connection Machine (CM-1), had 64,000 microprocessors and began shipping in 1986. Apple introduced Lisa, the first personal computer with a graphical user interface, which was inspired by Xerox's Star workstation. Compaq Computer Corp. introduced first PC clone that used the same software as the IBM PC. With the introduction of its PC clone, Compaq launched a market for IBM-compatible computers. The success of the ARPANET as a way for researchers in universities and the military to collaborate prompted its bifurcation into military (MILNET) and civilian (ARPANET) segments. This was made possible by the adoption of TCP/IP, a networking standard, three years earlier. ARPANET was renamed the "Internet" in 1995. The Musical Instrument Digital Interface (MIDI) was introduced at the first North American Music Manufacturers show in Los Angeles. MIDI is an industry-standard electronic interface that links electronic music synthesizers. Microsoft announced Word, originally called Multi-Tool Word, and the Windows operating system. Richard Stallman, a programmer at MIT's Artificial Intelligence Lab, developed a free alternative to the popular UNIX operating system called GNU (for Gnu's Not Unix), the precursor to Linux. Able to hold 550 megabytes of prerecorded data, CD-ROMs made their presence known. The Bernoulli Box emerged at this same time. It used a special cartridge-based hard disk technology system and allowed people to move large files between computers.

With a single $1.5 million commercial during the 1984 Super Bowl, Apple Computer launched the Macintosh, the first successful mouse-driven computer with a graphical user interface. IBM released its PC Jr. and PC-AT. IBM announced its new 3480 cartridge tape system to replace the traditional reels of magnetic tape in computer centers with a 4- × 5-inch cartridge that held more information and offered faster access to it.

In 1985, Richard Stallman founded the Free Software Foundation (FSF). Commodore released the Amiga 1000. The modern Internet gained support when the National Science Foundation formed the NSFNET, linking five supercomputer centers at Princeton University, Pittsburgh, University of California San Diego, University of Illinois at Urbana-Champaign, and Cornell University. Soon, several regional networks developed; eventually, the government reassigned pieces of the ARPANET to the NSFNET. (The NSF allowed commercial use of the Internet for the first time in 1991. NSF decommissioned the backbone in 1995, leaving the Internet a self-supporting industry.) The Whole Earth 'Lectronic Link (WELL), founded by Stewart Brand and Larry Brilliant, was an effort to create an online bulletin board system (BBS) to build a "virtual community" of computer users at low cost. The founder of Aldus Corp., Paul Brainerd, announced its program PageMaker, a desktop publishing application, for use on Macintosh computers. This created an interest in desktop publishing. Two years later, Aldus released a version for IBMs and IBM-compatible computers. Bjarne Stroustrup, at AT&T Bell Laboratories, published *The C++ Programming Language*; the C++ programming language emerged as the dominant object-oriented language in the computer industry.

In 1986, David Miller of AT&T Bell Labs patented the optical transistor, a component central to digital optical computing. Called Self-ElectroOptic-Effect Device, or SEED, the transistor involved a light-sensitive switch built with layers of gallium arsenide and gallium aluminum arsenide. Compaq beat IBM to the market when it announced the Deskpro 386, the first computer on the market to use Intel's new 80386 chip. At 4 million operations per second and 4 kilobytes of memory, the 80386 gave PCs as much speed and power as older mainframes and minicomputers. Daniel Hillis of Thinking Machines Corp. moved artificial intelligence a step forward when he developed the controversial concept of massive parallelism in the Connection Machine. The machine used up to 65,536 processors and could complete several billion operations per second. Each processor had its own small memory linked with others through a flexible network that users could be altered by reprogramming rather than rewiring. IBM and MIPS released the first RISC-based workstations, the PC/RT and R2000-based systems. Reduced instruction set computers grew out of the observation that the simplest 20 percent of a computer's instruction set did 80 percent of the work, including most base operations such as add, load from memory, and store in memory. Also in 1986, Apple Computer cofounder Steve Jobs purchased the Special Effects Computer Group from Lucasfilm and named it Pixar. The group had previously created the computer-animated segments of films such as *Star Trek II: The Wrath of Khan* and *Young Sherlock Holmes*. (Pixar was bought by Disney in 2006.)

In 1987, Motorola unveiled the 68030 microprocessor, which was built on a 32-bit enhanced microprocessor with a central processing unit core, a data cache, an instruction cache, an enhanced bus controller, and a memory management unit in a single VLSI device. IBM introduced its PS/2 machines, which made the 3½-inch floppy disk drive and video graphics array standard for IBM computers. IBM released a new operating system, OS/2, at the same time, allowing the use of a mouse with IBMs for the first time. Apple engineer William Atkinson designed HyperCard, a software tool that simplified development of in-house applications. HyperCard differed from previous programs of its sort because Atkinson made it interactive rather than language-based and geared it toward the construction of user interfaces rather than the processing of data.

In 1988, Compaq and other PC-clone makers developed enhanced industry standard architecture (EISA), which used a 32-bit bus. Apple cofounder Steve Jobs, who left Apple to form his own company, unveiled the NeXT. The computer he created failed, but was recognized as an important innovation because it was the first personal computer to incorporate a drive for an optical storage disk, a built-in digital signal processor that allowed voice recognition, and object-oriented languages to simplify programming. Robert Morris, the son of a computer security expert for the National Security Agency, sent a nondestructive worm through the Internet, causing problems for about 6,000 of the 60,000 hosts linked to the network. A researcher at Lawrence Livermore National Laboratory in California discovered the worm. Morris, who said he was motivated by boredom, programmed the worm to reproduce itself and computer files and to filter through all the networked computers. The size of the reproduced files eventually became large enough to fill the computers' memories, thus disabling them. Pixar's short film *Tin Toy* became the first computer-animated film to win an Academy Award, taking the Oscar for best animated short film.

In 1989, Intel released the 80486 microprocessor and the i860 RISC/ coprocessor chip, each of which contained more than 1 million transistors. It doubled the performance of the 386 chipset without increasing the clock rate. Motorola announced the 68040 microprocessor, with about 1.2 million transistors. The concept of virtual reality made its appearance in technologies designed by the computer-aided design software company Autodesk and the computer company VPL. Maxis released *SimCity*, a video game that helped launch of series of simulators. Maxis founders Will Wright and Jeff Braun designed a computer program that allowed the user to create their own city.

In the 1990s, an industry shakeout began with fewer surviving companies offering increasingly complex products at higher prices. Much development during this period centered on client tools for application development, such as PowerBuilder (Sybase), Oracle Developer, VB (Microsoft), and the like. Client–server model for computing became the norm for future business decisions. Development of personal productivity tools such as Excel/Access (MS) and ODBC also dominated the end-user tool landscape. This also marked the beginning of Object Database Management Systems (ODBMS) prototypes. By the middle of the decade, the usable Internet/World Wide Web appeared. Companies scrambled to allow remote access to computer systems with legacy data. Client–server frenzy reached the desktop of average users with little patience for complexity while Web/DB grew exponentially. By the end of the decade, the large investment in Internet companies fueled the tools market boom for Web/Internet/DB connectors. Active Server Pages, Front Page, Java Servlets, JDBC, Enterprise Java Beans, ColdFusion, Dream Weaver, Oracle Developer 2000, and so on were examples of such offerings. Open source solutions came online with widespread use of gcc, cgi, Apache, MySQL, and the like. Online transaction processing (OLTP) and online analytic processing (OLAP) came of age with many merchants using point-of-sale (POS) technology on a daily basis.

In 1990, NewTek introduced Video Toaster, a video editing and production system for the Amiga line of computers. Much more affordable than any other computer-based video editing system, the Video Toaster was not only for home use. Also that year, Commodore released the Amiga 3000, the first 32-bit Amiga, which featured the Motorola 68030 processor and the upgraded ECS chipset. The World Wide Web was born when Tim Berners-Lee, a researcher at CERN, the high-energy physics laboratory in Geneva, developed HyperText Markup Language. HTML, as it is commonly known, allowed the Internet to expand into the World Wide Web, using specifications he developed such as URL (Uniform Resource Locator) and HTTP (HyperText Transfer Protocol). Berners-Lee founded the W3 Consortium, which coordinates World Wide Web development. Microsoft shipped Windows 3.0, which offered multitasking capabilities and was compatible with DOS programs, the first successful version of Windows.

Adobe shipped version 1.0 of Photoshop, an image editing program developed by Thomas and John Knoll. Mark Washburn, working on an analysis of the Vienna and Cascade viruses with Ralf Burger, developed the first family of polymorphic virus: the Chameleon family. The programming language Haskell, named after logician Haskell Curry, was introduced by Simon Peyton Jones and colleagues.

In 1991, Linus Torvalds released Linux to several Usenet newsgroups. Almost immediately, enthusiasts began developing and improving Linux, such as adding support for peripherals and improving its stability. Also that year, Pretty Good Privacy (PGP) was introduced. PGP, an e-mail encryption program, was invented by software engineer Phil Zimmermann, who created it as a tool for people to protect themselves from intrusive governments around the world. The Michelangelo boot sector computer virus was first discovered in Australia. The computing language Python made its debut.

In 1992, DEC introduced the Alpha AXP architecture and the Alpha-based DEC 3000 AXP workstations, DEC 4000 AXP departmental servers, and the DEC 7000 AXP enterprise servers.

In 1993, Intel released its Pentium microprocessor line. The Pentium introduced several advances that made programs run faster, such as the ability to execute several instructions at the same time and support for graphics and music. Microsoft introduced Windows NT 3.1, which supported 32-bit programs. That same year, Id Software released *Doom*, an immersive first-person shooter-style game. The PC was morphing to become a platform for video games. The Mosaic Web browser, designed by Eric Bina and Marc Andreessen at the University of Illinois's National Center for Supercomputer Applications, was released. Mosaic was the first commercial software that allowed graphical access to content on the Internet. Also that year, the MP3 file format was published. Boot sector viruses "Leandro & Kelly" and "Freddy Krueger" made their appearance. The programming language Ruby, by Yukihiro Matsumoto, brought a new language designed to balance functional programming with imperative programming.

In 1994, Netscape Communications Corporation was founded by Marc Andreessen, Jim Clark, and others, and it is credited with developing the Secure Sockets Layer (SSL) protocol. Yahoo!, the popular Web portal, was founded by Stanford University graduate students Jerry Yang and David Filo that same year. Also at that time, the Iomega Zip Disk was released. The initial Zip system allowed 100MB to be stored on a cartridge roughly the size of a 3½-inch floppy disk. Commodore International declared bankruptcy and its assets were put up for sale. That same year, the first smartphone, the Simon Personal Communicator, was intoduced by Bell South. The OneHalf, a DOS-based polymorphic computer virus, made its debut.

In 1995, Sun Microsystems announced the Java software platform designed by James Gosling. PHP, a server-side scripting language designed for Web development by Rasmus Lerdorf, made it debut. Microsoft released Windows 95. The first macro virus, called "Concept," was created and attacked Microsoft Word documents. Sony introduced its first PlayStation. Amazon.com went online. 3dfx released Voodoo, the first consumer 3D accelerator, capable of rendering scenes in real time and in high resolution.

In 1996, Nokia introduced its Communicator line of smartphones with the Nokia 9000. Netscape Navigator became the first browser to support JavaScript with release of Navigator 2.0. Toshiba introduced the Libretto, the first subnotebook. IBM's Deep Blue supercomputer won one of six games of chess to reigning world chess champion Garry Kasparov. Hotmail was founded by Sabeer Bhatia and Jack Smith in Mountain View, California. The Ply virus arrived; Ply was a nonencrypted polymorphic virus with a built-in permutation engine.

In 1997, Microsoft bought Hotmail. Intel introduced the Pentium II product line. IBM's Deep Blue became the first computer to beat a reigning world chess champion, Garry Kasparov, in a full chess match by winning three and a half of the six games in the match. Microsoft bought 100,000 nonvoting shares of Apple's stock to provide Apple with critical funding. Distributed.net marked the first large-scale use of idle computing capacity to solve vexing computing problems.

In 1998, Compaq Computer Corporation bought DEC. Google was incorporated. Apple introduced the iMac, and Microsoft introduced Windows 98. The first version of the CIH virus appeared and was able to erase flash ROM BIOS content.

In 1999, peer-to-peer computing concepts were demonstrated at scale with the launch of Napster. The Happy99 worm first appeared. It invisibly attached itself to e-mails, displayed fireworks to hide the changes being made, and wished the user a happy New Year. It modified system files related to Outlook Express and Internet Explorer (IE) on Windows 95 and Windows 98. Also, the Melissa worm was released, targeting Microsoft Word and Outlook-based systems and creating considerable network traffic. The ExploreZip worm, which destroys Microsoft Office documents, was first detected. The Kak worm, a Javascript computer worm, spread itself by exploiting a bug in Outlook Express.

In 2000, Transmeta released the Crusoe microprocessor, which was designed for laptops. Microsoft released Windows 2000. Sony announced the release of PlayStation 2. AMD released the Athlon chip and Intel released the Pentium III and the Pentium IV. The RSA cryptographic algorithm entered the public domain. C# was announced, with Anders Heljsberg as its chief designer. The first USB flash drives were sold. The ILOVEYOU worm, also known as Love Letter, or VBS, or Love Bug worm, made its presence known by infecting millions of Windows computers worldwide within a few hours of its release.

In 2001, The Agile Manifesto, which defined a growing trend toward more "agile" processes in software development, was released. Apple released the iPod as well as Mac OS X, and Microsoft released Windows XP and the Xbox gaming system. Wikipedia was founded. The Anna Kournikova virus hit e-mail servers by sending e-mail to contacts in victims' Microsoft Outlook address books. The Sadmind worm spread by exploiting holes in both Sun Solaris and Microsoft IIS. The Sircam worm was released and spread through Microsoft systems via e-mail and unprotected network shares. The Code Red worm attacked the Index Server ISAPI Extension in Microsoft Internet Information Services. Code Red II began aggressively spreading onto Microsoft systems, primarily in China. The Nimda worm was discovered; it spread through a variety of means, including vulnerabilities in Microsoft Windows and backdoors left by Code Red II and Sadmind worm. The Klez worm was first identified. It exploited a vulnerability in Microsoft Internet Explorer and Microsoft Outlook and Outlook Express.

In 2002, Research In Motion (RIM) released the first BlackBerry smartphone. The Simile virus appeared; it was a metamorphic computer virus written in assembly language. Beast, a Windows-based backdoor Trojan horse, emerged; it was capable of infecting almost all versions of Windows. Mylife, a computer worm, spread itself by sending malicious e-mails to all the contacts in Microsoft Outlook. Optix Pro was a configurable remote-access tool, or Trojan.

In 2003, Skype was introduced as a way of completing video and voice calls over the Internet at low cost. Apple launched the iTunes store. NVIDIA released GeForce FX 3D cards, which provided extensive support for pixel and vertex shaders. Intel released the Pentium M for notebooks and the Centrino mobile platform. AMD released the Opteron line of server processors, which were based on a 64-bit K8 microarchitecture. AMD also released the Athlon 64, the first 64-bit processor for the consumer market. The SQL slammer worm attacked vulnerabilities in Microsoft SQL Server and MSDE and became the fastest-spreading worm of all time, crashing the Internet within 15 minutes of release. Graybird appeared as did ProRat, a Turkish-made Microsoft Windows–based backdoor Trojan horse. The Blaster worm rapidly spread by exploiting a vulnerability in system services present on Windows computers. The Welchia (Nachi) worm was discovered; this worm tried to remove the Blaster worm and patch Windows. The Sobig.F worm spread rapidly through Microsoft systems via mail and network shares. Swen was a computer worm written in C++. The Sober worm was first seen on Microsoft systems. Agobot, a computer worm, spread itself by exploiting vulnerabilities on Microsoft Windows. Bolgimo was a computer worm that spread itself by exploiting a buffer overflow vulnerability.

In 2004, Facebook was incorporated. Google's G-mail was launched. Mozilla introduced FireFox 1.0. Bagle, a mass-mailing worm affecting all versions of Microsoft Windows, appeared. The L10n worm, a Linux worm, spread by exploiting a buffer overflow in the BIND DNS server. The MyDoom worm emerged and currently holds the record for the fastest-spreading mass-mailer worm. The Netsky worm was discovered; it spread by e-mail and by copying itself to folders on the local hard drive as well as on mapped network drives, if available. The Witty worm was a record-breaking worm in many regards. It exploited holes in several Internet Security Systems (ISS) products. It was the first Internet worm to carry a destructive payload, and it spread rapidly using a prepopulated list of ground-zero hosts. The Sasser worm emerged by exploiting a vulnerability in the Microsoft Windows LSASS service and caused problems in networks. Caribe or Cabir was a computer worm designed to infect mobile phones that run Symbian OS. It was the first computer worm that can infect mobile phones; it spread itself through Bluetooth. The Nuclear Remote Administration Tool was a backdoor Trojan that infected Windows NT family of systems. The Vundo Trojan appeared and caused popups and advertising for rogue antispyware programs; it degraded service with some websites, including Google and Facebook. Bifrost, a backdoor Trojan, infected Windows 95 through Vista. Santy, the first known webworm, was launched and exploited a vulnerability in phpBB, using Google to find new targets. It infected approximately 40,000 sites before Google filtered the search query used by the worm, preventing it from spreading.

In 2005, Intel released the Pentium D and AMD released the Athlon 64 X2, both of which are dual-core 64-bit desktop processors. IBM sold its PC business to Lenovo. YouTube was incorporated. Apple announced that they were going to use Intel processors in upcoming Macintosh computers. Microsoft released the Xbox 360. The Zlob Trojan, masquerading as a required video codec in the form of the Microsoft Windows ActiveX component, was detected. The Bandook Remote Administration Tool, a backdoor Trojan horse, infected the Windows family. It used process hijacking and kernel patching to bypass the firewall and let the server component hijack processes and gain rights for accessing the Internet.

In 2006, Intel released the Core brand: mobile 32-bit single-core and dual-core processors. Apple Computer introduced the MacBook Pro, their first Intel-based, dual-core mobile computer, as well as an Intel-based iMac. Twitter was released. Sony released the PlayStation 3, and Nintendo released the Wii. The Nyxem worm was discovered; it was spread by mass-mailing. Its payload, which activated on the third of every month, attempted to disable security-related and file-sharing software and destroy files of certain types, such as Microsoft Office files. The discovery of malware for Mac OS X, a Trojan horse known as OSX/Leap-A, was announced.

In 2007, Apple introduced the first iPhone. Microsoft launched Windows Vista. ASUS announced the first ASUS Eee PC. Apple launched Mac OS X Leopard. AMD released the Phenom line of high-performance processors. Amazon launched the Kindle ebook reader. Estonian government networks were interrupted by a denial of service attack by unknown foreign intruders. Storm Worm, identified as a fast spreading e-mail spamming threat to Microsoft systems, began gathering infected computers into the Storm botnet. Zeus was a Trojan that targeted Microsoft Windows to steal banking information by keystroke logging.

In 2008, the first version of Android was introduced by Verizon Wireless. The HTC Dream was released, which was the first commercially available phone to run the Android operating system. Hulu was launched, marking the significant integration of computing and television viewing across a variety of platforms. Mocmex, a Trojan, was found in a digital photo frame. Torpig, a Trojan horse that affected Windows by turning off antivirus applications, was found. It allowed computer access to unauthorized persons, modified data, stole confidential information, and installed more malware on the victim's computer. Rustock.C, a spambot-type malware with advanced rootkit capabilities, was detected. Bohmini.A, a configurable remote access tool Trojan, exploited security flaws in Adobe Flash 9.0.115 with Internet Explorer 7.0 and Firefox 2.0 under Windows XP SP2. The Koobface computer worm targeted users of Facebook and MySpace. The computer worm Conficker infected anywhere from 9 to 15 million Microsoft server systems running everything from Windows 2000 to the Windows 7 Beta.

In 2009, Apple launched Mac OS X Snow Leopard; Microsoft launched Windows 7. W32.Dozer attacked the United States and South Korean government, financial, and media websites. Symantec discovered Daprosy Worm, which was intended to steal online-game passwords in Internet cafes and could intercept all keystrokes and send them to its author. In 2010, Apple released the iPhone 4 and iPad, which marked the first commercial success of tablet technology at scale.

This concludes our high-speed look at the history of computing. As one reflects on humanity's advances in computational capability, two broad observations are unavoidable. The first marks the sheer rate of growth in achievements. The second is the how these advances are changing the IT function's "traditional" role as caretaker of technologies, provider of structured analysis (systems analysis), solution provider, and steward of business data within the enterprise. Technology advances have occurred in such a way as to diminish many IT stovepipes and specialties. Programming languages moved from approaches designed for building data structures and algorithms (from the most elemental concepts to expansive representations) toward scripting language, which presumes the existence of valid, powerful components and is intended primarily for gluing or connecting them. Along the way, pro-gramming efficiency declined as trade-offs were made to promote understand-ability by business users at the expense of efficient use of the computing stack. The old joke "what Andy (Grove of Intel) giveth, Bill (Gates of Microsoft) taketh away" now has many more actors.

The role of internal IT has become increasingly focused on integrating these independent solutions, data models, and architectures to support the business need for speed. The ability of anyone to write a macro, "construct" a query, or write some HTML does not mean the result is meaningful or even useful. To push the argument to the edge, as long as a user avoids dividing by zero, Excel will calculate anything and produce a result. Hardware has moved from enormous fit for purpose structures to devices that contain many times more processing power but now fit on a laptop or desktop.

These shifts have deemphasized the technology as it pursues business goals, which is perhaps as it should be. However, as the technology recedes into the background, more careful reflection recognizes that the comparatively slow speed of developing solutions was not "synchronized" with the speed that organization change could be responsibly effected. To put this in context, we are able to generate new solutions faster than ever before, but we do so with a limited understanding of how to integrate the resultant morass into a valuable whole. Anyone who has ever called their financial institution will immediately recognize that the rate of solution creation has eclipsed integration. The companies within the financial services sector are generally unaware of the products consumers purchase from them. Bank accounts, mortgages, home equity loans, automobile loans, insurance products, and IRAs all gener-ate independent marketing mailers and statements while providing limited integration at call centers.

As humanity entered the 21st century, the Internet bubble of the 1990s burst, but new shoots have grown amid the carnage. It marked a decline for dubious Internet-based business models but also ushered in solid growth of database applications, as more and more data became accessible for analysis. Data mining, data warehousing, and data marts were already commonly used techniques. Now Big Data (terabyte scale +) was set to launch its own spending spree and arms race. Systems appeared, such as HADOOP and Netezza, that underscored a new level of complexity for handling and analyzing data. Organizations with access to large data sets were keenly interested in discov-ering the insights that these approaches created in fields as diverse as retail, pharmaceutical, national security, and space exploration. And yet the faster we computed and the larger the data sets we explored, the more we were exposed to new sources of turbulence.

In the world of Big Data, where data and its contextual meaning are sliding past one another, we risk making expensive judgments based on insufficient insight. A recent article in the *Harvard Business Review* entitled "Good Data Won't Guarantee Good Decisions," by Shvetank Shah, Andrew Horne, and Jaime Capellá, underscores this point. They observe, "For all the breathless promises about the return on investment in Big Data, however, companies face a challenge. Investments in analytics can be useless, even harmful, unless employees can incorporate that data into complex decision making." Their analysis identified the prerequisite skills for good decision making. These included the ability to "balance judgment and analysis, possess strong analytic skills, and listen to others' opinions but [be] willing to dissent." However, their research found that only 38 percent of employees and 50 percent of senior managers met this criteria. Massively expensive data to collect and process, stripped of context and placed in the hands of people who, on average, are not well equipped to make sound judgments on that data, appears to introduce new instability.

On the application front we are seeing more interactive applications appear with use of personal digital assistants (PDAs), POS transactions, smartphones, and tablets. Perhaps in response, "gamification" appears to be the next stage of development for business applications: immersive environments that display points, promote competition, and provide leader boards as employees execute transactions to advance enterprise goals. Like the downside of Big Data, this too has its unseemly attributes and implications for new pressure ridges on turbulence.

Most organizations use some key performance indicators (KPIs) to describe preferred outcomes. However, it is not unusual for the indicators to be measuring that which is easy to capture versus that which is truly important. This is before we explore the phenomena of KPI bloat. The underlying concept of KPIs is that they are *key*. As consultants, we frequently review KPI suitability and effectiveness. One of the first things clients are asked is to put their key ring in front of them and count the keys. Few have more than six or eight. None will have 40, 60, or more. All too often, KPI bloat simply confuses matters for employees as they attempt to maximize their performance. Gamifying weakly constructed KPIs will only create greater performance swings as the enterprise overachieves in one dimension and then lurches to overcorrect. The financial sector offers clear examples of the use of unbalanced incentives regarding financial trading. Despite growing regulation and scrutiny, ill-conceived trades that are contrary to policy and regulation continue to occur. Before embracing gamification concepts, perhaps there is more merit to ensuring that balanced goals and measures are firmly understood and actually promote the behaviors desired. The law of unintended consequences prevails.

Despite massive technical progress, turbulence grows in the issues surrounding outcomes, mission, privacy, ethics, security, and usability.

The Impact of Technology Turbulence

As we said at the beginning of this chapter, we consider turbulence to be a state of sudden disorder. It suggests unanticipated and abrupt changes in the status quo.

Technology change and resulting sudden disorder has always seemed to characterize information technology. In many respects the pace is accelerating, at least in terms of products and services, although some fundamental laws (e.g., Moore's Law) appear to remain as powerful as ever. Based on recent history, we make the general case that the pace of change will continue to accelerate and will affect every area of information technology. This adds to the turbulence, change, and uncertainty, as the traditional means of IT planning, development, and production are challenged by the continuously changing methods and capabilities available. This turbulence is even more pronounced in the ways in which IT is dispersed throughout the business and becomes an element of local organization and individual decision-making and use. This "democratization" of computing—as one observer put it—is by itself an extremely strong turbulent force in the enterprise and in the IT supply areas.

With Exhibit 1.1 in Chapter 1, we introduced a mental model for the relationship between IT and business. In adapting this as Exhibit 5.1, we make four basic generalizations:

1. Technology turbulence is accelerating and quickly expanding the kinds of things that are possible for the business.
2. Technology turbulence in the form of significant innovation makes new business strategies and operational strategies possible—and quickly.
3. Technology turbulence in the form of new methods of delivering IT (e.g., cloud) makes new IT relationships with the business outside the existing IT organization possible—and quickly.
4. Technology turbulence changes how IT organizations deliver IT services—and quickly.

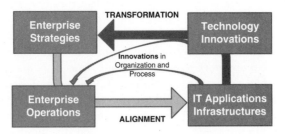

Exhibit 5.1   Impact of Technology Turbulence

Technology Turbulence Is Accelerating and Quickly Expanding the Kinds of Things That Are Possible for the Business

The first part of this chapter surely makes the case that technology turbulence in rapidly increasing.

The Gartner Hype Cycle[2] offers an interesting way to describe and regularly track the introduction of new technology, from research and development through to market acceptance. To understand the sense of turbulence, one can look via Internet search at the many Hype Cycle diagrams for the last few years, and note two things. First, specific technologies can march through the phases quite rapidly, demonstrating a fast pace from laboratory to application. But second, the number of technologies that appear in a given year and do not return in subsequent years is indication of the turbulent nature of things. Some of the changes are vocabulary and packaging, where items are more fully understood. But many come and go, adding to the sense of turbulence and uncertainty.

A large number of technology and application categories are tracked in separate Hype Cycle diagrams, thus expanding the actual number of technologies included. This adds to the sense of turbulence and uncertainty, but also to the sense of significant new opportunities. As we will emphasize in Chapters 18 and 19, this perspective adds to the leadership challenges for both business and IT. As we remarked in Chapter 1, it is not clear that business management always has a clear grasp of the opportunities and turbulent challenges in front of it, fueled by technology turbulence. The situation offers a leadership opportunity for CIOs and IT executives to make that case, but this depends on the ability of the technology leadership to make the connection to the business. As Exhibit 5.2

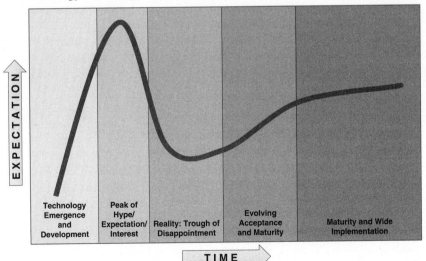

Exhibit 5.2 Our Simple View of the Gartner Hype Cycle

graphically suggests, this requires a strong relationship between IT and business. We expand on this CIO leadership requirement in Chapter 17.

(The Hype Cycle also emphasizes the downside of new technology: that the actual accomplishments lag expectations, and reality does set in in the form of disappointment, redeployment, and testing of the business–IT trust.)

Technology Turbulence in the Form of Significant Innovation Makes New Business Strategies and Operational Strategies Possible—and Quickly

Reviewing the first part of this chapter, the nature of the kind of business innovations made possible becomes apparent. Some generalizations include:

1. A growing and significant part of information processing by humans is taken over by computers. Among other things, the social implications of this phenomenon is readily observed in the kinds of jobs and professions available.[3]
2. An increasing impact of IT is made possible by lowering business costs, enabling new business models, and providing new services and trans-formational ways of interactions between business and its customers and supply chain.
3. Businesses find major shifts in their business models from solely product to services-enhanced products with information, increased accessibility, and maintainability and support.
4. Major shifts caused by disintermediation—the removal of the middleman in supply chains affects entire industries, as do the possibilities of new relationships, or reintermediation, enabled by technology.

These are simple generalizations but give a sense of the enormous changes we have been seeing and feeling for the last couple of decades. And we do not believe the pace will slow.

The business impact is expressed in business strategic planning and responses to the threats and opportunities. As noted earlier, this puts enormous pressure on the business, in terms of understanding what is possible and the business turbulence effects that may be happening, and at the same time puts pressure on the technology suppliers—the IT organization, CIOs, and so on—to articulate the coming opportunities in terms the business understands.

Technology Turbulence in the Form of New Methods of Delivering IT Makes New IT Relationships with the Business Outside the Existing IT Organization Possible—and Quickly

Many business functional areas have started to acquire IT services directly from suppliers. Examples are in sales force management and healthcare administration, where packaged solutions are available directly to those functional areas. Similarly, a significant component of outsourced services involves new ways to provide access to IT capabilities for the business. This complicates the enterprisewide perspective on a whole variety of issues, such as security, data integration, and cross-business-unit and cross-business-function initiatives.

It can be said that one consequence of technology turbulence is the movement of the networking components to the center of the business and IT concerns, rather than processing (the computer itself) or possibly the data/information. Networking is one area that is based on commonality across the enterprise; it is difficult to imagine different/incompatible voice connections being useful or attractive. The same consideration of commonality can apply to other common infrastructure services such as e-mail, as well as security. Nevertheless, even in these relatively protected domains of IT supply, the rapid changes in technology and supplier availability makes new relationships possible.

Technology Turbulence Changes How IT Organizations Deliver IT Services—and Quickly

While IT organizations have sought stability and well-engineered solutions to ensure service and reduce maintenance and related uncertainties, challenges to this exist, as suggested previously in this chapter. But even the fundamentals are changing in terms of IT–supplier relationships. Technology makes new ways of doing things possible; on a simple individual note, the rapid availability of cloud-delivered services, from basic storage (e.g., word processing) to data storage and backup to powerful analysis technologies, shows the patterns that become possible. The rapid diffusion of mobile devices throughout the enterprise demonstrates the forces involved.

Enterprise Implications Based on Turbulence in IT

While we aren't writing a book on IT management per se, we are interested in how IT turbulence adds to the issues of trust and partnership in general and to the broad capabilities IT (and business) require to sustain that trust and partnership to produce effective business–IT solutions for turbulence and uncertainty, as well as to provide superior business value.

There is a fundamental irony here. In some ways, alternative sourcing solutions (in contemporary terms, the cloud) reverse the relationships between the business units and IT organization(s). That is, the business unit—making independent decisions about sourcing—is the IT supplier, and the IT organization (in the sense of security, data integrity, data acquisition, and management for "Big Data" applications) is the business unit.

In some ways this is the same perspective as described in Chapter 3 for the business. There, the distinction was drawn between stable and turbulent business environments, with consequent differences on organization, governance, and so on. The same is probably applicable in the IT domain as well, with the lessons of Chapter 3 applied, but to the IT end of the process.

Similarly the lessons of Chapter 3 about turbulence, which raise the aspect of speed and adaptability (requiring the ability to find and implement solutions faster), come into play as well, as the technology turbulence introduces new technologies rapidly, challenging all the settled means of performing the elements of Strategic IT Management such as planning, operational excellence, financial management, and the like. In all cases, the turbulence requires the processes to adapt and to make decisions more rapidly. That was the case from the business perspective in Chapter 3, but the sources of the dynamics in technology here in Chapter 5 require the same adaptations.

These are starting point statements for organizational implications.

- *Governance.* The various ways decisions are made about IT are complicated enormously by the n to m nature of IT in its current form of turbulence. By "n to m," we refer to multiple business units (n) served by multiple IT providers (m). Exhibit 5.3, while assessing IT turbulence, may imply the issue is largely IT governance (i.e., the exercise of IT leadership), in fact it becomes much broader than that, to the level of corporate or enterprisewide business governance and leadership. The decisions being made affect all areas; in particular, they affect the manner in which business is conducted.
- *Software Development.* The prospect of multiple active sources of software, in a context of expecting integration and use of common infrastructure, is daunting. The questions are about things like jointly developed policies, standards, and the like.
- *Operational Excellence.* Who is responsible? What are the policies? Where is the support (e.g., help desk)?
- *Accountability.* The same questions about operational excellence apply here, but from an organizational perspective on both sides.
- *Cost Management.* Managing cost is a complex matter, particularly when there are aspects of centrally provided IT (e.g., networks) on top of which are cloud-sourced applications, and so forth.

- *Planning and Innovation.* (This area presumably includes enterprise architecture.) Again, this subject is a complex matter with the n to m relationships that can emerge.

The main point of this chapter is how the turbulence in IT significantly affects the things that have to be done to connect business and IT, to deal with turbulence, and to build trust and partnership. Some suggested principles: We aren't concerned per se about IT management itself; we're concerned about how the aspects of Strategic IT Management create and sustain the partnership/trust context that allows for effective decisions both in business and in IT regarding the issues caused by technology turbulence.[4]

Technology Turbulence Assessment

The reader is invited to self-assess (see Exhibit 5.3) how the impact of technology turbulence may be affecting the enterprise.

Exhibit 5.3   Turbulence Assessment

Technology Turbulence Impact	Current Impact on the Enterprise	Business Leadership Understanding	IT Leadership Understanding
Technology turbulence is accelerating and quickly expanding the kinds of things that are possible for the business.			
Technology turbulence in the form of significant innovations makes new business strategies and operational strategies possible—and quickly.			
Technology turbulence in the form of new methods of delivering IT (e.g., cloud) makes new IT relationships with the business outside the existing IT organization possible—and quickly.			
Technology turbulence changes how IT organizations deliver IT services—and quickly.			

Scale:
1. Little or no current impact on the enterprise; or little or no leadership understanding
2. A few areas of current impact, or some minor leadership interest and understanding
3. Beginning to see real impact, or leadership is beginning to ask serious questions
4. Current impact has spread into many areas, or leadership is paying attention
5. Significant changes have occurred, and management is devoting time and energy to the changes

References

The following sources contributed to the Technology Turbulence narratives.
Schumpeter, J. *Capitalism, Socialism, and Democracy*. New York: Harper & Row, 1942.
http://basicofcomputer.com/history_of_database_and_history_of_database_management_
   system.htm
http://ccvr.vrbandenpvs.nl/onderwerpen/rekenen2.html
http://cs-exhibitions.uni-klu.ac.at/index.php?id=222
http://hbr.org/2012/04/good-data-wont-guarantee-good-decisions/ar/1
http://history-computer.com/Babbage/LeonardoTorres.html
http://history-computer.com/People/People.html
http://invention.smithsonian.org/centerpieces/Quartz/inventors/clock.html
http://math.hws.edu/vaughn/cpsc/343/2003/history.html
http://oberlinsmith.org
http://oreilly.com/news/graphics/prog_lang_poster.pdf
http://plato.stanford.edu/entries/principia-mathematica
http://trillian.randomstuff.org.uk/~stephen//history
www.asugnews.com/2011/06/20/do-ceos-know-what-they-want-from-cios
www.ciodashboard.com/it-strategy/does-ceo-care-about-it
www.computer.org/cms/Computer.org/Publications/timeline.pdf
www.computer.org/portal/web/computingthen
www.computerhistory.org/semiconductor/timeline/1931-The-Theory.html
www.computerhope.com/history/2001.htm
www.conference-board.org/subsites/index.cfm?id=14514
www.dynamiccio.com/2011/12/should-ceo-understand-it.html
www.historyworld.net/timesearch
www.historyworld.net/timesearch/default.asp?conid=2&bottomsort=21808261&
   direction=NEXT&keywords=19thcenturytimeline&timelineid=
www.kean.edu/~rmelworm/3040-00/LuoDatabaseTimeLine.html
www.levenez.com/lang/lang_letter.pdf
www.smithsonianeducation.org/educators/lesson_plans/carbons/1920.html
www.thocp.net/index.htm
www.thocp.net/timeline/2005.htm
www.zdnet.com/blog/projectfailures/it-failure-blame-your-ceo/8401
http://www-groups.dcs.st-and.ac.uk/~history/HistTopics/Zero.html
Augarten, Stan. *BIT by BIT, An Illustrated History of Computers*. Houghton Mifflin, 1984.
British Multimedia Encyclopaedia, GSP.
A Chronology of Digital Computing Machines (to 1952). See http://www.davros.org/misc/
   chronology.html (1994).
Giscard d'Estaing, Valerie-Anne, ed. *The Book of Inventions and Discoveries*. Macdonald Queen
   Anne Press, 1991.
Moody, Glyn. *Rebel Code (Linux and the Open Source Revolution)*. Basic Books, 2002.
Ridge, Peter M., David M. Golden, Ivan Luk and Scott Sindorf. *Sound Blaster: The Official
   Book*. Osborne, 1994.
Southampton University Archaeological Computing Lecture Notes (AY3.86, 2000).
Tischer, Michael, and Bruno Jennrich. *PC Intern*, 6th ed. Abacus Software, 1996.

Notes

1. More information available at: SouthAfrica.info, "Border Cave Opens for Visitors," January 15, 2004, www.southafrica.info/travel/cultural/border-cave.htm#ixzz2LrRK2l4k; also, K. Kris Hirst, "Border Cave (South Africa)," About.com, http://archaeology.about.com/od/bterms/g/bordercave.htm

2. See, for example, Gartner, "Hype Cycles," Gartner website | Research Methodologies, www.gartner.com/technology/research/methodologies/hype-cycle.jsp. Since its origination in 1995, the Hype Cycle has grown to nearly 100 technology categories embracing nearly 2,000 technologies.

3. See, for example, "A Special Report: Manufacturing and Innovation—A Third Industrial Revolution," *The Economist*, April 21, 2012.

4. See, for example, *The Cutter IT Journal* 26, No. 7 (July 2013), which poses the question "Is IT Still Relevant?"

CHAPTER 6

The Effects of IT Sourcing

I T services may be provided by the internal IT department or by external suppliers. Both options impact the relationship between business and IT. We start with discussing this choice as a strategic concern and how this impacts strategic, tactical, and operational decision making with regard to IT. Next, the discussion continues with the effects of trust and turbulence. We conclude with a view on how internal versus external services delivery may evolve in the near future.

The IT Services Supplier as a Strategic Concern

A key strategic IT management concern is the question of who will supply the IT services that the business needs. This may be a corporate or business unit IT department, it may be one or more external IT service suppliers, and of course it may be a combination of both. This concern is not only typical for IT; other functions, such as human resources (HR), accounting, and logistics, face the same questions. IT, particularly considering the developments in Internet-based communication both from person to system and from system to system, has been one of the drivers of this development. Availability of bandwidth and Internet technology makes it possible for HR services to be delivered from a central location (e.g., London) to staff located worldwide; these can even be customized to a high degree using so-called á la carte services. Another example is delivering accounting services from Bangalore to Western companies with a global presence.

In many industries, there is a clear trend that enterprises are concentrating on core business areas and outsourcing other areas to specialized suppliers. Decisions about service provisioning and planning long-term relationships

---

This chapter is based on earlier publications of the results of a research program at Tilburg University: E. Beulen, P. Ribbers, and J. Roos, *Managing IT Outsourcing*, 2nd ed. (Routledge, 2011).

with suppliers have become a part of the strategic planning process. These decisions determine a firm's position in its competitive environment relative to its customers, suppliers, and other stakeholders. Of course, tactical make-or-buy decisions still exist concerning how the company can procure specific goods and services within the current planning period in a cost-efficient way.

We distinguish between strategic insourcing and strategic outsourcing. Strategic insourcing is based on long-term motives, such as keeping core competencies in house and safeguarding confidentiality. Strategic outsourcing is likewise based on longer-term motives such as creating a more agile organization and gaining access to important complementary resources that can be better supplied from outside than developed internally. The focus here is on a longer-term relationship, where companies collaboratively plan their moves in a common competitive environment. The intercompany dependency is consequently high, and contract periods will encompass a longer (strategic) planning horizon.

Strategic IT Outsourcing

Strategic IT outsourcing can be defined as handing over the responsibility for the execution of all or part of the organization's IT services to one or more external IT services suppliers, based on a long-term contract; this may occur with or without transfer of staff and assets. Examples of such relations are data center outsourcing, network operations outsourcing, desktop outsourcing, applications outsourcing services, help desk outsourcing, and disaster recovery. According to a recent study among 137 U.S. and Canadian companies by Computer Economics,[1] IT outsourcing has been rising in the past decade. Still, according to this study, in 2013 the portion of the typical IT budget that is allocated to outsourcing is up about 23 percent. In particular, software as a service, data center outsourcing, web e-commerce systems and application development, and help desk and desktop support are important in this respect.

Can every function within IT be outsourced? When discussing IT management, a distinction is made between demand management and supply management.[2] Demand management is business oriented. It is about specifying the organizational needs for information and information systems. Demand management is typically a business responsibility. Supply management has a technology focus. It is about managing information resources—people, assets, processes—in such a way that the organization's demand for information is met effectively in a cost-efficient manner.

As demand is an integral business responsibility, it is typically not a candidate for outsourcing. On the other hand, supply is about installing and managing the technology in order to deliver the needed information.

This is often an activity quite apart from the core business of the organization, and it requires different skills and knowledge bases. As such, supply management may typically be (but is not necessarily) a candidate for outsourcing. In the 1990s, Philips, an international producer of electronics headquartered in the Netherlands, decided to restructure their demand and supply management. They first outsourced the application part of the internal IT department and later outsourced their infrastructure management. The initial structuring and the phased approach enabled the implementation of an adequate demand management.[3]

There are three levels of decision making in the management of any business activity: strategic-level decisions, which relate to the long-term objectives of the organization; tactical-level decisions, which ensure that planned resources are obtained and used to accomplish the stated objectives; and operational-level decisions, which ensure tasks are carried out according to plan. This same distinction applies to IT. Outsourcing has different implications for each organizational level. Generally speaking, strategy cannot be outsourced. Day-to-day IT service delivery can potentially be outsourced, since it involves more operational tasks.

Strategic-Level IT Responsibilities

IT strategy relates to long-term plans with regard to demand and supply, and belongs on a strategic organizational level. The demand perspective focuses on the information and systems required to enable business strategy implementation. These views and plans are sanctioned by management and intended to support the objectives of the organization in the long run.

The supply perspective specifies how the required information provisioning and systems will be supported by technology. It encompasses choices with regard to hardware, software, databases, networks, and related standards, and it defines the services to be delivered, such as computer operations, data management, software development, maintenance, and user support. The supply perspective also addresses which IT services will be delivered by the company's internal IT department and which will be outsourced to external service providers. Both the demand and supply side of IT strategy relate to information, applications, and technology, but each from a different perspective.

Despite obvious difficulties, some strategic aspects are, in fact, sometimes supplied by service providers. Manning the strategic level can be difficult for many companies. Contracting external consultants may offer one solution. The company maintains responsibility for and control over strategy but hires external staff to fill the knowledge gap and/or provide extra capacity when there are peaks in the tasks to be carried out.

Tactical-Level IT Responsibilities

Planning the quantity and type of IT services to be delivered during the upcoming planning period and ensuring the proper utilization of these services (e.g., through training) is within the province of the tactical organizational level. With either outsourcing or in-house IT service delivery, tight agreements must be laid out in service-level agreements (SLAs). In the case of outsourcing, the need for watertight contracts is of course greater, since there is only a contractual relationship with the service provider(s) as opposed to a hierarchical relationship. Nevertheless, in practice it is often impossible to foresee every eventuality and cover it within the scope of a SLA.

Service providers increasingly offer tactical activities in their menu of services. This enables them not only to increase their turnover but to strengthen their grip on the client. For this reason, outsourcing tactical activities may not always be a good idea.[4]

Operational-Level IT Responsibilities

Responsibility for actual delivery and proper use of IT services is an operational matter. Outsourcing is primarily an issue for capabilities and activities on this level. Agreements and contractual obligations entered into on the tactical level control the relationship and service provision. Nevertheless, the dynamics of such obligations have always been a source of trouble and will continue to be so in the future.[5] This situation continues to grow even more complex with the increasing number of companies involved in mergers and acquisitions and new technological developments, like the rise of mobile applications and bring-your-own-device (BYOD) policies.

The Impact of Trust and Turbulence

Whether an internal IT department or an external provider is chosen for service delivery may depend on the effects of trust and turbulence.

Trust

Managing an IT partnership relationship is not a matter of the "hard side" only. Much attention must be paid to the "soft side," especially trust. Trust in IT partnerships reflects the confidence of the service recipient in the service provider to meet the agreed performance milestones and metrics stipulated in the SLA.[6] In general, from a trust perspective, outsourcing forms a bigger challenge than in-house production and delivery. Companies have their own profit and loss (P&L) statements and are driven by them. Opportunistic behavior lurks behind every potential outsourcing agreement. Not everyone is equally honest. Some people try to exploit situations to their own advantage. Not everybody does, of course, and not all of the time. But the problem is that some people do some of the time, and when you do business, it is difficult to distinguish between the honest and the dishonest. As a result, most transactions involve numerous inspections, controls, certifications, and the like, even if the partner involved is considered perfectly trustworthy. The occurrence of opportunism will therefore increase costs. This is especially important when there are few potential trading partners. These partners will care less about their reputations, as there are few alternatives to which their clients may turn if they are not satisfied. The fact is that outsourcing companies can never fully and accurately judge the quality of their potential suppliers, nor their true intentions. Therefore, it is important that they mitigate the risks involved in the selection stage by gathering as much independent information about their potential suppliers as possible. Sources for such information include market research, current and former clients who are familiar with the supplier's track record, and sometimes independent authorities or institutes, who may carry out benchmarking activities. Opportunism may also explain the rise of certification procedures in the past decade or two, such as the ISO certification process.

Once the contract has been signed, the recipient must ensure that the tasks he is paying for are carried out in his best interests. The service supplier, however, has a major information advantage, so his actions are difficult to assess from the recipient side. Service suppliers may boost their own profits, for example, by spending less time or utilizing fewer resources than agreed. Monitoring is one way of countering this risk, but it is costly, since one must set performance standards and measure the actual work performed or have it audited by an independent authority. Another method to combat this problem is to align the supplier's interests with those of the outsourcing company by introducing positive enforcement measures, such as incentive schemes, for example.[7]

For these and other reasons, the presence of trust improves the performance of interorganizational exchanges in general, as it allows free and flexible communication and fewer formal controls to be established. A targeted policy aimed at promoting confidence in an outsourcing relationship comprises several components. Of primary importance is a mutually agreed-upon method of conflict resolution, in which both parties view the decision process to be fair and just. This type of atmosphere supports feelings of fair treatment. Communication is a key in building trust, as two-way communication has been widely identified as a major contributing factor in trusting relationships. For example, service providers must provide clear and understandable reports on the services they have delivered; service recipients should give clear feedback on their suppliers' performance. Essentially, this is a matter of communication hygiene, and it applies to the parties' formal communication protocols. With respect to informal communication, trust may be generated through consultation prior to more formal discussion formats. In addition to trust between organizations and groups, trust must also be established between individuals. Both provider and recipient must get a feel for which personal profiles best fit the management of their partnership, and staff in both organizations need to take the time to get to know each other. Trust also plays a role in reporting. Reports should not only concern the services delivered but the degree of trust between partners as well. It goes without saying that these measures also apply when IT service delivery is the responsibility of an internal department; however, as said before, outsourcing makes it more difficult.

Turbulence

Next to trust, dynamic environmental conditions will affect the relationship, too. Change impacts the requirements and the volume of services needed. Hard-to-predict change makes this more critical, as there is little time to react, as we saw in Chapter 2. The possibility of swiftly adapting requirements and scaling the availability of services up or down is paramount under these circumstances. The level of flexibility required under these conditions may be a driver for outsourcing, as flexibility may be the added value of a supplier who is a big player in the IT services industry. However, what potentially may be expected from the supplier and what the supplier may be able to offer under these conditions is difficult, even impossible, to specify in detailed contracts. Close collaboration and flexible adaptation by both recipient and provider are paramount. Again, trust is the key ingredient that provides a flexible relationship between the organizations concerned, allowing them to sustain the relationship over the strategic planning horizon.[8]

Looking Ahead[9]

A few developments will play an important role in the near future, in the sense that they will significantly influence outsourcing relationships and their management. These are standardization and commoditization, the trend toward business process outsourcing, and cloud computing.

Increasing standardization makes IT a commodity. Commoditization takes place in two main areas: applications and IT services. Standardizing applications makes it easier for companies to communicate with each other, which is of special importance to companies collaborating in a network organization. IT services are increasingly becoming commodities. Unit pricing is not only common practice for desktop seats, but for ERP seats as well. Commercial off-the-shelf solutions (COTS) become the preferred option for many service recipients, who, by standardizing, reduce the number of customer-specific requirements to an absolute minimum. This contributes to low application management costs. Important suppliers of IT services, like IBM, Accenture, and EDS, are developing "on-demand" and "utility" types of service delivery.[10] The expectation is that recipients will have access to the kind of IT services they desire, when they need them, and in the volumes they need. Even when these volumes fluctuate, recipients are only billed for the types and volumes of services they purchase.

Business process outsourcing (BPO) began slowly in the 1980s and continued to develop throughout the 1990s. Essentially, it may be considered an extension of IT outsourcing: The provider not only delivers IT services but uses those services to carry out one or more of the recipient's entire business processes. This usually concerns processes in which IT plays a central role. To deliver those services, suppliers need a thorough knowledge of the process concerned and often of its industry-specific characteristics. Currently, BPO is found mostly in the financial industry.[11] This is a consequence of the information processing intensity that is characteristic of financial corporations. Another reason for this is the fact that financial institutions were among the first to computerize their business processes, which is now causing them legacy problems.

Cloud computing is a practice on the rise. The concept is founded on sharing the capacity of available resources. Clouds are large pools of easily usable and accessible virtualized resources, such as hardware, development platforms, and services. These resources can be dynamically reconfigured to adjust to a variable load (scale), allowing optimum resource utilization.[12] Trust is very important in cloud computing, since it involves letting go of the dedicated environment used for a single client.[13] This worries auditors, who must assess the way in which companies have organized their IT services.[14] Although expectations are high, the question remains whether the market will solve all the problems involved.

References

Cullen, S., and L. Willcocks. *Intelligent IT Outsourcing: Eight Building Blocks to Success.* Butterworth-Heinemann, 2003.

Weinhardt, C., A. Anandasivam, B. Blau, N. Borissov, W. Michalk, and J. Stosser. "Cloud-Computing." *Wirtschaftsinformatik* 51, No. 5 (2009).

Notes

1. "IT Outsourcing Statistics," Computer Economics, Inc., 2012.
2. S. Cullen and L. Willcocks, *Intelligent IT Outsourcing: Eight Building Blocks to Success* (Butterworth-Heinemann, 2003).
3. E. Beulen, P. Ribbers, and J. Roos, *Managing IT Outsourcing*, 2nd ed. (Routledge, 2011).
4. V. Grover and J. Teng, "The Decision to Outsource Information Systems Functions," *Journal of Systems Management* 44, No. 11 (November 1993).
5. M. Lacity and R. Hirschheim, *Information Systems Outsourcing* (Wiley, 1993).
6. Lacity and Hirschheim, *Information Systems Outsourcing.*
7. "IT Outsourcing Statistics," Computer Economics, Inc.
8. K. Sabherwal, "The Role of Trust in Outsourced IS Development Projects," *Communications of the Association for Computing Machinery* 42, No. 2 (1999): 80–86.
9. See Chapter 7, "Information Systems Sourcing," in Keri E. Pearlman and Carol S. Saunders, *"The Tools for Change," Managing and Using Information Systems: A Strategic Approach*, 4th ed. (Wiley, 2010), for a good description of alternative sourcing models. See also Beulen, Ribbers, and Roos, *Managing IT Outsourcing.*
10. J. Ross and G. Westerman, "Preparing for Utility Computing: The Role of Architecture and Relationship Management," *IBM Systems Journal* 43, No. 1 (2004).
11. J. Tas and S. Sunder, "New Architectures for Financial Services: Financial Services Business Process Outsourcing," *Communications of the Association for Computing Machinery* 47, No. 5 (2004).
12. L. Vacquero, J. Caceres, M. Linder, and L. Rodero-Merino, "A Break in the Clouds: Toward a Cloud Definition," *ACM SIGCOMM Computer Communication Review* 39 (2009).
13. C. Everett, "Cloud Computing: A Question of Trust," *Computer Fraud & Security* 6, No. 06 (2009).
14. Weinhardt, C., A. Anandasivam, B. Blau, N. Borissov, W. Michalk, and J. Stosser. "Cloud-Computing," *Wirtschaftsinformatik* 51, No. 5 (2009).

PART TWO

Principles for Transforming Business in Turbulent Times

C hapter 1 introduced the idea that the business–IT relationship has two distinct and related elements: first, the partnership element characterized by common goals and mutual trust, and second, the service element characterized by competent IT service delivery and appropriate business expectations for those services. Together, the partnership and service relationship describes how business and IT work to achieve the goal of superior business response to turbulence and superior business value from the use of information and IT in the business. Exhibit II.1 shows a simplistic view of the two elements of the relationship.

We'll focus more intensely on the service relationship element in Chapter 8 and the partnership issues in Chapter 9. But the main point is that both service and partnership aspects of the business–IT relationship apply.

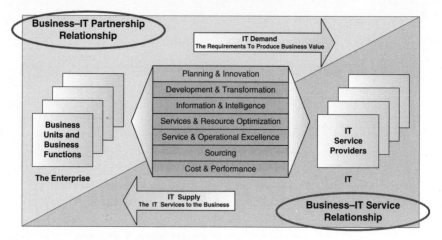

Exhibit II.1   Business and IT Relationships

Strategic IT Management Principles for the Business and IT Relationship

Strategic IT Management frames the requirements for the partnership and service relationship between business and IT.

1. **Service-Based Relationship:** *The business and IT relationship is based on IT services delivering value and building credibility and trust.* IT has to perform with credible and effective services, no matter its source (e.g., the IT organization, external providers and sources, and internal providers within the business). The IT organizational and personal culture needs to focus on services with business outcomes. Chapter 8 describes the requirements for a service-based relationship.

2. **Partnership-Based Relationship:** *The business and IT relationship is also a partnership.* Credible IT service is necessary to build trust, but this is not sufficient to support partnership. The challenge is that IT's culture, performance, credibility, and transparency typically do not encourage trust, and IT is not good at developing partnerships. Business typically does not fully participate as well. The challenge is that IT is typically overly IT-centric, and this creates barriers in partnering with business. Proactivity by IT in building this business-focused culture is required. Chapter 9 describes the requirements for a partnership-based relationship.

3. **Leadership:** *Senior business and IT management provides support for the business–IT relationship and provides leadership throughout the life of the*

relationship. IT leadership creates a business-focused culture and nurtures the best relationships within IT and with the business. The CEO and business leadership establish the environment for the partnership, the roles to be played, and the necessary commitment and motivation. Chapter 10 describes the leadership required.

4. **Engagement:** *Business and IT managers participate in business–IT partnerships.* Every management level is engaged in and provides leadership for joint business–IT activities. Chapter 11 connects the leadership, culture, and engagement required for business and IT leadership.

5. **Governance:** *The IT and business relationship is governed at all levels with effective decision-making processes.* These are characterized by transparency, trust, and business and IT and do not act as inhibitors and bureaucratic barriers.

6. **Outcomes:** *The enterprise produces outcomes at all stair steps of the Total Value Performance Model (TVPM).* Partnership, leadership, engagement, IT services, and governance produce superior business value and responses to turbulence and uncertainty. These outcomes include business adaptability and flexibility, data and process integration within and without the enterprise, and timely planning and decision capabilities. Chapters 2 and 4 describe the stair steps and outcomes necessary.

7. **IT Competencies:** *Business and IT have the tools and ability to execute the tasks and methodologies required within each capability.* The IT competencies can be deployed throughout the enterprise, engaging any IT provider (central IT organization, business IT activity, sourcing/cloud sources, do-it-yourself IT) and each business unit using IT. Chapter 7 describes these competencies.

8. **Enterprise IT Capabilities.** *The enterprise possesses the seven capabilities based on trust, leadership, and partnership to create superior value and responses to turbulence and uncertainty.* Exhibit II.1 shows the seven, and Chapter 11 introduces their characteristics and requirements. Part III describes each enterprise IT capability in detail.

That all of these conditions are important to the success of the systemic business–IT relationship is a given. They are particularly important when conditions of turbulence, change, and uncertainty plague the enterprise. Their absence cause significant barriers to achieving what's necessary.

In each chapter, we'll restate the relevant conditions for success and demonstrate what needs to be done. Note that these principles may be read as though "IT" is a single IT organization in the company that provides services to all elements of the company. As we'll describe through Part II, this is an oversimplification. IT sources (as shown in Exhibit II.2) can be multiple:

Exhibit II.2   Strategic Management Scorecard

Strategic IT Management Principles	CEO's and SLT's Perceptions	Business Unit Executive's Perceptions	IT Managers' and Professionals' Perceptions
Service-based Relationship: The business and IT relationship is based on IT services delivering value and building credibility and trust.	Don't know	No	Sometimes
Partner-based Relationship: The business and IT relationship is a partnership.	Don't know	No	Sometimes
Leadership: Senior business and IT management provides support for the business–IT relationship and provides leadership throughout the life of the relationship.	Unaware of the need	No	No
Engagement: Business and IT managers participate in business–IT partnerships.	No	No	Sometimes
Governance: The IT and business relationship is governed at all levels with effective decision-making processes.	Unaware of the need	Significantly Inhibit	Unaware of the need
Outcomes: The enterprise produces outcomes at all levels of the Total Value Performance Model (TVPM).	Uncertain	Uncertain	Uncertain
IT Competencies: Business and IT have the tools and ability to execute the tasks and methodologies required within each capability.	Don't know	Sometimes	Yes
Enterprise IT Capabilities. The enterprise possesses the seven capabilities based on trust, leadership, and partnership to create superior value and responses to turbulence and uncertainty.	Don't know	No	Certainly

outsourcers, the "cloud," the internal IT organization, business-unit-specific IT organizations, and "self-help" IT. But they all fall within these basic principles.

Scale

1. Unaware of Need or Don't Know or No
2. Significantly Inhibit
3. Uncertain
4. Sometimes
5. Yes, certainly

Note, however, that these principles are, substantively, process-oriented in nature. That is, they ask what should be done to cope with turbulence and so forth, and how those tasks should be accomplished. This process view overlooks a more fundamental issue that we'll deal with in Part III, namely, the critical role of the business and IT mental models that characterize the as-is and to-be of the business. We introduced them at the end of Chapter 1 to show the kind of changes involved. Mental models define where we are now and the fundamental changes moving to the future. This underpins the use of process (and principles) to actually get there.[1]

A Scorecard for Strategic IT Management Principles

We often use a scorecard to assess the current situation in a business and IT organization. The scorecard details are described in each subsequent section. Consider applying this scorecard to your current circumstances. We show this scorecard example with results that summarize the outcomes from a number of enterprises in North America.

The results we've produced through our workshops show the real problems: that the perceptions between IT and business not only are different, but they do not form the kind of foundation required for trust and partnership. This disconnect between business and IT reflects a compelling theme throughout Part II, in terms of the steps needed to close it.

We suggest the reader look at the scorecard (Exhibit II.2) and apply it to the reader's organization.

Finally, in Chapter 11, we begin to outline the specific requirements for enterprise IT capabilities. In Chapter 7, we focus on requirements based on turbulence and uncertainty, as well as the current under-performance of the IT activities. These, taken with what will come in Chapters 8, 9, and 10, will produce a summation of requirements, mapped to the enterprise requirements themselves. We'll define them and how they relate to the specific practices employed by the business and IT organization.

Note

1. Gary Hamel, with Bill Breen, *The Future of Management* (Harvard Business Review Press, 2007).

CHAPTER 7

Requirements for Strategic IT Management

I n this chapter, we wrap up the conclusions from the earlier chapters and discuss their consequences for (strategic) IT management. First, we focus on the impact that turbulence and trust have on strategic IT management, then we focus on their consequences for creating effective business–IT partnerships. We conclude with a discussion on the need for *relational governance*.

The Impact of Turbulence and Trust

IT management encompasses the entire management process with regard to information systems utilized by a business. It comprises the whole cycle: agreeing on objectives to be pursued via IT, making plans to reach those objectives, organizing resources so that plans can be realized, creating and monitoring conditions to ensure that realization occurs according to plans, and finally, controlling the outcome and intervening when realized results deviate from plans. The strategic component of IT management (strategic IT management) relates specifically to deciding on, implementing, and making appropriate use of information systems that support the long-term objectives of the company. These plans are typically sanctioned by senior management. The term *IT* is here being used in its broader sense; it does not only relate to the technology as such, but includes the whole "system" of organizational, procedural, human, and technological factors that enable organizations to gather, store, retrieve, and process data, and deliver meaningful information to users.

The premise of the earlier chapters has been that this process of strategic IT management is impacted, even impeded, by two major factors: the business and technological uncertainty and turbulence under which IT has to operate, and the lack of trust between business and IT professionals involved in the (strategic) management of IT. Although these two factors are independent of one another and could be discussed as such, they are interrelated. Working under conditions of high uncertainty and turbulence requires high levels of trust. One has to be able to count on the other, as there is no time for checks, negotiations, or anything else. On the other hand, the absence of trust leads to hoarding information—instead of sharing—and thus increases uncertainty for the other parties. When discussing the impact of these factors on strategic management of IT, we will start with the effects of turbulence.

The Impact of Turbulence

Strategic IT management is impacted by two general sources of turbulence: general business-related turbulence and IT-related turbulence. When a company is functioning under conditions of general turbulence, the whole organization is affected, not only IT. Shortening product life cycles, fickle customer behavior, changing supply markets, changing legal and regulatory conditions, new competition from emerging markets—all are sources of uncertainty and turbulence that directly affect the genes of the entire organization, not just a single department. Of course, they also affect the information services the company needs. Under these conditions, just making IT more flexible will not help; if an organization functions like a bunker while IT operates like a flexible jet fighter (or vice versa), the additional flexibility in one structure will not help the overall business very much.

So what are the characteristics of an organization functioning under turbulence? We concluded that turbulence causes two fundamental problems:

- The inability to make reliable forecasts
- The inability to react quickly enough

Let us discuss the impact of both on strategic IT management separately.

The inability to make reliable forecasts is inherent to uncertainty and, in particular, to turbulence. This does not imply, however, that organizations would have to be literally totally uninformed about what they may expect in the future. These organizations should develop capabilities that will help them survive under these conditions. They should develop an enterprise-wide strategy aiming at what Steve Haeckel calls "knowing earlier" when discussing the "sense and respond organization."[1] "Knowing earlier" is what we referred to as a *dynamic capability* in Chapter 3. We defined a dynamic capability as "the ability to sense and then seize new opportunities and to reconfigure and protect knowledge assets, competencies and complementary assets so as to achieve sustained competitive advantage."[2] Several technical, planning, and organizational measures contribute to this capability.

For being prepared for what may happen in the long-term or mid-long-term future, a company may apply scenario planning. Scenario planning, being "the art of the long view,"[3] does not produce forecasts; scenarios are possible futures that may result from interdependencies between known factors that have high impact, but which occurrences are highly uncertain. Scenario planning can be exercised at the enterprise level; for example, Shell[4] is known for integrating scenario planning into its enterprise planning systems. Scenario planning also can be exercised at the functional level, for example, for analyzing possible developments in the application of IT.

When forecasting is unreliable, the organization may develop the ability to "sense"—basically, to capture instant information about the current state of the environment and adapt quickly to it. Techniques like environmental scanning, early warning signals, and developing superior business analytics have proven to enable an organization to be responsive. Also, various information technologies that enable the capture of structured data and unstructured data support sensing.[5] An example of the former are data captured through point of sales terminals or barcodes; examples of the latter are data gathered from social sites, communities, blogs, and the like. The Spanish fashion chain Zara has been highly successful in applying these principles; it developed the most responsive supply chain in the industry.[6,7] Zara does not need nine months to design, produce, and deliver new designs to its stores, as is the norm in the industry. It manages to introduce new apparel designs from concept to stores within two weeks. Instead of relying on (unreliable) forecasts, it manages the supply chain by using up-to-date information. The habits and tastes of potential customers are continuously tracked and recorded. Sales figures, including information on what has not been sold, are communicated on a daily basis by all the store managers to the headquarters in La Coruna. As part of its continuous market research, Zara visits university campuses, discos, and similar youth-oriented locations to sense fashion trends. So when Madonna was touring in Spain, teenage girls at her last concert were wearing the outfit she wore for her first concert.[8] By working this way, Zara avoids profit-eroding yearly sales, which are caused by working with unreliable forecasts.

Besides the ability to know earlier, the organization must have the ability to react quickly enough, or putting it differently, to "respond."[9] This ability impacts the organization at large. The organization should be structured in such a way that it is prepared to act swiftly. We concluded that under uncertainty and turbulence, organizations are characterized by organic structures as opposed to traditional bureaucratic, mechanistic structures. Organic structures aim at realizing flexibility and responsiveness instead of predictable, efficient, and controllable behavior. Key ingredients of organic structures are delegation and empowerment as opposed to command and control; horizontal linking mechanisms and mutual adjustment as opposed to centrally imposed coordination and procedures; cross-organizational communication as opposed to predominantly vertical communication aimed at commanding, reporting, and controlling. Such a responsive system is what Steve Haeckel calls "a structure for action" instead of "a structure of action."[10]

Also, the installed IT can support or impede responsiveness. Information flows across departmental, functional, and geographical units should be facilitated by interoperable systems rather than restrained by architectural silos based on local standards. On an interorganizational level, IT systems should support easy information exchange and interfirm collaboration. The IT systems themselves also must be able to adapt quickly to the changing demands imposed on them. The available infrastructure capacity should be able to scale up or down flexibly. Easy modifications in available functionality, necessitated by fast-changing business demands, should be made possible by reconfigurable modular components. Mergers, acquisitions, and divestments impact the delivery of IT services. Information systems must be coupled and realigned or, in the case of divestments, disentangled. The ability to connect and disconnect quickly is a key characteristic of a flexible IT architecture.

As stated previously, business-related turbulence is not the only type of turbulence affecting IT. Irrespective of business-related turbulence, the IT function can experience turbulence because of (sudden) changes in available technology and in the supply market of IT services. These may affect the mere service provisioning by the IT department, but they may also directly or indirectly affect the business as well. New technologies and practices are being introduced with an increasing frequency, it seems, such as mobile infrastructures and applications, social media, cloud computing, and bring your own device (BYOD). New, easy-to-use applications, mashups, are downloadable from the Internet and challenge the position of the traditional IT department. The question is how a company should include these developments in its strategic IT management. Again, this is a question of being informed in a timely matter and acting upon that information adequately.

First, an organization should actively apply environmental scanning to be informed in a timely manner about developments that may affect it. Research organizations like Gartner provide views on developments in information technology and thus may be instrumental in this endeavor. As for acting upon information adequately, developments in applicable IT are uncertain, to a degree; however, it is quite predictable that the company, in the near future, will have to deal with some of them. So companies must be better prepared for this type of scenario. Practices need to be in place to assess emerging technologies on their added value and risks. There needs to be room for experimentation, both in terms of budget and resources. Results of experiments are documented for learning and further use and then assessed; experiments, by definition, do not necessarily lead to actual implementations. Of course, this policy can only foster change if it is embedded in a management culture that is tolerant of failures and open to outside ideas.

The Impact of Trust

Trust is the foundation upon which a business organization depends. Without trust, an extensive system of checks and controls becomes necessary, and operations become inefficient. Lack of trust impedes information and knowledge sharing, with all its consequential effects on performance. We concluded that trust is a multidimensional concept, encompassing competence, openness, caring, and reliability trust. Among these dimensions there is a hierarchy (see Exhibit 7.1). Competence-trust is a prerequisite: if there is no shown competence, there will be no trust. Openness-trust is the next prerequisite: if there are perceived, even suspected, hidden agendas, the basis for open communication and collaboration does not exist. For a true business–IT partnership, business trust in IT is dependent on a foundation of proven competency and openness. When occurring on an operational management level, the competency to have systems up and running as agreed is the dominant trust dimension. It also plays out on higher managerial levels, where the freedom for IT to act as a credible partner depends on this proven ability. On higher management strata, the other dimensions of trust (caring and reliability) grow in importance. Moreover, in higher management strata, next to organizational trust, person-based trust is a foundation for a true business–IT partnership. These conditions also apply to the business as seen

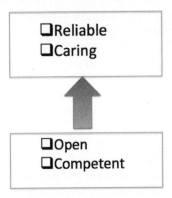

Exhibit 7.1   Hierarchy of Trust

from the perspective of IT, as trust is a relational concept. For the business–IT relationship to function well, trust needs to be reciprocal: IT needs to trust the business too, which finds its foundation on the same grounds.

Trust is an issue in its own right, in that it has an impact on the business–IT relationship no matter what the conditions are. However, under turbulence, it becomes a key concern. Successfully acting under turbulence conditions depends on the existence of open and effective relationships. The involved business and IT professionals must be able to rely on each other blindly. In other words, lack of trust slows an organization significantly and reduces its effectiveness.

Turbulence and Trust: Requirements for Business–IT Partnership

In this section, we address the question "What are specific requirements for an effective partnership between business and IT resulting from turbulence and trust?" Starting from the traditional framework of strategic, tactical, and operational management, we discuss the competencies for strategic IT management required at each level. As a result, this section provides a list of competencies for strategic IT management under conditions of challenging organizational change.

IT-Related Responsibilities, Planning Levels, and Competencies

There are many ways to describe strategy. We define strategy as a set of decisions that drives future plans and principle policies and defines the business in which the enterprise operates. In general, strategy refers to corporate strategy, which is the strategy that drives the enterprise as a whole. Business units within larger corporations have their own strategies related to their own product–market environment. From the corporate or business strategies is derived the notion of functional strategies. In every organization, responsibilities, activities, and roles are allocated to specific individuals and groups. This allocation is based on principles of division of labor, which aim at balancing the benefits of specialization and the costs of coordination. That is how regularly known functional areas have emerged, like marketing, finance, and HR.

These principles equally apply to all responsibilities and activities related to information and information technology. With regard to the latter, a distinction may be made between information systems (IS) and information technology (IT) and their respective management. Information systems is defined as "the means by which people and organizations, utilizing technology, gather, process, store, use and disseminate information."[11] IS strategy thus concerns total investments made in the application portfolio (e.g., strategic applications, business critical systems, infrastructure, etc.), the benefits expected from them, and the necessary organizational and other changes to deliver the benefits.[12] IS relates to the purposeful use and exploitation of IT. In that context, IT strategy refers specifically to how the application portfolio will be supported by technology. It encompasses hardware, software, databases, networks, and related standards, and defines the services to be delivered, such as computer operations, data management, software development, maintenance, and user support. In this book, we will conform to international standards and use the IT function as the responsible function for IS and IT. Making sure, through an appropriate IT strategy, that the needed information and information systems are available to the business functions is thus the responsibility of the IT function.

The management of any business activity can be described on the basis of Anthony's traditional planning and control framework. This framework distinguishes three levels of management decisions:

- *Strategic level:* Strategic decisions typically relate to the long-term objectives of the organization, changes in those objectives, resources needed to attain those objectives, and policies that govern the acquisition, use, and disposition of those resources.
- *Tactical level:* This level concerns the management activity through which managers ensure that the planned resources are obtained and used to accomplish the stated objectives.
- *Operational level:* Operational-level activities are about ensuring that specific tasks are carried out according to plan.

These planning levels form a hierarchy, with the strategic level at the top and the operational level at the bottom. The longer the effect of a plan, the more difficult to reverse and the more strategic it is. More judgment is needed the higher the importance of a decision and the more strategic it is. However, in practical situations, distinctions are not always that clear. Often the distinction is more relative than absolute.

Strategic-Level IT Responsibilities

Obviously, the strategy with regard to IS and IT belongs on a strategic organizational level. First, the appropriate alignment of business and IT requires the development of a vision of how IT should support the business and also how IT may enable new strategies and business models. The (out-) sourcing strategy is part of this; it defines which IT services will be delivered by the company's internal IT department and which will be outsourced to external service providers. The IT strategy also includes choices about architecture. The IS/IT architecture is part of a broader enterprise architecture. The enterprise architecture has a broad scope and encompasses the strategy, the organization structure, business processes, and information (and other) systems.[13] It may be defined as the deliberate design of the enterprise as a whole. Within that, the IS/IT architecture concerns, specifically, applications, databases, hardware, and networks, must fit the other layers of the enterprise architecture.

Tactical-Level IT Responsibilities

Planning the quantity and type of IT services to be delivered during the upcoming planning period and ensuring the proper utilization of these services (e.g., through training) is a matter for tactical organization levels. Agreements with internal departments and with external suppliers must be laid down in contracts and service-level agreements (SLAs).

Operational-Level IT Responsibilities

Finally, there is the challenge of delivery of low-cost and high-quality IT services. The responsibility for the actual delivery and use of IT services day to day is an operational matter. With its IT operations, the business finally realizes (or not) the value of its IT investments. Contractual obligations entered into the tactical level point the way here. Nevertheless, the dynamics of such obligations have always been a source of trouble. Should IT focus more on being proactive versus being reactive? How does IT deliver high quality while reducing costs? Is stability more important, or responsiveness to the business? All of these present a delicate balancing act that occurs every day.[14]

Competencies for Strategic IT Management

IT strategic management necessitates specific competences on each of the three planning levels. The competences required per planning level are further discussed in the following sections.

We presented Strategic IT Management principles for transforming business in turbulent times in the Introduction to Part II.

IT Competencies: *Business and IT have the tools and ability to execute the tasks and methodologies required within each capability.* The IT competencies can be deployed throughout the enterprise, engaging any IT provider (central IT organization, business–IT activity, sourcing/cloud sources, do-it-yourself IT) and each business unit using IT (Exhibit 7.2).

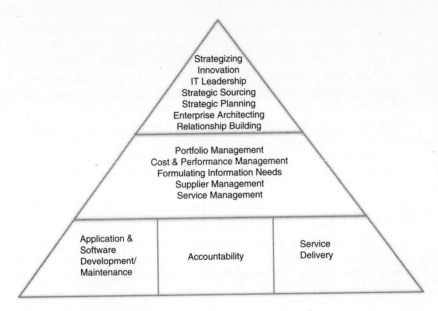

Exhibit 7.2   IT Competencies

Strategic-Level Competencies

Managing IT on a strategic level requires the competences of strategizing, innovation, IT leadership, architecture planning, strategic planning, and relationship building.

Strategizing. Strategizing encompasses devising a strategy or a course of action. Strategizing for strategic IT management is about envisioning how modern business management can be optimally supported, and how business models and processes can be reshaped by exploiting the possibilities of modern IT. The IT function's most important task is making sure the business information and support requirements are met. It must therefore deploy information technology so that it makes a maximum contribution to business management. As a consequence, the IT function must be aware of the developments in the field of information technology as well as in its company's markets.

Innovation. The IT function is a driver of business- and technology-related innovation par excellence. Dramatic changes in established ways of working and end-to-end business processes crossing organizational boundaries, with a tremendous downward effect on transaction costs, are only a few examples. However, innovations within the IT function with regard to ways that services are delivered also may have an unexpected impact on the business; examples of these are the introduction of cloud computing and mobile technology. Making innovation work and achieve its desired effects requires close collaboration with the business functions, as its eventual impact depends on complementary organizational and management changes.

IT Leadership. Leadership sets out the vision and the direction in which to go with IT. The business functions expect a reliable partner in discussions on the implementation and use of IT at all levels of management. Business and IT plans are the result of cocreation, in which shared understanding results in broadly supported IT plans. The IT function is expected to be a mainstay in all business discussions in which IT is an important topic. Closely related to this competency is the next one.

Strategic Outsourcing. Concentrating on core business has become the trend in many industries. This means that those activities that are not core to the business are outsourced to specialized suppliers. As a result, decisions on how to acquire the basic products and services required to meet the customers' needs have come to be of strategic importance. They define the company's position in the competitive environment. The long-term relationships with internal and external suppliers that are the result of such sourcing practices are therefore included in the company's strategic planning processes. In strategic outsourcing decisions, the dependence between the parties involved, their motives, and the contract periods are unlike those of traditional outsourcing. The parties involved are much more dependent on one another; strategic outsourcing concentrates on long-term motives, such as making one's organization more agile and gaining access to important resources that are better supplied by external parties; the decisions to be made concern the strategic planning horizons.

Architecture Planning. The enterprise architecture defines the deliberate design of the enterprise as a whole; this in contrast to the design of a part of the enterprise, such as an information system.[15] It encompasses the business level and the IT level, and each of them can be detailed in sublevels if needed. The business architecture is obviously the responsibility of business management; however, close collaboration with IT management is needed, as IT may enable or impede some business architectural designs. The responsibility for the IT architecture may be defined as bringing about the technical platforms that support current and future business models. It is a technical activity that is a part of IS and IT strategies. It involves an analysis of the development of current into future business management practice in order to establish an architecture that is adaptable to potentially changing business conditions. As such, the architecture defines and limits what the business can and cannot do. The close interplay of the development of modern technologies and the demands posed by new business models also require, in this respect, a close collaboration between IT groups and business management.

Strategic Planning. Strategic planning is the administrative and technical competency to realize the strategic intentions and plans of the IT function, through programs, project management, and the like.

Relationship Building. As argued, IT decisions cannot be made or implemented in isolation. Building collaborative relationships at all levels is a key ingredient for a successful deployment of information systems. For the people involved, this competency requires good interpersonal skills in order to succeed.

Tactical-Level Competencies

Managing IT on a tactical level requires the competencies of portfolio management, cost and performance management, formulating information needs, service management, and supplier management.

Portfolio Management. A portfolio is a collection of resources. Within the domain of IT, it represents a collection of IT resources and investments together with relevant information about them. The information includes specifics such as how many applications there are, where they are being used, quality and service levels, and information about the business impact. IT portfolios consist of, for example, applications, infrastructure components, or IT services. Typically in a portfolio, resources with similar characteristics are grouped together. These categories can use terms like "strategic," "key-operational," "support," "high potential."[16] Portfolio management is basically a management tool for planning and decision making about IT investments and resources. It enables management to look at the entire IT portfolio holistically. Portfolios represent 100 percent of IT costs in the company and identify the sets of resources that are the poorest performing or weakest in quality and so forth. It is basically the foundation for managing IT in the company.

Cost and Performance Management. Cost and performance management and portfolio management are closely related to each other. By defining how many resources are devoted to each portfolio category, and by providing information about service and quality, management can identify the least valuable (in business impact terms) and the least well-performing element of each portfolio. This allows cost-containment actions based on bottom-line impact and performance. This process is important in that it provides management a view of 100 percent of the costs, rather than the differential expenditures caused by new investments. This competency is particularly important as the project/development budget, on average, represents around 20 percent of the spend. By offering a management view on cost and performance of the entire IT spend, management has the ability to reallocate resources from low-performing to more promising opportunities or to focus on the low performers when they belong to critical applications for the company.

Formulating Information Needs. Knowing the information needs of the business units and business functions is essential for defining the right IT services. This competency will rest ideally with subject experts, who understand how a department or business unit functions, what its purpose and role are, and how it fits within the rest of the business. Formulating information needs is a key competency for assuring the right fit between business needs and IT service delivery.

Service Management. First, IT must ensure delivery continuity by applying attention to setting up, maintaining, and certifying service delivery processes as, for example, specified by the IT Infrastructure Library (ITIL). As one might expect, certifications such as ISO and CMM play an important role in service-provider selection. Certification is therefore essential in outsourcing and offshore outsourcing relationships. Next, service management includes establishing the expected performance for the coming period in terms of quantity and quality of services needed. The IT function must ensure that sufficient and adequate resources are available to guarantee the service delivery as expected.

Supplier Management. As stated previously, parts of the IT function may be candidates for outsourcing to external suppliers. Supplier management encompasses supplier selection, monitoring the supplier performance against expectations, and supplier development. Supplier selection requires market knowledge and insight in order to enable informed buying. Transparent tendering procedures and open communications are important to maintain good relations with the IT services suppliers. Once suppliers have been selected, the relationships have to be managed. Suppliers are kept on track by gearing their performance to the existing contracts and developments in the service market. For monitoring contracts, good periodic reporting in business terms is essential, usually monthly, and on the basis of key performance indicators. Service agreements and contracts are not perfect; neither are the suppliers nor the recipients. It is important that upcoming problems can be solved quickly and fairly within the framework of agreements and relationships. Trust, and in particular personal trust, is very important in that matter. Also, if recipient and provider trust each other, fewer checks are necessary.

Operational-Level Competencies

Finally, managing IT on an operational level requires the competencies of service delivery, accountability, application, and software development and maintenance.

The required processes as described by the ITIL can be of help here. Day-to-day service provisioning issues have to be discussed with business on a daily basis, if needed. Change requests, either from business or IT, have to be followed up. Similarly, in projects, upcoming issues have to be resolved. Key operational competencies of the IT function in this regard concern reliable service delivery, accountability for the operations, application and software development and maintenance, and operational excellence in all its operational service delivery activities. Frequent and uncertain changes—environmental turbulence—affect the competencies, particularly with regard to application and software development and maintenance. Traditional waterfall approaches become problematic. Agile approaches like Scrum are introduced, as they are expected to generate better results in highly dynamic environments.[17] The concept of Scrum is based on the concepts of incremental innovation strategies, lean manufacturing, and *kaizen* (continuous improvement). In line with our previous analysis, the application of Scrum as a framework directly impacts the organization. Key in Scrum is having small, flexible, cross-functional teams that contain all necessary expertise for delivering a shippable product,[18] as well as having the management support and vision to operate like this. These self-organizing teams are responsible not only for execution, but also for planning, reviewing, and decision making in close collaboration with the final client.

Next to the competencies discussed earlier, managing the IT professionals and creating and maintaining a skills base may be a challenge too. The supplier must have the right quantity and quality of resources available to deliver the contracted services, which may be a problem, especially in the current Western world. As for managing the IT professionals, there is a dilemma. The service recipient is interested in stability; to maintain the knowledge base needed for a proper service delivery, the personnel situation preferably should be stable. From the IT supply perspective, it is important to ensure sufficient career and development perspectives for the professionals involved. Assigning new responsibilities, which leads to unpleasant dynamics from the perspective of the service recipient, may do this.

Demand and Supply Management of IT

Some responsibilities and roles in strategic IT management reside in the business functions; some reside in the IT function. We referred to this distinction as demand and supply management. This section discusses these two types of responsibilities. Segregation of tasks and responsibilities creates the need for coordination. We conclude this section with an analysis of the ways demand and supply roles need to connect to make strategic IT management work.

Demand and Supply Responsibilities and Roles

With regard to the management of information and information resources, one can distinguish between demand and supply, and so between demand management and supply management.[19] Demand management is business oriented and deals with what to do with information and information systems, and how to manage them from a business point of view. Supply management has a technology focus and deals with how technology is to be applied in delivering information; it is about managing the information resources—people, assets, and processes—in such a way that that demand for information and support exerted by the organization is met effectively in a cost-efficient way. Being an integral business responsibility, demand is typically not a candidate for outsourcing. Supply is about installing and managing the technology in order to deliver the needed information, which often will be an activity quite different from the (core) business of the company. As this requires different knowledge bases and skills, it may be a typical candidate for outsourcing. Related to this distinction is the difference between information systems and information technology, which we established earlier in this chapter. The focus of the IS strategy is on demand management. IT strategy specifies how the required application portfolio will be supported by technology, and thus is related to supply.

For the execution of demand- and supply-side responsibilities, different functions may be defined. The IT function is typically led by the chief information officer (CIO), who carries the final responsibility for IT services and for the development and implementation of his/her company's IS and IT strategies. In the European context, the CIO tends to be more geared toward the demand side, less to the technology side. As a consequence, (s)he will be less involved with technology issues, but much more so with information needs of the organization and how they are met. The CIO is also a full partner of the business in discussions about how future business models and strategies may be enabled by various information technologies. The responsibility of a U.S. CIO tends to be more geared toward technology-side choices and issues, although we notice a tendency to orient more to the demand side.

The CIO is supported by various roles.[20] The roles for the demand-side activities are, for example, information managers, business analysts, and business managers. Information managers bear responsibility for defining the IT services and the implementation of the company's IS and IT strategies. In large companies, there may be several information managers, each with a responsibility for a part of the company. Business analysts implement the IS and IT strategies; they serve as liaisons to the business units (and business managers) who must define their information needs and who have final responsibility for the business processes. For the supply-side activities, typical roles are IT director, account managers, service delivery managers, process managers, and IT professionals. The IT director is the final responsible functionary for the delivery of IT services and for ensuring continuity in service delivery. Account managers are the provider's front office; they are the liaison officers who maintain relationships with demand management and with the company's recipients of IT services. Service delivery managers manage the IT professionals responsible for the day-to-day delivery of IT services. Process managers set up and maintain the processes and certification of the IT services delivered. IT professionals are responsible for the actual delivery of IT services.

Demand and Supply Linkage

The partnership relations between the business and IT functions, and the nature of the responsibilities by which these can be realized, are displayed in Exhibit 7.3.

On the strategic level, designing the business–IT strategy is a matter of shared responsibility and cocreation. IT discusses proactively with business the future options for an IT-enabled strategy, business models, and organization structures. The CIO should not wait until (s)he is asked to do so; (s)he is a permanent and active participant and driver of the discussion. Nor can the CEO and the management teams "throw" the business issues to IT and then lean back and wait. Success with IT is also their responsibility. Good teamwork is the key to success. Also, working on good relationships between business and IT through-out the company starts at the top. Supply management is involved in the discussions (e.g., represented by the IT director) when technology choices are on the agenda. Supply management bears a direct responsibility for designing the target IT architecture in alignment with the target business architecture.

The tactical level proactively plans for the quantity and type of service delivery for the upcoming planning period; it also reactively intervenes when problems or changes occur that put the daily service delivery at risk. Activities on this level require a close interplay between business functions and IT supply management; in this interaction, demand management is closely facilitated by demand management roles. In some organizations, to ensure a greater inde-pendence of demand management in relation to supply, the former may report directly to a business manager.

The operational level activities are the clear responsibility of supply management. Good working partnership relations are maintained with busi-ness functions for which the services are delivered. Whenever needed, they are consulted and informed about the status of current operations (Exhibit 7.3). Essential in this stage is the reporting about the service delivery to business and demand management (on a tactical level) in business terms.

Exhibit 7.3   Responsibilities and Accountabilities

	CIO and IT Managers		CEO and Business Management
	Demand Mgmt*	Supply Mgmt*	
Strategy Level			
Strategizing	R		R/A
Innovation	R	C	R/A
IT leadership	R/A	C	R/A
Strategic Sourcing	R	C	R/A
Enterprise Architecting:			
Business Architecture	C		R/A
IS/IT Architecture	R/A	R	
Relationship Building	R/A	C	R/A
Tactical Level			
Portfolio Management	R	C	R/A
Cost & Performance Management	R/A	R	
Formulating Information Needs	R	C	R/A
Service Management	C	R	C
Supplier Management	R/A	C	C
Operational Level			
Service Delivery	C	R/A	C
Accountability	C	R/A	C
Application & Software Development/Maintenance	A	R	C

*R: responsible; A: approves; C: consulted

Demand and Supply Impact on Outsourcing

Sourcing IT services, and deciding whether or not to outsource them (either fully or partially), is a key component of strategic IT management. Outsourcing has implications for strategic IT management competencies at each of the planning levels. We discuss these consequences in the following section. We conclude this section with an analysis of how turbulence and trust affect sourcing.

Operational Supply Activities as a Potential Candidate for Outsourcing

As we said in Chapter 5, strategic sourcing is about deciding for the long term which competencies and activities should be developed and kept in-house and which ones should be acquired from external providers. Several arguments related to the competitive position of the company play a role in this discussion. In principle, a company should focus on its core competencies. As for the non-core competencies, competitive pressures may force the company to have a top-level performance on those activities as well. This may be an argument to "unbundle the value chain" in this respect and to develop long-term partnerships with one or more external suppliers for which these activities are part of their core competence.

Outsourcing IT has different implications for each of the organizational levels discussed and displayed in Exhibit 7.3. IT service delivery (the supply) can potentially be outsourced, as it is a pure operational task. Ensuring the correct delivery of the required services may be considered a technology-specific activity that a company would leave with an external party. Generally speaking, strategy cannot be outsourced. As strategy relates to the future needs of the company, it cannot be a primary candidate for outsourcing. Service delivery, accountability, and application and software development and maintenance are all areas that may be placed outside the company. As follows from Exhibit 7.3, good collaborative relations with the service recipient's demand organization and business functions are needed, especially for handling upcoming problems and coordination needs in the process of service delivery. The identities of the contact officials on both sides must be perfectly clear, because setting up good interfaces between client and supplier is key for a good relationship. Steering organizations with regular meeting frequency are instrumental in this regard for discussing day-to-day service provisioning issues and upcoming change requests.

Provider-related tactical-level responsibilities, such as managing cost and performance and setting up reliable (and certified) delivery processes, are related to making sure that service delivery on the operational level will meet the client's expectations. The service recipient's required competence on a tactical level will be influenced by outsourcing also. Contracts must be managed and monitored; continuous collaboration with the supplier is needed to ensure alignment between what the supplier can offer and what the company needs. Formulating information needs is a tactical-level responsibility that requires close coordination between the recipient's demand organization and the supplier. Coordination between recipient and provider is needed for planning near-future service delivery and for reviewing the provider's performance for the previous period. Also on this level, steering organizations help to structure these discussions.

As we said before, strategic-level responsibilities of the service recipient, in principle, cannot be outsourced. Strategizing, innovation, IT leadership, enterprise architecting, and relationship building belong to the core of the recipient's responsibility. Designing the IT architecture as part of the enterprise architecture is, however, an exception in this list; being a supply-side responsibility, it is an activity that may be sourced externally. Another example is innovation, when a company can link up with a major IT supplier. Although strategy is the responsibility of the service recipient, suppliers can be involved in strategic planning. Steering committees that involve senior managers from both the recipient and the provider are instrumental in this respect. They also deal with escalated issues from the tactical level.

We summarize the foregoing discussion in Exhibits 7.4 and 7.5. As presented, the services supplier's responsibilities concern mostly operational-level

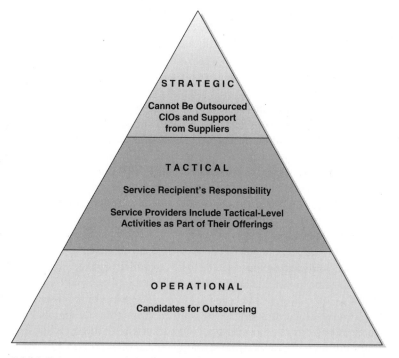

Exhibit 7.4 Management and Strategic Outsourcing

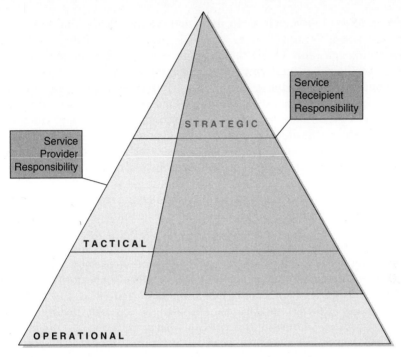

Exhibit 7.5   Demand and Supply Responsibility of IT Management

activities, and they are candidates for outsourcing; the service recipient's responsibilities are mostly related to strategic- and tactical-level responsibilities. Strategy cannot be outsourced; tactical-level responsibilities also should remain with the service recipient. The line dividing both domains in Exhibit 7.5, however, indicates a need for collaborative efforts on the three planning levels, though with a different emphasis. While ensuring a reliable service delivery on a day-to-day basis is obviously the main responsibility of the supplier, also the recipient has its share here; making plans about the required services in the near- or longer-term future is a responsibility of the service recipient that also needs input from and collaboration with the service supplier(s).

The Impact of Turbulence and Trust

Rapid and uncertain change is expected to have an effect on a company's outsourcing strategy. The question is, how can a company ensure availability of the right types of services in sufficient amounts, without being able to give an accurate enough forecast about them? Rapid change limits the ability of any single organization to have all resources needed to sustain its competitive position. Under these circumstances, having access to the right resources becomes more important and economically more efficient than building and owning them. Acting in a one-to-many model, suppliers can potentially benefit from scale advantages and offer lower prices. Acquiring the services externally turns fixed costs into variable costs and creates the ability to meet flexible capacity needs. To conclude, being strategically flexible[21] becomes one of the primary drivers for outsourcing, next to considerations with regard to non-core competencies and cost and quality of service delivery.

Again, trust is a key ingredient of any outsourcing relationship; it is all the more important under conditions of rapid and unexpected change. Trust allows the parties to go beyond the formal contract, as they may expect fair behavior, reciprocity, and future business. For example, under uncertainty, service agreements will rarely be based on agreed-upon volumes. Trust also makes open communication possible, where information and knowledge is freely exchanged, which enables new insights, shared views, and reasonable adjustments in formal agreements. The truth is, however, that outsourcing makes trust more difficult. Service delivery happens by one or more independent companies. Contracts can never be "complete"; they entail risks, which necessitate additional controls to monitor for possible opportunistic behavior. Also, these controls add to the costs—agency costs, as economists call them. Trust between organizations may be organization-based trust but needs to encompass personal trust as well. Organizational trust is important in the selection stage of the service provider and will be supported by certifications, prior experiences, and the like. Personal trust becomes important during the actual service delivery. Socializing, open communication, and stability in staffing are all ingredients of a trustful relationship. Personnel who do not show or promote trustworthy behavior may even be removed from the relationship.

To Conclude: The Need for Relational Governance

A general conclusion of the discussion in this chapter is that relationships are a foundation for strategic IT management. Effective relationships are needed both within the organization—between business functions and IT—and with external organizations, as far as IT services are outsourced. Relationships are critical to making the organizational machinery work properly; they are also necessary for the creation of an organization-wide "shared view." This shared view among business and IT functions concerns the direction in which the business ought to develop and the ways IT should support or enable this. Relationships are needed at all planning levels:

- The strategic level, to establish the long-term view
- The tactical level, to ensure the availability of the right IT services in the upcoming planning period
- The operational level, for solving problems in the actual service delivery

And finally, relationships are needed between the planning levels, to assure proper alignment between planning and operations.

There is probably an inverse relationship between the planning level and the difficulty in establishing effective relationships: the lower the planning level, the more difficult it gets, and the more effort it requires. It is easier to achieve agreement among the members of a senior management team than among all concerned on an operational level.

Organizational relationships can be established by formal measures and structures.[22,23] There are different ways to establish organizational relations that do not mirror the established hierarchy. Cross-departmental horizontal and lateral direct contacts between managers jointly affected by a problem may be stimulated and should not be hindered by unnecessary procedures and regulations. If more frequent meetings and negotiations are necessary, this requires committees and task forces, with a formal charter and way of working. The responsibility of handling frequent communication between parts of the organization may be assigned to specific liaison roles or departments. An example of this organizational form in European firms is the information management department, which interfaces between business functions and IT. Special linking roles may facilitate communication, in particular, between parts of the organization that are highly differentiated in knowledge bases, culture, and environments. Again, in a European company, the CIO acts often as a managerial linking role between IT and the business functions.

Formal arrangements are a necessary condition for effective relationships; however, they are not sufficient. On a person-to-person basis, open, participative, and collaborative relationships are needed, too. Without them, the organization deteriorates to a malfunctioning machinery, with poor coordination and probably no shared views to be established. So-called relational mechanisms[24] are instrumental in creating these conditions. Examples include offering the possibility of job rotation (IT-staff working in the business units and vice versa), co-location (physically locating business and IT people close to each other), cross in-company training, and informal meetings between IT and business staff. Southern Californian Edison (SCE), a Californian utility company, was known for these practices. It applied job rotation (e.g., IT management assuming the final responsibility for a part of the business, IT staff was forbidden to speak

"IT-language" outside the IT department, etc.).[25] When, for efficiency reasons, IT was organized into a shared service center, additional complementary measures were needed to enable better integration of business and IT and thus compensate for the additional "distance" created.

As we have argued extensively, trust is the glue that makes all of this work; if trust is absent, distrust will function like sand in complex machinery. The machinery slows down and in the end stops functioning. We discussed the foundations of trust between business and IT. The proposition that we want to take is that organizational trust, and in particular business–IT trust, should be an active management concern for the senior management team. Trust should be operationalized, objectives should be formulated, plans and actions should be in place to promote trust, and finally, trust should be measured on a regular basis. Decisions about whom to place in particular positions should be also based on existing trust between the employees who have to work together. The composition of the team, no matter on which level, is critical.

Good formal arrangements complemented by measures to support good person-to-person working relations are required for an effective business–IT relationship. This is true under conditions of change and uncertainty as well under more stable conditions. The external conditions do not make a difference here, as we showed in earlier publications.[26] However, this being said, conditions of turbulence put much more stress on the relationship. There is a need for mutually supported interpretations of (near) future uncertain events and their business and IT impact, and there is not much time to plan and organize. As Steve Haeckel says, in a "sense and respond" organization, structuring relationships is a key concern and a senior management responsibility.[27]

To conclude this chapter, acting under turbulence requires "relational governance" as a senior management responsibility. Relational governance encompasses practice-based measures, as we discussed, sanctioned by management to promote a desired collaborative organizational behavior.

Self-Assessment: IT Competencies

It is helpful to consider the current status of the IT competencies described in this chapter. To review, *competency* describes the specific knowledge, skills, and experience foundation needed for performing the processes and methodologies required. So, for example, strategic competency may include command of the specific methodologies required, such as strategic IT planning, scenario planning, and innovation planning. Competency is a characteristic of the organizations charged to perform the processes and methodologies. These may be business and/or IT organizations, including those external to the enterprise (e.g., sourcers).

Exhibit 7.6 is an opportunity to assess where the enterprise is today for each of the defined IT competencies. The assessment applies to the various possible

Exhibit 7.6   Strategic IT Competencies in the Enterprise

	Scale 1 Below	Scale 2 Below		
	Current Importance to the Enterprise	Central or Corporate IT Organization	Business Unit IT Activities	Sourcers Involved in Delivering IT
IT Strategic Competencies				
Strategizing				
Innovation				
IT Leadership				
Strategic Outsourcing				
Architecture Planning				
Strategic Planning				
Relationships Building				
IT Tactical Competencies				
Portfolio Management				
Cost & Performance Management				
Formulating Information Needs				
Service Management				
Supplier Management				
IT Operational Competencies				
Service Delivery				
Accountability				
Application				
Software Development & Maintenance				
Professional Management				

Exhibit 7.7   Assessment Scale 1 for Exhibit 7.6

Description	Current Importance to the Enterprise	
The *Importance* reflects the extent to which the status of this competency influences current success in applying information and IT in the enterprise	0	Not applicable to this enterprise
	1	Not important to the enterprise
	2	Management is interested, but with no relevant activities
	3	Somewhat important to the success of information and IT in the enterprise
	4	Very important to the success of information and IT in the enterprise
	5	Critical to the success of information and IT in the enterprise

Exhibit 7.8   Assessment Scale 2 for Exhibit 7.6

Scale	Current Status of the IT Competency in the Enterprise	
0	Not applicable	Don't know or not applicable
1	Incompetent	IT (corporate, or business unit based, or sourced/cloud) is incompetent, with bad results
2	Mostly incompetent	IT (corporate, or business unit based, or sourced/cloud) is mostly incompetent, with some bad results
3	None	No competence, but without good or bad results
4	Some competence	IT (corporate, or business unit based, or sourced/cloud) has some competence
5	Competent	IT (corporate, or business unit based, or sourced/cloud) is competent

sources of IT, including the central IT service–providing organization, any business unit–based IT activities, or external sourcers, including cloud providers.

The scales for this assessment are shown in Exhibits 7.7 and 7.8.

Notes

1. S. Haeckel, *Adaptive Enterprise: Creating and Leading Sense-and-Respond Organizations* (Harvard Business School Press, 1999).

2. David J. Teece, *Dynamic Capabilities and Strategic Management* (Oxford University Press, 2011).
3. Peter Schwarz, *The Art of the Long View: Planning for the Future in an Uncertain World* (Currency Books/Doubleday, 1991).
4. Kees van der Heijden, *The Art of Strategic Conversation* (Wiley, 1996).
5. Marcel van Oosterhout, *Business Agility and Information Technology in Service Organizations* (Erasmus Research Institute of Management, 2010).
6. R. Dymond, "Four Weeks," www.innovel.net/?p=26 (as cited in Van Oosterhout, *Business Agility and Information Technology in Service Organizations*).
7. van Oosterhout, *Business Agility and Information Technology in Service Organizations*.
8. Dymond, "Four Weeks."
9. S. Haeckel, *Adaptive Enterprise: Creating and Leading Sense-and-Respond Organizations* (Harvard Business School Press, 1999).
10. Haeckel, *Adaptive Enterprise*.
11. John Ward and Joe Peppard, *Strategic Planning for Information Systems*, 3rd ed. (Wiley, 2004).
12. Ward and Peppard, *Strategic Planning for Information Systems*.
13. Mark P. McDonald, *Architecting the Enterprise: An Approach for Designing Performance, Integration, Consistency and Flexibility*, Ph.D. dissertation, Delft University of Technology (Life Reloaded, 2005).
14. See "ITIL: Best Practice Management" at www.best-management-practice.com/Knowledge-Centre/Publication-Reviews/ITIL/?DI=630982
15. McDonald, *Architecting the Enterprise*.
16. John Ward and Joe Peppard, *Strategic Planning for Information Systems*, 3rd ed. (Wiley, 2004).
17. R. Mac Iver, *Scrum Alliance*, 2009.
18. See: "Agile Manifesto," http://richd.me/wp-content/uploads/2011/05/Agile-Manifesto.pdf
19. Ward and Peppard, *Strategic Planning for Information Systems*.
20. Erik Beulen, Pieter Ribbers, and Jan Roos, *Managing IT Outsourcing*, 2nd ed. (Routledge, 2011).
21. David R. King, "Implications of Uncertainty on Firm Outsourcing Decisions," *Human Systems Management* 25 (2006).
22. Jay R. Galbraith, *Organization Design* (Addison-Wesley, 1977).
23. Richard L. Daft, *Understanding the Theory and Design of Organizations* (Thomson–South-Western 2007).
24. W. Van Grembergen and Steven de Haes, *Business Strategy and Applications in Enterprise IT Governance* (Springer, 2012).
25. Michael L. Mushet and Marilyn Parker, "Coping with Business and Technological Change," in *Strategic Transformation and Information Technology: Paradigms for Performing while Transforming*, ed. Marilyn M. Parker (Prentice Hall, 1996).
26. Ryan Peterson, Pieter Ribbers, and Marilyn Parker, "Information Technology Governance Processes under Environmental Dynamism: Investigating Competing Theories of Decision-Making and Knowledge-Sharing," (2002). *ICIS 2002 Proceedings*, Paper 52 (2002). http://aisel.aisnet.org/icis2002/52.
27. S. Haeckel, *Adaptive Enterprise*.

CHAPTER 8

The Service Relationship

I T Service Management is a core element in providing credible IT services. This is required to build the business trust leading to business–IT partnership. The principles from Chapter 1:

- **Service-Based Relationship:** *The business–IT relationship is based on IT services delivering value and building credibility and trust.* IT has to perform with credible and effective services—no matter its source (e.g., the IT organization, external providers and sources, and internal providers within the business). The IT organizational and personal culture needs to focus on services with business outcomes.
- **Partnership-Based Relationship:** *The business–IT relationship is also a partnership.* Credible IT service is necessary to build trust, but this is not sufficient to support partnership. The challenge is that IT's performance typically does not encourage trust, and IT is not good at developing partnerships. Chapter 10 describes the partnership requirements.

In other words, the business–IT relationship is built on two interrelated components: 1) IT as a set of services to the business, and 2) IT as a partner with the business (see Exhibit 8.1). Both relationships are impacted by issues such as business and IT culture, role ambiguity in terms of what business and IT expect in the partnership, and characteristic (less-than-perfect) performance and utilization of the IT services.

This chapter describes the necessary service-based relationship between business and IT. IT Service is also the foundation for how IT and the business in practice deal with turbulence, uncertainty, and value creation. It should be noted that our references to "business" may suggest a single monolithic enterprise. We cannot forget that as Exhibit 8.1 shows, the enterprise has multiple business units and functional units; consequently the service-based relationship is with each of the units, and can take on somewhat different characteristics for each.

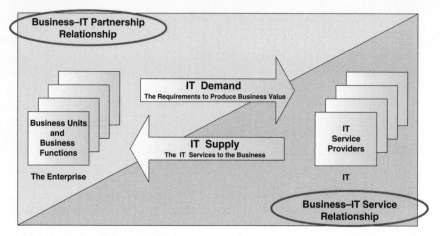

Exhibit 8.1   Business and IT Relationships

IT Is a Service Business

IT is fundamentally a service business. That is, the IT managers managing *IT Supply* are really managing the *supply of IT services* to the business.[1] And we can see it as the word *service* crops up all over the information technology world. There's service-oriented architecture, managing IT like a business (meaning a service business), the "service catalog" coming out of the the IT infrastructure library (ITIL) community, "service-level agreements," and so forth.

Some of the current trends include the following:

- Ongoing adoption of IT service language occurs within many IT organizations. The newest thinking (represented for example by ITIL[2]) is that IT is internally comprised of many services and that managing these services is the way to successfully manage IT.
- For many companies, the "rate card" covering billing for IT is framed in service terms. E-mail, PC support, and application operations are good examples of line items on user bills. For others, service-level agreements (SLAs) are used to define the requirements for IT deliverables to the business.
- The IT architects adopt a "service-oriented" view of the technology, albeit at a lower level of abstraction than "application operations." This view makes it easier to construct the technologies and manage applications making up the services ultimately delivered to the business.

So it appears that concepts of "service" have taken over elements of IT management. And business is receptive to this process, as business expects services. Any business CEO or vice president expects IT to deliver business-focused deliverables. This means running applications (as a service), delivering additions and changes to applications (as a development service), and offering technology-delivered services like e-mail. These expectations are framed in service terms. Just think of the ways performance expectations are expressed by business: on time, within budget, keep costs down, reliable, available, and easy to use. These are exactly the sort of expectations one has of *any* service, be it accounting services, marketing services—or IT services.

So What Is the Problem?

Unfortunately, the problem is misunderstanding, inconsistency, and even worse, a culture and practice based on technology management rather than service management. For example, IT managers still think of the application, project, and infrastructure portfolios as *resources* or *assets*, not as *services*. "Software Asset Management" is an example of current thinking.[3] (Note the word "asset."). In ITIL, the service catalog has commonly included things like storage management and server management. In performance measurement, the metrics typically are of resources consumed (e.g., space, servers) and not services delivered in business terms.

So the problem is that IT uses the *service* term, but most often as an internally focused (on IT) component of managing assets and resources rather than an externally focused (on the business) part of delivering services to the business. The inconsistency problem comes from employing some parts of service such as ITIL, but not consistently carrying through with the other aspects of service management such as planning, billing, and (most importantly) expectation management.

But there's a more important point. So much of the value of the *service* idea—for example, in service-oriented architecture (SOA) and in the ideas of service catalogs—is based on the notion of flexibility and choice. Using service ideas in architectures, for example, allows more fluid and flexible and hopefully less costly solutions. This is good. However, the notion of service for purposes of development of trust and partnership and credibility is not the result of choices of services from a menu or in SOA; it is the achievement of the necessary characteristics of the *performance* of the service. It simply requires the other aspects mentioned earlier—planning, expectation management, appropriate behaviors, and in general, all the things we typically expect from really competent service companies (e.g., doctors, lawyers, accountants, or engineers).

The point in the context of this book is that the level and quality and competency of services to the business—covering all of the IT services discussed in the following section—is the basis for the IT's credibility and ultimately for trust, which itself is the foundation of the partnership relationship.

The Five IT Service Portfolios

We've been applying the concept of *service* to IT for a long time. But it evolved from portfolio (asset) management, not from a foundational understanding of IT as a service. Bob Benson's first book, *Information Economics* (1988),[4] focused on the project portfolio and its governance. His more recent book, *From Business Strategy to IT Action* (2004), emphasized the concept of five basic portfolios comprising the entire IT spend for the enterprise. These five portfolios were described as the project portfolio and four "lights-on" portfolios, described as resource pools: applications, infrastructures, services (meaning the help desk et al.), and management.[5]

When we applied these portfolio concepts to real enterprises (both government and for-profit) in North America and Europe, we almost immediately recognized that while these are resource portfolios with costs, they are also the foundation for the actual services provided from IT to the business. So application and information, (direct) infrastructure services, project services, technical (user) services, project services, and management services comprise the IT service portfolios, reflecting 100 percent of IT costs, the basis of their service performance, and the source of IT's value to the business.

(It should be noted that, even in that 2004 book, the whole discussion of the portfolio "assets" took on service characteristics almost immediately. For example, the portfolio assessments described in that book included factors like service level, quality, performance, etc. . . . which are certainly aspects of services.)

Formally, the five IT service portfolios, shown in Exhibit 8.2, are defined as the following. Note that the specifics of each portfolio may vary in a given enterprise, but the overall framework applies.

- *Application and Information Services.* Consists of installing, operating, maintaining, and providing break-fix services to the business for each business application. The cost of these services includes all staff and infrastructure required.
- *Direct Infrastructure Services.* Consists of the direct-to-the-user services such as e-mail and Internet attachment. The cost of these services includes all staff and infrastructure required.

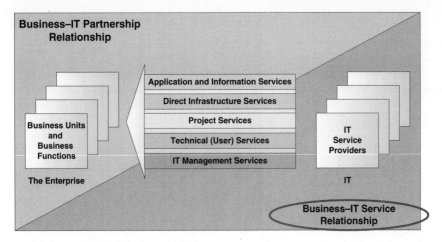

Exhibit 8.2   The Five IT Service Portfolios

- *Project Services.* Consists of the full life cycle (whether traditional, agile, or other methodologies) of project development. The costs include all staff and infrastructure required.
- *Technical (User) Services.* Consists of the direct-to-the-user services such as help desk, PC and workstation support, and training.
- *IT Management Services.* Consists of the CIO and all related management services to the IT organization and to the services that may be directly provided to users, such as IT procurement, IT human resources (HR).

One hundred percent of IT costs are found somewhere in at least one of these IT service portfolios.

The point being emphasized here is that the relationship with business—using terms of trust and partnership—*exists in an IT service context.* This concept will be a characteristic of much of the discussion in the following chapters. The goal, of course, is to deal effectively with turbulence and uncertainty, to enable superior business responses to them, and to achieve superior business value from the use of IT.

It should be noted that several great advantages to the IT service portfolio framework became immediately apparent to us in its utilization since 2004. First, from the business perspective, the service framework broadly reflects what business expects to receive from IT. In application and information services, for example, business expects the delivery of the application and its information and functional capabilities, together with the operational, support, and management activities behind the scenes. This really simplifies some aspects of the IT "role" question we've introduced in this chapter: IT's role (limited in this discussion just to applications) is delivering the application service (including all the aspects mentioned previously).

Second, again from the business perspective, the set of IT services deployed in the business (e.g., applications) can be managed holistically without regard to their exact source. In other words, whether a corporate IT organization provides them, or the business acquires the services externally (e.g., direct from a vendor), or the business provides them internally within the business unit, they are all applications and information available to the business unit. This gives a holistic perspective of IT services in the business, together with the potential for acquiring and managing them consistently. For example, we note that many enterprises employ IT in such a way as less than half of the total IT spend is in a formal, separate IT organization. From the IT and business perspective, this holistic perspective on IT in the enterprise gives very important capabilities for dealing with the turbulence and uncertainty of today; viewed this way, at least the problem of multiple providers and multiple users can be understood.

Third, the IT service portfolio framework provides a powerful way to think about the many IT sources available to the business. As an aside, Cutter Benchmark work on IT budgeting[6] has consistently revealed (from now more than 500 respondents) that, on average, the percentage of enterprise IT costs held in the central or corporate IT organization is around 40 percent. The remaining amounts are in business unit–based IT activities, or sourcers (e.g., cloud), or do-it-yourself IT activities. However, all these sources have critical roles to play, both in the service relationships and in providing comprehensive partnership relationships to deliver superior IT results to the enterprise. For example, Exhibit 8.3 gives the reader the opportunity to think about the breadth of IT service sources in his/her enterprise.

The answers shown in Exhibit 8.3 might reflect a "yes" or "no" as to whether IT services are provided to the business units from each of the service sources. Or an estimate of the percentage for each service, across the four sources would be useful. Or even an estimate of the costs incurred from each of the IT sources for each of the services would be especially enlightening. Overall, however, simply thinking through the complexity of sources is a useful exercise. As we think about the business unit–IT service and partnership relationship, this becomes important. And when we discuss the enterprise IT capabilities in Part III, this array of IT sources becomes a critical part of defining the capabilities required to deliver strategically and operationally significant IT to the business.

Exhibit 8.4 portrays a single enterprise and its five service portfolios with annual costs. These costs include services from all IT sources, and it offers a great holistic view of the IT activity in support of the business. It should be emphasized that this is an "all-in" view—with all providers of IT reflected,

Exhibit 8.3 IT Service Portfolios and Sources

	Central or Corporate IT Services	Business Unit–Based IT Activities	Sourced IT Activities (Direct to Business Units)	"Do-It-Yourself" IT Activities
Application & Information Services				
Direct Infrastructure Services				
Technical (User) Services				
IT Management Services				
Total "Lights On" IT Services				
Project Services				
Total IT Services				

including outsourcers, "cloud," and local providers from inside the business unit. In this specific case, only about 50 percent of the enterprise IT cost is found in the central IT organization; the rest of it is in the costs of IT services from these other sources.

So we'll say it again: the business–IT relationship may be a partnership, but it is one built on the service relationship created in the five service dimensions: applications, direct infrastructure, projects, technical support, and management. Said another way, the business–IT relationship *should be* a partnership; in its absence, the relationship is solely a service relationship of provider and consumer. But even so, that service relationship is a necessary condition, but not a sufficient condition, for a partnership.

Our objective here is to describe the components of good service relationship needed to enable the partnership relationship. This is how we can effectively deal with the issues of turbulence and uncertainty and mistrust described in Part I.

Service Performance Is the Foundation for IT Credibility and Trust

Part I led us to understand that trust is vital to the business–IT partnership. We also stated that agility and speed are the required outcomes to deal with

Exhibit 8.4 Example Costs in IT Service Profiles

IT Service Portfolio	Personnel	Operations & Infra- structure	Other	Outsourcing	Gross Costs	Adjustment for Operations & Infrastructure	IT Service Portfolio Costs
Application Services	183,764	2,528,786	0	356,138	3,068,688	0	3,068,688
Direct Infrastructure Services	656,300	3,160,982	540,040	7,835,039	32,192,361	9,031,378	3,160,982
Technical (User) Services	393,780	270,941	0	1,424,553	2,089,274	0	2,089,274
Management Services	866,315	993,452	0	237,425	2,097,192	0	2,097,192
LIGHTS-ON SUBTOTAL	2,100,158	6,954,161	540,040	9,853,155	19,447,915	9,031,378	10,416,136
Project Services	525,040	2,077,217	0	2,018,116	4,620,373	0	4,620,373
TOTAL IT SERVICE COST	2,625,198	9,031,378	540,040	11,871,271	24,067,887	9,031,378	15,036,509

turbulence and uncertainty. But we cannot overlook the practical issues of IT's service performance as an integral element of building trust. We discussed this in terms of the Total Value Performance Model (TVPM) in Chapter 2 and Chapter 6. That is, IT service performance builds on the stages of IT's effectiveness and competencies to produce the necessary business outcomes across the five service portfolios.

But the TVPM also introduces the notion of performance expectations by the business and the consequence that IT's credibility is based on competent production of outcomes in each of the six TVPM stair steps. Most important: trust comes on *credibility based on demonstrated ability to perform*.

Exhibit 8.5, the TVPM, shows outcomes, not IT processes per se. These outcomes are produced by one or more IT organizations via its IT Services using one or more IT processes (e.g., the IT competencies described in Chapter 7). For example, a project development team (executing one of the methodologies in Project Services) may be focused on software development, and not business change. The point is that the TVPM focuses on the ability of the IT organization(s) to produce the outcomes. The idea is that IT organizations can't productively move "up" the TVPM without first demonstrating competence to produce the lower-level outcomes.

Silos within an IT organization, and the multiple sources of IT (per Exhibit 8.4), introduce complexity and fog in thinking through IT services and related competences required. The requirements for clarity are that the business expectation for, say, the outcomes of IT project services most likely

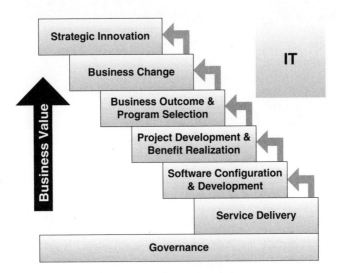

Exhibit 8.5   IT Total Value Performance Model

includes the actual development activity (operational excellence), the software development, and the deployment . . . and from a business value perspective, the business changes and strategic innovation outcomes. These are outcomes generally understood by the business to be part of the project. But the actual accountability for these outcomes may be not so clearly identified as spread across the IT silos and multiple IT sources. Typically the project team might finish the software and turn it over to a project implementation group, and probably not get engaged in the actual business changes themselves. The point is, when a business thinks in terms of the IT services obtained from IT (say, application and information services), the packaging of the outcomes (operational excellence, perhaps support to business change, etc.) is critical to establishing expectations and performance. And this does not account for the role the business managers themselves need to play in producing the outcome.

Given this, it is no wonder that IT credibility might be uncertain. And this does not account for the possibility that IT performance in delivering the outcomes in the TVPM may be in question. Note that the actual IT services matrix shown in Exhibit 8.6 may well be different for individual organizations and that it may involve more than one IT source (e.g., various silos in the IT organization, outside sources, and internal-to-the-business sources).

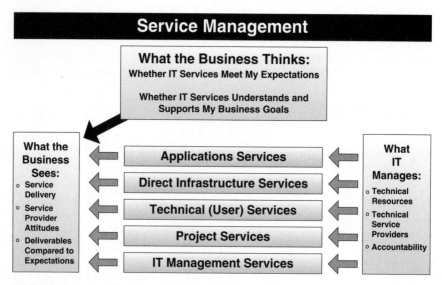

Exhibit 8.6   Service Management Perspectives

IT Service Management Is Critical

We stated the Strategic IT Management principle about Service Management in the Part II Introduction:[7]

> **Service-Based Relationship**: *The business and IT Relationship is based on IT services delivering value and building credibility and trust.* IT has to perform with credible and effective services, no matter its source (e.g., the IT organization, external providers and sources, and internal providers within the business.) The IT organizational and personal culture needs to focus on services with business outcomes. Chapter 8 describes the requirements for a service-based relationship.[8]

IT simply has to perform well on the services it promises the business. This is the core idea, but begs the question of what exactly is promised and what constitutes competent, credible performance. The answer to this requires *service management*. While this book is not about service management per se—there are a number of excellent books on this subject[9]—it is important for us to understand the critical role that service management plays in achieving the credible IT performance required to foster trust. Of course, we're also crossing into the realm of *operational excellence*, the most basic and fundamental outcomes required of IT (refer to the TVPM). We will describe service management as a main component of the operational excellence capability required of IT in Chapter 15. We'll discuss the details there.

But here, we're focusing on the importance of service management to the concept of credibility and trust. Simply, IT has to manage its services to the businesses to meet expectations of the business. This connects two simple ideas. The first is the setting of expectations as a critical (business) capability for IT. But the second is to reflect that meeting those expectations is not just a reality question (did we actually meet those expectations?) but a question of perception by the business (Do they believe or perceive that we met their expectations?). We saw a bit of this in a previous paragraph where we noted that in the example we cited, business expectations for project services likely include elements of business change and innovation, whether or not these were formally a part of the project plan or agreements. What counts is what management believes, and management's perspective forms the basis for accepting IT's performance and, ultimately, the credibility of IT's performance—leading to trust.

Exhibit 8.6 shows the three perspectives of IT services management. First, it shows what IT actually delivers in the five service portfolios. This perspective establishes, with metrics, the actual services required and provided. As the figure shows, this is essentially an operational perspective. Second, the exhibit shows what IT manages, which is the setting of the standards and culture within the IT organization (or other providers) for excellence in performance produced. But third—and most critical—it shows "What the Business Thinks." (Note that this exhibit formalizes the idea that we're essentially talking about *operational excellence* in the IT and business perspective; however, the details of this will wait for Chapter 15.).

We emphasize that we're talking about service management as it applies to the IT services provided to the business, not just the narrow service description and application in, for example, ITIL. It is instructive to consider ISACA's definition of service management: "The management of end-to-end delivery of business-aligned, quality IT services." While this is a good narrow definition, it is tends to be IT Supply focused and not customer focused, and does not consider the critical element of business expectations for the services (alignment is not it, nor is quality).[10]

This definition also does not help us in our consideration of what's needed in IT under conditions of turbulence and uncertainty. And as one more side note, the definition does not explicitly cover the "value" of the services delivered (and again, alignment is not it.) And oh, why don't we believe alignment is "it"? Our view is that this is the "aim" of the service direction— is it headed in the right direction? But this view does not include whether we also delivered the expected value to the customer.[11]

Again, while this is not an IT service management book, we will apply much of what has been learned about the subject as applied in business. This is difficult for IT, for this discussion does not stay within the narrow bounds of "best practices," things like meeting requirements and specifications, establishing formal SLA agreements, and the like. Yes, these are helpful and important, and will be covered later. But for our purpose, which is establishing trust and credibility through service delivery performance, more is needed.

Let's go back to the alignment discussion to illuminate what we're after here. Consider a fast-food restaurant and the application of service management. There, the operational excellence desired might include cleanliness, timeliness, capable staff at the order desk, capable staff at the stove, good packaging, and of course a good hamburger. If we apply alignment and quality measures to the services delivered, we might be happy that we have supplied services that measure up to the specifications. There might be a small problem though: The tendency is for us (as IT people) to make the service specifications explicit for each of the piece parts: the chef, the staff, the food produced, and the eating area. The customer does not care about the piece parts; he cares about the holistic experience—coming in, getting swift service, hot food, and a place to eat it. In effect he cares about the outcome, not the means of production.

From a services perspective, the first question is what the customer expects—and here we might add two basic ideas. First is value: Does the customer get value for money? Value is largely based on expectation: Is a sirloin steak expected? Are candles expected on the table? Of course, the answers may be part of the specifications and requirements. But are they what the customer expected? The second is the quality of the service interaction itself. Does the customer perceive the service as friendly? Helpful?

Service expectation theory is a cornerstone of service management. A leading researcher, Valarie Zeithaml, has with others evolved a set of service management standards and measures that have been operationalized across many industries.[12] As she put it, it is the difference between what has been promised (through specifications, SLAs, etc.) compared to what—without any reference to these promises—is actually experienced.[13] As we've put it, what the user expects sets the basis for service performance; what the user experiences is the basis for unhappiness (and ultimately lack of trust).

The core idea is that service management is about focusing on five basic parameters of the service:[14]

- *The tangible deliverable.* In the case of the fast-food restaurant, this is the hamburger, the seat and table, the condiments, the napkins. In effect, this is the value proposition of the restaurant.
- *The reliability of the service.* This primarily means that the service experience is the same each time; this forms the basis for the expectation. This is the consistency of the service.
- *The responsiveness of the service.* This is not a timeliness variable, but rather whether the customer believes the service as expected can be adapted to his specific requirements. This encompasses willingness to help customers and provide prompt service.
- *The empathy of the service provider to the customer.* "Are we in this together?" Ultimately, this means care and individualized attention to customers.
- *The assurance of the service provider.* This is based on the ability to convey trust and confidence.

Of course, these are not absolute, immutable measures; they'll differ with each enterprise. Again, thinking of the fast-food restaurant (compared to a high-end French restaurant), these parameters in practice would be vastly different between the two of them . . . yet within the context of the basic service business, both businesses would have aspects of each of the five. It is the expectation that counts. And, as we'll see, it is their uniqueness within each enterprise that is the main point: IT generally has little idea of what they should be in the business units they serve.

Service Management Is Also about Culture and Attitude

As we'll discuss later, it should be noted that only the first two service parameters—the tangible deliverable and the service reliability—are strictly speaking about the substance of the delivered service. The other three parameters, responsiveness, empathy, and assurance, are characteristics of the "how" the service is delivered. And these will come back as fundamental in the requirements for trust and partnership, in Chapter 9.

But the ramifications are much more than idealizing IT as a fast-food restaurant. It turns out that in all our IT consultative and research experience, this issue of service management ultimately turns on *knowing the customer*. Just as it does in the restaurant business, knowing the customer, understanding the customer, communicating with the customer, is central to defining and delivering credible services and hence trust. To have empathy, to project assurance, and therefore to define the limits of responsiveness, establish the reliability, and ultimately define the characteristics of the deliverable—all of this requires intimate customer knowledge. And it is here that IT has its greatest failing. In our consulting experience, we ask IT professionals, "Have you actually talked with a real customer of the company?" or "Have you actually visited the place of work of your users, watched them work with your applications, and discussed the ramifications of possible changes or improvements?" We ask the same of our IT management students. It is amazing—depressing, actually—the enormous percentage of responses that are "no." We're not talking here of the CIO, or even the CIO's direct reports; we're talking about the folks in the line who provide the real services—data center folks, project members and managers, and help-desk providers, for example. The amount of noninvolvement with the business (and hence failure to understand these issues) is staggering.

It is extremely doubtful that any IT organization has trained its entire staff to understand these service elements, let alone execute them across all five IT service portfolios. In our nearly 50 years working with hundreds of firms, we've never seen it. And, as we'll discuss in Chapter 9 on partnership, there's a lot in the way, namely IT culture, history, and behavior.

Please note we're not beating up on ITIL and ISACA.[15] What is done there is very important, effective, and appropriate. From the perspective of building trust and partnership, though, the issues from their perspective (which is mostly IT Supply) are necessary . . . just not sufficient. And we're going to see a lot more of this in Chapter 9, the partnership discussion, because there we will be focusing on matters such as IT culture, behavior, and in general the human gaps between business and IT.

But so what? It is our view that IT will never achieve the level of credibility and trust required without awareness and acceptance of the fundamental notions of service management, This requires two basic things: first, acceptance of the proposition that IT is in the service business. And second, this means—in addition to simply being able to perform the service well—that the elements of what defines quality are based on expectations, and these include the elements described previously.

We're now at the heart of the Strategic IT Management contribution to the creation of business value generally and the capacity to respond to turbulence and uncertainty in particular. Packaged as *service management*, it is really more fundamentally hands-on knowledge and awareness of the business user, the business context, the customers they deal with, the problems they have. This is the core of service management and, ultimately the basis for credible IT performance leading to trust and partnership. And, as an aside, this is the area of weakness of "best practices" in IT management. They—and the leading books in the field—rarely if ever discuss this most critical element of IT service management.

Jim Clifton, the chairman of Gallup, refers to the 11 questions Gallup uses to relate customers to their service providers. He writes about what businesses must do to prosper, namely, recognize what it takes to create "billions of new global customers."[16] The service management of his message emphasizes that "talent and relationships can almost always beat low price—they inspire customer engagement." This of course is the core of our story, that business and IT have a service relationship but also a partnership relationship within which the services are provided and consumed (see Exhibit 8.7). This, as Clifton says, requires full engagement of the business. Some of the key questions Gallup uses to measure customer engagement include (we'll substitute "IT" for "the company" here, and adapt the wording for our purposes):

- How satisfied are you with IT overall?
- How likely are you to recommend the IT organization to a friend or associate?
- The IT organization is something I can always trust.
- IT always treats me fairly and with respect; IT is perfect for people like me.

The questions in that list were written toward a single manager. Clifton goes on how Gallup understands the standards for customer engagement, with four key metrics (we mention three here and again adapt the wording for our purposes):

- IT (as a supplier to me) has a clear understanding of our business issues.
- IT is an easy firm with which to do business.
- I consider IT's representatives to be trusted advisors.

To achieve these conditions and outcomes is what he calls *Customer Science*, and it is what we mean by service management applied to IT!

As one more aside, we may also be at a point where North American and European views are significantly different. It comes down to the role and

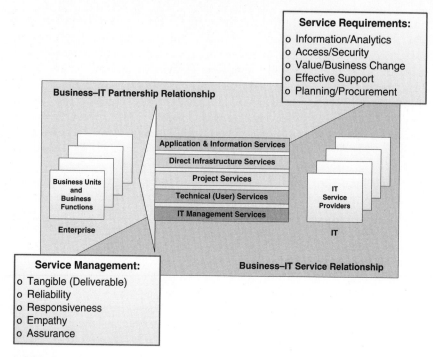

Exhibit 8.7   Service Relationship—Requirements and Performance

mission of IT—is it to provide the actual service to the business units (e.g., planning, project development, etc.) or is there another unit in the business that does this? For the North Americans, the answer is that IT provides the service. For the Europeans, there may be another unit in the business. However, even so, it does not change the nature of the challenge.

Let's review our view of Strategic IT Management. Exhibit 8.8 shows the basis for interactions between business and (all sources of) IT. This ranges from *Planning & Innovation* down through *Service & Operational Excellence*. Note these are not services per se; these are the enterprise IT capabilities that must be provided (whether from IT or business or both) in order to effectively manage the development, use, and exploitation of information and IT in the business. Recall our own value proposition:

> To define how "transformational ways to do business" are successfully envisioned, achieved, and exploited, especially in times of turbulence and uncertainty. The goal is to enable superior business response to turbulence and uncertainty, and to create superior business value from the use of information and IT in the business.

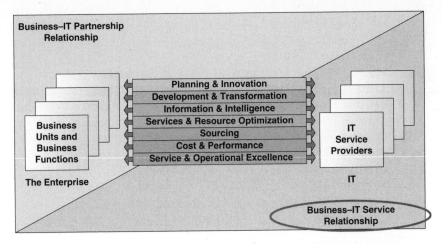

Exhibit 8.8   Enterprise IT Capabilities Required in the Business–IT Service Relationship

These capabilities are actually components of each of the five service portfolios: application, infrastructure, project, technical support, management services. Each service portfolio has, more or less, requirements for each of the capabilities. Exhibit 8.8 shows which capabilities are most oriented to service (as distinct to partnership). This will be discussed at length in Part III.

The point here is that business perceptions of IT services apply to each of the five service portfolios and the relative success in carrying out the appropriate elements of these capabilities. This is how Strategic IT Management functions to deliver on the value proposition.

One of the more persuasive presentations about these topics was given in a California State Government management forum.[17] There, the distinction between an *IT Demand* and *IT Supply* focus of IT services (our terms, not theirs) included the following dichotomy.

IT Demand Focus	IT Supply Focus
Service	Technology
End-to-end service quality	Technical components
Relationship with customers	Internal organization
Being proactive	Reactive
Business best practices	Ad hoc
Continuous improvement	Break/fix
Group capabilities	Heroes

There's quite a bit more to this set of dichotomies than we are discussing here; we're really narrowly focused on the service idea, the customer relationship idea, and the proactive idea. But the discussion of the dichotomy is quite compelling, and suggests the degree of the challenge for IT.

As an aside, we remark from time to time about the multiple sources of IT services available to the enterprise, meaning cloud, sourcers, inside-the-business-unit activities, and "do-it-yourself" IT. While this adds to the IT capabilities available to the business, it also adds a competitive aspect for the IT organization. In other words, poor service management can have consequences for the IT organization.

So What?

We continuously shift our discussion between two highly correlated goals. The first is repairing and strengthening the basic IT service performance received by the business. We have talked throughout Part I as to the need to do this, not the least of which is to enable—through the credibility of IT performance—the trust and partnership between business and IT. The second is to better enable business and IT to deal with the increasing turbulence and uncertainty, in both the business and the technology domains.

The first goal, strengthening IT's performance, requires recognition that IT is a service, effective execution of IT services in each of the five IT service portfolios, and an IT organization, accountabilities, and capabilities consistent with IT services. We will be exploring this in detail in Part III, where we'll consider how the five basic IT services portfolios each require the seven Strategic IT Management capabilities.

This leads to two core ideas about credibility and by extension how trust flows from this. The idea is that IT needs to set expectations—and the business needs to understand and accept them—for performance for each area of service, and then meet those expectations consistently.

Academics and consultants in the field of "service management" have researched the concepts of expectations and performance for more than three decades. Based on their conclusions and our experience, we establish the core elements of service quality on which the credibility of the IT organization depends. The key question: does IT set and meet expectations for each element of services, from operations to systems development to planning to business changes to innovation? Sadly, the answer is often no. For example, many organizations simply can't get projects done competently (on time, on budget, meeting business needs). This completely erodes any hope for credibility (who would believe the promises made by IT?) and consequently trust, and then, of course, partnership.

Exhibit 8.9   Example IT Service Outcomes

Enterprise IT Capability	Examples: The Enterprise Is Capable of These Service Outcomes (IT Perspective)
Planning & Innovation	Finding the best business opportunities and innovations for IT
Development & Transformation	Ensuring business outcomes; producing value with every project
Information & Intelligence	Applying analytics and data
Service & Resource Optimization	Managing IT assets; managing value and risk
Sourcing	Making the best decisions among the alternatives for IT sourcing
Cost & Performance	Understanding the cost and value of all Information and IT
Service & Operational Excellence	Performing service excellence in all five IT service portfolios

But the implications go further. The second core idea is that IT is unable to meet service expectations for services beyond the level of simple operational excellence. That is, the Strategic IT Management objectives noted in Exhibit 8.9 (e.g., ensure business outcomes; identify and control cost; make the best decisions about value and risk; produce value with every project, find the best opportunities for IT) are all fundamental to service management; and well beyond the current capabilities of most IT organizations. This point will be explored at length in each of the chapters of Part III.

The overall point is that service management is critical throughout the execution of the five service portfolios. The seven Strategic IT Management capabilities provide the required content specific to each IT service area.

What's the Connection between Service Management and Partnership?

We've set up this dual characteristic of the relationship between business and IT (see Exhibit 8.1) made up of service and partnership. Here in Chapter 8 we've focused on the service aspect in general and on the concept of performance and meeting business expectations for service. It turns out, however, that—as briefly introduced in the section about service characteristics—a large part of good partnership is also part of good service management. In Chapter 9 we'll explore these in detail, including the fundamentals of trust and mutual respect, the challenge of different business–IT cultures, the difficulty of IT adapting to the business, the requirement for establishing common goals, and the requirement for clarity on the mutual roles played by business and IT. This is alluded to in the prior discussion about empathy, assurance, and responsiveness. These are also a fundamental part of trust, a component of partnership as well as of service. So the dichotomy between service and partnership is not stark; in fact, partnership depends on the credibility of service, and this is largely dependent on these common elements mentioned here.

What's the Connection between Service Management and Turbulence and Uncertainty?

All the previous discussion applies to IT no matter what the external conditions. But what is the significant when adding turbulence and uncertainty the mix?

It is a question of readiness to respond quickly, as suggested in Chapter 7, with quick solutions and changes to the services being provided. But this requires something else—having good data, good base performance, and good relationships across the business and IT silos.

Consider how other kinds of service businesses deal with turbulence and uncertainty—service businesses like architects, engineers, health care, and for that matter, food service. It is instructive to understand the key points used there.

Requirements for Strategic IT Management

The scorecard that follows gives a template for scorecarding for existing practices (why they don't address the problems and requirements identified in this chapter) and the innovations found in Strategic IT Management. It results in a scorecard to be used in both.

Conclusion and Scorecards

Chapters 8 and 9 together describe the relationship between business and IT as service and partnership.[18] The service relationship is primarily a provider/consumer relationship, though with mutual obligations and responsibilities and expectations. Chapter 8 defines this relationship.

An IT Service Management Scorecard

Service performance covers each of the five IT service portfolios. Exhibit 8.10 is a scorecard, determining how well the current services correspond to the standard (business) service management parameters.[19]

Exhibit 8.10 IT Service Management Scorecard

Service Management Parameter	Service Management Description	Application & Information Services	Direct Infrastructure Services	Project Services	Technical (User Support) Services	IT Management Services
Tangible/Deliverable	The value proposition for the actual deliverable meets expectations					
Reliability of the Service	The service meets performance expectations and is consistent					
Responsiveness of the Service	Willingness to help customer; whether customer believes service will meet requirements					
Empathy of the Service Provider to the Customer	Care and individualized attention to the customer					
Assurance of the Service Provider	Ability to convey trust, competence, and confidence					

Exhibit 8.11 Service Management Scorecard

Strategic IT Management Goals	Strategic IT Management: The Systemic Capabilities for Producing the Outcomes with Service Management		Current Status for IT Services
Build Trust and Partnership Among Business(s) and IT(s)	A-1	IT services build credibility through execution and performance	
	A-2	IT services add to and trust between organizations	
	A-3	IT services add to stakeholder trust	
Provide Business and IT Leadership, and Personal Responsibility	B-2	IT leadership provides necessary leadership about service management, with emphasis on culture, trust, and partnership	
	B-5	IT service management establishes accountability for processes and outcomes	
Adapt to Enterprise and Leadership Culture	C-2	IT service management applies holistically across silos, organizations, and other processes	
	C-4	IT service management produces forecasts, measurements, and monitoring	
Strategic IT Management IT Goals	**Strategic IT Management: The Business Outcomes**		
Produce or Support Superior Business Value	D-3	IT service management delivers or supports business operational effectiveness	
	D-4	IT service management delivers or supports cost mitigation and risk mitigation	
Produce or Support Superior Response to Turbulence and Uncertainty	E-3	IT service management enables or supports the deployment of solutions faster	
	E-4	IT service management delivers or supports adaptability and flexibility in its solutions	

This scorecard is based on a five-point scale:

1. The service performance is unacceptable.
2. The service performance is poor.
3. The service performance is acceptable, but does not build the partnership or relationship with the business
4. The service performance is good.
5. The service performance is outstanding.

Scorecard Evaluation[20]

The success or failure of IT (business) service management is the backbone of IT's credibility, and consequently trust, with the business. Scores of less than 4 on this rating signal significant difficulties. And, harking back to Chapters 2 and 4, failure of service particularly in terms of reliability and the deliverable creates significant hurdles to trust and partnership.

A Second Service Management Scorecard

Chapter 1 introduced the five enterprise IT capability goals regarding the IT vlue to be delivered and the means for delivering it. Exhibit 8.11 examines the manner in which the IT services connect to the business with trust, leadership, and the production of business value.

The scale for the Service Management Scorecard is shown in Exhibit 8.12.

Exhibit 8.12   Service Management Scorecard Scale

Scale	Extent to which the Described Outcomes Are the Result of Enterprise IT Activities	
5	Often Produce Outcomes	The enterprise IT activities, overall, perform to produce the outcomes.
4	Rarely Produce Outcomes	The current enterprise IT activities often produce the descried outcomes.
3	No Effect	The current enterprise IT activities, overall, have no effect in terms of the described outcomes.
2	Occasionally Make It Worse	The current enterprise IT activities occasionally perform in such a way as to make the described outcomes worse.
1	Often Make It Worse	Current enterprise IT activities often perform in such a way as to make the described outcomes worse.
NA	No Response	Not applicable, or do not know.

Notes

1. See Jim Clifton, *The Coming Jobs War: What Every Leader Must Know about the Future of Job Creation* (Gallup Press, 2011).
2. See, for example, the ITIL V3 Guide to Software Asset Management, and John D. Campbell et al., eds., *Asset Management Excellence: Optimizing Equipment Life-Cycle Decisions*, 2nd ed. (CRC Press, 2011).
3. See Office of Government Commerce, "Service Delivery," *IT Infrastructure Library* (The Stationery Office, 2001).
4. Marilyn M. Parker, Robert J. Benson, and Edward Trainor, *Information Economics* (Prentice-Hall, 1988).
5. Robert J. Benson, Thomas L. Bugnitz, and William B. Walton, *From Business Strategy to IT Action* (Wiley, 2004): 88.
6. See *Cutter Benchmark Review*, which has IT Budget Surveys from 2006 to present, at Cutter.com.
7. See the Introduction to Part II.
8. See the Introduction to Part II.
9. See, for example, the foundational books: Dwayne Gremler, Mary Jo Bitner, and Valarie A. Zeithaml, *Services Marketing*, 6th ed. (McGraw Hill/Irwin 2012); Valarie A. Zeithaml, Mary Jo Bitner, and Dwayne Gremler, *Services Marketing*, 5th ed. (McGraw Hill, 2008); and Valarie Zeithaml, A. Parasuraman, and Leonard Berry, *Delivering Quality Service: Balancing Customer Perceptions and Expectations* (Free Press, 1990).
10. In the organization and management literature, organizational alignment has a broader connotation. There are different meanings of alignment dependent on the chosen perspective: alignment as commitment, as cultural alignment, as shared understanding, as organizational linkage, as congruence, as attunement, and as shared understanding expressed congruently. In general, the term refers to actions, processes, states of the organization that ensure that the organization will achieve its purpose.

    Henderson and Venkatraman also used the term in the broader organizational sense. With *quality*, there are typically two definitions: "fitness for use" and "conformance to specifications." The second is most often associated with the ISACA definition.

    Brent Demoville, *The Dynamics of Organizational Alignment*. PhD dissertation, The Fielding Institute, 1999. Retrieved from demovillefamily.com on 15 December 2013.
11. One of the authors asked, as we were writing this section, "Do you really want to include all of this in the definition of service? For example, they are also not included in the definition of *product*; the definition of a product does not include the value of the product delivered either." The answer: This is exactly the issue in IT service management—failing to include the necessary elements of service quality from the business perspective.
12. See Chapter 15 for a more thorough description of the details of service management and the key gaps with IT practices.
13. Zeithaml et al., *Services Marketing*, 5th ed. and Zeithaml et al., *Delivering Quality Service*.
14. This has been applied to all industries under the rubric SERVQUAL. See Zeithaml et al., *Delivering Quality Service*.
15. See Gad Selig, Section 6.4, "What Is ITIL and Why Is It Different," in *Implementing IT Governance: A Practical Guide to Global Best Practices in IT Management* (Van Haren Publishing, 2008). This is, incidentally, a great resource for referencing all the many acronyms and processes involved in IT management.
16. Clifton, *The Coming Jobs War*: 121–123.
17. Tom Jones, "Creating Business Value Through IT Operational Excellence (OpX)," a presentation to the California Legislative Council, 2007.

18. See Mark D. Lutchen, *Managing IT as a Business* (Wiley, 2004) for a long discussion of the implications of IT as a service business.
19. We present a much more complete scorecard in the Operational Excellence portion of Chapter 14.
20. Note that we have classified these parameters into the service deliverables (the first two) and the service contexts (three through five).

CHAPTER 9

The Partnership Relationship

This chapter describes the business–IT partnership as a collaboration of equals seeking to achieve common, mutual goals. The partnership is not just at the organizational level; it describes every situation where business and IT staff work together, such as in project teams, governance processes, and planning groups (Exhibit 9.1). (Note, again, we talk here as though partnership is one on one, engaging just two organizations: a single business unit and a single IT organization. As we've mentioned throughout, this is a simplification. The reality is often that more than one business partner and more than one provider partner are engaged in the pursuit of the common goals.)

The Introduction to Part II stated a Strategic IT Management principle:

Partnership-Based Relationship: *The Business and IT Relationship is also a Partnership.* Credible IT service is necessary to build trust, but this is not sufficient to support partnership. The challenge is that IT's culture, performance, credibility, and transparency typically do not encourage trust, and IT is not good at developing partnerships. Business typically does not fully participate as well. The challenge is that IT is typically overly IT-centric, and this creates barriers in partnering with business. Proactivity by IT in building this business-focused culture is required.[1]

This chapter describes the essential character of partnership applied to business and IT, with guidance to how this can be strengthened and matured with business and IT. But even more importantly, this chapter presents the "why" of partnership—why partnership is necessary to achieve superior results, particularly in the context of turbulence and uncertainty.

The chapter is organized in four sections:

1. Reasons for Business–IT Partnership
2. Defining the Business–IT Partnership

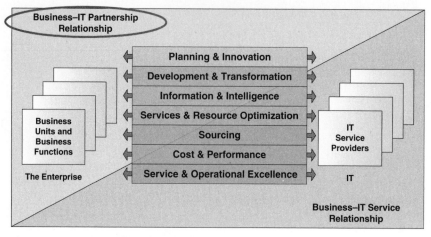

Exhibit 9.1   The Partnership Relationship

3. Dealing with Culture, Behavior and Silos
4. Implementing the Business–IT Partnership

Reasons for the Business–IT Partnership

Partnership is one of those words widely applied to practically every area of business and government. One easily finds reference material in such diverse areas as tax law, health care systems, public/private joint activities, professional services organizations (e.g., doctors, lawyers), construction, engineering, real estate, and so forth. Practically every professional area has evolved distinct concepts as to what partnership is, what it requires, what constitutes success compared to failure. We can simply adapt those concepts, those models of partnership, to the business–IT relationship.

But this overlooks a more fundamental question: *Why exactly do we need partnership between business and IT?* If IT is simply a service provider, perhaps we don't need a partner relationship; as Piet Ribbers has remarked, he does not need a partnership with his hairdresser or his telephone company to get quality services meeting his requirements. Is not the service relationship described in Chapter 8 sufficient?

In reviewing Part I and Chapters 7 and 8, we identify a number of concerns about the business and IT relationship and about the services provided to business, such as trust and credibility. Turbulence and uncertainty are the backdrop for these services, and complexity of the business and technology involved adds factors. So perhaps these sorts of issues make the required relationship between IT and business resemble more of a partnership.

For example, uncertainty, the need for customization (asset specificity), and the complexity of the services themselves may make partnership necessary. The complexity in itself demands an understanding of and commitment to common goals between business and IT. Complexity also requires sharing of knowledge, hence trust. Uncertainty and complexity bring the need to make decisions and plans that contribute optimally to the combined objectives of the parties involved, rather than target one single party. In the enterprise-wide perspective, this means identifying and reaching goals across business units and IT sources, or eliminating duplicate or overlapping services, all of which are more beneficial to the enterprise as a whole. In other words, building the business–IT relationship as a partnership can make real sense when one or more of these kinds of conditions exist.

Partnership sure sounds like a good idea. When examining the business professional and social science literature—and reviewing one's personal experience working with service companies—five key words stick out as characterizing successful partnerships. The first, of course, is the *partnership* relationship itself and the requirements for effective relationships, which will be covered in this chapter. The second is *trust*, something we introduced in Chapter 2, elaborated on in Chapters 7 and 8, and will further discuss here. The third is *proactive*, which means that the actions IT people take throughout the relationship and the execution of the partnership need to be driven by a sense of purpose and hoped-for outcomes, and enabled by the energy brought to it by the staff involved. The fourth is *understanding*, which requires mutual awareness of the business (and of IT), its issues and its goals, along with a comprehension of what the partnership can deploy to carry out those initiatives and goals.

And, of course, *common goals* are the heart of partnership; developing these goals with understanding, proactive behavior, and trust is what builds the capabilities of the partnership. Michael Eisner said in his book, "Partnerships . . . encourage a series of characteristics—trust, teamwork, a regard for someone else, and continuing checks and balances—that run counter to the factors that contributed to the sequence of economic messes of the last ten years."[2] Well, that's the economic scene: We're more interested in the same sense in applying IT in business, and running counter to factors that cause messes (or perhaps more important, failing to miss opportunities) sure sounds good.

Of the words and phrases that describe partnership here, two stand out: *common goals* and *trust*. Every partnership has to have common goals (and commitment to meeting them). Partners with different agendas, different hoped-for outcomes, simply don't work. Of course, there are critical aspects of business and IT goals that are distinct one from another, but they can certainly be common. Common goals are a part of *trust*, but there are many other aspects that need further attention. And overall, we have *leadership* . . . that capability of individuals to build the partnership, define the common goals, and engender trust among all concerned.

But again, why do we need it? We blithely started out in Part I to identify "partnership and trust" as a central goal, the central characteristics of what we need in the relationship of business and IT. But exactly what is this goal? And why do we think it valuable?

It might be questioned why a strong service relationship is not by itself sufficient to satisfy business requirements. After all, when we add the service management characteristics of empathy, responsiveness, and assurance (as we discussed in Chapter 8) to the delivery of IT services, shouldn't this be enough?

This is a key question. And for some organizations, perhaps it is. We simplify it a bit with Exhibit 9.2, which serves to classify the business–IT relationship. The original is a classic, of course, discussed in the early 1980s by MacFarlan, McKenney, and Pyburn.[3] We have adapted the original diagram here.

The point, though, is that for some business situations, service management might be sufficient to meet business requirements for IT. The *support* quadrant might be these businesses. But even there, it is possible that changes are still required and that therefore partnership, in terms of the description in the previous paragraphs, is required. And turbulence can appear anytime. Furthermore, this figure applies to business units; a given enterprise and IT organization may well have business units in each of the quadrants.

In the academic world, the *service management* field has apparently morphed into a "service marketing" field. This field, its courses, and its research look at all aspects of service, particularly when a service is the product

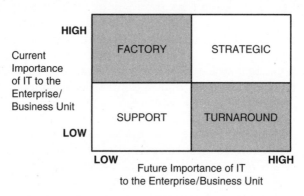

Exhibit 9.2   Role of IT in the Enterprise/Business Unit

a company sells. A key concept taught is "know the customer." And often IT organizations have followed this concept.

One way this can happen is for the service provider, in this case IT, to participate with the business in their planning meetings, engaging them in business-based conversations about requirements, getting traction on what their business strategies really are, and so forth. This is thought to be a great way to know the customer. To this end, we often observe IT managers and professionals participating in business unit planning meetings. They presumably hope to better understand and respond to the business's spoken requirements, concerns, and strategies. This approach is, of course, a good thing. But it seems to be a challenge. The IT spirit is willing, but the task is apparently difficult. What is the indicator for this conclusion? We almost always observe technology managers and professionals (other than the CIO, of course) completely silent in business meetings. They seem to believe they are there to listen, but not to engage or participate. That is, they're behaving like service providers, not partners.

This is problematic from several perspectives. First, they might as well not be there; they could otherwise just read reports and summaries of the planning meeting. Second, they don't use the opportunity to ask questions in areas they don't understand, or seek clarification where things are not clear. Third, they don't behave with the business managers as partners or contributors might behave; not as equals in any sense. Fourth, they miss the opportunity to suggest exactly how IT or information might contribute solutions or directions to the business matters under discussion. They seem unwilling to display that perhaps they don't quite understand the business, and therefore are unwilling or unable to contribute to the business discussion.

This is part of a larger problem: They indeed may not understand the business. Two dimensions dominate this. First, there are the operational, transactional, and process elements of the business: How exactly does work get done? Who does it? What represents successful and unsuccessful execution and supervision of the operational or transactional activities? Second, there are the strategic issues: Exactly how does the firm make its money? What is the basis of competition within the industry(ies) in which the company participates?

It is not that IT managers and professionals don't see the work and the industry factors. Certainly, they are familiar with the outlines of the business and its processes. What they have difficulty internalizing is the "so what" question—what captures the essence of what managers and organizations need to do, change, improve, and transform? It is the commonsense and instinctive judgments about the business that IT managers (and professionals) lack. Oh sure, they see the operational systems, the enterprise resource planning (ERP), the business intelligence (BI), and analytics that go on. They just do not know what constitutes real success in their use. But more importantly, they're reticent to talk about it with their business peers.

This behavior may be all right for a simple service provider, but realistically, more is necessary. The whole point is to enter into useful conversations about business direction, along with the opportunity for information/IT to provide significant innovations and improvements. Something more than service management is necessary.

Defining the Business–IT Partnership

Partnerships require partners. Certainly this is obvious. But can the IT organization and IT managers and professional perform the partner role effectively? And the same question applies to the business. We raised questions about the business and IT relationship as service receipient and providers in Chapter 8 and as early as the third paragraph of the Preface voiced concerns about the effect of silos between business and IT and within each domain. We note in the following sections that IT and business are often physically separate, not just culturally and behaviorally. The question of whether either IT and business can perform as partners is highlighted by the extent of their separateness.

The question does center on culture and behavior. We're all familiar with the anecdotal business complaints: IT does not speak our language. IT is located in another building and we never see them. They don't understand our problems. They only are interested in nifty technical solutions. They impose solutions that are not fit for our business issues. They're arrogant—or worse, uncaring. They can't deliver projects on time. Their applications break. They're unreliable. These of course are examples of comments made by a variety of individuals; they do not specifically apply to every circumstance. But there's enough truth in them to worry about, and if culture, behavior, and performance are not positive factors, they certainly are negatives to relationships in general and partnership in particular.

We have conducted studies about the business–IT relationship for several years under the sponsorship of the Cutter Consortium. We've looked at matters ranging from governance to IT's value delivery to cost. In this effort, we've engaged more than 500 organizations in several of these studies. While we'll report on many of the details in later chapters, the overall result of the studies and direct hands-on experience is to support the message that these anecdotal comments deliver. That is, IT is not a good partner (for that matter, neither is the business). At the same time, we've conducted direct assessments and studies in more than 100 organizations. Now, of course, these aren't formal statistics but, broadly speaking, the comments leading this section accurately characterize much of the results we've encountered.

We also conduct training and development programs for IT professionals and managers, aimed at improving their relationship with the business. With few exceptions, these participants fully agree with the three basic issues: "We're guilty," they exclaim. Of course, the issue is now "So what, and what's to be done?"

(Note that while this discussion sounds like we're describing a single IT organization and a single business unit, these propositions apply to every aspect of the business enterprise and every way in which IT is delivered to the organization, whether in-house, corporate IT organizations, outsourcing, or self-help IT. Similarly, the propositions apply to the service relationship with *each* business unit and functional area.)

Consider other business partnerships. There is general agreement on the key attributes of successful partnerships. By "general agreement," we mean in professions organized as partnerships (e.g., law, medicine, engineering, architectures) and in social science literature talking about people-to-people partnerships. Further, the literature about business partnership that describes how two companies come together to create a new product, or a new company, or a new relationship for distributions, and the like uses most of the same words we've already used. This is not surprising, since any partnership, whether between business and IT to achieve business goals, or between business organizations, or for that matter between individuals such as professionals (e.g., lawyers, CPAs) or performers (e.g., bands) do indeed share the same basic characteristics.

Conditions (and Reasons) for Successful Partnership

While we are focused on the business–IT partnership, researchers and managers in other professions generally describe three partnership facets that are keys to success as well as reasons for doing partnership in the first place.

Ability to Work Together

This can be to share expertise, build the capability to do things each individual partner could not do alone, bring disparate communities together, or simply to get things done. This covers:

> *Collaboration.* For example, IT may have done the easy things over the last decades, like the automation of back-office functions. These could be and mostly were done without business partnership. But the requirements for advanced business values, such as reaping the benefits

of business intelligence, providing superior customer contacts throughout the customer–business life cycle, advanced integration of business functionality within the enterprise and throughout the enterprise value chain, transformations of manufacturing and distribution—the list of wonderful opportunities goes on. And they all require the effective contribution of skills capabilities from both business and IT. (As an aside, one of the real challenges is convincing both—that is, all—parties to partnerships that the collaboration is required. We'll discuss this later.) The idea of "transforming business in turbulent times" raises the collaboration stakes even higher.

Coordination. With the increasingly complex environment for business advancement—integration, speed, multiple business relationships, and the like—there are a *lot* of moving parts.

Communication. This ties with collaboration and coordination, with the additional factor of trust, described below.

Responsiveness. Given turbulence and uncertainty, the values of coordination, communication, and sharing may lead to improved responsiveness to those issues.

Gaining Agreement on Goals and the Means to Accomplish Them

Partnerships founder on misunderstanding on goals, roles, and commitment to working together.

Common Goals. This of course is paramount. There's no point to a partnership that does not share the same goals. Oh sure, a partnership can undertake actions that may benefit one side more, but that's part of understanding what the common goals are. Between business and IT, the focus is on the common business goals being pursued, whether overall (e.g., governance and prioritization) or specific (e.g., within individual projects.) There may be IT goals as well—perhaps simplification, enhanced infrastructure, and the like. But the point is, these all are sought after as common goals for the group as a whole—common goals for the partnership.

Sharing. This covers a lot of ground: sharing expertise between the business and IT, sharing resources, sharing cost, sharing risk. The specifics, of course, are dependent on the partnership context.

Inclusive Behaviors. This is a consequence of the trust discussion. If partners act with hidden agendas and with activities that do not engage the other partners, the consequence to the partnership is detrimental.

Roles. While this seems minor, having clarity about the specific role each partner is to play defines the ability to work together and, ultimately, the trust between the partners.

Commitment. This is reflects the aspect of agendas. All parties should be perceived as being committed to the common goals and to the activities of the partnership.

Ownership. This is an offshoot of the *commitment* requirement that all partners own the partnership and, more importantly, the common goals and actions needed to achieve them.

Trust

Trust. We talk about this as a requirement for partnership; but when looking over the given reasons for partnership, we determine that trust is also an important *outcome* of partnership. Organizational development and design theorists and commentators have extensively studied how business units work together effectively in partnerships. One common theme is that partnership depends on trust and respect. It is a simple idea: Organizations work well together as partners when each mutually enjoys the trust and respect of the other.

Breaking Down the Silos. Both business and IT have silos, and having effective communication and sharing and planning across the silos is always problematic. Partnership, engaging the multiple silos in both domains, can be a terrific strategy to overcome the gaps, particularly when considering the other aspects of partnership mentioned previously.

Transparency and Openness. This is part of trust, of course, but the idea is that partnerships prosper when the partners are open and transparent about relevant matters. Sometimes this is financial, sometimes in actions and other considerations. But secrets are certainly barriers.

Hidden Agendas. Again, this is part of trust and transparency. It is clear that partners with hidden agendas can torpedo the partnership. With IT this can be problematic, at least as perceived by the business. Here's where IT culture (discussed later) really plays an important role. If IT is perceived to be driven by technical agendas that are not apparent or transparent, business does not want to play.

While these are just a few of the typical discussions found in partnership descriptions, whether in social science research or in practical guides to partnership, they are very inclusive. The striking thing, of course, is that they all revolve around trust—that all partners are in it together, without hidden agendas, secrets, or behaviors that prevent achieving the common goals. Trust—certainly important when considering IT's performance in services—is even more important in characterizing the behavior and commitment of all the partners.

Partnership Is a Good Idea

Given these reasons, partnership sounds like an even better idea.[4] The underlying proposition of this chapter is that partnership and service relationships are based on mutual clarity of role, values, culture, performance, and ultimately trust. However, one size does not fit all: Each IT organization and business can have a distinctive profile that affects the character of the relationship between IT and business.[5]

So what is this thing called partnership? It is business and IT coming together to achieve the common goal of competitive and operational excellence. As we say in our introduction, our book's objective is to define how "transformational ways to do business" are successfully envisioned, achieved, and exploited. This is a challenge in general, but particularly so in times of turbulence and uncertainty, with business and IT working in concert. The outcome is to enable superior business response to turbulence and uncertainty, and to create superior business value from the use of information and IT in the business.

So while we talk later about the requirements for partnership, equally important is the reason for needing partnership: breaking down the barriers between IT and business and finding common goals and purposes.

Dealing with Culture, Behavior, and Silos

Both IT and business culture and stereotypical behaviors can be a significant barrier to trust and thus to partnership. While this is most often thought of as an IT problem ("they don't speak our language, they don't understand our business, they have only technical goals"), it is clear that business has its own cultures.[6] This is not in itself bad; every business area and IT organization needs culture and behavior to be effective.[7] The challenge is to understand culture and not let it be, unintentionally, a significant inhibitor to partnership.

The challenge is the significant differences between typical business and IT cultures and behaviors. Most importantly, the challenge is business's expectations for culture and behavior and IT's failing to measure up to those expectations.

It seems sometimes that business is on Mars and IT on Venus. Many commentators have noted the problems of different language and vocabulary, different ways of approaching problems and solutions, considerable difference in comfort in working with people, and so forth. It appears that, at least stereotypically, IT folks are different, and this can get in the way of building trust with business. That is, one's personal behavior patterns, whether as an organization as a whole in terms of culture or by individuals, matters. It matters from the business side as well.

Exhibit 9.3   Attitude in Communication

Culture/ Behavior	Typical IT Attitudes Expressed in Communication with Business
Defensive compared to **Supportive**	Not my job. Not me! *You* chose that vendor! Your people rejected this. Can I help you? Let me find out and get back to you.
Control compared to **Spontaneity**	Who authorized that? You can't have security approval. No! Sure! Great idea, let's try it. Let's look at this possibility.
Closed compared to **Open**	No. Table that. (Silence.) Let me check with my manager. Here are our ideas to help. Here are some options. What are your ideas?
Judgmental compared to **Neutral**	What did you do that for? No. We can't do that. What are your thoughts? That might work. Here are some options
Competitive compared to **Cooperative**	Can't let them do it. Can't let the business do that. Can't let AppDev do that. Let's do it. How can we help?

Source: Adapted from Jack Gibb's work; see, for example, J. R. Gibb, "Defensive Communications," *The Journal of Communication* 2, No. 3

The concept of trust in partnership and relationships has been well defined in research; Jack Gibb, for example, wrote a leading book named *Trust*[8] and made it the foundation for understanding how organizations and people work well together (or not). But how do IT and business organizations measure up in terms of this? How do individual IT professionals measure up? It would be informative to take a culture/behavior inventory of both business and IT. A considerable part of organizational behavior lies is in the way organizations, their managers, and their staff relate to each other.

Exhibit 9.3 provides an example of a culture/behavior assessment framework.[9] It is expressed in terms of five opposites in culture/behavior, in effect an organizational personality. The table shows results from a business–IT team that was asked to provide examples of behavior in each of the opposites. This example is done in the context of a service provider to a customer. But these behaviors apply equally in a partnership relationship.

One can easily see that these five characteristics, presented as dichotomies, might have positive and negative impact in building both trust and respect and impede or support partnerships. If the goal of a partnership is working together, seeking common goals, and building trust, one side would be more helpful than the other. In effect, one side (defensive, controlled, closed, judgmental, competitive) would seem to be inhibitive to trust at least and probably to respect.

Often this discussion is about the IT folks, those bad guys. For example, if one asked a business manager which of the end points of each dichotomy describes the typical IT professional, would we be surprised that these "negative" patterns might be the descriptors? Put another way, these dimensions would seem to describe the nature of the wall between IT and business, from the business perspective. Furthermore, it is equally likely that the various business organizations might exhibit some of these "negative" behaviors as well. One is compelled to think of the stereotypes of accountants, for example. And of course, an underlying element of the sample behaviors is vocabulary. The use of technical and/or business terms and acronyms is a great way to display defensive, control, closed, judgmental behaviors.

Exhibit 9.4 provides an example of a scorecard we use in our engagements to discuss IT behavior and culture.

Now of course while this is beating up on IT, the business organizational culture/behavior may well exhibit similar results and differences between how IT perceives the business and how business perceives itself.

In this example, two things matter. First is the difference in perceptions from the two organizational perspectives. But the second is the consistency of the business view. From everything we've experienced and the relevant research, the defensive/control/closed/judgmental/competitive culture and behavior is not a positive thing for a partnership. To the extent the business assessment as shown in the table is the primary characteristic of IT behavior, it would be unusual to think that it would lead to successful partnership and trust and respect. Worse, we believe that most IT organizations that find themselves in a bad relationship with business are typified by these behavior patterns.

Of course it is more complex than this. Partly the business itself has varying characteristics (e.g., one might consider the culture and behavior

Exhibit 9.4   IT Culture/Behavior Scorecard

Culture/ Behavior	Business Management Assessment of IT's Culture/Behavior	IT's Self-Assessment of Culture/Behavior
Defensive vs. Supportive	Defensive	Supportive
Control vs. Spontaneous	Control	Control
Closed vs. Open	Closed	In Transition
Judgmental vs. Collaborative	Judgmental	Neutral
Competitive vs. Collaborative	Competitive	Collaborative

of the financial area or the engineering area or the marketing area of the business). The point is that this matters: understanding the perceptions on both sides of culture/behavior is a positive thing, and, of course, considering how to rethink the IT culture/behavior and how to improve it with an eye toward the development of trust and then partnership is useful.

But we do make it difficult. An interesting symptom is the physical separation of the IT organization from the rest of the business. Often we'll see IT in a separate building, or perhaps a separate floor. This creates a silo mind-set with no regular social or interpersonal contacts between separate departments. Often we'll see governance processes based on impersonal interactions in paper or electronic forms, limiting person-to-person contact. The "processillization" of IT (e.g., the IT Infrastructure Library [ITIL]) can markedly contribute to this. Sometimes we think that if we "just had the right process" (e.g., planning, prioritization), we'd be golden. Or even worse, if we could just measure it, we'd really understand it.

Work closely with the business? Break down these cultural and behavioral barriers? It turns out this is ultimately a personal commitment, something that each IT manager and professional has to work out. A lot of the work involved includes learning about the business, the industry, and business's perspective on IT. And a lot of the work is simply and persistently communicating and interacting with business and IT people about their concerns and goals. But all of the work is based on accepting the commitment to perform the work, and this is a strongly personal thing. It is also a strong cultural thing, affected by leadership. We'll spend time on this in Chapter 10.

As an aside, in Chapter 16 we will present a plan for doing just this, with a series of activities intended to create the climate for trust and partnership. And again, why do we care? Because we believe that partnership is central to dealing with trust and uncertainty. And even more vital, we think that culture/behavior plays a significant role in successful service management as well.

(Note that we take a very simplistic view of the concept of culture. One has only to read researchers such as Schein[10] to realize the complexity and extensiveness of culture concepts. For our purposes, however, we simply focus on the basis for trust and partnership, and that "culture"—meaning shared beliefs and the like—is something to be addressed through building credibility and relationships.)

Overcoming Silos

"Breaking down the silos" is, ultimately, a prime purpose of business–IT partnerships. But we continue to work with IT organizations that, by and large, have disdain for even talking with the business, much less occupying the same conceptual space with them. Most recently, we worked with senior IT project and management individuals who continue to see their future solely in technical terms: doing projects and managing IT. In another case, we worked with IT managers for whom the thought of including senior business managers in an IT planning and governance exercise was deemed irrelevant and was very strongly resisted. "Oh no," they said, "we [the IT folks] can provide the business input." In a third example, the IT managers couldn't exactly identify the appropriate business managers who might be included in a planning exercise. They didn't know anyone other than their "business contact" in the organization.

Our point is that the IT organization does not seem to be getting any closer to the business. It certainly is no better than 10 or 20 years ago. We use the following four informal measures to diagnose the distance between IT and business:

1. What percentage of the IT training budget is spent on the host business organization's issues (the things that are important to the business) as compared to IT topics? (Our experience: zero.) For example, in a financial institution, how much training do IT folks get in banking?
2. What percentage of the IT management and project staff has actual business experience anywhere in their career?
3. What percentage of time do the IT management and project staffs spend in the same physical space as the business organizations that use their services?
4. What percentage of the IT strategic plan discusses exactly what IT is doing to contribute to specific business objectives (as distinct from the means to achieve IT objectives)?

The same question applies to the business. What percentage of training is spent on topics related to the use of IT in the business?

In either case, we find that in most organizations with which we deal—and in the research we've conducted, primarily in North America—the answers tend to be "zero" or close to it. Note that we do *not* misunderstand that organizations do indeed invest in education—for example, sending key managers to executive MBA programs. But this is generic (e.g., about general business topics, not specific to the host organization) and does not apply to the majority of the staff.

In other words, focusing on IT, we see little evidence that IT has the desire or, more importantly, the capability to successfully partner with the business, to break down the silos. All the evidence we see on the ground is in the other direction—that the IT organizations and its professionals are becoming more distant. So what? Of course, there's clearly something going on. All the wonderful developments in the air—social networks, business 3.0, cloud, BI, and the like—portend significant and turbulent changes. And all us consultants and commentators and wannabe CIOs surely can't be wrong about the future of IT as being more closely integrated with the business. But where's the evidence that the IT organization and its professionals are getting closer to the business?

A further challenge lies in the fact that the current IT leadership cadre is aging and, in the coming decade, will be retiring in large numbers. That is not the problem—but the fact that the younger IT staff members exhibit even more of the distance between business and IT is. As we think through our client experiences, we realize that the younger generation of IT people is even more into the technology and less into the business than is the current leadership. And this really is bothersome.

The point is that this behavior—separation, reticence to engage business, limited business knowledge—may be perfectly acceptable in an IT services role and service relationship with the business (although we cannot overlook the importance of service management and its values, such as empathy and responsiveness, that have similarities to partnership values). But this is not sufficient to achieve our aim, which is to define how "transformational ways to do business" are successfully envisioned, achieved, and exploited. Especially in times of turbulence and uncertainty, this is not sufficient.

To meet our goals of enabling superior business response to turbulence and uncertainty and to create superior business value from the use of information and IT in the business requires partnership. Most fundamentally, it requires common goals with the business and a full understanding of the business. This requires more than (just) service management. Do not misunderstand: the tenets and practices of service management (Chapter 8) are required. They're not, however, sufficient to meet the goals.

But What about Business?

Again, the sections presented thus far in this chapter focus on IT. While the same discussion can be had about business and its commitments to partner with IT, here the situation is somewhat different. This difference lies in business's ability to source its IT in a variety of ways, not usually constrained to just one IT organization. Recent developments such as cloud sourcing and increased "do-it-yourself" capabilities make it possible to bypass the in-place IT organization. So while the issues described earlier are the same, the circumstances may be different when viewed on the business side. This difference of view may be unfortunate, as it means the stakes in building the business–IT partnership can be much greater from the IT organizational side; more is to be lost if the partnership does not flourish.

This situation emphasizes the need for IT to be particularly aware of the partnership, culture, and behavior issues. It is not necessarily balanced, but that is in the nature of it.

What about the Intrabusiness and Intra-IT Silos?

Just a word here; we'll further develop this issue later. But this is perhaps as important a challenge as the more general business versus IT silos. Within the business, every business unit and functional area can be a distinct silo, with all the attributes of differing culture, behaviors, goals and agendas. Within IT, the same certainly applies; for example, the operations, development, user services, and architecture areas often function as silos. In some ways, the five service portfolios described in the last chapters represent potential silos organizationally.

Implementing the Business–IT Partnership

From our research and practical experience, we generalize three basic issues about IT as a partner with business.

- *Agreement on the Need for Partnership.* Do both business and IT agree that partnership in general, and a partnering behavior, is necessary?
- *Mission.* Do IT and the business organizations have the same view of what IT is expected to do for the business? (By extension, does business understand what it must do as a consequence?) The issue is that there is often confusion as to IT's mission, and this vastly complicates having an appropriate and effective culture to bring to the business–IT relationship.
- *Partnership Requirements.* Can IT in general, together with the business units, behave in a manner required for success?
  - There is confusion about IT's role as a partner.
  - IT culture and behavior gets in the way.
  - IT's (poor) service performance gets in the way of trust and hence potential partnership.

The question is: Do business and IT agree that partnership in general, and partnering behavior from both, is necessary? This question applies to all levels, whether organizational or individuals. And this is a difficult challenge, particularly from the IT side, where the culture tends to be self-reliant and exclusive. "We know what's needed" is often the IT position. But the business, too, can be reluctant to agree on the need. IT folks, after all, are simply the plumbers.

Our experience with clients really reinforces this. For example, when we conduct strategic IT planning exercises with IT organizations, it seems to come as a surprise that we should include business folks in the discussion. It comes as more of a surprise to think that business should be thought of as partners, not simply grateful recipients of IT's services. When we conduct planning sessions with business, we get the same (mirror) reactions. Yet when we do conduct joint sessions, we get the reaction that, wow, this is the first time we've really had good conversation (across the business–IT gap) about mutual needs, common understanding of the problems, and potentially the nature of the (business and IT) solutions.

In some ways the problem is greater from the business side. In our client work, we see the attitude from business that "that's what we hire IT to do" . . . meaning that they (the business folks) haven't the time or inclination to talk with IT. Just throwing the problem over the transom and getting the result back—hands-off—is a common attitude.

Engaging the Business

Partnership does not work unless business management is fully engaged and holds up its end of the bargain. This particularly applies to the practices involved in Strategic IT Management. In the Part II Introduction, we set out a principle:

> **Engagement**: *Business and IT managers participate in Business–IT partnerships.* Every management level is engaged in and provides leadership for joint business/IT activities. Chapter 11 connects the leadership, culture, and engagement required for business and IT leadership.

This management engagement is part of governance activities but applies to every one of the Strategic IT Management enterprise IT capabilities in such activities as planning, prioritization, project development, operational excellence, and financial management. Partnership and trust—in the relationship between business and IT—is not possible unless both parts are fully engaged.

In many ways, the previous sections also apply to the business. All the dimensions of trust, including credibility, apply. But the most serious in this case is the issue of business's accountability to be the proper "receiver" of IT services. And IT behavior gets in the way. All of the TVPM discussions in Chapters 2 and 5 focus mostly on the performance credibility, or competency, of the IT organization. That's certainly what we describe in this chapter.

It turns out that the business organization is equivalently described in performance and credibility terms. In fact, this is one the key contributions of this book, to reflect and recognize on the importance the business organization plays in everything that IT purports to do for them. More to the point, it is the *use* of information and IT that brings on business success. In many ways, the business does not care about the IT Supply aspects of IT management. Those aspects are seen as "their" problem and therefore not of real interest or concern. But it is the translation of business opportunity and utilization that makes the difference.

So when one considers the basic competency—IT's service delivery— when looking at the IT Supply side, of course we can identify some key components, such as reliability, functionality, ease of use, flexibility, and so on, that the IT services delivered. But—and here's the real point—unless the business also is competent and capable of managing the use of information and technology and translating that into operational excellence capabilities, it simply does not matter.

And this is the real point. The most wonderful IT organization has little or no impact on the business, unless the business is capable of using and applying the IT being provided. Of course there are examples where IT itself is the point of contact for "real" customers, the point of delivering "real" products and services, and so on. But even this misstates the basic proposition. In these cases (e.g., the ATM, the kiosk, the self-service, the web sites), IT is certainly the delivery medium, *but it stands for the business, and it operationalizes the business processes.*

Key question: who's accountable?

Example 1: Business Engagement

To illustrate how business is engaged, consider the example of the roles to be played in business-driven project prioritization. For any IT governance to work, we need the active participation and decision making of business management in these areas:

- *Project approval* (e.g., project sponsorship)
- *Decision-making processes* (e.g., setting the ground rules for making prioritization decisions)
- *Prioritization decisions* (Which are the most valuable projects in terms of impact on the business?)
- *Confirming prioritization decisions* (Which projects should actually be done? What are the "mandatory" or "compliance" projects?)
- *Scheduling decisions* (Which projects should be done first?)

- *Content participation* (e.g., agreements on business strategic intentions, business goals, business change management)
- *Monitoring and mitigation* (e.g., developing and agreeing to the mitigation plans—including project stoppage, deferment, etc.—as risks are recognized in a project or in the portfolio)

While we describe these participative roles here with respect to managing the project portfolio, we can develop similar "need" lists for the other IT governance activities, such as IT planning, financial management, and cost containment. In all these areas, we need business management to focus on balancing functional silos with enterprise needs and on enforcing standards and process definitions.

A critical challenge is that business managers often don't want to spend the time and energy or risk the political exposure to participate in this way in an ongoing fashion. We often find that business management's views of how governance works are limited to these perspectives:

- "Approval" is a rubber-stamping review of individual projects.
- Senior managers say, "This is what we hire you to do," leaving IT to make the decisions.
- Business managers see their role in IT governance as shepherding their individual projects, not making decisions for the good of the enterprise.
- "Prioritization" is treated as a matter for individual business units and individual projects. Business managers ask, "When will our project be done?" rather than "What is the optimal set of projects to be done?"[11]
- Few business managers care whether projects for managers in other business units are high priority. The siloization of business is very apparent. Every organization struggles with cross-silo prioritization, and most fail, with the result that IT resources become silo-specific.

How many of us have sat through steering committee dog-and-pony shows in which everything is approved? ("After all, how can we turn down his project knowing that he's about to vote on ours?") How many of us have gone to governance meetings only to encounter not the designated manager but her "representative"—even though that representative didn't attend previous meetings or bother to read the support material? These situations arise partly because current IT governance schemes focus only on participation, not on actual decision making. They are also partly due to the zero-sum-game aspect of project governance decisions; they require saying no to other parts of the business, which is not easily done.

How do we change all this effectively in project portfolio management? Over the last 25 years, the most pressing problem our clients have faced is getting business management to engage in an ongoing fashion in IT portfolio management and IT planning. Everyone gets participation for the first cycle, but it declines from there. The upshot is that IT managers end up driving the portfolio management and IT planning processes—and making the decisions.

The basic dilemma is that it is easy to say we need to establish effective governance roles, engage business management in them, and demonstrate that the result is better than what we have now. What's hard is doing so in ways that encourage and reward participation and gain enthusiastic support. Simply telling management to participate has never worked.

Example 2: Getting Management Involved

In working with a recent client, we made the point that getting and keeping business involvement in any aspect of IT governance is a serious difficulty. We noted that this is true for every client with which we've worked over the last 25 years.

For this client, this understanding allowed us to lead them to a "three-phase" approach to successfully gain management involvement, focusing on portfolio management for applications and infrastructure services as a start.

Phase One: Giving business management a clear example of exactly what IT governance in general and portfolio management in particular will give them. An academic argument does not work—they need complete set of examples of their specific applications and the kind of reporting and analysis that's possible. This will lead to understanding of what value they'll get. Note this is a relatively passive phase; we aren't asking them to do anything; rather, we're giving them concrete examples of the outcomes. Note also this means that the IT organization has to provide the basic data for this phase.

Phase Two: Going to business management with a complete costing of applications and infrastructure services. While it is interesting to know the applications on which they depend and to know how they might be aligned or how well they're performing, nothing gets attention as much as cost. Giving insight into where costs are, which applications and infrastructure services are the most costly, does get attention. Even though IT may be a small cost overall (2 to 5 percent of the overall revenue stream), it is a major cost to the business unit.[12]

Phase Three: Getting their participation in a complete business-value assessment of their applications and infrastructure services. This is a value assessment to lead them to more optimally manage their IT efforts and obtain better business impact. This of course is the point of IT governance. But once they've seen what's possible—and seen the cost—the barriers to their engagement are significantly reduced.

Phase Three gets us to an initial level of participation. Keeping this participation over time requires a governance cycle that revisits the value assessment, probably as a part of the annual budget cycle.

In our experience, the points about the importance of IT governance and business management involvement are very difficult to make in the abstract. This is why the three phases are so critical. Phases One and Two provide examples that business managers will recognize, but also show the value of the effort. This will reduce the hurdles to their involvement in Phase Three. Further, seeing what the possibilities are will encourage them to contribute the necessary realistic data (e.g., business-focused assessments).

Implementing Partnerships Requires Agreement on Roles for the Partners

The challenge is to have business and IT managers agree on the mission IT is to play in the business unit and the enterprise as a whole. The reason, of course, is that a business–IT partnership would exist to meet common goals with the appropriate allocation of responsibility and effort. This is difficult if there's no agreement, explicit or assumed, on exactly what those goals are and what is to be done to meet them.

The simple test is: What would each business and IT executive say would be the priority for the primary IT mission, particularly viewed from the role that's to be played in a partnership? From the perspective of business, the IT organization can play four roles. These roles differ significantly on the focus and primary objectives sought. (Note these roles may include aspects that are outsourced.) This helps establish the expectations business may have for IT (particularly for partnership with IT) and the expectations IT has in how it deals with the business.[13]

The question is, what is the priority view for IT's mission in the business? It is not that these are mutually exclusive, but there is a fundamental priority among them. Exhibit 9.5 summarizes our results in obtaining answers from executives from mid-sized companies (median revenue $1 billion) and from government agencies in North America. (Recall the discussion in Chapter 1

Exhibit 9.5 Mission

IT Mission	CEO/Senior Leadership Team (SLT)	Business Unit Executives	IT Executives and SLT
Operate IT Services. Provide operations and technical support for the applications and services used by the business.	Last—Least Important	Last—Least Important	Highest—Most Important
Transform IT. Introduce the latest technologies; provide leadership for the adoption of new technologies throughout the business.	Third Highest	Third Highest	Second Highest
Support Business Processes. Provide direct support—even perform business tasks—for the business and its processes.	Second Highest	Highest—Most Important	Third Highest
Transform Business. Provide leadership and direction for competitively and operationally significant transformations in the business organization.	Highest—Most Important	Second Highest	Last—Least Important

about possible differences between Europe and North America in these discussions about IT mission.) The question is: What are the most important to least important business development and partnership roles for IT to play in the business? Exhibit 9.5 summarizes our experience in firms in North America. For any given enterprise, however, the expectations may be quite different.

Of course, this is not to say that technology operations aren't vital to the business. The whole idea of *service and operational excellence*, discussed later, says it is. And the business is highly dependent on IT.

Rather, this says that the developmental and partnership roles of IT may be well beyond simple operations, in the view of management. So while technology operations may be vital—a necessary condition—it is not nearly a sufficient condition to warrant the sort of trust and partnership that would propel the business forward in general and, as we consider the issues, that would deal successfully with turbulence, change, and uncertainty.

These are not mutually exclusive by any means. However, the primary expectations for business make enormous differences in expectations for IT and, by extension, the nature of the common goals and joint responsibilities. By the same token, the business is expected to perform different functions and responsibilities based on the expectations for these IT roles. This may explain some of the current barriers between business and IT. If we can't agree on what our most important mission might be, that gets in the way of partnership.

So we have three basic points. First is that understanding the mission expectations, as shown in Exhibit 9.5, is an important first step for the development of partnership and trust. Second is that the likelihood of disagreement among the management groups (CEO, business unit, IT) is very large, and this in and of itself gets in the way of developing trust and partnership. But third, the recognition of IT's mission leads to different configurations of Strategic IT Management. We'll be paying attention to this in Chapter 12.

Consider the seven basic areas of Strategic IT Management, as shown in Exhibit 9.6, and then consider what their characteristics need to be depending on the priority for mission.

The point we're making is not whether this is the right answer when the IT role is *Operate IT Services*. Rather, it is whether there is agreement among the management players as to what the mission is. And while this is simple test in terms of specific executives (CEO, CFO, etc.), the real question is how each manager, supervisor, and professional throughout the enterprise views the mission and who is responsible for what. If there are misunderstandings and

Exhibit 9.6 Mission and Strategic IT Management

IT's Role in the Enterprise IT Capability	Business Transformation	Business Support	IT Transformation	Operate IT Services
Planning & Innovation	High		High	
Information & Innovation	High	High		
Development & Transformation		High		
Service & Resource Optimization			High	High
Sourcing			High	
Service & Operational Excellence				High
Cost & Performance Management				High

Exhibit 9.7 Mission Example

Primary Role and Mission for IT	CEO	CFO	Business Unit Executives	CIO and IT Executives
Operate IT Services	1	1	1 (tie)	2
Transform Technology	2	3	3	1
Support Business Process	3	2	1 (tie)	4
Transform Business	4	4	4	3

differing expectations between IT and business, the foundation for an effective partnership is weak. This example shows only one possibility for the *Operate IT Services* role. A similar table would exist for the other roles.

An example of the possible differences in one company is shown in Exhibit 9.7. Each business and IT executive is asked to rank order their understanding and perspective of the mission IT is expected to perform.

For this particular company, there's some agreement but considerable room for disagreement and misunderstanding, even if there are attempts to clarify. This difference of opinion dramatically influences the development of partnership and trust. When individuals expecting to work together have different views on what IT is expected to do and emphasize, there's no surprise when mistrust arises, with thoughts that the individuals have different agendas—because in fact, they do.

Is This a Real Problem?

One might wonder whether what we've described here actually exists in real organizations. One only has to walk into a typical IT organization and ask the first-line supervisors or project managers, "What is the role you play with respect to IT?" "What are the outcomes you are expected to produce?" and "What roles do business managers play?" Then go out to the business units and ask the same questions of the business unit executives and direct reports. Not surprisingly, perhaps most typically IT folks target their role as technical production of software and the operation of the infrastructure and applications, and they expect business management to clearly define their requirements and do whatever is necessary to effectively use the technical IT results. The business managers either don't have an opinion or expect IT to support business and understand their needs, in addition to their development and operational roles; and they are pretty blank about their own role in IT. This gap in understanding is indeed real. What's interesting is that alternative forms of sourcing, whether formal outsourcing or cloud, only exacerbate the understanding gap; the business tends to think of outsourcing or cloud as much more than just the technical IT deliveries.

One might imagine that service-level agreements (SLAs) would solve the problem. While there's some value to this, they tend also to widen the gap as SLAs will certainly focus on operations and development and not too much, if at all, on the business focus aspects. We encourage readers to conduct a self-assessment on this issue of business and IT expectations for the role and mission of IT and the related business accountability and responsibility issues. See Chapter 1 for self-examination instruments.

The danger is this discussion is abstract, interpreted to be applicable only to the business–IT organization at the highest level. "Of course, we have a partnership!" leadership might exclaim.

The tangible aspects of partnership, however, require coordinated, joint action on the part of the parties and real goal achievement. More to the point, this notion of *partnership* applies at *all levels of the interaction* between business and IT. Each project team is a partnership. Each governance group (e.g., for service management, for prioritization, etc.) is a partnership. Each working group in architecture, or in an agile activity, or in planning is a partnership.

"Teaming" Is the New Partnership

Amy Edmondson's work[14] focuses on the notion of *teaming* as a critical element of multi-organization and multi-individual efforts—in short, partnerships. Here are examples of what she is describing.

> Most people recognize that the knowledge-based twenty-first century organization depends on cross-disciplinary collaboration, flattened hierarchies, and continuous innovation.
>
> With flattened hierarchies and distributed leadership, is the need for strong leadership fading?
>
> Type One—Formal Leadership
> Type Two—Staff leadership . . . throughout the organization . . . at the front lines where crucial work affecting customer experiences is carried out.

This is exactly what we're about—establishing the capability to partner, to team, between business and IT. And it is for everyone—staff leadership at the forefront. Everyone who's engaged in developing IT's capabilities for the benefit of the business is necessarily engaged in teaming.

Partners Exist at Every Level

We have the tendency to talk about partnership and partners as though it is a one-on-one between two organizations. The concept of partnership, however, applies to each interaction between business and IT, even at the individual level. The notion of partners applies even to two individuals working together on a project. The notion also incorporates every potential participant, meaning multiple sources of IT and multiple locations from the business. We've said this before: the overall business–IT partnership is all inclusive.

The challenge is a bit more subtle than just multiple levels of partnership. It is not uncommon to have CIOs and senior business executives talk about the business/IT partnership. This idea gets into the rhetoric pretty easily. The challenge is to have the requisite acceptance of the idea, and the resulting behaviors at all levels of both business and IT, actually occur. Getting nominal agreement at the top level seems easy. Getting the behavior is not.

Having said all this, it is good to remind ourselves why we want partnership. Collaboration, communication, cooperation, common goals, sharing, trust, responsiveness—these are highly desirable when considered in the context of "transforming business in times of turbulence and uncertainty." But these are also desirable in extending the basic service management relationships as well.

Summary

Successful partnership-based business and IT relationships require everything any business or personal partnership requires. We require trust, common goals, clear roles and missions for each partner, mutual respect, collaborative effort, inclusive behaviors, leadership, and culture.

At the same time, these important partnership characteristics also define why a business–IT partnership relationship is not just a good thing but critical to dealing with the challenges of turbulence and uncertainty. Unless these descriptions of the relationship exist, the challenges of finding credible, flexible, and quick solutions to the problems facing business may be insurmountable.

Partnership Scorecards

In Exhibit 9.8, we present a simple scorecard for the current level of partnership between the business and IT.

Exhibit 9.8   Partnership Scorecard

Partnership Parameter	Partnership Description	Business View	IT View
Collaboration	Business and IT collaborate effectively, seeking common goals and with clear roles and accountabilities.		
Coordination	Business and IT exhibit good coordination in activities that affect one another.		
Sharing	Both business and IT share necessary information, skills, and personnel as required.		
Responsiveness	The collaborated and coordinated efforts operate quickly and responsibly to turbulence and change.		
Trust	The important characteristics of trust are exhibited in the behavior of business and IT: sharing, transparency, common goals, clear agendas.		
Breaking Down the Silos	Business and IT have successfully reduced the bureaucracies. Activities, solutions, and efforts seamlessly cross organizational boundaries in business and IT.		

The scorecard is based on a five-point scale:

1. This Partnership Description rarely characterizes the behaviors of business or IT.
2. This Partnership Description sometimes characterizes the behaviors of business or IT.
3. This Partnership Description occasionally characterizes the behaviors of business or IT.
4. This Partnership Descript often characterizes the behavior of business or IT.
5. This Partnership Description almost always characterizes the behavior of business and IT.

The same scorecard applies to each of the IT service areas, as shown in Exhibit 9.9. The same five-point scale operates as used in Exhibit 9.8.

Exhibit 9.9 Service Portfolio Scorecard

Partnership Parameter	Partnership Description	Application & Information Service	Direct Infrastructure Services	Project Services	Technical (User) Services	IT Management Services
Collaboration	Seeking common goals and with clear roles					
Coordination	Coordinating activities that affect one another					
Sharing	Sharing necessary information, skills, and personnel					
Responsiveness	Operating quickly and responsibly to turbulence					
Trust	Sharing, transparency, common goals, clear agendas					
Breaking Down the Silos	Reducing the bureaucracies, seamlessly crossing boundaries					

Notes

1. See Chapter 3, "IT Management Is about Relationship Management," in Mark Lutchen, *Managing IT as a Business: A Survival Guide for CEOs* (Wiley, 2004): 57.
2. Michael D. Eisner, with Aaron Cohen, *Working Together: Why Great Partnerships Succeed* (HarperCollins, 2010): xv.
3. F. Warren McFarlan, "Information Technology Changes the Way You Compete," *Harvard Business Review* (May 1984).
4. So are teaming and collaboration. See Amy Edmondson, *Teaming: How Organizations Learn, Innovate, and Compete in the Knowledge Economy* (Jossey-Bass, 2012).
5. A partnership scorecard is located at the end of this chapter.
6. See Edgar H. Schein, *Organizational Culture and Leadership*, 4th ed. (Jossey-Bass [Wiley], 2010). As he states in the preface: "Culture defined: pattern of shared basic assumptions learned by a group as it solved its problems . . . which has worked well enough to be considered valid . . . as the correct way to . . . think" (p. 18). We believe this applies equally to "considered valid as the correct way to behave." We adopt this view. This defines our use of the culture term.
7. Lawrence and Lorsch call this "differentiation." P. Lawrence and J. Lorsch, "Differentiation and Integration in Complex Organizations," *Administrative Science Quarterly* 12 (1967). The point is that each functional group needs its culture and behavior to be effective and that these differences should not get in the way of good partnership.
8. Jack Gibb, *Trust: A New Vision of Human Relationships for Business, Education, Family, and Personal Living* (Newcastle Publishing, 1991), p. 223. For example, four "fundamental propositions" are 1) Personal behavior produces trust, 2) Authentic openness produces integration of . . . process; 3) Internal realization results in high productivity; 4) Interdependence produces synergy.
9. Adapted from Jack Gibb's work; see, for example, J. R. Gibb, "Defensive Communications," *Journal of Communication* 2, No. 3 (1961): 141–148, and J. R. Gibb, "Climate for Trust Formation," in *T-Group Theory and Laboratory Method*, ed. L. P. Bradford, J. R. Gibb, and K. Benne (Wiley, 1964).
10. Dorothy E. Leidner and Timothy Kayworth, "A Review of Culture in Information Systems Research: Toward a Theory of Information Technology Culture Conflict," *MIS Quarterly* 30 No. 2 (June 2006): 357–399.
11. Lutchen, *Managing IT as a Business*, Chapter 3.
12. See Cutter.com for Cutter Consortium Advisors. See, for a discussion of this, our Cutter Consortium Advisor "Knowing the Cost of IT," September 12, 2006, and "If You Don't Know Cost, You Don't Know Anything," August 23, 2006).
13. J. F. Rockart, M. J. Earl, and J. W. Ross, *The New IT Organization: Eight Imperatives* (Center for Information Systems Research, Sloan School of Management, Massachusetts Institute of Technology, 1996). http://18.7.29.232/handle/1721.1/2623
14. Edmondson, *Teaming*.

CHAPTER 10

The Leadership Required

The Introduction to Part II defines the Leadership principle for Strategic IT Management as:[1]

Senior business and IT management provides support for the business–IT relationship and provides leadership throughout the life of the relationship. IT leadership creates a business-focused culture and nurtures the best relationships within IT and with the business. The CEO and business leadership establishes the environment for the partnership, the roles to be played, and the necessary commitment and motivation.

Leadership is not only about the CEO and CIO and their roles, it is about everyone involved in applying information and IT in the enterprise, both business and IT staff.[2] But what is it? Some of it seems like simple good management, making things happen. A lot more is setting the direction for moving forward, up to and including what we've defined as *strategic management*—motivating and mobilizing the available resources to achieve the enterprise's strategic aims.

We find the two fundamental leadership aspects vital to Strategic IT Management. The first aspect, namely the proactive initiatives to achieve short- and long-term goals for IT in the enterprise, is indeed connected to management. Some researchers call this *transactional* leadership. The second aspect is the leadership necessary to achieve fundamental change in the mission or structure in business or IT activities. Some researchers call this *transformation* leadership.[3] Both aspects are required of the CEO, the CIO, and the rest of the business and IT organizations as well.

Both leadership aspects require all the things important to strategic IT management: trust, partnership, and a reflection of the business and IT culture. They also require, for those exercising leadership, confidence in the direction and goals being sought and the trust and credibility needed to influence others to participate in the necessary actions.

This chapter describes the organizational and individual leadership needed to make trust and partnership, and the successful responses to turbulence and uncertainty, possible. The organizational leadership requirement has four focal points: the CEO, the CIO, the IT staff, and business executives. The individual leadership by IT and business staff reflects the requirement for proactive behavior on the part of all IT managers and professionals. We elaborate on these requirements in Chapters 17 and 18.

Our leadership goals are to *enable superior responses to the turbulence in business and IT* and *produce superior business value* with the use of information and IT. Doing so requires partnership and trust, as well as basic management capabilities. The challenge is that there are barriers to overcome, such as culture, lack of trust, and lack of performance. Passivity will not overcome them; it requires proactive leadership on the part of all concerned. Again, leadership is key.

We make five points about leadership, its role in Strategic IT Management, and its necessity to achieving our basic goals:

1. Leadership is required for partnership, trust, and common goals.
2. Leadership requires leaders and a good understanding of the requirements.
3. (Proactive) Transactional leadership is required.
4. Transformational leadership is required.
5. Leadership is earned through credibility, trust, and culture.

Chapters 17 and 18 discuss recommendations for CEOs and CIOs (as well as other business and IT executives), which include dealing with the requirements for leadership. As those chapters make clear, the real application, and implication, for leadership is making change possible, making change happen.

Goal #1: Leadership Is Required for Partnership, Trust, and Common Goals

A simple review of literature and various Internet sources reveal a very simple leadership definition, said in our words: *Leadership is a process where an individual influences a group of individuals to achieve a common goal*. Others add the leadership process of setting those goals; in our words, *leadership establishes direction and influences others to follow that direction.*[4]

The interesting thing, of course, is most books focused on business descriptions of leaders and leadership and partnerships tend to focus on the highest management levels: CEOs and management teams.[5] But what we're talking about is more fundamental than that. It is the leadership skill needed throughout the IT organization—and mirrored in every part of the business organization—to achieve the partnerships and the results cited throughout the book. These skills focus on building the business–IT relationships, producing the required outcomes, and resulting in recognition that IT is a core business function. That is, every project manager, every supervisor, every IT director needs these leadership qualities. Why is that? Because the premise of Strategic IT Management is the establishment of partnerships for the achievement of common goals *throughout* the relationship between business and IT. This leadership requirement works at planning, project development, operational excellence, and service management—all the things that IT does (IT Supply) to meet business requirements (IT Demand).

The idea that effective leadership is needed for IT to prosper in its mission of serving the business is, of course, an old one. In particular, the belief that IT (and the CIO) needs the leadership support of the CEO began somewhere in the 1960s and 1970s.[6]

Why is leadership so important? And who should exercise it? We will make the case here that leadership is necessary for every level of business and IT management, and in the context of achieving our goals of successfully dealing with turbulence/uncertainty and delivering superior business value, it is required to achieve these goals.

But what is it exactly? There's a lot written about it in business journals and academic research reports. Some common themes are in the contemporary literature: leadership is successfully encouraging people to follow you, leadership is setting a vision and moving the organization in that direction, leadership is enabling all within the organization to contribute to its success. And on and on.

We posit a simple leadership requirement: *The ability to encourage others to adopt a goal and a course of action, and to motivate and provide support for them to execute to achieve it.* There can be many subcategories, such as the "Cs" of leadership: catalyst, collaboration, cheerleader, coach, collaborator, cooperation, candid, caring, communicator. Those "C" words certainly characterize elements of *encouragement* and *motivation*.

We choose this broad requirement because this is what the enterprise requires to achieve our goals: superior response to turbulence and superior value from IT. As we'll say from time to time, there are a lot of moving parts in the business–IT relationship, some wholly business, some in technology, many in the space between them. These moving parts are at all levels: executives, managers, supervisors, and associates. The moving parts may be part of another organization, for example, partners, sourcers, suppliers. To deal with turbulence and to create superior applications of information technology, all these moving parts need to work together toward common goals (recall *partnership* in Chapter 9), deliver and exploit information/IT (recall *service performance* in Chapter 8), and hopefully introduce transforming change in how business is done in response to turbulence and uncertainty. As we'll see, this takes leadership.

One of the better statements about leadership is "Management is coping with complexity; leadership is coping with change."[7] But it is more than just coping. Leadership is proactively marshaling the resources to achieve the superior responses to turbulence, faster and better. And it is producing the necessary superior services to supply the information and technology needed for those responses in a proactive manner. And it is applying information and IT in the business to create the transformational changes proactively. And perhaps most importantly, leadership is establishing the context within which the ability to "persuade others on a course of action, and motivate them to execute it" can be effectively exercised.

Goal #2: Leadership Requires Leaders—and a Good Understanding of the Leadership Requirements

Much of the business and research literature describes two classes of leadership: transactional leadership and transformational leadership.[8] The first is task-oriented and the second is directional- or change-oriented. Our requirement—to have the leadership ability to encourage others to adopt a course of action and motivate them to execute it—tends to bridge between the two: the transactional in terms of the details of execution; the transformational in terms of the significant change in the overall goals being sought and all of the consequential things that need to be done.

This comes down to two fundamental Strategic IT Management leadership requirements:

- *Transactional leadership*, to marshal the resources, motivate others to work together in partnership, and provide context and motivation to achieve the desired business goals.
- *Transformational leadership*, to marshal the factors needed to identify the fundamental changes required and develop the partnership and capabilities needed to achievement them.

These are closely related, of course.

The problems are many. They begin with incompatible cultures and belief systems. The problems can't be solved without accepting the need to change (i.e., of course, what turbulence is about). Setting the direction, communicating it, and encouraging its adoption—all of these tasks are required. It is about leadership, which requires leaders.

The Required Leadership Outcomes:

- IT culture, behavior, and performance focuses on business.
- CIOs and IT's senior leadership teams (SLTs) provide leadership for trust and partnership.
- Business unit managers fully participate in the IT processes, producing trust and partnership.
- CEOs and enterprise SLTs provide the right context and leadership for trust and partnership.
- Organizations are motivated to work together and to work toward common goals.

Overall, the key is this: Someone has to provide all this leadership. Whether in business or IT, leadership comes from leaders. And everyone has a leadership role.

Goal #3: The Requirements for (Proactive) Transactional Leadership

In many ways, transactional leadership is simply good management. For example, a typical web site developed to describe management and leadership says: "Leadership is an important function of management which helps to maximize efficiency and to achieve organizational goals." This includes actions such as initiating action, providing motivation and guidance, creating confidence, building morale, enabling coordination and cooperation.[9]

And these are surely important goals. But this does not scratch the surface on the significant aspects of partnership, trust, common goals, and credibility. Leadership must create a combination of the strengths of all IT sources and all involved business organization: in effect, leadership must build the larger partnership to achieve the needed goals.

Anyone involved in any of the IT competencies described in Chapter 7 requires this form of leadership—at least to understand that these are the things the leadership has to accomplish. For example, simply achieving good partnership requires leadership for collaboration, coordination, communication, sharing, and overall, breaking down the silos (see Chapter 7). And simply achieving the basic characteristics of partnerships requires leadership to establish common goals, transparency and openness, lack of hidden agendas, inclusive behaviors, commitment, and ownership (see Chapter 9).

But it is more than just transactional leadership, the accomplishment of the tasks involved. This leadership requires proactivity, an energetic seeking out of the opportunities and ways to overcome the challenges in achieving the goals. Proactive transactional leadership accomplishes these outcomes in the context of both business and IT behavior and culture barriers. This form of leadership puts the spotlight on the things that prevent partnership, such as defensive, control-oriented, closed, or judgmental behavior.

Goal #4: The Requirements for Transformational Leadership

As we described earlier, transformational leadership identifies the transforming goals, marshals the enterprise factors needed to identify the fundamental changes required, and develops the partnership and capabilities needed to achievement them. That latter part dovetails with proactive transactional leadership, but here is focused on helping identify and achieve the innovative and breakthrough visions, that is, transforming the business. One core element is consideration for the mental models current existing and how they must change. This applies to both business and IT, as described in Chapter 9 on partnership.

We should step back from all the rhetoric and ask the simple question: What issues require the development of leadership? We're dealing with two related threads of ideas here. From the IT perspective, the first of course is the identification of required competencies and capabilities to deal with turbulence and delivery of business value. The competencies can be dynamic themselves but, as we described previously, can be such (relatively) simple things—for example, in the IT Supply domain, as "agile" or "architecture." The second is the ability to adopt the changes required. These two threads exist in the business as well, in terms of the capability to apply information and IT in ways to deal with business turbulence and uncertainty. So we're dealing with vision (what we need) and change (how do we get there.)

So the issues are simple: Transformational leadership includes these abilities:

- *Vision:* Identify the end-state that's desired, and clearly communicate the vision and its importance.
- *Mental Models:* Identify the necessary changes to accommodate the vision for the enterprise and/or for IT.[10]
- *Mission and Roles:* Identify who's to be engaged in achieving the vision and the teaming (partnerships) needed. We visited this in Chapter 9, with attention to the problem of inconsistency and ambiguity in the role IT is to play (and by extension the business).

- *Resolve Friction:* Identify the barriers to achieving the vision and the importance of addressing them.
- *Rules:* Identify the conditions for success.
- *Urgency:* Identify why all of this is necessary.

Recall our definition of the leadership requirement: *It is the ability to encourage others to adopt a course of action and to motivate and provide support for them to execute it.* The leadership scorecard in the next section explores the level of leadership provided for each ability.

Goal #5: Leadership Is Earned through Credibility, Trust, and Culture

One does not simply proclaim leadership. While one may desire to be a leader, the acceptance of the "led" is earned. While this is a topic covering decades of research and an outpouring of books and materials, the earning of leadership can be boiled down to credibility and trust. Some dimensions include the following.

Interpersonal Trust (Based on Respect)[11]

- Expertness
- Reliability
- Dynamism

Organizational Trust (Based on Respect)

- Competence
- Integrity
- Rapport

Here, too, the possibility of behaviors that do not reflect positives in these dimensions would certainly get in the way of respect.

Performance Credibility[12]

- *Execution* leads to operational excellence.
- *Transparency* is the basis for trust and respect.
- *Partnering* means finding a common mission.
- *Competence* is not just execution but command of the subject matter. This leads to the problem of IT competence versus business competence.

When one puts these interrelated facets together and judges IT's collective and individual capabilities against them, the challenge is easily seen. But the fundamental point is that leadership is earned and ultimately is based on individual and organizational behavior as it is perceived by others.

What Does the Past Teach Us about Leadership?

The leadership required of business and IT is not a permanent thing, unchanging. Business and IT turbulence introduces new elements and at a faster pace than in the past. In effect, the basis for earning leadership through credibility and trust changes. For example, it required perhaps five years for personal computers (PCs) to become a stable, recognized, significant part of IT activities, fully integrated with the rest of the (then centralized) IT activities. A collision of decentralized/centralized behaviors occurred then, with the ultimate movement toward centralization based on the learning curves, and consistent with what the two learning models introduced previously. The pendulum swings, but at different cycles for different technologies and technology applications.

Applied to leadership, the point is that in each of the major technology changes, culture and "best practices" and sheer inertia created barriers to change, tumult in the organization, questions about organization and practices and leadership (where should the CIO report?), and great opportunity for organizations that could overcome the barriers. As a secondary point, it is clear that every major technology change was not permanent: Something else would occur that would affect the previous settled technology patterns.

We recognize this section is IT-centric in its description of turbulence and the resulting leadership issues. Much the same kind of patterns exist on the business side as well, though some might argue that the broad-scale business changes are much more fundamental and certainly not characterized by the kind of centralization/decentralization pendulum often used to portray turbulence in IT. The "speed" chart in Chapter 4 is a fundamental aspect of change: Making needed progress requires significant business change, perhaps reminiscent of the "reengineering" discussions a few years ago. That experience, as a pattern, leads to the same recognition: that proactive leadership is required on the business side as well.

Leadership Scorecard

We encourage the reader to assess the current leadership capabilities in the enterprise as they relate to IT and Strategic IT Management. The scorecard in Exhibit 10.1 shows the areas of leadership needed.

Exhibit 10.1 Leadership Scorecard

	CEO and SLT	Business Unit Executives	CIO	IT Staff
Vision	Business outcomes—the common goals	The use of information and IT in the business to meet the common goals	The capabilities required to meet the common goals	The outcomes for initiatives, projects
Mental Models	Acceptance of new mental models	Acceptance of new mental models	Acceptance of new mental models	Acceptance of new mental models
Mission and Roles	Accountabilities	The business roles necessary	The IT roles necessary	Service management, development
Resolve Friction	Establish the culture; empower the actions needed	Establish the culture; empower the actions needed	Establish the culture; empower the actions needed	Service management, project teams
Rules	Confirm requirements	Confirm requirements	Standards	Standards
Urgency	Confirm and communicate	Confirm and communicate	Confirm and communicate	Confirm and communicate

Scale:

1: No leadership for this occurs.
2: Discussion occurs.
3: Leadership occurs unevenly.
4: Good communication.
5: Good communication with clear motivation and expectations.

Notes

1. Edgar H. Schein, *Organizational Culture and Leadership*, 4th ed. (Jossey-Bass [Wiley], 2010).
2. See Chapter 8, "Leadership," in Amy C. Edmondson, *Teaming: How Organizations Learn, Innovate, and Compete in the Knowledge Economy* (Jossey-Bass, 2012).
3. James MacGregor Burns, *Leadership* (Harper Collins, 1978). See, for example, Edmondson, *Teaming*, Chapter 8.
4. The job of a manager can be summarized in one sentence: "Create an atmosphere where good players want to do the right thing." That is how Terry Francona described it while winning two World Series with the Boston Red Sox. See "Girardi Stands, and Jumps Up, for What's Right," *New York Times*, August 20, 2013, www.nytimes.com/2013/08/20/sports/baseball/girardi-stands-and-stands-up-for-whats-right.html?hpw
5. For example, see Warren Bennis, *Leaders: Strategies for Taking Charge*, 2nd ed. (Harper-Business, 2007), and David A. Heenan, and Warren Bennis, *Co-Leaders: The Power of Great Partnerships* (Wiley, 1999).
6. For example, John Dearden, "MIS Is a Mirage," *Harvard Business Review* (January-February 1972): 90–99.
7. John P. Kotter, *Force for Change: How Leadership Differs from Management* (Free Press, 1990).
8. Begun, of course, with Burns, *Leadership*.
9. www.managementstudyguide.com/importance_of_leadership.htm
10. We have consistently emphasized the importance of mental models in business and IT. See Peter Senge, *The Fifth Discipline: The Art and Practice of the Learning Organization* (Doubleday, 2006).
11. See Pamela Shockley-Zalabak, K. Ellis, and R. Cesaria, *Measuring Organizational Trust* (New York: IABC Research Foundation, 2000).
12. See, for example: James C. Emery, *Organizational Planning and Control Systems: Theory and Technology* (Macmillan, 1969), and James C. Emery, *Management Information Systems: The Critical Strategic Resource* (Oxford University Press, 1987).

CHAPTER 11

Enterprise IT Capabilities

Too many books, articles, academics, and consultants take the view that difficulties and distrust between IT and business (and disappointment in the IT value received) are the fault of the IT organization and the various processes used to plan, manage, and execute IT. The "fix" to them is to upgrade the processes, restructure the IT organization, and focus more attention on the business. "If IT could only understand the business better!" Perhaps it is described as a governance problem as well, where *governance* is meant as the way business controls what IT does and determines on what IT spends. And, perhaps, the solution is viewed as business and IT becoming partners in the common goals of superior IT value and superior response to turbulence and uncertainty.

Three problems complicate this simple perspective of an IT organization–focused solution to what ails the business/IT relationship. First, this is indeed an IT-centric perspective. As we pointed out earlier, partnership requires partners, and both business and IT have to be capable of acting as partners. Somehow, even in the expression of "partnership," it seems as though the initiative and energy and structure has to come from IT. The evidence is the strong tendency to view the processes that connect business and IT as "IT processes." Second, every enterprise is in the throes of an enormous dispersion of IT activities, both within the enterprise and in the supplier/customer environments in which it operates. We talk of the "cloud" and sourcing and "do-it-yourself" IT as symptoms of this great IT dispersion, and very likely other forms of IT provisioning will quickly appear. Think, for example, of the implications of ideas like crowdsourcing, micromanufacturing, and organizational virtualization, from the perspective of corralling (optimizing) the use of and supply of information and technology in the business. This creates a much broader context for any partnership, including a potential multiplicity of IT actors in terms of where IT is sourced. There's not so much a single IT organization as a collection of providers, one of which may be the existing corporate IT organization. Third, the main subtext of this book is turbulence and uncertainty, and the absolute requirement of faster and more adaptable forms of everything, both in business and IT.

In other words, the "fix" applies to both business and IT. The aim is not just to "fix IT" but to fix the business–IT relationship.

While it is comforting to think of well-structured governance and processes and (from the IT view) architectures, the challenge is to view these so-called solutions through the lens of speed and adaptability and, of course, necessarily balance them with the same issues that need solutions in the business. It becomes clear that solutions that merely address processes, governance, or architecture, for a start, really are not enough; this sounds like the simple reworking of the standard enterprise. The threats of massive disruptive innovations, industry transformation, and huge but unforeseen dislocations affect almost every enterprise. We aren't about rearranging the desk chairs; we're about responding to the challenges of unknown and uncertain waters, and prospering in the process. *What we need is for the enterprise as a whole to be capable of the fundamentals: the IT capabilities needed to deliver superior business value and superior response to turbulence and uncertainty.* Simply, these enterprise IT capabilities have three fundamental requirements: 1) deal holistically with the business and with all forms of IT, 2) provide adaptability, 3) create the context and climate for partnership. All this requires seven enterprise IT capabilities that can deploy and execute the IT competencies described in Chapter 7.

The Introduction to Part II stated the Strategic IT Management principles, including:

> *The enterprise possesses the seven capabilities based on trust, leadership, and partnership to create superior value and responses to turbulence and uncertainty.*

And lest you think all this is just a phenomenon of and response to turbulence, let us be clear. The enterprise IT capabilities are fundamentally the fix for the current malaise of the IT–business relationship, irrespective of dealing with turbulence and uncertainty. We have remarked previously that, in any respect, most IT processes don't seem to be working well. This is seen in distrustful business–IT relationships, in governance, in strategic planning, and even in project development. Chapter 2, for example, makes the point that IT simply has a problem of performing. Chapter 6 puts this in the context of performance levels, the six levels of demonstrated outcomes needed to be achieved before IT can, indeed, participate in strategic business innovations (in other words, provide superior IT value). As a result, these seven enterprise IT capabilities are certainly required to deal with turbulence and uncertainty, but even more fundamentally, they are required to achieve IT's promise in the

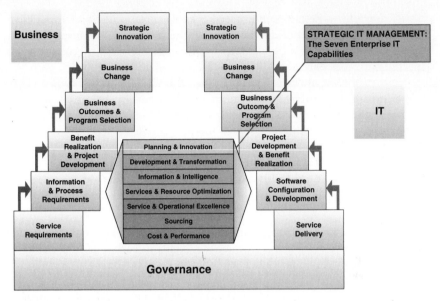

Exhibit 11.1   The Seven Enterprise IT Capabilities that Connect Business

enterprise, namely, providing superior IT value. Simply, they are required to build the trust and partnership required.

Exhibit 11.1 connects with the Total Performance Value Model (TVPM) and positions the enterprise IT capabilities as connecting, coordinating, and enabling the business–IT partnership to accomplish the tasks necessary. As Chapters 2 and 3 defined this model, the IT and business stair steps reflect what each organization needs to accomplish competently, in order to move up the staircase. Enterprise IT capabilities both make this possible and also are shaped by the current status of the enterprise in terms of the ability to perform.

Connecting IT Value, IT Competence, and Enterprise IT Capabilities

IT's TVPM describes the enterprise's current success (or lack thereof) in producing the actual outcomes required for superior IT value and, perhaps more importantly, the specific performance outcomes and therefore credibility that are the foundation for business–IT trust. The TVPM describes this for both business and IT, and also reflects an ordering of these outcomes (performance and trust is built up from step to step in the model).

IT competency describes the specific knowledge, skills, and experience foundation needed for actually performing the processes and methodologies required. Competency is the demonstrated command of tasks producing the specific outcomes expected

Enterprise IT capability describes the *overall ability of the enterprise* as a whole to perform the partnership efforts and tasks necessary to create superior business value from investments that exploit IT and superior response to turbulence and uncertainty.

Connecting IT Capability with IT Methodologies and Processes

Plenty of IT-centric processes, introduced in the Chapter 7 discussion of IT competencies, are available to execute the details in each area. For example, some of these available processes are listed in Exhibit 11.2.

We emphasize that these and similar examples of processes represent the typical IT competencies of organization management and professionals— corporate, business unit, and IT—to understand, communicate, partner, lead, and execute in each area. We also emphasize these IT competencies are not defined exclusively solely within either the business or IT domains. While the execution of many of the processes may be in either domain, this is a happenstance of the particular organizational culture (see, for example, the

Exhibit 11.2   IT Competencies

Strategic IT Planning	Project Management Office (PMO)	IT Finance
Scenario Planning	Software Development Life Cycle (SDLC)	IT Metrics
Enterprise Architecture	Agile	Architecture
Business Intelligence	Project Portfolio Management	Strategic Sourcing
Business Analytics	Application Portfolio Management	IT Infrastructure Library (ITIL) and Control Objectives for Information and Related Technology (COBIT)
Data Architecture	Infrastructure Portfolio Management	Service Management

discussion of North American versus European views on IT organization, in Chapter 1). The key is that someone within the enterprise takes the lead, is accountable for overseeing the key activities, and brings about the needed partnership, service, and operational activities.

This is not to say the IT competencies aren't important—they are critical to carrying out IT's services to the business.

Of course, there are already a lot of processes and methodologies that engage some elements of both business and IT. We listed a few of them in Exhibit 11.2. These have evolved through the decades and, generally speaking, do a good job within the confines of their specific objectives. We've used the term "best practices" to characterize many of them. And there's certainly plenty of information available about them, in books, consulting organizations, and so forth.

Problems get in the way, however. The "siloization" of the methods typically means very little coordination and commonality across them. Rarely, for example, do the same expressions of business strategy defined in, say, scenario planning reach into the specifics of ITIL or IT metrics. The execution of the methods can be very IT-centric. And generally, they aren't built with expectations of turbulence, trust, partnership, and complete business focus. Most importantly, these processes and methodologies typically are executed within the specific domains of business or IT and don't generally reach out to the other's domain. Culture, objectives, and basic vocabularies tend to restrict partnership transparency and trust as components of the methods themselves.

Breaking Down the Barriers between IT and Business: Enterprise IT Capabilities

Strategic IT Management is based on a holistic set of seven overarching enterprise IT capabilities necessary to produce superior business value and response to turbulence and uncertainty. As we will describe in the next section, these enterprise IT capabilities are not themselves the processes or methodologies of IT competencies. *Rather, they are the areas of enterprise IT capability— engaging both business and IT—to apply those processes or methodologies successfully and holistically.* And "successfully" means achieving the basic goals for applying IT in the business: superior business value and superior response to turbulence and uncertainty.

Taken together, Strategic IT Management results in a systemic capability to manage and apply IT throughout the enterprise for superior business value and superior response to turbulence and uncertainty.

We adopt the term *enterprise IT capability* with guidance from Hagel and Brown, as they said about their terminology: "We use the term *capability* rather than *competence* because the latter's common usage has tended to denote technology and production skills. We use the term *capabilities* broadly to refer to the recurring mobilization of resources for the delivery of distinctive value in excess of cost."[1] They're talking broadly about strategic management and competitive success and specifically about dynamic specialization, a product of the kind of turbulence we've been describing. The point is that this is exactly what's necessary: the holistic ability for an enterprise to mobilize the (IT) resources to deliver distinctive value from the use of information and IT.

As we introduced them in Chapter 1, the enterprise IT capabilities reflect the things the enterprise needs to be able to do, in business and IT partnership.

The Enterprise IT Capability for Strategic Thinking and Action about IT in the Business

Planning & Innovation. An enterprise requires the capability for business and IT (together) to define the future of the business and its use of information and IT.

This capability requires the ability to establish strategies, products/ services, and business models; to describe the turbulence and uncertainty affecting the business; to forecast its requirements or means for reacting to uncertainty; to understand competitive and performance requirements; and to respond to its requirements and uncertainty with viable plans, goals, and roadmaps for all its IT, as well as to do so successfully in conditions of turbulence.

The Enterprise IT Capabilities to Deliver Value through Information and IT

Service & Resource Optimization. An enterprise requires the capability to optimize the sourcing, development, and application of all its IT services and resources, from all sources: internal IT, business-unit IT activities, sourcers, and "do-it-yourself" IT activities.

Development & Transformation. An enterprise requires the capability develop, implement, and apply information and IT capabilities to change and transform business with superior returns.

Information & Intelligence. An enterprise requires the capability to acquire, manage, analyze, and apply its vast information resources in all relevant enterprise areas.

The Enterprise IT Capabilities to Execute IT in Partnership with the Business

Service & Operational Excellence. An enterprise requires the capability to perform its IT services with operational excellence and the right balance of adaptability/flexibility toward standards and stability (and, overall, holistically covering the enterprise and all its IT).

Sourcing. An enterprise requires the capability to define, plan, acquire, manage, and effectively employ IT services from all sources: internal IT, business-unit IT activities, suppliers, and "do-it-yourself" IT activities.

Cost & Performance. An enterprise requires the capability to capture and analyze the complete IT costs for all sources and applications of information and IT, and to describe its IT performance requirements and metrics, from the business perspective

All seven play critical roles in the overall performance and contribution of IT in the enterprise. And again, we are not talking narrowly about the process and methodologies, the IT competencies, themselves. Those processes are typically within the province of the technology manager in the IT organization or in the business domain. Recall our observation that there are many different practices, for example, between the United States and Europe, as to who is primarily engaged in the oversight and the enterprise IT capabilities. The crucial idea here is that the enterprise, taken as a whole, possesses and performs each of these enterprise IT capabilities. And, moreover, that the multiplicity of activities in the enterprise, the business units on the business side and all the sources of IT on the IT side, are engaged in and participate in the execution of the activities within each of the enterprise IT capabilities.

Enterprise IT Capability Overview

Exhibit 11.3 displays the seven capabilities with a summary of outcomes required and a set of examples of IT competencies, processes, and methodologies. Chapters 12 to 14 will describe each in detail.

The Risk of Strategic IT Management

Exhibit 11.3 effectively illustrates what we mean by Strategic IT Management—seven vital enterprise IT capabilities and examples of business outcomes and

Exhibit 11.3 Outcomes and Competencies within the Seven Enterprise IT Capabilities

Enterprise Capability	Example Strategic IT Management Objective for the Enterprise Capability	Example Business Outcomes Required for Superior Value	Example Business Outcomes Required for Superior Response to Turbulence	Example IT Competencies (Chapter 7)
Operational: Enterprise IT Capabilities to Execute IT in Partnership with the Business				
Cost & Performance	Create trust with transparency in IT cost and performance	Complete business-based visibility on cost and performance	Comprehensive cost and performance in changing conditions	• IT Service Finance • IT Performance Metrics
Sourcing	Match IT sourcing (internal and external) to business requirements	Sourcing matched to achieving business competitive and operational excellence, with standards	Adaptability, responsiveness, partnerships. Frameworks (e.g., responsive architectures)	• Architecture • ITIL • Supplier selection and management
Service & Operational Excellence	Manage to expectations for service and operational excellence	Superior performance matched to business requirements. Competence.	Adaptability, responsiveness, partnerships	• ITIL • COBIT • Service Management
Tactical: Enterprise IT Capabilities to Deliver Value with Information and IT				
Information & Intelligence	Transform the business through use of information and analysis	Superior use of information; competitive and innovative business forecasting and decisions	Rapid, comprehensive, responsive intelligence, forecasting	• Business Intelligence • Business Analytics • Data Architecture
Development & Transformation	Deliver business value— transformation and change— with every IT investment and project	Every project delivers business value linked to business strategic intentions and goals	Adaptability, responsiveness, partnerships, collaboration	• PMO • SDLC • Agile/Scrum • BPR

(continued)

Service & Resource Optimization	Make effective business-value and risk-based IT investment decisions	Optimized service and resource portfolios for cost, performance, and risk	Adaptable, responsive service and resource portfolios, with reduced risk.	• Portfolio Management for Applications, Infrastructure
Strategic: The Enterprise IT Capability for Strategic Thinking and Action about IT in the Business				
Planning & Innovation	Provide leadership and support for business transformation and change	Business competitive and operational excellence	Business adaptability and responsiveness Collaboration	• Strategizing • Scenario Planning • Enterprise Architecture

IT competencies needed. We have seeded these examples throughout the book, for example, in each of the detailed enterprise IT capability descriptions that follow. The problem is that this gives the strong impression that Strategic IT Management is an end point. In fact, we do use the term *end point* in the enterprise IT capability descriptions. And an end point implies a destination, a cessation of further development.

This raises two critical risks for us. First, our description of Strategic IT Management suggests end-point stability, a fully realized vision that itself will not change further. We fall into this by combining two ideas in Strategic IT Management. First, there is a notion that current IT "best practices" are not by themselves satisfactory largely because of poor focus on the business instead of IT (i.e., they're IT-centric), and the seven enterprise IT capabilities overcome this problem. Second, our descriptions of change, turbulence, and uncertainty can be interpreted as a second-level concern subordinate to fixing the inadequacies of current practices by closing the gaps with business.

Turbulence and uncertainty forms the overall background, and Strategic IT Management addresses this as the key outcome, but it's a continuous process, not simply creating an end point. Similarly, addressing current practices is an ongoing process, as circumstances, organizations, and requirements change driven by business and technology turbulence. So we emphasize to the reader not to think of these enterprise IT capabilities as a fixed unchanging end point. Rather, we are creating an environment that links business and technology in an ongoing, always-changing process of addressing business requirements and opportunities in the condition of turbulence and change.

The risk is *not* taking turbulence and change seriously.

Enterprise IT Capabilities Requirements

Partnership, trust, leadership, and holistically addressing the entire enterprise characterize the requirements for enterprise IT capabilities and their deployment of IT competencies. The real challenge is to specify exactly what a specific enterprise should actually do to change and add to how it manages IT. It is not like waving a wand and declaring that the processes and methodologies currently in use (e.g., ITIL, Strategic IT Planning, agile development, et al.) are sufficient and capable. And not every enterprise has the same requirements. So in our description of requirements here, while we need to focus on the characteristics and outcomes of the enterprise IT capabilities, we have to be able to recommend actual action to make them happen.

These characteristics focus largely on trust, partnership, and turbulence. We'll use them to describe each of the enterprise IT capabilities and provide a self-assessment checklist for the reader. These are, however, not specifically tied here to any of the specific IT competencies. That is, the basis for assessment and discussion does not, for example, consider the specific performance of a particular IT planning methodology. It's taken as a given that each methodology or process works. The issue here is whether, even if a particular methodology or process does work well, it does so with the characteristics critical to Strategic IT Management.

Overall, partnership and leadership connected to culture dominate as the critical contributors to success (or, with lack of, for failure) for the IT business relationship in general and the capability to deal with turbulence and change in detail. The context for this is the underlying service relationships between IT and business. These three critical elements—partnership, leadership and culture, and service—are treated in Chapter 8, The Service Relationship; Chapter 9, The Partnership Relationship; and Chapter 10, The Leadership Required.

In the meantime, the lessons of Chapters 1 through 7 are crystallized here in terms of specific requirements for the enterprise IT capabilities covered later. These are described generally in the following paragraphs and are discussed in detail in the context of each of the enterprise IT capabilities in Chapters 12, 13, and 14.

Requirements for Enterprise IT Capabilities

The requirements reflect the discussions in previous chapters, covering the factors of 1) business outcomes, 2) response to turbulence, and 3) business IT partnerships, 4) applicable holistically through the enterprise and all its sources of IT services. We state the general requirements in this section. We describe in Chapter 12 through 14 exactly how each enterprise IT capability in fact meets the requirements. More importantly, we describe in Chapter 15 how a specific enterprise can determine its current status in so doing and take action to improve its activities.

The thing to keep in mind is that we're talking about these enterprise IT capability requirements for the enterprise as a whole, holistically covering all sources of IT (corporate, business-unit, sourcing, do-it-yourself) and integrated through all business units. While a given business and/or IT silo may be effectively applying a particular IT competence, such as application development, the stakes are much higher when considering how that fits all the activities in the enterprise IT capabilities *Development & Transformation*, or *Information & Intelligence*, along with the rest of the enterprise, and particularly in times of turbulence and uncertainty.

A sometimes overlooked aspect is how the respective enterprise IT capability activities are tracked and measured: that is, how does management know the performance level and effects of improvement initiatives? This is in addition to the tracking of business impact; here we're also interested in understanding how well the IT efforts themselves are performing. This is an important component of our discussions in Chapters 12 and 13.

Finally, these requirements apply to each enterprise IT capability (e.g., *Planning & Innovation, Sourcing*, etc.). However, not every requirement applies with equal force to each capability. So, for example, while the first one in Group D below, "Business Strategic Effectiveness Is Sought and Delivered," is certainly important, the force of its application to, say, the enterprise capability for *Service & Operational Excellence* might be somewhat less than its application to *Planning & Innovation*. And each might be differently applicable to one enterprise compared to another. These differences are taken into account in subsequent chapters.

The Core Ideas for Enterprise IT Capabilities

We've spent considerable time talking about the importance of enterprise IT capabilities and the problems and challenges they need to overcome. These all are summarized into five fundamental ideas, the core ideas of Strategic IT Management.

Strategic IT Management—The Systemic Capabilities for Producing the Outcomes

A. Build trust and partnership between business(es) and IT(s): methodologies and processes

- Credibility is established through IT's execution and performance. (A1)
- Trust increases between organizations. (A2)
- Stakeholder trust increases. (A3)
- Partnerships are enabled at all levels with common goals, engagement. (A4)
- Processes support decision making, overcoming bureaucracy. (A5)

Of course, these seem obvious. But the core issue is the degree to which the processes and methodologies within an enterprise IT capability *add to* or *build barriers to* the building of trust, partnership, and so forth. Significant numbers of factors influence the development of trust and partnership, including:

B. Provide business and IT leadership and personal responsibility: methodologies and processes

- Processes focus on business, strategic intentions, and goals. (B1)
- IT leadership provides necessary leadership for trust and partnership. (B2)
- Business leadership provides necessary leadership for trust and partnership. (B3)
- Process is characterized by proactivity in addressing business environment. (B4)
- Accountability is established for the process and outcomes. (B5)

Again, the question is, in the context of a particular enterprise IT capability, the degree to which the methods and processes add to or detract from these factors. Often individual processes and methodologies have specific limitations, as do the mental models of the participants in planning and innovation activities.

C. Adapt to enterprise and leadership characteristics and culture: methodologies and processes

- Apply business domain and industry perspectives. (C1)
- Apply holistically across silos, organizations, and other processes. (C2)
- Match to enterprise and business unit cultures. (C3)
- Produce reliable forecasts, measurements, monitoring. (C4)

One size does not fit all. Each enterprise is different in culture, leadership, and the industry/business context in which it operated. The question is the degree to which enterprise IT capabilities match to each unique enterprise.

Strategic IT Management—The Business Outcomes

D. Deliver superior business value

- Business strategic effectiveness is sought and delivered. (D1)
- Business operational effectiveness is sought and delivered. (D2)
- Risk mitigation is included in the result. (D3)
- Cost mitigation is included in the result. (D4)

These four outcomes comprise IT's value. The question is the degree to which the enterprise is capable of producing them with IT.

E. Deliver superior responses to turbulence and uncertainty

- Recognize projects and requirements faster. (E1)
- Develop solutions and plans faster. (E2)
- Deploy solutions faster. (E3)
- Ensure that solutions emphasize adaptability and flexibility. (E4)

To contribute to IT's value, each capability requires the ability to achieve these process characteristics. These focus on the capability to respond to turbulence. The key word is "faster," and it requires consideration of the impediments to doing so. This is a big challenge, and depends on the following characteristics of how the IT competencies (e.g., planning methodologies, etc.) actually work. It is about encouraging and building on the character of the relationships between the individuals and organizations involved. This is, of course, foundation for the focus on trust and partnership.

Not every factor here is critical to every enterprise IT capability. We will further describe this later. But they all deal with the fundamentals of trust and partnership, and dealing with turbulence and uncertainty.

Assessing Enterprise Performance against Requirements

It is helpful to think about the relative importance of each requirement to a particular enterprise. We encourage readers to consider a simple question: "To what extent does my enterprise exhibit these characteristics?" This sets the stage for Part III's discussion in detail of each enterprise IT capability and of the steps to be taken to produce the desired results. An assessment table and scale are provided for each section; a summary of results is presented at the end of this section.

Requirements for Strategic IT Management: Systems Capabilities for Producing the Outcomes

A. Build Trust and Partnership between Business(es) and IT(s)

This consists of building the foundation for working together for common goals, the essence of Strategic IT Management.

Build credibility through IT's execution and performance. Chapter 2 confirmed the importance of IT's performance in building trust and partnership, a necessary condition for strategic IT management. (A1)

Build trust between organizations (e.g., credibility, performance). As part of the competent execution capability, the business and IT partnership is capable of performing the enterprise IT capabilities, executing the specific IT services, delivering value with IT, and thinking strategically about IT in the enterprise. In particular, the goals for the specific capability (e.g., for the *Planning & Innovation* capability, effective, achievable plans) are produced. Is the enterprise capable of this? (A2)

Build stakeholder trust (e.g., transparency, openness, credibility). The same questions apply to the ways in which the various organizations involved interact in process, in management styles and decision making, in organizational approach to performance measurement and management, and in problem solving.

Throughout this book we reiterate the essence of trust: based on credibility—itself based largely on performance meeting expectations—but also based on transparency, openness, and collaboration. And this is a give-and-take situation: does business trust IT? Does IT trust business? Do the culture and organizational context for both enable the kind of openness and transparency needed? (A3)

Enable partnerships at all levels with common goals, engagement of all stakeholders. The key to partnership is (in addition to trust) common goals and commitment to meeting them. For example, while sourcing may be characterized by service management principles, which tends to think in terms of suppliers and consumers, the context is fundamentally to advance the performance of the business. Recall that a key notion of service management is empathy and assurance (per Chapter 8). The treatment of IT services as a pure service can very much obscure the larger relationship issue of seeking to achieve business objectives. It just is not sufficient to provide a good service (though that surely is required); it is necessary to understand and work toward overall business performance. We've emphasized the problems of silos in business, within IT, and between business and IT. This is the critical barrier to partnership. (A4)

Processes and methodologies support decision making, overcoming bureaucracy.
The phrase "overcoming bureaucracy" is the essence of enterprise IC
capabilities; that, along with mitigating the consequences of silos and
perhaps a legacy of relatively low turbulence, creates the contexts for
complex decision and/or complex decision vetting. Also, processes and
methodologies are a means of supporting relational governance. The
traditional hierarchical organizations, together with the silos within business and IT, create a lot of the problems; being capable of using a more
horizontal, engaging framework for dealing with planning, decision
making, and so forth, is vital. The term *relational governance*, introduced
in Chapter 7, covers this. (A5)

Consider how enterprise IT activities, described with the seven enterprise IT capabilities (as listed in Exhibit 11.1), are currently performed with
existing methodologies and processes and organization structures. Using
Exhibit 11.4, assess the extent to which the desired outcomes (e.g., A4:
"currently enable or strengthen partnerships") are the result of the enterprise
IT capabilities.

Often, enterprise IT activities not only do *not* result in a positive improvement in trust, or partnership, or decision making, they make things worse. For
example, poor planning activities may corrode trust and partnership; poor IT
services can certainly do the same. These possible outcomes are reflected in the
assessment.

Use the scales shown in Exhibit 11.5 for each of the following groups.

Exhibit 11.4 Trust and Partnership Assessment

Business Trust and Partnership between Business(es) and IT(s)	Scale
To what extent do current enterprise IT activities build credibility through IT's execution and performance?	
To what extent do current enterprise IT activities add to trust between organizations?	
To what extent do current enterprise IT activities add to stakeholder trust between organizations?	
To what extent do current enterprise IT activities enable or strengthen partnerships and collaboration at all levels and with all IT sources?	
To what extent do current processes and methodologies support decision making and overcome bureaucracy?	
Average Current Assessment: Build Trust and Partnership between Business(es) and IT(s)	

Exhibit 11.5 Scales for Use with Assessments

Scale	Extent to which the Described Outcomes Are the Result of Enterprise IT Activities	
5	Routinely Produce Outcomes	The current enterprise IT activities, overall, perform to produce the desired outcomes.
4	Often Produce Outcomes	The current enterprise IT activities often produce the desired outcomes.
3	No Effect	The current enterprise IT activities, overall, have no effect in terms of the described outcomes.
2	Occasionally Make It Worse	The current enterprise IT activities occasionally perform in such a way as to make the described outcomes worse.
1	Routinely Make It Worse	Current enterprise IT activities routinely perform in such a way as to make the described outcomes worse.
NA	No Response	Not applicable, or do not know.

B. Provide Business and IT Leadership and Personal Responsibility

This includes individual accountability for results, as well as both business and IT leadership to overcome culture and trust barriers to the partnership

> *Methodologies and processes focus on business, strategic intentions, and goals.* While this may be more an issue of development and portfolio alignment, it clearly has implications for the culture and context for adopting the results of new requirements, new developments, and new means of production. (B1)

> *IT leadership provides necessary leadership for trust, partnership with the business.* Chapter 10 highlights the requirements for leadership, to deal with the culture and relationship issues, to set the stage for improving the enterprise capability to create value and cope with turbulence end change. (B2)

> *Business leadership provides necessary leadership for trust and partnership with IT.* Chapter 10 also highlights the requirements for the CEO, CxO, and business executives to create and support the climate for enterprise IT capabilities. (B3)

> *Process characterized by proactivity in addressing business environment.* Too often, IT management processes are reactive in nature, waiting for stimulus, direction, or leadership. (B4)

> *Accountability established for the process and outcomes.* Too often, all concerned fail to understand the role of personal responsibility in achieving the goals for enterprise IT capabilities. (B5)

Exhibit 11.6 Business and IT Leadership Assessment

Provide Business and IT Leadership, and Personal Responsibility	Scale
To what extent do the current enterprise IT activities employ methodologies that focus on specific business, strategic intentions, and goals?	
To what extent does IT management provide necessary leadership for, with emphasis on culture, trust, and partnership with, the business?	
To what extent does business management provide necessary leadership for, with emphasis on culture, trust, and partnership with, IT?	
To what extent do business and IT proactively address the business environment?	
To what extent do business and IT establish accountability for the processes and outcomes?	
Average Current Assessment: Provide Business and IT Leadership	

Using Exhibit 11.6, consider how the seven enterprise IT capabilities (as listed in Exhibit 11.1) are currently performed. (Use the scales shown in Exhibit 11.5.)

C. Adapt to Enterprise and Leadership Characteristics and Culture

One size does not fit all, and Strategic IT Management approaches deal with the uniqueness of each enterprise.

Apply business domain and industry perspective. The strong tendency is to focus on the business and IT internal to the enterprise. It can be unusual for IT professionals and business supervisors and first-line managers to have a strong vision into what happens outside the specific enterprise and its specific customers and supply chain participants. The need to improve and optimize the functioning of the enterprise gives rise to this limit to perspective. To deal with turbulence effectively requires more than that. (C1)

Apply holistically across silos, organizations, and other processes. The strong tendency in enterprises is for silos to impede processes, reducing understanding and trust with all the stakeholders and organizations. (C2)

Match to enterprise and business unit cultures. Chapter 10 introduces ways in which to consider culture. IT has to perform and produce IT services meeting business expectations. Business organizations similarly work with the context of culture, which is sometimes different for business units and lines of business. But as we often say, one size does not fit all, and there are

Exhibit 11.7   Assessment of Leadership and Culture

Adapt to Enterprise and Leadership Characteristics and Culture	Scale
To what extent do the current enterprise IT activities apply business domain and industry perspectives?	
To what extent do the current enterprise IT activities apply holistically across silos, organizations, and other processes?	
To what extent do the current enterprise IT activities match to enterprise and business unit cultures?	
To what extent do the current enterprise IT activities produce forecasts, measurements, and monitoring?	
Average Current Assessment: Adapt to Enterprise and Leadership Characteristics and Culture	

many variations of enterprise culture. Understanding that, and adapting to the variations, is a key capability. (C3)

Produce reliable forecasts, measurements, and monitoring. This relates to the remarks made earlier about the need for tracking the performance of each enterprise IT capability and the business outcomes produced. (C4)

Using Exhibit 11.7, consider how the seven enterprise IT capabilities (as listed in Exhibit 11.1) are currently performed. (Use the scales shown in Exhibit 11.5.)

Requirements for Systems IT Management: Enterprise Outcomes

D. Produce Superior Business Value

Value is increasing the enterprise's *strategic effectiveness* and *operational effectiveness*, as defined in business competitive literature.[2] Value also includes business and technical cost and risk mitigation. The question for the enterprise is: How capable are its strategic IT management activities in focusing on and achieving improvements in delivered business value?

Business strategic effectiveness is sought and delivered. Whether for the enterprise as a whole or for individual business units, we expect the use of information and IT to create success in strategies, to strengthen competitive performance, and to distinguish the enterprise for its competition. The question is whether the enterprise has the capability to develop and deploy IT for these purposes. That is, for each enterprise IT capability and its accompanying IT competencies, to what extent can it produce business strategic effectiveness? Each enterprise IT capability has the potential for improving IT's contribution to enterprise strategic effectiveness; the issue is whether, as currently understood and used within the enterprise, this potential can be realized. (D1)

Innovation and change are delivered or supported. We expect change to occur in the business, whether process, organization, product, customer interface, and so forth. This requires change management and commitment to follow through on the business and organizational implications.[3] (D2)

Business operational effectiveness is sought and delivered. From process improvement through service management, this addresses all aspects of how the business operationally achieves its goals for excellence. The question is about the enterprise's capability to deploy IT focused on these desired operational results—that is, to what extent each enterprise IT capability will contribute to this outcome.[4] (D3)

Risk mitigation is included in the result. Risk includes business risk, strategically and operationally, and IT risk in performance and development. The question is the enterprise capability to focus on risk in its IT efforts, both operationally and in deployment: to what extent will each enterprise IT capability contribute to risk mitigation?

Cost mitigation is included in the result. IT, of course, can be dominated by cost reduction objectives, both for itself and for the business activities applying IT. The question is about the enterprise IT capability to manage and deploy IT that delivers on cost mitigation, especially across silos and in times of turbulence and uncertainty: to what extent will each enterprise IT capability contribute to cost mitigation? (D4)

At first reading, one might question why the Group D requirements are included in this discussion of enterprise IT capabilities, as they are outcomes, not necessarily characteristics of the processes or methodologies. And, of course, these outcomes are certainly expected of any IT investment or business planning effort. The critical point to be made is that IT processes and methodologies have mixed records in enabling, compared to being barriers or impediments to, the achievement of these goals. It is a question ultimately of priority: Are these outcomes the primary goal of everything being done to connect business and IT? The discussion of each enterprise IT capability will make it clear how this priority perspective needs emphasis; moreover, the reader, when asked to assess the current situation of the enterprise, may discover that current behaviors are not as firmly focused as one might desire.

Exhibit 11.8 Assessment of Business Value

Produce Superior Business Value	Scale
To what extent do the current enterprise IT activities deliver or support business strategic effectiveness?	
To what extent do the current enterprise IT activities deliver or support innovation and change?	
To what extent do the current enterprise IT activities deliver or support business operational effectiveness?	
To what extent do the current enterprise IT activities deliver or support cost and risk mitigation?	
Average Current Assessment: Produce Superior Business Value	

Using Exhibit 11.8, consider how the seven enterprise IT capabilities (as listed in Exhibit 11.1) are currently performed. (Use the scales shown in Exhibit 11.5.)

E. Produce Superior Responses to Turbulence and Uncertainty

This group consists of faster responses to conditions (as emphasized in Chapter 4), as well as adaptability and flexibility. Being fast and flexible is good. Being fast and flexible in providing viable solutions, useful forecasts, more capable business processes, better customer experiences, and the like in the face of turbulence and uncertainty is better. Again, "we need to be better than our competition."

Recognize projects and requirements faster. Producing reliable forecasts is good, but it is even better to know earlier, when forecasting is difficult, by capturing instant information and applying superior business and operational analytics. The whole notion of turbulence and the requirements for speed can undercut the idea that forecasts remain important. Nevertheless, acquiring the data and having the analytical capability to use that data in forecasting is actually even more important. The notion that forecasting is not limited to specific enterprise issues relates to the requirements for business domain and industry perspective. The question is, does the enterprise IT have the capability to work to recognize problems faster? (E1)

Develop solutions and plans faster. This goal is focused on the capability to respond quickly enough with solutions and designs. Turbulence requires speed of response. Long cycles, long approval processes, and long coordinating activities within and without the enterprise all get in the way of the fast response. Bureaucracy and no-longer-relevant technology practices may do so as well.[5] (E2)

Deploy solutions faster. This goal is focused on the capability to *respond quickly enough with solution implementation.* The same may be said for change management and implementation; long cycles and the like really get in the way of good responses to turbulence. (E3)

Solutions emphasize adaptability and flexibility. The goal is for the enterprise to enhance its adaptability and flexibility,[6] which is strongly related to the previous statements. The overall capability to embrace new and changed circumstance, whether organizational, service demands, service sourcing and resourcing, or integration and combinations, all this is the environment needing support. This goal also addresses the capability to enable unbundling and sourcing. Here, the issue is not so much whether sourcing is an outcome to be sought as a part of planning or responses to turbulence. Rather, when sourcing does occur, the same characteristics of doing sourcing well are achieved. Further, the ability to modify and respond to change in the context of operations becomes critical. A critical message is that turbulence causes change; change causes the requirement to respond, quickly. The capacity for doing operations simply can't be in the way; unbundling capabilities in order to respond quickly to change is paramount. An example is enterprise architecture, oriented toward adaptability and change, as distinct from technical architecture, which if not done well to enable change can be an impediment to change. (E4)

Using Exhibit 11.9, consider how the seven enterprise IT capabilities (as listed in Exhibit 11.1) are currently performed. (Use the scales shown in Exhibit 11.5.)

Exhibit 11.9   Turbulence and Change Assessment

Produce Superior Responses to Turbulence and Change	Scale
To what extent do the current enterprise IT activities enable the understanding of requirements more quickly?	
To what extent do the current enterprise IT activities enable the development of business solutions and plans quickly enough?	
To what extent do the current enterprise IT activities enable or support the deployment of solutions more quickly?	
To what extent do the current enterprise IT activities deliver or support adaptability and flexibility in its solutions?	
Average Current Assessment: Produce Superior Response to Turbulence and Change	

Reviewing the Initial Enterprise IT Capability Assessments

An overall assessment can be done for each of the seven enterprise IT capabilities in Chapters 12 to 14. Not all assessment factors apply to every enterprise IT capability, which is taken into account in the individual section describing them.

We describe the main objectives and example processes and methodologies for each of the seven enterprise IT capabilities in the following chapters. We listed some of these IT competencies, processes, and methodologies in Exhibit 11.2. The main point is that simply performing the processes or methods is not enough to deliver superior business value and superior responses to turbulence and uncertainty. For example, simply performing a competent SDLC does in fact deliver projects to requirements and on time and on budget. But delivering superior business value requires the enterprise IT capability to be focused on transformation and change, which is a broader requirement.

The focus is holistic. All these enterprise IT capabilities need to work together with common purpose and common views of the business problems and the technology solutions. It is paramount that we avoid the silos that can exist among these activities. How often, for example, do the expressions of business strategy used in strategic IT planning also get used in portfolio management, project prioritization, and descriptions of project objectives? Our experience is almost never; such expressions appear in one of these silos but are reinvented into different expressions in other areas.

What does this mean? It means being driven by the fundamental issues of the business and IT relationship: trust, partnership, leadership, and service orientation. Performing the SDLC without these characteristics is not sufficient. It means achieving the characteristics like credibility, transparency, and so forth. In other words, the example processes and methodologies are just that: mechanical steps to be followed, outcomes specified in producer guides and manuals. It is necessary, to be sure. But to be sufficient, the underlying characteristics must be present—producing results in partnership, with the focus always on achieving fundamental business objectives and dealing with the issues of turbulence and uncertainty.

Leadership, as described in Chapter 10, is a key component. This elevates mere process and methodology to the kind of problem-solving and value-delivering activity required. It is not just leadership to make things happen; it is leadership that matches the activity to the culture, to the context, to the realities of the organization and the organization's culture. And this approach to leadership applies to all involved: from the business, from the IT leadership, and from every IT professional involved in the activity. It is reaching out proactively to the stakeholders in the partnership to ensure the conditions for success.

Exhibit 11.10 Current Enterprise Status

Current Assessment of Enterprise IT Activities	Scale
Group A. Build Trust and Partnership between Business(es) and IT(s)	
Group B. Provide Business and IT Leadership and Personal Responsibility	
Group C. Adapt to Enterprise and Leadership Characteristics and Culture	
Group D. Deliver Superior Business Value	
Group E. Deliver Superior Response to Turbulence and Uncertainty	
Overall Average	

Summation of Enterprise IT Activities

By entering the scores from the prior exhibits into Exhibit 11.10, an overall picture of current enterprise IT activities can be obtained.

IT's Capability to Change: The IT Dynamic Capability

It is worthwhile to explore for a moment IT's capability to change, particularly in response to business and technology turbulence. In business terms, we might call this dynamic capability. Academic researchers in this area define this something like "the capacity of an organization to purposefully create, extend, or modify its resource base."[7]

Continuing the business perspective, an increasing amount of attention is being paid to the idea that companies, depending on their circumstances, will increasingly compete on their ability to change in response to quick-changing environmental and customer requirements. An entire part of business strategic management research has focused on just this idea. Enterprises will differ in their need, and willingness, to embrace dynamic capability as a significant component of their fundamental strategy and organizational commitments. Information technology plays a big role in this, of course; for example, if one considers manufacturing (robots, etc.) and service organization (customer information, quick product developments), it is pretty clear that IT is in the center of an enterprise's dynamic capability.

In looking at IT organizations, however, it is certainly the case that IT has its own issues with dynamic capability. That is, depending on the situation, IT has requirements to respond to business demands that may be turbulently changing. If IT is in fact the enabler of the business dynamic capability, this adds another dimension to the need to be able to change. Actually, we are talking about two different characteristics of IT's dynamic capability. Paul Pavlou, a leading IT-orientated academic who's studied this area for a long time, has concluded that dynamic capability in IT really is two distinct things:

1. *Dynamic Capability* (using the same term, but more narrowly) is a designed capacity to support rapid change. This designed capability can have its own restrictions and limitations. For example, a modular architecture can be used to make change easy, as long as the parameters of the architecture aren't themselves to be changed. In effect, there's a certain amount of designed and engineered aspects to this class of IT dynamic capability. The nature of the expected changes is, broadly speaking, known.

2. *Improvisational Change*, which is the ability to respond quickly in new, unanticipated ways. Being unanticipated, this is not a designed or engineered approach; rather, it is the ability (and willingness) to act outside of the normal parameters for the development and use of information and IT in response to the new requirement.

These are very different things. In the first case, all the strengths of architecture, good software design practices, perhaps agile methodologies, can be deployed. In the second case, in effect it is "whatever will work." In the first case, adherence to standards (for the enabling technologies) and processes is a good thing. In the second case, adherence to things like standards and processes may not be such a good thing.

From the Strategic IT Management perspective, we have not until this point paid much attention to the details of IT Supply management issues. That is, the choice of SDLC or agile, the deployment or not of ITIL, and so on are all within the black box and not necessarily of critical interest. Now, however, we need to pay some attention to the ways in which the IT organization prepares for and is capable of either form of dynamic capability as defined by Pavlou. Because, of course, the answers will either support or inhibit IT's capability to be responsive to business requirements.

IT's culture can very much get in the way here. Making a general statement, IT's culture is oriented to stability and engineering: Perfection is good; failures are bad; risk to good performance is bad. For example, for operational excellence purposes, any new thing that risks reliability and good service performance is bad. Again, this culture may be all right for the narrow form of dynamic IT capability, but it may be quite bad for improvisational change.

As an aside, this whole area may be a critical driver for the appeal of "cloud," software-as-a-service (SaaS), and do-it-yourself computing to the business units. If one can be freed from the bureaucracy of things like project development methods, PMOs, operational excellence in the data centers, and the like, the business can gain a lot more ability to be dynamic. Never mind, of course, the penalties involved: security, data integration, and so on, not to mention things like user support (help desks) and the like.

So, from an IT Supply perspective, some serious questions need to be asked.

- What is the commitment of the IT organization to support either the dynamic capability (the narrow version) or the improvisational change? This will be reflected in architecture, processes, decision making, budgets, and personnel training.
- What are the risks involved?
- What are the interactions with well-established enterprise practices like procurement, sourcing, security, and the like?
- What architecture capability exists? Can the kind of dynamic changes needed be accommodated?

Reference

Lutchen, Mark D. *Managing IT as a Business*. Wiley, 2004.

Notes

1. John Hagel III and John Seely Brown, *The Only Sustainable Edge* (Harvard Business School Press, 2005).
2. Michael E. Porter, *The Competitive Advantage: Creating and Sustaining Superior Performance.* (Free Press, 1985; republished with a new introduction, 1998.) Michael E. Porter, *On Competition, Updated and Expanded Edition.* (Harvard Business School Publishing, 2008). Also see Robert J. Benson, Thomas Bugnitz, and William Walton, *From Business Strategy to IT Action: Making Right Decisions for a Better Bottom Line* (Wiley, 2004).
3. See Gary Hamel, 2012, *What Matters Now: How to Win in a World of Relentless Change, Ferocious Competition, and Unstoppable Innovation* (Jossey-Bass, 2012).
4. Keri E. Pearlman and Carol S. Saunders, "The Tools for Change," from *Managing and Using Information Systems: A Strategic Approach*, 4th ed. (Wiley, 2012): 141.
5. See Chapter 7, "Stopped: First Beats Best," in Dave Ulrich and Norm Smallwood, *Why the Bottom Line Is Not: How to Build Value Through People and Organization* (Wiley, 2003).
6. See, for example, a section titled "Structural Flexibility" in Hamel, *What Matters Now*, pp. 128–132.
7. "The ability to sense and then seize new opportunities, and to reconfigure and protect knowledge assets, competencies and complementary assets so as to achieve sustained competitive advantage," S. Winter, "Understanding Dynamic Capabilities," *Strategic Management Journal*, 24, No. 10, 2003.

PART THREE

The Road to Strategic IT Management

n Part I (Chapters 1 through 6) we focused on current conditions affecting business and IT, with particular attention given to turbulence, the resulting uncertainty it brings, and the resulting pressure on both business and IT to do things faster. The outcome we need is adaptability: the rapid capability of business and IT to react to new conditions. We also focused on trust and partnership, the necessary conditions between business and IT that permit working tougher to achieve adaptability, the response to turbulence and uncertainty. And we introduced the notion that the enterprise in general and the business units in particular have many opportunities and means for acquiring information and IT. The ability to identify them and make the right decisions about sourcing is increasingly vital as these opportunities flourish. At the same time, we acknowledge that the current "best practices" that purport to connect business and IT aren't working well. As a result, the conditions of trust and partnership between business and IT, which are needed in order to respond to turbulence and uncertainty, simply don't exist there.

In Part II (Chapters 7 through 11), we focused on the conditions necessary to build that trust and partnership in ways that promote the capabilities needed for adaptability and response to turbulence and uncertainty (Exhibit III.1). We group these conditions in ways that also address the current limitations of the

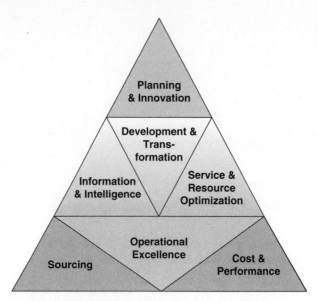

Exhibit III.1   Enterprise IT Capabilities

"best practices." The sum of these conditions is Strategic IT Management, and consists of factors such as credibility and trust.

In Part III, we explore in detail the seven enterprise IT capabilities every organization needs to overcome the difficulties and what initiatives can be taken to strengthen them. These are the practical methods to carry out the requirements described in Part II and to respond to the problems and opportunities described in Part I. While we have introduced the enterprise IT capabilities in earlier chapters, we now look in detail at the requirements for each, along with the IT competencies required to carry them out, and make the case for why each is critical.

Our purpose is not to spell out in detail how each of these practical methods needs to work. Of course, there are numerous detailed processes and methodologies that cover the topics well. We're intent, rather, on specifying the Strategic IT Management principles that must be satisfied in order to successfully nurture trust and partnership, address the problems of turbulence and uncertainty, and achieve the overall objective, namely better IT perform- ance in delivering transformative value to the business.

As we said in Chapter 11, the essential conflict is between processes and methodologies that work toward structured and engineered solutions together with well-defined governance, and the requirement for innovation, flexibility, and response to turbulence. At heart is the underlying requirement for the enterprise: developing trust and partnership between business and IT and together enabling superior responses to turbulence. This is the core requirement.

Seven Fundamental Capabilities of the Enterprise

The seven enterprise IT capabilities described in Exhibit III.1 were introduced in Chapter 1, further described in Chapter 11, and are described in detail here:

Strategic: The Enterprise IT Capabilities for Strategic Thinking and Action about IT in the Business

Planning & Innovation

Tactical: The Enterprise IT Capabilities to Deliver Value through IT

Development & Transformation

Service & Resource Optimization

Information & Intelligence

Operational: The Enterprise IT Capabilities to Execute IT in Partnership with the Business

Service & Operational Excellence

Sourcing

Cost & Performance

The enterprise IT capabilities focus on the fundamentals of value delivery and response to turbulence. Of course, every enterprise is in a different situation, unique to the culture, history, and position(s) in the industries in which it is active. So this is not a one-size-fits-all proposition; rather, these seven capabilities should be fitted to the specific characteristics and circumstances of the specific enterprise.

Chapter 11 presented five core ideas forming the foundation for Strategic IT Management. Every enterprise requires the seven IT capabilities listed previously, and each needs to be capable of responding to these five basic requirements.

Strategic IT Management: The Systemic Capabilities for Producing the Outcomes

A. Build Trust and Partnership among Business(es) and IT(s)
B. Provide Business and IT Leadership and Personal Responsibility
C. Adapt to Enterprise and Leadership Characteristics and Culture

Strategic IT Management: The Business Outcomes

D. Deliver Superior Business Value

E. Deliver Superior Response to Turbulence and Uncertainty.

How each IT capability responds to these requirements is described in the chapters of this section. The reader should note that, while we've defined 21 requirements in the five groups listed in this chapter, each of the enterprise IT capability descriptions only use a subset.

Good Methodologies and Processes Aren't Enough

Competent, effective methodologies are sprinkled throughout this book (see Chapter 7 on competency and its extended notes of books and articles, all offering great methods). Examples are shown in Exhibit 11.2.

Our message is that the use of these methodologies has to be combined with the requirements of partnership, trust, leadership, and service orientation described here. They also require a focus on business strategies, requirements, and organization, which often are lacking in practice. These characteristics are different within each enterprise IT capability; for example, planning requires a different set of these characteristics than, say, operational excellence or cost management. The principles are the same; the priority may be different, and the symptoms and prescriptions different.

But the main message is that a great methodology (e.g., scenario planning), though it is terribly important, simply will not by itself address the problems that can be addressed by Strategic IT Management.

The Challenge to CEOs and CIOs: What Exactly Should Be Done?

Much of the discussion that follows in Chapter 12 is about the characteristics of each of the seven enterprise IT capabilities. What do they look like? What outcomes should they foster? What values are inherent in the required IT competencies (methodologies, processes) and their execution (partnership, trust, leadership)?

However—and this is important—our book is not intended as a discussion of specific processes or methodologies. As we will describe, many[1] books, articles, consulting practices, and academic courses cover the specific details of processes and methodologies. These processes and methodologies represent technical and business competencies necessary, and we introduced these competencies in

Chapter 7. But we do not specify the details here. For example, we discuss planning and innovation, but do not expect a description of exactly how to perform specific methods. Rather, our purpose is to specify the outcomes required and the specific characteristics of trust, partnership, and leadership needed.

Said another way, our concern is not so much for the methodologies as it is for the capability of the enterprise to execute the methodologies with the characteristics of partnership, trust, and so forth. The real challenge is to determine what a specific enterprise and its leadership should actually do. It is not like waving a wand and declaring the process and methodologies currently in use are good enough (e.g., IT Infrastructure Libraries [ITIL], strategic IT planning, agile development, et al.). And it is not the same for every enterprise.

So while it is critical to focus on the characteristics and outcomes of the capabilities, we have to be able to recommend actual action to make them happen. This is our challenge!

The Challenge to Individuals—And It Matters!

While the enterprise IT capabilities are described in enterprise terms and imply that actions are necessary by CEOs and CIOs, *every business and IT professional has a critical part to play*. Whether it is in understanding and responding to the effects of culture, behavior, or skills, individuals whatever their role are the prime actors in achieving the Strategic IT Management objectives. The chapters in Part III (as well as those in Part II describing service, trust, partnership, and leadership) define the desired *end point* for individual behavior. Every business and IT professional improves his/her performance and the capability of the enterprise to exploit IT by paying attention to the messages in each section. Individual behavior and skills matter!

One Size Does Not Fit All

A core element of our approach is one size does not fit all. We have introduced a few specific tests that result in classifying the enterprises in previous chapters. A lot of contingencies are described in other books and articles. We have chosen five to apply here, although one can choose from many more. The point overall is to be sensitive to the enterprise characteristics in determining the course of action to be taken.

Let us be clear on this, however. The overall goals—creating value and dealing with turbulence and change—apply to everyone. It is just that enterprise readiness for adoption-appropriate solutions will differ. In fact, it may differ between various parts of the enterprise. We emphasize this because it is too easy to assert that every enterprise needs every specific recommendation we make. But it simply is not true; while the seven enterprise IT capabilities may be a desirable goal, an end point, certainly the starting point is different and the priority for achieving each capability is different. And for some enterprises, not all capabilities may be needed.

We suggest that an enterprise can be classified in ways that provide the groundwork for deciding exactly which enterprise IT capability is the priority, along with the specific characteristics fitted to the enterprise. We explain these in Chapter 16, and will mention and apply them as appropriate throughout the book.

Enterprise classification according to demonstrated performance capability. Chapters 2 and 3 introduced the six-step Total Performance Value Model (TVPM). By assessing where an enterprise stands and which of the six steps represents the highest level of good performance, guidance as to priority of enterprise IT capabilities is provided.

Enterprise classification according to complexity. We introduce a quadrant assessment describing the complexity of enterprise governance (multiple business units, annual versus responsive planning cycles). This classification helps identify the difficulty of achieving enterprise IT capabilities and links them to the specific governance patterns.

Enterprise classification according to turbulence. We introduce a quadrant assessment describing the business-related and IT-related turbulence an enterprise faces. This classification helps to identify the degree of agility an enterprise needs in its business organization and in IT.

Enterprise classification according to the role IT plays. We apply the classic MacFarlan analysis of operational versus competitively distinct IT roles as an example, with the now-famous classifications of *factory, support, turnaround,* and *strategic.*[2] This very directly identifies the current as-is situation for a particular enterprise, with the notion that a) turbulence may cause rapid change in the situation, and b) the situation may be different for each business unit and function within the enterprise. The classification clarifies not only where the enterprise is today, but the possible consequences of complexity and turbulence.

Enterprise classification according to IT governance practices. Chapter 2 introduced a seven-factor governance activity map that included the kinds of decisions to be made, along with a self-assessment as to how the enterprise is currently performing these governance activities. This classification system provides guidance as to the context in which enterprise IT capabilities are operationalized and linkage to building the governance capability.

Enterprise classification according to the current and future likelihood of turbulence. While it is a given that environment turbulence affects all, its significance to the enterprise will differ. We provide a self-assessment, and each enterprise capability is described in the context of this classification.

Enterprise classification according to enterprise/management culture. Chapter 10 opens the discussion and demonstrates the importance of management culture as it affects governance and decision making, respective to the kinds of things enterprise IT capabilities offer.

There is plenty of overlap in these classifications. Enterprise/management culture, for example, surely overlaps with the role of IT and demonstrated performance capability. We do not intend to provide a mechanical process for reconciling all these factors. But we expect to be sensitive to the one-size-does-not-fit-all mantra and provide several self-assessment opportunities for determining where, exactly, a particular enterprise falls. And at the conclusion, we bring these back into suggested roadmaps for further action.

Two important ideas stand out. First, we emphasize the concept of *fit* throughout, consistent with the idea that one size does not fit all. That is, how an enterprise achieves the appropriate set of enterprise IT capabilities is based, largely, on how they fit to the specifics of the enterprise. Chapter 13 introduces several tests for enterprise characteristics, the results of which can be used to tailor the specific enterprise IT capability requirements to the specific organization. Second, the related concepts of speed and adaptability loom throughout, as this is a priority for the achievement of Strategic IT Management for each enterprise. But the specifics will differ according to the kind of enterprise involved.

However, irrespective of how an enterprise is positioned in the given classifications, trust, partnership, and IT as a service between business and IT are prerequisites for any successful operation.

Strategic IT Management Applies to More than Just the Current IT Organization(s)

Exhibit III.1 pictures the seven enterprise IT capabilities that connect business and IT. These are not described as better IT processes or better IT management activities. While better processes and activities, as described as the IT competencies in Chapter 7, may certainly be desirable, they are IT-centric and do not get at the basic issues in Strategic IT Management: business partnership, trust, turbulence, and uncertainty, as well as the dispersion of IT resources throughout the enterprise. This requires enterprise IT capabilities,

Exhibit III.2   IT Competencies and Methodologies Examples

Strategic Competencies	Tactical Competencies	Operational Competencies
Strategizing Innovation IT Leadership Strategic Outsourcing Architecture Planning Strategic Planning Relationships Building	Portfolio Management Cost and Performance Management Formulating Information Needs Service Management Supplier Management	Service Delivery Accountability Application Software Development and Maintenance Professionals Management
Example Methodologies	**Example Methodologies**	**Example Methodologies**
Strategic IT Planning Scenario Planning Enterprise Architecture	Business Intelligence Business Analytics Data Architecture Portfolio Management for Applications, Infrastructure System Development Life Cycle	ITIL COBIT Service Management Architecture System Development Life Cycle IT Financial Management

not just IT competencies or methodologies. An example of the IT competencies and methodologies is shown in Exhibit III.2.

Strategic IT Management applies not only to the IT organization but to all sources of IT and, of course, the business units. In other words, the enterprise IT capabilities apply to all business units and IT organizations, overcoming the silos that typically separate them.

Business Outcomes Are Required

Chapters 2 and 3 introduced the TPVM. There, the purpose was to describe with stair steps the increasing levels of performance affecting credibility and trust among business unit(s) and IT organization(s). Exhibit 11.1 displayed the six stair steps along with the seven enterprise IT capabilities that connect the stair steps in business and IT.

Chapters 3 and 4 described some examples of business outcomes expected with the effective performance of each stair step. These are summarized in Exhibit III.3 for emphasis.

Scale for Current Status

1. None of these business outcomes occurs.
2. One or two outcomes currently are produced.

Exhibit III.3   Example Business Outcomes for Strategic IT Management

TVPM (Combined IT and Business Perspective)	FROM CHAPTER 3 Examples of Business Outcomes: Execution and Performance for Superior Business Value	FROM CHAPTER 4 Examples of Business Outcomes: Execution and Performance for Superior Business Value	Current Status
Strategic Innovation	• Business strategic effectiveness, direct support for strategic intentions • Transformative changes to the business model • Transformative changes in relationships to market and customer	• Strategic innovation done faster • Flexible, adaptable, integratable business and IT platforms • Enterprise-wide applicability	
Business Change	• Improvements in business operational effectiveness • Changes to the business organization and processes • Changes to relationships in the supply chain	• Requirements and changes done faster • Flexible, adaptable results	
Business Outcomes and Program Selection	• Effective business change management • Priorities based on business strategies and requirements	• Established platforms for change • Adaptability beyond individual business units • Enterprise-wide applicability	
Benefits Realization/ Project Development	• Business requirements across the enterprise are defined and met • Successfully implemented and business-operationalized projects	• Adaptable solutions • Integratable solutions • Dynamic capabilities	
Requirements and Development	• Projects meet business requirements • Successfully developed/ completed projects • Successfully acquired software and solutions	• Adaptable business solutions • Dynamic business capabilities	
Service Requirements and Delivery	• Cost and risk mitigation is supported • IT services meet business requirements • IT services support and do not disrupt business processes	• Services are flexible and adaptable	

3. Many of the outcomes currently are produced.
4. Most of the outcomes currently are produced.
5. All of the outcomes currently are produced.

These example outcomes are certainly not exhaustive, but do portray the kinds of things to be expected. In Part III, we link these outcomes to the enterprise IT capabilities necessary to produce them.

Again, this is not a process or methodology description, though they are certainly necessary to produce the outcome. Rather, these outcomes require the enterprise-wide capabilities described here, that link the business unit(s) and IT organizations(s) required, along with the elements of service, partnership, and leadership described in Part II.

Notes

1. See for example: Wendy Robson, *Strategic Management and Information Systems: An Integrated Approach* (Pearson Education Limited, 1997).
2. F. Warren McFarlan, "Information Technology Changes the Way You Compete," *Harvard Business Review*, (May 1984).

CHAPTER 12

Strategic Enterprise IT Capabilities and Competencies

U ntil this point we have been focusing on the broad requirements for Strategic IT Management in general and for the enterprise IT capabilities in particular. In Part I, this meant turbulence, uncertainty, trust, and demonstrated performance, summarized into requirements for Strategic IT Management in Chapter 7. In Part II, this meant the general enterprise IT capabilities required for effective IT services, partnership, and leadership. In addition, specific requirements of holistic perspective, business focused, and commonality of core concepts and information about the enterprise and its IT activities were presented.

The enterprise IT capabilities match up with the Anthony Triangle[1] classification of management activities as strategic, tactical, and operational, as shown in Exhibit 12.1. This overview description shows the objective, general outcomes, the specific outcomes needed to deal with turbulent times, and example methods. For the guidance of enterprise managers, a self-test for current enterprise IT capabilities is shown here in summary and later on in detail. The overall idea is that by assessing where the enterprise is today, a sense of gap and potential improvements can be developed.

Chapter 7 describes the IT competency requirements for business–IT partnership, with emphasis on strategic, tactical, and operational responsibilities and strategic-level competencies. Chapter 7 goes on to identify the management roles involved. Here we expand those requirements to focus on how, exactly, the methodologies and processes making up the enterprise IT capability satisfy those requirements and produce superior IT value and superior responses to turbulence and change.

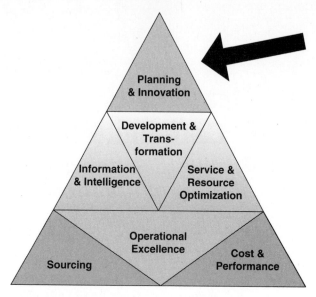

Exhibit 12.1　Strategic Enterprise IT Capabilities

Enterprise IT Capability: *Planning & Innovation*

This enterprise IT capability connects business and IT planning, from strategic through operational planning. Typical methodologies include strategic business planning,[2] balanced scorecard,[3] strategic IT planning,[4] scenario planning,[5] and enterprise architecture.[6]

Most enterprises typically use one or more of these example methodologies.[7] Whether they have the specific competencies needed—for example, in enterprise architecture—is always a question. But this is not the challenge.

Consider the challenges of partnership, trust, leadership, and turbulence, all in the context of innovating and planning for IT in business. For example, many enterprises do strategic IT planning in silos: focusing on individual business units or, even more problematic, doing planning as an IT-focused activity. The enterprise IT capability for *Planning & Innovation* requires 1) engagement of all the business, 2) clear focus on business innovation, 3) ability to enable change during turbulence, and 4) achieving all this partnering with the business and with all the IT sources. Exhibit 12.2 summarizes the objectives, outcomes, and example methodologies for planning and innovation. But these aren't methodology issues: the tools such as scenario planning and enterprise architecture can work well. Rather, these are capability issues, indicating whether the culture, leadership, organizational understanding, and willingness to perform are there.

Exhibit 12.2 Examples of *Planning & Innovation* Objectives and Outcomes

Enterprise IT Capability	Strategic IT Management Objective	Example Outcomes for Superior Value	Example Outcomes for Superior Response to Turbulence	Example Methods
Planning & Innovation	Provide leadership and support for business transformation and change	Business competitive and operational excellence	Business adaptability and responsiveness. Collaboration	• Strategizing • Strategic IT planning • Scenario planning • Enterprise architecture

Yet even with the availability of good methodologies, enterprises often fail at producing effective innovation and effective planning. Again, these are not methodology issues; rather they are failures of the key trust, partnership, and leadership provided, both in IT and business.

So the overall problem is that an enterprise's planning and innovation efforts confront many problems, such as silos, cycle-time challenges, limited vision, requirements for adaptability and flexibility, and impediments to quick solutions. How to overcome these is the challenge. Of all of these, silos are perhaps the biggest challenge, restricting the impact of any planning effort to the sponsoring silo and creating warring (or nonexistent) foundations for enterprise actions.[8]

What Is the *Planning & Innovation* Enterprise IT Capability?

We say an enterprise requires the capability for business and IT (together) to define the future of the business and its use of information and IT.

The *Planning & Innovation* capability is about responding to challenging requirements in times of turbulence. The capability is more than simple methodology; it is marshaling the business and IT resources to be engaged in the planning, and extending the scope of the planning across the business and IT silos. It is the holistic exercise of defining the business, its use of IT and information, and its opportunities to achieve strategic success and overcome turbulence.

Business and IT must be able to establish strategies, products/services, and business models; describe the turbulence and uncertainty affecting the business; forecast its requirements or means for reacting to uncertainty; understand competitive and performance requirements; and respond to its requirements and uncertainty with viable plans, goals, and roadmaps for all of its IT—and do so successfully in conditions of turbulence.[9]

Broadly, this enterprise IT capability connects three planning regimens: business planning, IT planning, and innovation processes. Competency in executing this capability requires the ability to do the three planning regimens in a silo-free context, connecting the results, engaging the stakeholders, producing solutions that can be done with speed and adaptability and produce the best value responses.

Plenty of methodologies exist to help, such as scenario planning, strategic IT planning, or the planning components of balanced scorecards. An enormous challenge is to integrate the outcomes with the other aspects of governance, planning, budgeting, project development, and the like. The silos are intense in this context; it is not unusual to find that IT planning, for example, is unaware of any business scenario planning efforts. Often an enterprise employs several methodologies, perhaps in different business areas, though this can exacerbate the silo effect. Similarly, each methodology can function as a silo of its own. For example, does enterprise architecture directly employ the outcomes of scenario planning? However, these methodologies *are* important. So, for example, scenario planning is something every enterprise facing turbulence should consider applying.

The End Point

So what do we require from the enterprise IT capability for *Planning & Innovation*? While our concerns about turbulence, trust, leadership, and partnership define the means for *accomplishing* the end point, the objectives *for* the end point are a realization by business and IT about the actual business goals and the role IT plays in achieving them. To return to the definition of strategic management, it is the ability of the enterprise to, as we said in Chapter 1, "take a holistic view of the assets and resources available to them, and optimally deploy them in pursuing of the strategic objectives and outcomes desired."

End points for *Planning & Innovation* include:

- Clear connections between business, IT, and innovation planning, across all business units and IT sources
- Understanding of the business and technology environment, opportunities, and forces for change
- Clear explication of business (enterprise and business-unit) strategic goals and strategic intentions, and how IT helps achieve them
- Appropriate involvement of business (i.e., the entire enterprise and each business unit) and IT (including corporate, business unit, external sourcers, and do-it-yourself IT) in their description

■ Clear accountability for, decision making about, and plans for, achieving the desired outcomes
■ Clear attention to speed and responsiveness and adaptability as the environments changes[10]
■ Focus on the entire information cycle, from acquisition to utilization[11]
■ Business outcomes, such as those listed in Exhibit 12.2, are achieved

The reader can ask whether these end-point attributes accurately describe the current practices in the enterprise and whether they apply to all IT sources in the IT ecosystem (e.g., sourcers, cloud).

This list does not describe the attributes of specific planning methodologies or processes, though they certainly play a critical role in achieving them. Rather, this list describes the capability of the enterprise—through all its related methodologies and processes and governance and organizations, together with the necessary resources, leadership, and commitment—to achieve this end point.

The Total Value Performance Model (TVPM; see Chapters 2 and 3) describes actual performance outcomes for superior business value and therefore credibility that is the foundation for trust. Exhibit 12.3 shows outcome

Exhibit 12.3   Examples of Business Outcomes for *Planning & Innovation*

	Execution and Performance — Business Outcomes	
TVPM Steps (IT Perspective)	**Examples of *Planning & Innovation* Execution and Performance Business Outcomes for "Superior Business Value"**	**Examples of *Planning & Innovation* Execution and Performance Outcomes for "Superior Response to Turbulence and Uncertainty"**
Strategic Innovation	• Strategic analysis • Transformative strategic effectiveness • Direct support for strategic intentions • Transformative changes to the business model • Transformative changes in relationships to market and customer	• Strategic innovation done faster • Flexible, adaptable, integratable business and IT platforms • Enterprise-wide applicability
Business Change	• Improvements in operational effectiveness • Changes to the business organization • Changes to business processes • Changes to relationships in the supply chain	• Requirements and changes done more quickly • Flexible, adaptable results

examples for *Planning & Innovation*. These examples give a general idea of what the *Planning & Innovation* capability should be capable of producing.

These examples are, of course, the point. While not every outcome is necessary all the time, they should be possible. We said at the outset of this chapter that *an enterprise requires business and IT (together) to 1) define the future of the business, with its strategies, products/services, business models, 2) forecast its requirements and/or adapt requirements to change, 3) understand competitive and performance requirements, and 4) respond to its requirements with viable plans, goals, and roadmaps for all its IT, and 5) do so in conditions of turbulence and uncertainty.* Here we've added enumeration for emphasis. The outcomes in Exhibit 12.3 display what we mean, what the enterprise capability should be able to produce.

We had introduced these outcomes in Chapter 3, with a self-assessment template about the current situation in the particular enterprise. Perhaps now would be a good time to review the status using that template.

Enterprise IT Capability Requirements

As we have emphasized, we're not concerned here about the specific details or methodology of strategic IT planning, scenario planning, and so forth. Rather, it is whether the enterprise possesses the *capability* to apply them effectively, to produce the value and response to turbulence required. The following tests the enterprise IT capability of *Planning & Innovation*. Again, it is not the competence to pursue the specific methodologies; the critical thing is whether the capability exists connect business and IT with trust and partnership.

We introduced the five groups of enterprise IT capability requirements in Chapter 11.

Strategic IT Management: The Systemic Capabilities for Producing the Outcomes

A. Build Trust and Partnership among Business(es) and IT(s)
B. Provide Business and IT Leadership and Personal Responsibility
C. Adapt to Enterprise and Leadership Characteristics and Culture

Strategic IT Management: The Business Outcomes

D. Deliver Superior Business Value
E. Deliver Superior Response to Turbulence and Uncertainty.

Here, we specifically apply them to *Planning & Innovation*. As we noted in Chapter 11, not every one of the requirements applies with equal force to a given enterprise; nevertheless, it is instructive to consider each of them. But the overall issue is the ability to exercise this capability across the enterprise, to engage business and all IT together, to collaborate and partner on the road to achieving better value and response to turbulence. This, more than the technical details or methods, is the paramount concern.

The following are the 11 most relevant "requirements" from those we defined in Chapter 11, with focus on the trust, partnership, and leadership issues. These requirements come in two parts: those that reflect how *Planning & Innovation* is carried out in the enterprise, and those that reflect the business outcomes expected from the enterprise efforts in *Planning & Innovation*. These do not reflect specific methodologies; for example, we do not specify how a given Strategic IT Planning methodology might be done. But if it is done, and if *Planning & Innovation* methods are used, these are the Strategic IT Management requirements.

Strategic IT Management: The Systemic Capabilities for Producing Outcomes for *Planning & Innovation*

Chapter 11 listed and described the three key characteristics of process and methodology required for Strategic IT Management. As summarized previously, these characteristics include trust, partnership, leadership, and adaptability to the enterprise circumstances. Fourteen detailed characteristics flesh out the requirements. In this section we apply nine of particular importance to successful *Planning & Innovation*.

Builds Credibility through IT's Execution and Performance (A1)[12]

This one is simple. Do planning and innovation occur in the enterprise, engaging business units and IT sources, and are they working? *Specifically, are the end points achieved?* That is, do the various participants, both in business and IT, believe it works well and produces results? As we've emphasized throughout, credibility comes largely through demonstrated performance.

Enables Partnerships and Collaboration at All Levels and with All IT Sources (A3)

The key to partnership is common goals and commitment to meeting them along with the other attributes of partnership, described in Chapter 9. In practice, though, hurdles exist.

- The business folks aren't so involved. Often, the strategic planning associated with IT is done without significant business participation.

- The lack of good partnership makes innovation difficult to discuss without it becoming an IT-centric conversation.
- Partnership requires trust, common goals, transparency, and commitment to achieving the goals. Whether the exercise of the planning methodologies encourages this, whether the culture of both business and IT support this, and whether enterprise and IT leadership promote this, are always in question.

Partnership is a desirable characteristic, but the real effort is the communication and agreement on the business goals to be achieved. While methodologies provide for goal setting, it is often questionable whether these are taken to heart in terms of acceptance by all concerned and a transition to action toward their achievement.

We mention the IT sources in this partnership context. This means all IT, whether corporate, business-unit, external providers including cloud, and do-it-yourself IT in the business units. They are all players and prospective partnership participants.

Employs Methodologies that Focus on the Specific Business, Strategic Intentions, and Goals (B1)

While this may be considered more an issue of development and portfolio alignment, it clearly has implications for the culture and context for adopting the results of new requirements, new developments, and new means of production. Too often, IT planning and resulting solutions target the technology side of the problem. Moreover, too often the actual strategic intentions and goals are not apparent to the folks doing the planning.

This issue becomes more significant when multiple business units and functional business areas are included in the scope of innovation and planning methodologies. For example, strategic planning processes are typically "one size fits all," with little adjustments for specific enterprise or business unit characteristics, culture, or history. These processes may be tied into governance structures, which can also apply a "one-size-fits-all" orientation to the enterprise.

The enterprise IT capability goal, linked to partnership that looks toward common goals between IT and business, is adapting to the specific requirements of each unique business context. The expectation of "common" goals does not mean the same goals for everyone; rather, it means connecting the relevant business and IT components into common goals for them.

Applies Business Domain and Industry Perspectives (C1)

The strong tendency is to focus on the business and IT issues internal to the enterprise. It can be unusual to have IT professionals and business supervisors and first-line managers with strong vision into what happens outside the specific enterprise and its specific customers and supply chain participants. The need to improve and optimize the functioning of the enterprise gives rise to this limited perspective. To deal with turbulence effectively requires more than that, as the factors involved come from without the enterprise.

Enterprises are often challenged to encourage perspectives outside the specific business context. This becomes a substantial inhibitor to innovation, which often requires just that sort of external perspective. Culture, practice, and governance can be significant inhibitors. The meaning of the enterprise IT capability is, through common views, goals, and partnership, to escape these limitations.

Applies Holistically across Silos, Organizations, and Other Processes (C2)

It is common for enterprise silos to impede processes, reducing understanding and trust with all the stakeholders and organizations. Being blind to what's happening in the other parts of the enterprise and the industry is a self-limiting characteristic that dooms planning and innovation.

The consequence of silos is that the planning effort is also siloed; typically, it focuses on one or two business units or a functional area, and almost always is limited to the sponsoring IT organization. Rarely (unless it is something like an ERP planning initiative) is the enterprise considered; we've never seen a planning initiative that embraced all sources of IT (corporate, business unit, sourcing/cloud, do-it-yourself IT). And in cases where IT is sometimes provided by industry or outside-agency government sources, these are often not included.

Strategic IT Management: The Business Outcomes for *Planning & Innovation*

These requirements reflect the business outcomes expected. Exhibit 12.3 gives examples of these outcomes.

Delivers Business Strategic Effectiveness (D1)

It seems obvious that all planning and innovation should do deliver business strategic effectiveness. In practical terms, enterprises have great difficulty in moving beyond a relatively tactical perspective and a primary focus on the IT supply opportunities. Any management bias toward action can favor short-term and tactical solutions. So many strategic IT plans, for example, target the ways in which IT can be delivered and not, for example, the explicitly defined transformative effects on business.

In particular, the enterprise IT capability needs to focus on IT as a solution to and enablement for the strategic intentions for the business. Again, this seems obvious, but some of the following are practical barriers:

- In planning, the most fundamental requirement is to identify the business strategic intentions management is pursuing and produce the transformative ways in which IT can be deployed to achieve them. This applies to both corporate and business-unit strategic intentions. But—and this is huge—business often has very unfocused statements of strategy, and IT in particular is unaware of them. In particular, there's little transition from broad high-level strategy statements to the "how" management intends to achieve them.
- Underlying all this are the overall business and IT partnership and trust requirements, whether the enterprise *Planning & Innovation* activities add to or subtract from them. The planning and innovation activities really emphasize the requirements for common goals and for transparency. In terms of common goals, it is easy for the IT side to emphasize IT concerns and the innovative technologies, for example, while the business side is targeted on fundamental issues of strategy and innovation.
- Business and IT folks engaged in innovation and planning often lack significant understanding of the turbulence that can afflict the enterprise and the opportunities that information and IT can provide. Often the IT folks involved can't "think strategically" from the business perspective.
- There's little real understanding of the competitive challenges, particularly by the IT participants.
- Business and IT leadership can be unfocused, providing little vision or support for the outcomes.

The fundamental question is whether the processes and methodologies employed actually result in identifying and achieving the business strategic effectiveness and the strategic intentions that management proposes and, in doing so, building on the partnership and trust relationships. Is the enterprise—both business and IT—capable of doing so? We say again, it is not the actual methodologies in question here: so many strategic planning, scenario planning, and enterprise architecture processes exist, each promising to produce the desired strategic outcome. The question is whether the enterprise is capable of doing it; that's the meaning of *enterprise IT capability*.

Supports Business Innovation and Change (D2)

The enterprise's culture, practice, governance, and leadership sometimes serve as hurdles to innovation.[13] The problem of silos contributes to these innovation hurdles, as does the normal bias toward short-term business performance improvement. The answer to overcome these hurdles depends on mutual trust and, very significantly, on the leadership provided by business and IT. Innovation does not happen without support and partnership.

Develops Business Solutions and Plans Quickly Enough (E3)

Specifically, to what extent does the existing enterprise have the capability of producing results quickly enough to respond to turbulence and uncertainty?

- Turbulence requires speed of response. Long cycles, long approval processes, and long coordinating activities within and without the enterprise all get in the way. Bureaucracy and no-longer-relevant structure and processes add hurdles.
- The problem is largely one of cycle and of governance. Often planning processes are tied to an annual business planning and budgeting cycle. The process for gaining management support and approval for the results can be enmeshed in company politics and lengthy procedures.
- The silos of business and IT planning can add to the overall cycle times.

The question is whether the methodologies, processes, and governance—both business and IT—work quickly enough and work together effectively.

Emphasizes Adaptability and Flexibility in Its Solutions (E4)

While well-engineered solutions are appealing, and while practices like architecture can be critical to achieving successful solutions, beginning with the focus on these is putting the cart before the horse. In conditions of turbulence, any new solution simply must be able to respond to future change requirements, which surely are coming.

- Part of the issue is culture: The IT side tends to focus on engineering and stability, particularly in infrastructure. And this is certainly necessary for most enterprises. This can be a challenge to balance with adaptability and flexibility. This is one area in which enterprise architecture can be especially valuable if focused on adaptability.
- The strategic planning efforts are divorced from other management processes, both in business and IT. Architecture, on one hand, and business annual planning and project plans, on the other, often are not connected to any strategic planning results.

This is also related to the planning and management cycles mentioned earlier. A big hurdle to adaptability is the need to satisfy many audiences, and silos make this particularly difficult.

The question is whether the enterprise can mobilize its *Planning & Innovation* activities to overcome the burdens of things like siloed processes and governance and emphasize the necessary architectures and solutions with the ability to adapt. This certainly underscores the importance of processes like scenario planning and enterprise architecture, requirements to enable adaptability.

What Is the Current Status with *Planning & Innovation*?

Understanding the problem is a good start. A self-assessment is helpful to position an enterprise's current situation and its capability to plan and innovate. We began this with the prior discussion on building credibility through IT's execution and performance (A1), in which the assessment is about the current actual performance in the sense of producing desired business outcomes. Here, we've noted the nine factors listed earlier as specifically of interest. We offer our perspective on their relative importance to superior value and their response to turbulence based on our research and client experience, although a particular enterprise may differ. The current status is measured from 1 to 5, with 1 reflecting little or no matching to the requirement and 5 reflecting strong matching to the requirement. Note that we have adapted this assessment to include only those factors deemed most applicable to *Planning & Innovation*. The reader can apply all to *Planning & Innovation*. Chapter 11 also presents a complete scorecard for enterprise capabilities, which we will reference again in Chapter 13. A short version with the 11 requirements described previously is contained in the next section.

Planning & Innovation Scorecard

This scorecard gives quick insight into the current importance and status of *Planning & Innovation* in a particular enterprise. Note, however, that the scorecard is simplistic in three dimensions. First, the importance and status may be different for each of the enterprise lines of business. Second, while the scorecard is intended to reflect all IT sources (corporate, BU, sourced, do-it-yourself), it is too easy to think in terms of a single IT organization (probably corporate) and consider how the questions apply to it alone. Third, only 11 of the 21 requirements described in Chapter 11 are included; we have selected those most applicable to, in this case, *Planning & Innovation*.

The objective is to apply the Strategic IT Management requirements to the enterprise's current *Planning & Innovation* practices (Exhibits 12.4 through 12.6).

Exhibit 12.4   Strategic IT Management: The Systemic Capabilities for Producing the Outcomes

Requirements for Trust, Partnership, Leadership, and Service Management	Importance	Current Status
To what extent does the existing *Planning & Innovation* enterprise IT capability build credibility through IT's execution and performance? *Specifically, are the end points achieved?*		
To what extent does the existing *Planning & Innovation* enterprise IT capability enable or strengthen partnerships and collaboration at all levels and with all IT sources?		
To what extent does the existing *Planning & Innovation* enterprise IT capability employ methodologies that focus on specific business, strategic intentions, and goals?		
To what extent does the existing *Planning & Innovation* enterprise IT capability apply business domain and industry perspective?		
To what extent does the existing *Planning & Innovation* enterprise IT capability apply holistically across silos, organizations, and other processes?		
Average for Trust, Partnership, Leadership, and Services		

Exhibit 12.5   Strategic IT Management: The Business Outcomes

Requirement for Outcomes	Importance	Current Status
To what extent does the existing *Planning & Innovation* enterprise IT capability deliver or support business strategic effectiveness?		
To what extent does the existing *Planning & Innovation* enterprise IT capability deliver or support innovation and change?		
To what extent does the existing *Planning & Innovation* enterprise IT capability enable or support the deployment of solutions faster?		
To what extent does the existing *Planning & Innovation* enterprise IT capability deliver or support adaptability and flexibility in its solutions?		
Average for Outcomes		

Exhibit 12.6   Scales for Self-Assessment

Importance to the Enterprise			Current Status of *Planning & Innovation*	
The *Importance* reflects the degree management is concerned, and the extent to which this requirement will influence business success in the future.	0	Not Applicable	0	Not Applicable
	5	This requirement is critical to the enterprise	5	Current *Planning & Innovation* activities often produces the required outcome
The *Status* reflects the extent to which the requirement's statement is achieved today.	4	This requirement is very important to the enterprise	4	Current *Planning & Innovation* activities sometimes produces the required outcome
	3	This requirement is of some importance to the enterprise	3	The outcome requirement is not produced through *Planning & Innovation* activities
	2	This requirement is interesting but not important	2	Current *Planning & Innovation* activities sometimes makes the outcome worse than required
	1	This requirement is not important to the enterprise	1	Current *Planning & Innovation* activities often makes the outcome worse than required

The reader is encouraged to revisit Chapter 11 section "Assessing Enterprise Performance against Requirements" and apply all 21 requirements to *Planning & Innovation*.

Bottom Line: *Planning & Innovation* Performance

Performance comes down to three fundamental questions:

1. Does whoever participates in *Planning & Innovation* (IT, business, consultants, etc.) actually perform the activities well and produce desired business outcomes?
2. Will *Planning & Innovation* activities add to trust and partnership?
3. Do the *Planning & Innovation* outcomes address change and flexibility sufficiently?

Strategic IT Management and enterprise IT capabilities aim to get positive answers to the three questions.

What Is the Enterprise to Do about *Planning & Innovation*?

Chapter 16 will emphasize the options for short-term and long-term actions available. Note, however, that we will not delve into the specific details of the available process and methodologies (e.g., balanced scorecard, scenario planning). The point here is that as these processes are undertaken in any specific enterprise, serious evaluation of their performance with the given requirements is critical.

What Are the Implications for the Individual Manager and Professional?

The key question for the reader: Am I capable of contributing to *Planning & Innovation*, especially with the requirements reflecting credibility, trust, and partnership? Individual managers or professionals can perform the self-assessment to identify the contribution he or she can make toward achieving the required outcome. The key issue is the extent to which the individual contributes to business–IT partnerships, developing trust, and focusing on business and not technical outcomes.

Once the individual self-assessment is complete, consider how to develop the required capabilities. Chapter 19 provides some suggestions.

Notes

1. Robert N. Anthony, *Planning and Control Systems: A Framework for Analysis* (Harvard University Press, 1965).
2. Henry Mintzberg, Bruce Ahlstrand, and Joseph Lampel, *Strategy Safari: A Guided Tour Through the Wilds of Strategic Management* (Prentice Hall, 1998).
3. R. S. Kaplan and D. P. Norton, "Using the Balanced Scorecard as a Strategic Management System," *Harvard Business Review* (January–February 1996).
4. R. J. Benson, T. L. Bugnitz, and W. B. Walton, *From Business Strategy to IT Action: Right Decisions for a Better Bottom Line* (Wiley, 2004).
5. Nicholas C. Georgantzas and William Acar, *Scenario-Driven Planning: Learning to Manage Strategic Uncertainty* (Quorum Books, 1995). Also, Peter Schwartz, *The Art of the Long View: Planning for the Future in an Uncertain World* (Doubleday, 1991).
6. Jeanne W. Ross, Peter Weill, and David C. Robertson, *Enterprise Architecture as Strategy: Creating a Foundation for Execution* (Harvard Business School Press, 2006).
7. See "Brief Overview of Business Strategy Frameworks" in Keri E. Pearlson and Carol S. Saunders, *Managing and Using Information Systems: A Strategic Approach* (Wiley, 2009).
8. The issue is not that strategic planning, for example, is not fully understood by most enterprises. Plenty of books and articles describe a wealth of concepts and methods. The

problem is in execution and in connecting the planning outcomes and results to the rest of the enterprise's management activities, particularly those associated with IT.

9. See Chris Bradley et al., "Have You Tested Your Strategy Lately?" *McKinsey Quarterly*, (January 2011). Among his questions are "Does your strategy embrace uncertainty?" and "Does your strategy balance commitment and flexibility?" We describe this latter point as part of Chapter 18's messages to the CIO and IT managers.

10. The reader should review "The Risk of Strategic IT Management" in Chapter 11, which focuses on the risk of not taking turbulence and uncertainty seriously.

11. See Chapter 2, "How We Use Information Strategically," in Pearlman and Saunders, *Managing and Using Information Systems: A Strategic Approach* (Wiley, 2009).

12. The letter prefixes (e.g., A2, B4, etc.) refer to the enterprise IT capability descriptions in Chapter 11, and are used in the scorecard self-assessment charts in this chapter and in the roadmap chapters that follow.

13. Considerable literature exists on these points; for example: Clayton Christensen, *The Innovator's Dilemma: The Revolutionary Book That Will Change the Way You Do Business* (Harper Collins, 2011).

CHAPTER 13

Tactical Enterprise IT Capabilities and Competencies

The Enterprise IT Capabilities to Deliver Value with Information and IT

W e defined *Strategic IT Management* as an application of strategic management principles. Among the definitions introduced in Chapter 1 is "marshaling all relevant enterprise resources to achieve success in enterprise strategies." Marshaling all relevant enterprise resources is the foundation of the three tactical enterprise IT capabilities (Exhibit 13.1). These focus on:

- *Information & Intelligence*: The information and analytical resources in business and IT
- *Service & Resource Optimization*: The process, service, and technical resources throughout all IT in the enterprise
- *Development & Transformation*: The enterprise's total developmental resources, ranging from business process change through technical development and implementation

The challenges in the three areas are the same. In particular, the scope of the resources in each is larger than traditional IT-related processes normally consider. For example, the information resources are spread throughout the enterprise and beyond, to customers and supply chain and the economic environment. The developmental resources include traditional software development methods but also embrace culture, process, organizational, and individual development. The IT service resources include all IT sources, both within and without the enterprise. In all these cases the challenge is to

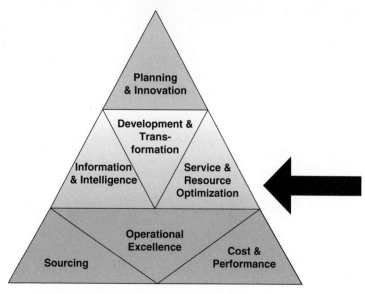

Exhibit 13.1   Tactical Enterprise IT Capabilities

understand the scope, providing means to fully engage the resources (and stakeholders) in the process of delivering value, and dealing with the enterprise, business, and IT silos and cultures.

This means attention to the same basics—partnership, trust, leadership, IT services—that have occupied us in this book. In this case, these are exercised in the context of marshaling and managing the resources and providing the integrative common view of objectives and outcomes required.

Enterprise IT Capability: *Information & Intelligence*

This capability emphasizes the business's ability to marshal its vast information resources, including those that are externally obtained, and apply management, decision-making, control, and analytical techniques to extract maximum meaning and impact on business performance. This capability connects the business's ability with the technology required to manage and deploy information and appropriate tools to the business. (Exhibit 13.2 summarizes the objectives, expected outcomes, and examples of methodologies widely used.)

From its beginnings as "data processing," IT has been a two-sided coin: process versus data. In the old days, systems analysis practitioners argued which came first: Did one analyze the business processes and then define the data

Exhibit 13.2   Examples of *Information & Intelligence* Objectives and Outcomes

Enterprise IT Capability	Strategic IT Management Objective	Example Outcomes for Superior Value	Example Outcomes for Superior Response to Turbulence	Example Methods
Information & Intelligence	Transform the business through use of information and analysis	Superior use of information; competitive and innovative business forecasting and decisions	Rapid, comprehensive, responsive intelligence, forecasting	• Business Intelligence • Business Analytics • Data Architecture

needed, or did one define the data required for reports and transactions and then define the processes needed to produce the data? Of course, the answer is "yes." Currently, with big data and analytics, attention is tending toward the data side.

Process is certainly vital, leading to optimization, cost reduction, and customer service; a lot of planning processes, such as enterprise architecture, devote considerable energy to the process side. But *data*, the addition of intelligence (e.g., analytics, "big data," etc.), has added a significant new dimension to the power of information technology. (It is, of course, "information" technology.) The purpose of this enterprise IT capability is transforming the use of information and analysis in the business.

Methodologies have been packaged under terms such as *business intelligence* and *business analytics*. These are reflected in a plethora of tools and technical enterprise capabilities. And data architecture is an important subspecialty within enterprise architecture. The goals are the superior use of information (compared to the competition), providing competitive and innovative business forecasting and decision making. The challenge of turbulence adds the requirement for rapid, comprehensive, and responsive intelligence and forecasting.

The key to the *Information & Intelligence* enterprise IT capability is to mobilize the enterprise's understanding of the vast information resources of the enterprise, and to connect these resources to their use in propelling the business forward. This is not a technical matter; it involves culture and significant engagement of the business.[1]

We do have a significant definitional problem that we need to clarify. We'll assert, a little later, that there's no one really in charge of enterprise

Information & Intelligence, in spite of the concept of the CIO, and that an enterprise has activities throughout its business organizations that deal with information, but not in a focused enterprise-wide fashion. A problem is that the word *information* is not often, perhaps never, used by itself in contemporary IT literature; rather, *information* is attached to words like *management* and *organization* and *architecture*, which are primarily the means of acquiring, managing, and delivering said information.

In short, it is largely an IT Supply discussion. Practically every current book and article about information and IT uses phrases like *information strategy*, *strategic information plan*, or *information management*, and what most of them mean is the IT enterprise, inclusive of planning, development, and delivery. An example definition is "an information strategy can be looked upon as a plan which sets the objectives and framework for the sustainable long-term development of an organization's information and communication capabilities."[2] Our co-author and his colleagues wrote this definition:

> A complex of implicit or explicit visions, goals, guidelines, and plans with respect to the supply and the demand of formal information in an organization, sanctioned by management, intended to support the objectives of the organization in the long run, while being able to adjust to the environment.[3]

The "use of information" is in there, but the large majority of attention is on information management. A couple of good CIO-targeted books don't mention information as such at all; the books are instead about the role, function, and effectiveness of the CIO and the IT organization.[4] Of course, these are critical issues—but they are not the point of *Information & Intelligence*.

So the question of enterprise IT capability is not one of structure or organization or control over information. Rather, the question is whether all the participants, whether business or IT, have the perspective of looking outside of their particular box, of understanding the opportunities and power of information—and the intelligence that can be deployed with it—for the benefit of the business. This is a holistic, cross-silo, integrative question, and not per se an architectural or structural one.

But a real challenge lies in the very strong interest in *Information & Intelligence* from every area of the business. It seems every business function (e.g., marketing, sales, customer services, logistics, and manufacturing, just to name a few) has developed real appreciation for information's role in their activities, and this increases day by day as the appeal of mining company or industry data becomes more apparent. This creates colossal, but siloed, energy—and significant incentives to bypass what may be thought of as the bureaucracy and limits of an enterprise's (and IT organization's) decision-making processes. Vendors add to this, offering specific solutions directly to the business. While exciting, competitively important, and effective, the cumulative effect can be a mess. Moreover, the real value of the data may actually lie in cross-functional and cross-line-of-business acquisition and analysis, which makes the silo issues more significant.

As a modest example, an IBM web site[5] posted a four-stage measure of analytics capability:

1. *Novice*—individuals or teams are analyzing their own data with spread-sheets or basic query tools
2. *Builder*—teams are operating more collaboratively in analyzing data and trends
3. *Leader*—analytics are being carried out from multiple systems and the organization is defining operational and financial metrics across departmental lines
4. *Master*—data-driven decision-making is pervasive and the organization can set goals and allocate resources based on real-time insight

This shows the character of the enterprise IT capability for *Information & Intelligence*: not so much tools and techniques as the holistic, cross-organizational character of the activity. This example focuses on the decision and analytics aspects. The cross-enterprise aspects of data acquisition, beyond the limitations of individual silos and applications, remain; these, too, are a significant aspect of the capability.

What Is the *Information & Intelligence* Enterprise IT Capability?

We said in Chapter 1 that "an enterprise requires the capability to acquire, manage, analyze, and apply its vast information resources in all relevant enterprise areas." Two related domains comprise this capability: one is related to the technology itself, the other related to the application of information in the business, from simple applications to enterprise-wide analytics. The more technical capabilities relate to the full information life cycle, from acquisition to analysis. The business-side capability is how these resources are applied.

So the challenge is to maximize the availability of data and the ability of the enterprise to apply it. Players in these domains include those inside IT, such as enterprise architects and data architects, as well as business functional analysts in places like marketing. Vendors are a big factor as well. So the overall problem is that an enterprise's *Information & Intelligence* efforts confront many problems similar to those we mentioned in *Planning & Innovation*, such as silos, cycle-time challenges, limited vision, requirements for adaptability and flexibility, and impediments to quick solutions. How to overcome these is the challenge. What's necessary is the ability to transform the business use of information and analysis and provide rapid, comprehensive, responsive intelligence and forecasting.

But the problem is much more serious in the following way: There's no real overarching set of existing processes or methodologies—whether in business or IT—that focus specifically on *Information & Intelligence*, unlike for example the plethora of processes for planning in *Planning & Innovation* and the other enterprise IT capabilities. With the possible exception of data architecture (a subset of enterprise architecture), everything dealing with information is a part of another process or methodology, such as systems (project) development, software engineering, business process management, development operations (devops), market research, product development, and on and on. Everything has a piece of *Information & Intelligence*; no one owns it. This is a real problem that the enterprise IT capability—the connection between IT and business, across the silos of both—has to understand, and accordingly develop awareness of the issues. This is not a "control" issue; it is a coordination, awareness, partnership, common goals exploitation issue.

This leads to real opportunity and, at the same time, real risks. Every IT activity—and every business activity—deals with information in some fashion, perhaps as transactions, perhaps as web interactions, perhaps as databases maintained, perhaps as data collected throughout otherwise simple activities (as minor examples, meters, cameras, monitors, etc.). The enterprise is full of data passing through its processes, its facilities. The opportunity is to aggressively move toward understanding and capitalizing on all this, in ways not necessarily foreseen in more traditional views of information technology. This opportunity is both highly siloed—each functional and business area has the opportunity to exploit its data, and one sees this in the euphoric writing in professional and industry journals—and highly holistic; it is only when data is put together across the enterprise, across functional and business silos that the transformative insights and capabilities are perceived.

While these statements tend to emphasize the intelligence and analytic side of data, the underlying skills for managing data are as important. Indeed, a second major problem—sustainability and risk management—lurks in the background, with such matters as security, integrity, and architecture involved. Much of the power of *Information & Intelligence* is based on the assumption that its implementation will include necessary sustainability and characteristics. However, silos get in the way of providing these qualities; partnership and trust are part of the successful picture. (Of course, some aspects of analytics involve use of the enormous amounts of raw, unstructured data an enterprise collects. Nevertheless, the structural issues can still be hurdles.) This problem will be explored in more detail in the *Service & Operational Excellence*, *Sourcing*, and, to a certain extent, *Service & Resource Optimization* enterprise IT capabilities.

A third, less crystallized problem was raised earlier in the Part III Introduction, having to do with the cultural collision between structure/engineering on one hand and flexibility/speed/turbulence on the other. The desire to strive for stability and certainty (e.g., control, security, data structure, architecture) is endemic to IT, yet there is also a requirement to be flexible and even accept something less than perfection, as in data analytics, using unstructured, perhaps even unreliable (in traditional terms) data.

The point ultimately is that enterprise IT capability requires both business and IT to be aware of and coordinate the solutions that exist throughout the enterprise. While some problems exist in areas such as application development and infrastructure (e.g., standards, security, etc.), their significance (and largely based on the seductiveness of the information solutions) is felt strongly here. In some ways it is overcoming what we might call the "data culture" in IT–for example, the current and ultimately narrow emphasis on big data and analytics treated as technical matters—to unleash the full power of information applied throughout the enterprise, but at the same time not giving up the important virtues of certainty, control, and so forth in the "engineering" culture.

The real enterprise IT capability is found in coordinating and setting expectations. But it is somewhat more complicated. While enormous interest is expressed throughout business and IT about things like big data and analytics, the voices in the background are saying things like "well, to really do these things one has to change the culture and the assumptions (mental models) business management has about the use of information in decision making." For that matter, the whole business of decision making itself has to be changed. The real enterprise IT capability is therefore a much more holistic requirement that bundles together the technical issues (e.g., security) with the business issues (e.g., strategic opportunities in responding to customer wants and needs) with the practical issues (who exactly is going to do all this) and, more to the point, how the skills needed can be spread throughout the enterprise.

Traditionally these skills combine database, data collection, and data analysis resources, typically comprising infrastructure, software, and the technical skills to apply them. Of course this approach has exploded with the onset of "big data" and analytics, in which the resources include very nontraditional information sources and willingness to use less-than-perfectly structured data. These resources certainly cross silos in IT, and cross business units, extending to outside-the-enterprise sources. At the same time, the opportunities also cross business unit silos and outside-the-enterprise sources. While business units and business functional groups (e.g., marketing) possess significant energy and pursue opportunities within their domains, the future lies in cross-domain, cross-silo opportunities.

Accordingly, building the people resources in this area is a major challenge and raises all the trust/partnership/common goals challenges possible. At the same time, all forms of IT are involved—not just the traditional transactional system but all of the outside acquired (e.g., cloud) and do-it-yourself IT solutions have significant roles to play in collection and analysis of data, across all the domains. Yet people resources are needed.

The End Point

Information becomes the critical resource; management ability to access, maintain, and analyze gives meaning to the wealth of information available to the enterprise. Examples of business-based outcomes are shown in Exhibit 13.3. Overall, however, the enterprise IT capability to execute in terms of the life cycle of data—all forms of data—is critical. But simply being

Exhibit 13.3   Example Business Outcomes for *Information & Intelligence*

TVPM (IT-Centric)	Execution and Performance: Business Outcomes as the Basis for Credibility and Trust	
	Information & Intelligence Examples: Execution and Performance Business Outcomes for "Superior Business Value"	*Information & Intelligence* Examples: Execution and Performance Business Outcomes for "Superior Response to Turbulence and Uncertainty"
Strategic Innovation	• Strategic analysis • Providing information foundation for strategic analysis • Transformative strategic effectiveness • Direct support for strategic intentions • Transformative changes to the business model • Transformative changes in relationships to market and customer	• Strategic innovation done more quickly • Flexible, adaptable, integratable business and IT platforms • Enterprise-wide applicability
Project Development & Benefit Realization	• Access to a universe of relevant and valuable data	• Adaptable solutions • Integratable solutions • Dynamic capabilities
Software Configuration & Development	• Successfully developed projects • Successfully acquired software and solutions	• Adaptable solutions • Dynamic capabilities

able to get the data is not enough; producing the real business outcomes is critical, as shown in the exhibit.

But what constitutes competency in execution in *Information & Intelligence?* We look at this in two dimensions. First, we are concerned about the competency of the execution in terms of the desired results for the enterprise, especially in the context of turbulence and uncertainty. Second, we examine how its performance matches up with the general partnership/trust/characteristics necessary.

The key end point for *Information & Intelligence* includes the following attributes:

1. Understand business information throughout the enterprise and in its competitive or government context
2. Reflect an enterprise-wide view of information—a holistic perspective that crosses business units and functions
3. Connect to business strategic planning processes and outcomes
4. See the connection between information and business processes
5. Understand the potentials for information in decision making, enterprise planning, and strategic thinking
6. Demonstrate awareness of external sources for information, including industry sources, and the strategic information related to customers and supply chain
7. Develop sources of trusted information
8. Achieve business outcomes such as those listed in Exhibit 13.3

The reader can ask whether these end-point attributes accurately describe the current practices in the enterprise and whether they apply to all IT sources in the IT ecosystem (e.g., sourcers, cloud).

This is a challenge for most IT organizations and providers in the IT ecosystem. While the business organizations may have great awareness of business information and its potential power, IT managers and professionals may not. The culture tends to focus on information delivery, relying on the business for understanding what it all means. And this may be a challenge for business as well, particularly as familiarity with the technical means for accomplishing the goals may be lacking.

The Total Value Performance Model (TVPM; see Chapter 2) describes actual performance outcomes for superior business value, and therefore credibility, that form the foundation for trust. Exhibit 13.3 shows outcome examples for *Information & Intelligence.*

The inherent nature of cross-domain, cross-silo business issues and similar cross-domain, cross-silo IT sources forces success in building the partnership. This heightens the requirement for aggressive business and IT leadership. For example, commentators on advanced analytics—where the goal is to affect how decisions are made and to provide tools to support making those decisions—point out that this in itself is a significant leadership and culture challenge. It is not technical; it is the underlying business environment.

While technical issues such as architecture, security, and technical data management exist, the core values come from exploiting information throughout the enterprise. This process requires, at the least, trust founded on credibility of performance, transparency, common goals, common (business) language, and all the attributes of partnership and collaboration. It's unlikely that business units share their information, that business functional areas partner across silos, or that business and IT work together without the foundation of trust. At the same time, business and IT leadership sets the context and culture for the partnership. This strongly influences the assessment of the enterprise IT capability in *Information & Intelligence* and applies the lessons of Chapters 9, 10, and 11.

The exploding sources of data change the partnerships as well. It is certainly not limited to traditional forms of transactional systems or even traditional online or Internet-driven applications. The typical enterprise is awash in all forms of data, instrumented, surveilled, and acquired through routine activities in all business pursuits. Exploiting this data requires partnership and leadership.

Enterprise IT Capability Requirements

In some ways, these requirements mirror those for *Planning & Innovation*. They need to be holistic, connect information to achieving business results, and so forth. Differences lie in the concept of marshaling resources, in this case information resources, and the recognition of processes to acquire manage and utilize information.

We introduced the enterprise IT capability requirements in Chapter 11, in five groups.

Strategic IT Management: The Systemic Capabilities for Producing the Outcomes with *Information & Intelligence*

A. Build Trust and Partnership among Business(es) and IT(s)
B. Provide Business and IT Leadership and Personal Responsibility
C. Adapt to Enterprise and Leadership Characteristics and Culture

Strategic IT Management: The Business Outcomes with *Information & Intelligence*

D. Deliver Superior Business Value
E. Deliver Superior Response to Turbulence and Uncertainty

In considering these requirements, we should recognize that many of the underlying methodologies and processes don't yet exist in many enterprises, that accountability is diffused, and that considerable activities are outside the orbit of the traditional IT organization. Accordingly, more than the other enterprise IT capabilities, there's much more of a discovery, a developmental aspect of these issues. It is not so much restructuring or organizing a lot of existing activities (as it might be in planning, e.g.) as it recognizing the need to have these activities in the first place. At the very least, we should recognize the need to corral the nascent activities in many business areas, to maximize their value and move more rapidly up the learning curve. At the same time, many existing methodologies and process do have a significant information component, such as software development, design, web support, or customer service. These too need to be included in the consideration for these requirements.

But what exactly are we asking about here? Again, in *Planning & Innovation* we had a pretty good sense of our concern, namely the ways in which the enterprise conducts its various planning activities. Yes, planning is not a control or governance question, as many separate planning activities undoubtedly go on throughout the enterprise. Nevertheless, we understand what's meant by the enterprise IT capability, to be applied to all planning activities. Here, the understanding is not quite so clear, given that information-related activities are embedded in other activities, and given that in practical terms there's no one in charge. Although, is that not what a CIO does?

However, it is precisely the diffuse nature of information-related activity that places such a premium on understanding and developing the enterprise IT capability for *Information & Intelligence.*

Strategic IT Management: The Systemic Capabilities for Producing Outcomes with Information & Intelligence

Builds Credibility through IT's Execution and Performance (A1) IT's basic contribution to business is making accurate, appropriate information available in ways the business can effectively and efficiently use. *Specifically, are the end points listed in the prior section achieved?* Failure here is fundamental to lack of credibility and trust.

Adds to Trust between Organizations (A2) Sharing information between organizations breaks down the barriers and overcomes the silos. Much of the power of business analytics is based on holistically applying data across all organizations and business units. Failure here, with bad data or with hurdles to sharing, damages trust among the business organizations and between business and IT.

Enables Partnerships and Collaboration at All Levels and with All IT Sources (A3)   At least two elements come into play here. First is the relationship between IT and business; the information management process is not solely a technical matter but engages the business in understanding the opportunities and requirements for the entire information life cycle, from collection through analysis and reporting. This applies equally to the value of direct customer interaction and customer access to relevant customer data.

The second element is the collaboration across all IT sources. The strong silo tendency for IT implementation, whether in applications, databases, cloud-sourced capabilities, or even do-it-yourself IT, makes it challenging to integrate and share information across the boundaries. Yet collaboration is a core capability.

Supports Decision Making and Overcomes Bureaucracy (A5)   Experience has shown that effective use of information in analytics, planning, and decisions requires more than simple access to information; it requires a change in how decisions are made. Some commentators have talked about how it requires a basic change in business management decision-making culture.

At the same time, the business and IT silos make cross-silo decisions difficult, including the governance processes that apply.

IT Management Provides Necessary Leadership, with Emphasis on Culture, Trust, and Partnership with the Business (B2)   Overcoming the culture and partnership hurdles we've discussed in Chapters 9, 10, and 11 requires leadership. Overcoming the silos in information sharing, and providing direction for seeing the power of information analysis across the organization, requires leadership.

Business Management Provides Necessary Leadership with Emphasis on Culture, Trust, and Partnership with IT (B3)   Business leadership is perhaps more critical than IT leadership, as the major challenges lie in overcoming the cultures and silos in the many business organizations. As information analysis and business analytics become more widespread, overcoming the reluctance to change how decisions are made requires strong business leadership; it is a cultural change.

Applies Business Domain and Industry Perspective (C1)   While cross-silo information sharing is powerful, linking internal enterprise information to that acquired from the economic environment, from value chain, from end customers, and from the customers of the end customers represents enormous power and potential.

Applies Holistically across Silos, Organizations, and Other Processes (C2)   As described previously, sharing information across the silos and among the business units adds significant power and opportunity. It in many ways defines the opportunities.

Strategic IT Management: The Business Outcomes with Information & Intelligence

Chapter 11 defined two sets of outcomes required for enterprise IT capabilities, summarized as "produce superior business value" and "produce superior responses to turbulence and uncertainty." Of the eight detailed requirements, the following apply particularly to *Information & Intelligence*.

Delivers Business Strategic Effectiveness (D1)   This emphasizes the role of business leadership. The whole point is to use *Information & Intelligence* for competitive and performance purposes. Simply having it available is not enough.

Supports Innovation and Change (D2)   Providing insight into business opportunities—new products and services, different ways to interact with the customer, restructuring the supply chain, any aspect of business—is the point. Without this capability, the information is valueless.

Delivers Business Operational Effectiveness (D3)   Insights into cost, customer satisfaction, and new ways to transform how business is done are central to *Information & Intelligence*.

Information & Intelligence Scorecard

The following scorecards offer the opportunity for self-assessment as to the importance and current status of each stated required. Exhibit 13.4 covers the system requirements as described earlier in the chapter; Exhibit 13.5 covers the business outcomes needed. Exhibit 13.6 provides the scales to be used in the self assessments.

The reader is encouraged to revisit the Chapter 11 section named "Assessing Enterprise Performance against Requirements" and apply all 21 requirements to *Information & Intelligence*.

Bottom Line: *Information & Intelligence* Performance

Information & Intelligence performance comes down to three fundamental questions:

Exhibit 13.4   Strategic IT Management: The Systemic Capabilities for Producing the Outcomes with *Information & Intelligence*

Requirements for Trust, Partnership, Leadership, and Services	Importance	Status
To what extent does the existing *Information & Intelligence* enterprise IT capability build credibility through IT's execution and performance? *Specifically, are the end points achieved?* (A1)		
To what extent does the existing *Information & Intelligence* enterprise IT capability enable partnerships and collaboration at all levels and with all IT sources? (A4)		
To what extent does the existing *Information & Intelligence* enterprise IT capability support decision making and overcome bureaucracy?		
To what extent does IT management provide necessary leadership for the *Information & Intelligence* enterprise IT capability, with emphasis on culture, trust, and partnership with the business? (B2)		
To what extent does business management provide necessary leadership for this *Information & Intelligence* enterprise IT capability, with emphasis on culture, trust, and partnership with IT? (B3)		
To what extent does the existing *Information & Intelligence* enterprise IT capability apply business domain and industry perspective? (C1)		
To what extent does the existing *Information & Intelligence* enterprise IT capability apply holistically across silos, organizations, and other processes? (C2)		

Exhibit 13.5   Strategic IT Management: The Business Outcomes with *Information & Intelligence*

Requirement for Outcomes	Importance	Status
To what extent does the existing *Information & Intelligence* enterprise IT capability deliver business strategic effectiveness? (D1)		
To what extent does the existing *Information & Intelligence* enterprise IT capability support innovation and change? (D2)		
To what extent does the existing *Information & Intelligence* enterprise IT capability deliver business operational effectiveness? (D3)		
To what extent does the existing *Information & Intelligence* enterprise IT capability deliver cost and risk mitigation? (D4)		

Exhibit 13.6   Scales for Self-Assessment

Description	Importance Column		Status Column	
The *Importance* reflects the degree management is concerned, and the extent to which this requirement will influence business success in the future.	0	Not Applicable	0	Not Applicable
	5	This requirement is critical to the enterprise	5	Current *Information & Intelligence* activities often produce the required outcome
The *Status* reflects the extent to which the requirements statement is achieved today.	4	This requirement is very important to the enterprise	4	Current *Information & Intelligence* activities sometimes produce the required outcome
	3	This requirement is of some importance to the enterprise	3	The required outcome is not produced through *Information & Intelligence* activities
	2	This requirement is interesting but not important	2	Current *Information & Intelligence* activities sometimes make the outcome worse than required
	1	This requirement is not important to the enterprise	1	Current *Information & Intelligence* activities often make the outcome worse than required

1. Do those who participate in *Information & Intelligence* activities (e.g., IT, business, consultants, etc.) actually perform well and produce the required business outcomes?
2. Will the *Information & Intelligence* activities add to trust and partnership?
3. Do the *Information & Intelligence* activities address change and flexibility sufficiently?

This is what Strategic IT Management and enterprise IT capabilities are about: getting positive answers to the three questions.

What Is the Enterprise to Do about Information & Intelligence?

Undoubtedly there's great interest in things like big data and business analytics. The question here is how best to mobilize the enterprise's capability for doing these sorts of things successfully. As we and others have remarked, this is as much a cultural issue as a technical one, and more of a cross-silo capability than a simple functional or business unit initiative. These are discussed in Chapter 16.

What Are the Implications for the Individual Manager and Professional?

The key question for the reader: Do I have the perspective and visibility about the information of the enterprise, how it can be used, and the role that I as a manager or professional play in making progress in this area? The self-assessment can be used as a method for beginning to address this question. Chapter 16 will offer some thoughts on steps to be taken.

Enterprise IT Capability: *Development & Transformation*

This capability marshals the enterprise resources to develop and deliver business transformation and change through application, business process, and software development. Exhibit 13.7 summarizes the objectives and outcomes required for *Development & Transformation*, together with example methods commonly used.

Project development is the cutting edge of IT services to the business and, of course, an area of challenge for many enterprises. Chapter 2 reported on the current state of success, which is not so good in terms of successful completion of projects. This is particularly problematic in two ways. First, successful project development is a primary indicator of the business IT relationship in terms of partnership, trust, credibility, and so forth. We focus on this in Chapter 3 (regarding the Staircase to Trust) and the TVPM. But second, it is the primary activity in terms of responding to turbulence and uncertainty. Everything that's difficult in doing projects well is even more

Exhibit 13.7 Examples of *Development & Transformation* Objectives and Outcomes

Enterprise IT Capability	Strategic IT Management Objective	Example Outcomes for Superior Value	Example Outcomes for Superior Response to Turbulence	Example Methods
Development & Transformation	Deliver business value— transformation and change— with every IT investment and project	Every project delivers business value linked to business strategic intentions and goals	Adaptability, responsiveness, partnerships, collaboration	• PMO • SDLC • Agile • Project Portfolio Management

difficult when times get short and speed is required. And as an aside, this is the area that often feeds into the "do-it-yourself" phenomenon—when projects are difficult, slow, or not successful, the motivation for doing something else becomes strong—again bolstered by considerations of turbulence and uncertainty.

The overall purpose is to deliver business value, meaning transformation and change, with every IT investment and project. While every project needs to deliver business value, turbulence adds requirements for adaptability, responsiveness, and more attention to partnership. The many methods and processes include traditional software development life cycle (SDLC) means and agile and similar processes. But the role of the project management office (PMO), both in terms of governance and in terms of overall project performance and risk mitigation, is critical, along with overall project portfolio management.

A relatively recent *Development & Transformation* discussion has introduced the term *technical debt* to the issues. This reflects the degree to which development produces results with ongoing costs and risks, particularly maintenance and inability to change.[6]

What Is the *Development & Transformation* Enterprise IT Capability?

We say in Chapter 1 that "an enterprise requires the capability to develop, implement, and apply information and IT capabilities to change and transform business with superior returns." The *Development & Transformation* enterprise IT capability focuses on more than just the completion of the project development steps, though that's important. It also extends to the objective of actually achieving the business change promised by projects. This is where the partnership and significant business–IT roles comes in. Change management has always been problematic, and is a prime concern to make the overall goals. Stepping back, though, the need for robust enterprise IT capability in this area—ensuring the overall performance of the methodologies employed in both the IT and business domains—is required.

A particular problem is that IT projects tend to be the most silo-intensive activity. Projects are typically sponsored by a single business unit or function, and tend to be owned in IT in the systems development group, or if externally sourced, by a particular vendor. The exception, of course, is an enormous project (read enterprise resource planning, or ERP) involving almost everyone. In this case, the silos don't go away but can be a significant impediment in a variety of ways. And, for better or worse, the really significant things, the innovations that drive the enterprise and responses to turbulence, are enterprise-wide or, at least, cross silos.

This leads to a second major problem: Projects by themselves don't accomplish anything. The successful implementation and adoption of the fruits of the development is what matters. This means effective change management at the detail level, but more broadly means organizational change, process change, and all the accouterments of transformation in the business. This can be a marked weakness in most organizations, particularly when the scope of change crosses silos.

The third problem area is the existence of a lot of IT-centric methodologies and processes, which may compete or may not be completely implemented. These range from agile, to SDLC, to PMO, to the particular methods for project prioritization. These too are silo intensive and tend to be technology intensive, which increases the problems of coordination, trust development, and partnership building. Added to this mix are the various roles of the PMO in enterprises. In some cases, the PMO is focused solely on IT and IT projects; in other enterprises, it has evolved into "program" management, including both business and IT components.

A fourth area of concern is the tendency for do-it-yourself and vendor-provided solutions to be active in the business units, bypassing the more formal aspects of IT project management such as architecture reviews, testing, and, in general, aspects of risk management. Here, though, we see clearly what the enterprise capability needs to include, in terms of the performance required of the business organization(s) and IT organization(s). The insight is that they are needed together, and need to be holistic across the affected organizations on both sides.

The End Point

Key elements of the *Development & Transformation* enterprise IT capability include:

1. Provide transparency to all development efforts: cost, performance, and risk, throughout the IT ecosystem.
2. Carry projects through to actually achieve business change.
3. Get the size of projects right, avoiding enormous and unending project development.
4. Clearly link business cases and projects to business strategies and strategic intentions.
5. Provide speed to implementation of solutions; increase speed of response.
6. Give significant attention to information and its capture, management, and use.
7. Prioritize properly, linking to business strategies and strategic intentions.

Exhibit 13.8 Example *Development & Transformation* Outcomes

TVPM (ICT Context)	Execution and Performance: The Actual Outcomes as the Basis for Credibility and Trust	
	Development & Transformation Examples: Execution and Performance Business Outcomes for "Superior Business Value"	**Development & Transformation Examples: Execution and Performance for "Superior Response to Turbulence and Uncertainty"**
Business Outcomes & Program Selection	• Effective business change management • Priorities based on business strategies and requirements • Clarity and agreement on business priorities	• Establish platforms for change • Adaptability beyond individual business units • Enterprise-wide applicability
Project Development & Benefit Realization	• Successfully implemented and operationalized projects • Access to a domain of relevant and valuable data	• Adaptable solutions • Integratable solutions • Dynamic capabilities
Software Configuration & Development	• Successfully developed projects • Successfully acquired software and solutions	• Adaptable solutions • Dynamic capabilities

8. Integrate development efforts across all sources of IT in the IT ecosystem.

9. Provide for appropriate standards without bureaucracy.

10. Do not add to "technical debt."

11. Achieve business outcomes such as those listed in Exhibit 13.8.

The reader can ask whether these end-point attributes accurately describe the current practices in the enterprise and whether they apply to all IT sources in the IT ecosystem (e.g., sourcers, cloud).

The point to all of this is to emphasize that enterprise IT capability is more—a lot more—than simply the ability to get projects done on time and on budget, although that's certainly a part of the TVPM we introduced in Chapter 2. More fundamentally, it is the enterprise's capability of really doing *Development & Transformation* the right way, and responding to turbulence quickly.

As projects are the cutting edge of delivering value and corresponding to turbulence, all of the overall enterprise IT capability requirements (see Chapter 11) apply. But some are more vital than others, as shown in Exhibit 13.8.

Enterprise IT Capability Requirements

The following assessment questions apply to all the ways *Information & Intelligence* activity—from technical design and implementation through the information life cycle—is conducted now in the enterprise. Our purpose is to show the gaps, thus providing guidance for future improvement. We are not focusing on the methodology and process details themselves, but rather the consequences of the specific methods and processes used.

Strategic IT Management: The Systemic Capabilities for Producing the Outcomes with Development & Transformation

Six of the 14 detailed systemic enterprise IT capability requirements, as defined in Chapter 11 apply particularly to *Development & Transformation*. Seven of the business outcome requirements apply.

The Enterprise *Development & Transformation* Capability Builds Credibility through IT's Execution and Performance (A1)   Chapter 2 made the point that failing to deliver IT projects damages credibility; simply getting projects done reflects itself in the TVPM (review Chapter 4, on the staircase to value). Enterprises simply have to get projects done. So development and transformation are vital requirements. The challenge extends well beyond having projects completed by IT; it extends to all sources of IT.

But it is more than simply credibility. Does *Development & Transformation* really produce the business outcomes? *Specifically, are the end points listed in prior sections achieved?* Is the software built successfully, or procured properly? Are the external services contracted effectively? Does the change management get done?

So this is also more than simply IT's execution. It is the execution in the context of the enterprise, engaging the business and other stakeholders. Simply, can the enterprise get it done?

The Enterprise *Development & Transformation* Capability Enables or Strengthens Partnerships and Collaboration at All Levels and with All IT Sources (A4)   The tendency in many enterprises is to keep projects in silos, engaging only one business unit or functional area. The exception is enterprise-wide projects. But generally, even the development activity for a single business unit is significantly strengthened by involvement of other units or, in the case of IT, other parts of the IT organization.

However, this adds to the potential for difficulties with competing agendas, lack of transparency, and all the attributes of mistrust between organizational units. The question here is the degree to which the existing processes for development understand these issues and actively work to overcome them.

The Enterprise *Development & Transformation* Capability Supports Decision Making and Overcomes Bureaucracy (A5) Part of governance is prioritization and project portfolio management, often through a PMO or similar activity. This can add time and barriers to decision making. Similarly, business units and the enterprise as a whole can use business planning or IT planning processes to govern basic investment and performance management decisions, which can also add time and barriers to decision making. Other review processes, such as architecture review boards and procurement processes, in the case of acquired software or sourcing contracts, can have similar effects.

The challenge arises from the desirability of these sorts of governance and review processes: Architecture is good, procurement standards are good, planning is good, project portfolio management and oversight are good, and so on. The question here is whether, taken together, the enterprise has the capability to minimize the bureaucratic character of these processes, optimize the decision-making activities, and reduce the time required.

The Enterprise *Development & Transformation* Capability Employs Methodologies that Focus on Specific Business, Strategic Intentions, and Goals (B1) In this context, this is key. Project development can be based on wish lists and squeaky-wheel responses rather than careful attention to (real) business requirements. One indicator is the degree to which the project documentation (e.g., business cases) refers to business strategy. Overall, the question is whether prospective IT investments are vetted based on documented connection to that which is important to the business of the enterprise.

The Enterprise *Development & Transformation* Capability Applies Business Domain and Industry Perspective (C1) This relates to the previous requirement, the degree to which development processes used in setting and prioritizing requirements are based on the business context in which they apply.

The Enterprise *Development & Transformation* Capability Applies Holistically across Silos, Organizations, and Other Processes (C2) This relates to the previous requirement emphasizing the engagement of business units, functions, and IT silos in the development of projects. This also raises issues of standards and consistency of the ways in which new development is done, both in-house development and procurement of sourced capabilities (e.g., software, cloud-based functionality, etc.).

Strategic IT Management: The Business Outcomes with Development & Transformation

The Enterprise *Development & Transformation* Capability Delivers or Supports Business Strategic Effectiveness (D1)　The heart of *Development & Transformation* is just this—produce real change to the business. It goes to the processes for identifying the opportunities through the entire cycle of change management, resulting in sustainable business strategic performance improvement, even transformation.

This requires more than just software development or procurement. And it requires more than just IT providing the technical aspects. This is an enterprise all-in capability and significantly tests whether the systemic capabilities for producing the outcomes spelled out in the previous section are achieved.

The Enterprise *Development & Transformation* Capability Delivers or Supports Innovation and Change (D2)　This extends the question of enterprise IT capability expressed previously. Here the focus is on the actual changes made possible through innovation development and the dramatic changes that may be necessary to successfully implement them.

The challenge is twofold. The first emphasizes the methods used to engage business and IT in the innovation thinking and planning. The second emphasizes the enterprise's will and capacity for actually doing what's necessary. Both are enterprise IT capability issues, not simply the methods themselves. This has to engage all needed stakeholders, in both business and IT.

The Enterprise *Development & Transformation* Capability Delivers or Supports Business Operational Effectiveness (D3)　This is the other side of the coin to business strategic effectiveness, namely the achievement of significant business performance improvement.

Development & Transformation Delivers or Supports Cost and Risk Mitigation (D4)　This too is related to business operational effectiveness, but with a specific focus on cost and risk.

The Enterprise *Development & Transformation* Capability Enables the Faster Understanding of Requirements (E1)　Turbulence and uncertainty demands the capability of fast response. Does the enterprise have this capability, or do the processes, methodologies, governance, and decision making bog things down?

The Enterprise *Development & Transformation* Capability Enables the Development of Business Solutions and Plans Quickly Enough (E2) While the prior requirements focus on understanding the issues, this issue is related to delivery. Whether through methods like agile, or simple development processes, does the enterprise have the capability to do things fast enough?

The Enterprise *Development & Transformation* Capability Delivers or Supports Adaptability and Flexibility in Its Solutions (E4) The predominant IT culture tends to emphasize engineering, perfection, and standards. While these are good, these may also impede flexibility and adaptability. Similarly, architecture is a very important activity, but in this context needs to specifically focus on adaptability and flexibility.

Development & Transformation Scorecard

Exhibits 13.9 and 13.10 provide a self-assessment of the current status of *Development & Transformation*. Exhibit 13.11 gives the scales to be used.

Exhibit 13.9 Strategic IT Management: The Systemic Capabilities for Producing the Outcomes with *Development & Transformation*

Requirements for Trust, Partnership, Leadership, and Services	Importance	Status
To what extent does the existing *Development & Transformation* enterprise IT capability build credibility through IT's execution and performance? *Specifically, are the listed end points achieved?* (A1)		
To what extent does the existing *Development & Transformation* enterprise IT capability enable or strengthen partnerships and collaboration at all levels and with all IT sources? (A4)		
To what extent does the existing *Development & Transformation* enterprise IT capability support decision making and overcome bureaucracy? (A5)		
To what extent does the existing *Development & Transformation* enterprise IT capability employ methodologies that focus on specific business, strategic intentions, and goals? (B1)		
To what extent does the existing *Development & Transformation* enterprise IT capability apply business domain and industry perspective? (C1)		
To what extent does the existing *Development & Transformation* enterprise IT capability apply holistically across silos, organizations, and other processes? (C2)		

Exhibit 13.10 The Outcomes for *Development & Transformation*

Requirement for Outcomes	Importance	Status
To what extent does the existing *Development & Transformation* enterprise IT capability deliver or support business strategic effectiveness? (D1)		
To what extent does the existing *Development & Transformation* enterprise IT capability deliver or support innovation and change? (D2)		
To what extent does the existing *Development & Transformation* enterprise IT capability deliver or support business operational effectiveness? (D3)		
To what extent does the existing *Development & Transformation* enterprise IT capability deliver or support cost and risk mitigation? (D4)		
To what extent does the existing *Development & Transformation* enterprise IT capability enable the faster understanding of requirements? (D5)		
To what extent does the existing *Development & Transformation* enterprise IT capability enable the development of business solutions and plans quickly enough? (E2)		
To what extent does the existing *Development & Transformation* enterprise IT capability enable or support the deployment of solutions faster? (E3)		
To what extent does the existing *Development & Transformation* enterprise IT capability deliver or support adaptability and flexibility in its solutions? (E4)		

While all 22 Enterprise IT Capability requirements are important, we've applied only those that in our experience are most important for *Development & Transformation*. The reader is encouraged to revisit Chapter 11 section titled "Assessing Enterprise Performance against Requirements" and apply all 21 requirements to *Development & Transformation*.

Bottom Line: *Development & Transformation* Performance

It comes down to three fundamentals questions:

1. Do those who participate in *Development & Transformation* activities (e.g., IT, business, consultants, etc.) actually perform well and produce the required business outcomes?

Exhibit 13.11 Scales for Self-Assessment of *Development & Transformation*

Description	Importance Column		Status Column	
The *Importance* reflects the degree management is concerned, and the extent to which this requirement will influence business success in the future.	0	Not Applicable	0	Not Applicable
	5	This requirement is critical to the enterprise	5	Current *Development & Transformation* activities often produce the required outcome
The *Status* reflects the extent to which the requirements statement is achieved today.	4	This requirement is very important to the enterprise	4	Current *Development & Transformation* activities sometimes produce the required outcome
	3	This requirement is of some importance to the enterprise	3	The outcome requirement is not produced through *Development & Transformation* activities
	2	This requirement is interesting but not important	2	Current *Development & Transformation* activities sometimes make the outcome worse
	1	This requirement is not important to the enterprise	1	Current *Development & Transformation* activities often make the outcome worse

2. Will the *Development & Transformation* activities add to trust and partnership?
3. Do the *Development & Transformation* outcomes address change and flexibility sufficiently?

This is what Strategic IT Management and enterprise IT capabilities are about: getting positive answers to these three questions.

What Is the Enterprise to Do about Its Development & Transformation Capabilities?

Development & Transformation is the cutting edge of IT in the enterprise. It is the vehicle for introducing change into the business and certainly the vehicle for responding to turbulence and change. It is often the primary means of interactions between business and IT, but it also suffers from the effects of silos, within business (among business units) and within IT (different IT sources, different parts of the IT enterprise). As a result, enterprise management responses to the issues raised here are important, but it extends throughout business and IT management. The leverage of effective actions is large, and the importance of doing so significant.

What Are the Implications for the individual Manager and Professional?

Practically everyone participates at one time or another in *Development & Transformation* activities, either as a part of requirements setting and managing implementation or as a part of developing the solution. As a result, practically everyone has some impact on all the issues raised here: culture, partnership, trust, timely responsiveness, and so forth. So take the self-assessment to see how one contributes or impedes the requirements achievement, an effective first step. Then consider how to strengthen the contribution, in partnership, trust, credibility, and speed terms. Chapter 19 gives advice on how to go about this.

Enterprise IT Capability: *Service & Resource Optimization*

Optimization covers all the IT services (e.g., the applications, infrastructure services, user services) and the underlying resources needed to provide them. Exhibit 13.12 summarizes the objectives and example outcomes to be produced and lists example methodologies commonly employed.

The complete IT investment in the enterprise—both ongoing "lights on" and projects—is described in five service portfolios:

1. Applications and Information Services
2. Direct Infrastructure Services
3. Technical (User) Services
4. Management Services
5. Project & Development Services

We describe these at length in Chapter 11.

Exhibit 13.12   *Service & Resource Optimization*

Enterprise IT Capability	Strategic IT Management Objective	Example Outcomes for Superior Value	Example Outcomes for Superior Response to Turbulence	Example Methods
Service & Resource Optimization	Make effective business-value and risk-based IT investment decisions	Optimized service and resource portfolios for cost, performance, and risk	Adaptable, responsive service and resource portfolios, with reduced risk	• Portfolio Management for Applications, Infrastructure

Optimized service and resource portfolios based on cost, performance, risk, and value are the outcome for investment optimization, from the perspective of IT Supply. Optimized service portfolios also address quality and value from the business perspective. In turbulent times, this optimization extends to include factors such as adaptability, responsiveness, and flexibility. The processes and methodologies typically focus on the central IT organization's portfolios, but the investment and portfolio optimization coverage includes all IT, even outsourced and do-it-yourself IT in the business units.[7]

What Is the *Service & Resource Optimization* Enterprise IT Capability?

In Chapter 1, we say that "an enterprise requires the capability to optimize its sourcing, development, and application of all its IT services and resources, from all sources: internal IT, business-unit IT activities, sourcers, and 'do-it-yourself' IT activities."

We look at optimization in two ways. The first focuses on the IT services actually provided to the business. Exhibit 13.13 shows the five services provided by IT sources. Optimization works to establish that the cost and value of the services are, in fact, optimized, meaning that they meet business requirements at an appropriate cost. It is considerably more involved, however, in that considerations such as risk and total cost of ownership are part of the optimization mix, as well as those mentioned in the turbulence context, namely adaptability, responsiveness, and flexibility. An even more interesting problem is that multiple IT sources are possible (e.g., in-house IT, in-business-unit IT, sourcers, "cloud," do-it-yourself services provide by a business activity or

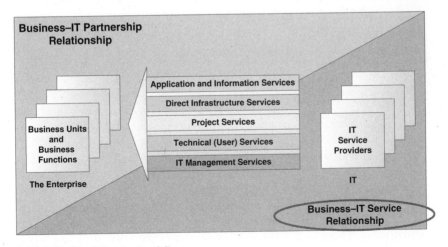

Exhibit 13.13   IT Service Portfolios

individual). And, certainly, multiple business units are the destination for these services, which further complicates the basis for assessment/evaluation. For example, optimization explores the alignment of IT services to business strategy and needs; multiple business targets makes the assessment multi-faceted at best.[8]

The End Point

Key Elements:

1. All IT services and resources are included, from throughout the IT ecosystem.
2. The technical and business risks in the IT services are documented.
3. The costs of IT services are documented.
4. Low-performing services are identified for mitigation planning. This covers value, quality, performance.
5. IT services are identified and described, from all IT sources in the IT ecosystem.
6. The IT service portfolios are inclusive of all IT sources in the IT ecosystem.
7. Analysis and decision making are supported for all IT services.
8. The resources needed to deliver and support IT services are optimized.
9. There is information transparency about services and resources; decision making is encouraged for each service and resource (e.g., cost mitigation, risk mitigation, value enhancement.)
10. Business outcomes, such as those listed in Exhibit 13.14, are achieved.

The reader can ask whether these end-point attributes accurately describe the current practices in the enterprise and whether they apply to all IT sources in the IT ecosystem (e.g., sourcers, cloud).

For the enterprise, from a holistic perspective, fundamental questions focus on overall risk (e.g., security exposures in the services, such as application services, project services), performance (e.g., stopping waste on low-performing services), and (perhaps most importantly) duplication. Any reasonably sized enterprise has multiple versions of many applications and services; cloud and do-it-yourself IT compound the problem.

The second way of looking at optimization is the underlying set of "pieced parts" that comprise the whole of the IT enterprise, wherever found in the organization. These pieced parts can be hardware, software, staff, contractual arrangements (e.g., contracted maintenance), or external services. This

Exhibit 13.14   Example Outcomes for *Service & Resource Optimization*

TVPM	Execution and Performance — the Actual Outcomes as the Basis for Credibility and Trust	
	Service & Resource Optimization Examples: Execution and Performance Business Outcomes for "Superior Business Value"	*Service & Resource Optimization* Examples: Execution and Performance Business outcomes for "Superior Response to Turbulence and Uncertainty"
Business Outcomes & Program Selection	• Effective business change management • Priorities based on business strategies and requirements • Clarity and agreement on business priorities	• Establish platforms for change • Adaptability beyond individual business units • Enterprise-wide applicability
Project Development & Benefit Realization	• Successfully implemented and operationalized projects • Access to a domain of relevant and valuable data	• Adaptable solutions • Integratable solutions • Dynamic capabilities
Software Configuration & Development	• Successfully developed projects • Successfully acquired software and solutions	• Adaptable solutions • Dynamic capabilities
Service Delivery	• Supports cost and risk mitigation • Meets requirements • Provides cost transparency • Provides performance transparency	• Flexible and adaptable

approach looks at the collections of piece parts from a portfolio perspective and asks questions, for example, about optimal levels, means of financing (buy/lease, e.g.), and risks. In both cases, the core capability includes a) knowing what the component parts are (e.g., the exact services, the applications, the piece-parts); b) knowing who provides them; c) knowing who the users are; and d) adopting the appropriate methods for assessment and decision making.

A lot of this is old hat; IT organizations have always paid attention to their portfolios of resources and have applied appropriate means for assessment, including ferreting out duplication and underperforming components on which resources are wasted—or at least they should have been. Considerable ranges of tools and methodologies are available to make this possible. The problem now is itself twofold. First, given the dispersion of IT sources in the IT ecosystem (e.g., sourcers, cloud, et al.) and IT utilization, an enterprise perspective rather than a silo perspective (IT source silo, business unit user silo) for optimization gives significant insight and leverage for making cost and value contributions. But even more so, the turbulence and uncertainty in today's environment ask for assessment and optimization capabilities beyond what most organizations have been doing.

Enterprise IT Capability Requirements

This enterprise IT capability is the core of governance and collaboration in the enterprise, because it identifies exactly the services being provided the business, their performance and cost, and provides the tools for determining whether they are successful in producing business value.

Chapter 8 devoted considerable time to describing what these services are. This capability applies that information in specific ways to ensure that these services do, in fact, perform as needed and as promised. Moreover, this capability pays attention to accountability and whether the services viewed from the business in fact meet those requirements.

Systemic Capabilities for Producing the Outcomes with Service & Resource Optimization

Five of the 14 systemic requirements for Enterprise IT Capabilities, defined in Chapter 11, apply particularly to *Service & Resource Optimization*.

The Enterprise *Service & Resource Optimization* Capability Builds Credibility through IT's Execution and Performance (A1)   A fundamental question is whether *Service & Resource Optimization* activities happen in the enterprise at all and whether they apply to all sources of IT (central/corporate, business unit, sourced, do it yourself). *Specifically, are the end points achieved?*

The governance processes with optimization provide monitoring and decision making about the services and resources. To the extent this is collaborative with the business units and the IT organizations, the transparency provided is a strong factor in documenting and communicating IT's execution and performance. The question here is the degree to which this occurs.

The Enterprise *Service & Resource Optimization* Capability Supports Decision Making and Overcomes Bureaucracy (A5)   The essence of *Service & Resource Optimization* is portfolio management applied to services and IT assets. This is executed in governance and review processes and perhaps in annual planning exercises, budgeting exercises, and similar activities. Whether these work in a timely fashion and avoid the problems of bureaucratic behavior is the question here.

The Enterprise *Service & Resource Optimization* **Capability Employs Methodologies that Focus on Specific Business, Strategic Intentions, and Goals (B1)**   Any optimization necessarily involves connecting services and resources to the business requirements, strategies, and goals. The issue here is the degree to which this happens.

The Enterprise *Service & Resource Optimization* **Capability Applies Business Domain and Industry Perspective (C1)**   Comparability to other businesses and industries, together with awareness of elements such as risk and cost, becomes part of the optimization decision processes. The issue here is the degree to which this perspective is part of the optimization processes.

The Enterprise *Service & Resource Optimization* **Capability Applies Holistically across Silos, Organizations, and Other Processes (C2)**   The nature of enterprise-level *Service & Resource Optimization* activities is to permit contrasts and comparison across silos, resulting in effective decision making.

Business Outcomes with Service & Resource Optimization

Three of the eight business outcome requirements for Enterprise IT Capabilities, defined in Chapter 11, apply particularly to *Service & Resource Optimization*.

The Enterprise *Service & Resource Optimization* **Capability Delivers or Supports Business Strategic Effectiveness (D1)**   The nature of *Service & Resource Optimization* is to analyze the connection of current deployed services and resources against business requirements, in this case to determine support of the business strategies. This is central to optimization.

The Enterprise *Service & Resource Optimization* **Capability Delivers or Supports Business Operational Effectiveness (D3)**   Similarly, the analysis applies to current requirements for business operations and costs. This too is central to optimization.

Service & Resource Optimization **Delivers or Supports Cost and Risk Mitigation (D4)**   The optimization decision making includes risk and cost as a core element of the factors to be considered.

Service & Resource Optimization Scorecard

The system and business outcome requirements for *Service & Resource Optimization* are listed in Exhibit 13.15 and Exhibit 13.16, for self-assessment. Exhibit 13.17 provides the scales to be used.

Exhibit 13.15   Strategic IT Management: The Systemic Capabilities for Producing the Outcomes with *Service & Resource Optimization*

Requirements for Trust, Partnership, Leadership, and Services	Importance	Status
To what extent does the existing *Service & Resource Optimization* enterprise IT capability build credibility through IT's execution and performance? *Specifically, are the end points achieved?* A1		
To what extent does the existing *Service & Resource Optimization* enterprise IT capability support decision making and overcome bureaucracy? (A5)		
To what extent does the existing *Service & Resource Optimization* enterprise IT capability employ methodologies that focus on specific business, strategic intentions, and goals? (B1)		
To what extent does IT management provide necessary leadership for these *Service & Resource Optimization* enterprise capabilities, with emphasis on culture, trust, and partnership with the business? (B2)		
To what extent does business management provide necessary leadership for this *Service & Resource Optimization* enterprise IT capability, with emphasis on culture, trust, and partnership with IT? (B3)		
To what extent does this *Service & Resource Optimization* enterprise IT capability proactively address the business environment? (B4)		
To what extent does this *Service & Resource Optimization* enterprise IT capability establish accountability for the processes and outcomes? (B5)		
To what extent does the existing *Service & Resource Optimization* enterprise IT capability apply business domain and industry perspective? (C1)		
To what extent does the existing *Service & Resource Optimization* enterprise IT capability apply holistically across silos, organizations, and other processes? (C2)		

Exhibit 13.16   Strategic IT Management: The Business Outcomes with *Service & Resource Optimization*

Requirement for Outcomes	Importance	Status
To what extent does the existing *Service & Resource Optimization* enterprise IT capability deliver or support business strategic effectiveness? (D1)		
To what extent does the existing *Service & Resource Optimization* enterprise IT capability deliver or support business operational effectiveness? (D3)		
To what extent does the existing *Service & Resource Optimization* enterprise IT capability deliver or support cost and risk mitigation? (D4)		

The reader is encouraged to revisit Chapter 11 section titled "Assessing Enterprise Performance Against Requirements" and apply all 21 requirements to *Service & Resource Optimization*.

Exhibit 13.17   Scorecard for This Assessment

Description	Importance Column		Status Column	
The *Importance* reflects the degree management is concerned and the extent to which this requirement will influence business success in the future.	0	Not Applicable	0	Not Applicable
	5	This requirement is critical to the enterprise	5	Current *Service & Resource Optimization* activities often produce the required outcome
The *Status* reflects the extent to which the requirements statement is achieved today.	4	This requirement is very important to the enterprise	4	Current *Service & Resource Optimization* activities sometimes produce the required outcome
	3	This requirement is of some importance to the enterprise	3	The required outcome is not produced through *Service & Resource Optimization* activities
	2	This requirement is interesting but not important	2	Current *Service & Resource Optimization* Activities sometimes make the outcome worse
	1	This requirement is not important to the enterprise	1	Current *Service & Resource Optimization* activities often make the outcome worse

Bottom Line: *Service & Resource Optimization* **Performance**

Service & Resource Optimization comes down to three fundamental questions:

1. Do those who participate in *Service & Resource Optimization* activities (e.g., IT, business, consultants, etc.) actually perform well and produce business outcomes?
2. Will the *Service & Resource Optimization* activities add to trust and partnership?
3. Do the *Service & Resource Optimization* outcomes address change and flexibility sufficiently?

This is what Strategic IT Management and enterprise IT capabilities are about: getting positive answers to these three questions.

What Is the Enterprise to Do about Its Service & Resource Optimization*?*

Most enterprises do not pay as close attention to ongoing IT activities as they do to project prioritization. This is understandable, given that projects are the cutting edge for IT innovation, but the real money is in the ongoing services and costs. Further, as Chapter 8 pointed out, conceiving of IT as a set of services is relatively new in the sense of service management principles applied from the business perspective. Consequently, enterprise response has culture and practice challenges, made more complex by the proliferation of IT sources available to the business. Corralling all that for management/governance purposes is a significant step. Chapter 16 and Chapter 18's Message 5 offer some suggestions.

What Are the Implications for the Individual Manager and Professional?

The notion of IT as a business service viewed from the business perspective is helpful to the individual manager for understanding and managing IT. Practically everyone in the business is either a provider or a consumer of IT services. Understanding this and the implications for performance improvement that can occur thought resource optimization is a key contribution to the success of IT. Self-assessment makes this possible.

Summary: Tactical Enterprise IT Capabilities and Competencies

Marshaling the relevant enterprise resources to achieve success in its strategic and operational strategies forms the foundation for Strategic IT Management. Tactical management capabilities focus on the management of these resources, engaging business and technology managers in working to achieve the business goals.

The challenges are larger than those of simple IT management, as the resources come from all IT sources and all business units involved. These include the information and analysis resources, the developmental resources, and the service and technical resources. Understanding and deploying them on behalf of superior business value and superior response to turbulence and uncertainty is the goal. Assessing their current capability and planning for their improvement is the goal; achieving this is made possible through the tools set out in this chapter.

Notes

1. See Chapter 2, "Strategic Use of Information Resources," in Keri E. Pearlman and Carol S. Saunders, *Managing and Using Information Systems: A Strategic Approach*, 4th ed. (Wiley, 2012), page 46.
2. Page 156 of Robert D. Galliers, Dorothy E. Leidner, Bernadette S. H. Baker, *Strategic Information Management: Challenges and Strategies in Managing Information Systems* (Butterworth Heinemann, 2001).
3. M. T. Smits, K. G. van der Poel, and P. M. A. Ribbers, "Information Strategy: Assessment of Information Strategies in Insurance Companies," in *Strategic Information Management: Challenges and Strategies in Managing Information Systems*, 3rd ed., ed. R. D. Galliers and D. E. Leidner (Butterworth Heinemann, 2003): 64.
4. See Richard Hunter and George Westerman, *The Real Business of IT: How CIOs Create and Communicate Value* (Harvard Business Press, 2009); Dean Lane, *The Chief Information Officers' Body of Knowledge: People, Process, and Technology* (Wiley, 2011).
5. http://www-01.ibm.com/software/analytics/aq/index.html?i.user1=-web_ibm_mte%20&mc=-web_ibm_mte
6. See, for example, Joshua Kerlevsky, *Refactoring to Patterns* (Addison-Wesley, 2004).
7. See "IT Portfolio Management" in Keri E. Pearlman and Carol S. Saunders, "The Tools for Change," in *Managing and Using Information Systems: A Strategic Approach*, 4th ed. (Wiley, 2012): 291. This does not cover service portfolios but describes ways to do the costing.
8. Stephanie Overby, "RIP. IT Value," *CIO Magazine*, May 15, 2011, pp. 21–26. "IT value is dead. Business outcomes are the only things important." And metrics have to be consistent "in concert with the values of the business." This requires moving from traditional to measured items, such as cost of service interruptions, cost of risks averted, revenue, market share, and speed of service compared to competitors.

Operational Enterprise IT Capabilities and Competencies

G iven the importance of operational competences are to trust, credibility, performance, and execution, it's possible that this set of three enterprise IT capabilities should come first.

Chapter 14 describes the three operational enterprise IT capabilities, as shown in Exhibit 14.1:

1. *Cost & Performance*
2. *Service & Operational Excellence*
3. *Sourcing*

While operational in character, these capabilities equally contribute to the issues of response to turbulence and uncertainty, trust, and partnership. It can be argued they are foremost in both, as the inflexibilities of bureaucracy and unwillingness to change often loom largest in these kinds of operational capabilities. Similarly, *Sourcing* raises all the relationship questions between the business and the sources, as well as among the IT organizations (e.g., issues like security, use of networks, and so forth).

Enterprise IT Capability: *Service & Operational Excellence*

This enterprise capability covers IT services and includes the elements of operational excellence (Exhibit 14.2).

The phrase "operational excellence" often dominates business and IT management conversations. In our context, we use this phrase to describe the first of the six stages of demonstrated IT performance for the enterprise, as

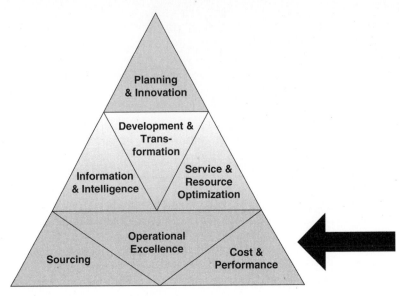

Exhibit 14.1   Operational Enterprise IT Capabilities

described in the section on Trust and the Total Value Performance Model (TVPM) in Chapter 2. The issue here is whether the enterprise is capable of specifying and delivering IT services to a standard of operational excellence.

Major parts of frameworks like the IT infrastructure library (ITIL) and Control Objectives for Information and Related Technology (COBIT) are devoted to the managing the foundations of IT's operational excellence. In the business context, service management focuses on operational excellence as an outcome of good service practices. Even in the business strategic domain,

Exhibit 14.2 *Service & Operational Excellence*

Enterprise IT Capability	Strategic IT Management Objective	Example Outcomes for Superior Value	Example Outcomes for Superior Response to Turbulence	Example Methods
Service & Operational Excellence	Manage to expectations for service and operational excellence	Superior performance matched to business requirements. Competence.	Adaptability, responsiveness, partnerships	ITIL COBIT Service Management

operational excellence (or operational effectiveness) is one of the two competitive outcomes[1] and one of the three strategic thrusts.[2]

So *Service & Operational Excellence* is important, perhaps even critical, as the foundation of both business performance and IT performance. Of course, it is helpful to define exactly what the concept covers. From an IT Supply perspective, operational excellence generally covers reliability, ability to respond to interruptions or defects, cost efficiency, and similar provider-oriented concepts. These concepts apply to the business, its processes, and the services it extends to customers as well.

From an IT Demand or IT user perspective, these concepts are also certainly important. But equally important are business-based service perspectives: whether the (IT service) provider is in tune with the business requirements, the people-to-people aspects of services, and similar concepts. Again, these issues are important in the business in its own processes and services as well: The business has *Service & Operational Excellence* concerns with its customers and its supply-chain partners. From the business perspective, IT can be a critical component in delivering business-to-consumer and business-to-business services.

Perhaps Operational Excellence is an unfortunate choice of words, as it tends to imply only data-center operational services. As we discussed in Chapter 8, IT services runs the entire gamut of the activities IT does for the business. Exhibit 8.2 showed the five basic service groups, which include applications, project development, infrastructure, and user support. But within these categories are also the services associated with strategic planning, information delivery and analysis, and so forth. So although we refer to "basic" services, we are focusing on everything IT does . . . from wherever this full range of IT services is delivered.

What do we expect from this enterprise IT capability? This is not, per se, a process question answered by structures like ITIL or (in business) service management processes. Those are the operational details; important to be sure, and certainly affected by the enterprise IT capability to perform them. But we're asking a more fundamental question.

What Is the *Service & Operational Excellence* Enterprise IT Capability?

In Chapter 1, we say, "an enterprise requires the capability to perform its IT services with operational excellence and the right balance of adaptability/flexibility toward standards and stability (and, overall, holistically covering the enterprise and all its IT)."

This is not an IT organization–centric question or capability; it is an enterprise question combining the business and IT perspectives. In Chapter 2, we introduced the six-step TVPM (Exhibit 14.3), which is based on a

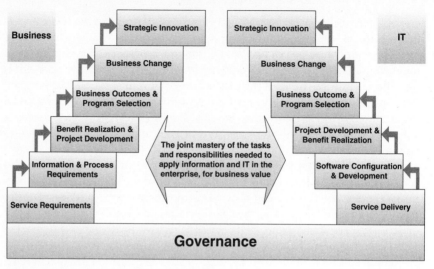

Exhibit 14.3   Total Value Performance Model

foundation of service delivery and service requirements. Note, though, that each of the successive steps also involves services, whether developmental, planning, or analytical in nature. This engages both IT (as the supplier) and business (as the consumer) of IT services; the enterprise IT capability of performing requires the full participation of both. But as an aside, it is interesting how few IT professionals are aware of the business-based service management connections to IT operational excellence. It is as though the concept of service is behind the IT wall, and not in the context of the IT "customer." Chapter 11 devoted considerable attention to this connection to service management. In another aside, recall that the relationship is n to m: That is, multiple IT sources and multiple business users may exist in the enterprise. The IT Sources/IT Supply Profile exhibit seen later in this chapter provides a simple way to understand the relationships among the various IT service provides and the services they deliver.

While we aren't focusing on specific processes (like ITIL's set of internal IT service management processes,) it is instructive to think about the pain points in operational excellence. In Chapter 2, we discussed the elements of credibility leading to (dis)trust between business and IT. If IT is simply unable to do the job right, both in operations and in project development, this is the source of pain. Costs can focus this pain—"IT costs too much"— and the ill feeling does not decline even once the data centers are managed better. The traditional means of measuring performance from the IT Supply perspective include: reliability (interruptions) and performance/response times. The business-focused means of measuring performing include functionality, ease of use, and similar user-focused issues. Failures in any of these areas are significant pain points. Without question, IT has to perform. (And the business has to perform with respect to its customers.) This is core to achieving the kind of IT performance reflected in our TVPM in Exhibit 14.3. Shortcomings in IT and business processes must be remedied to improve operational excellence.

Incidentally, lest the reader think these issues are in the past (so 20th century!) and are well addressed in current practice, this is certainly not our experience, whether in the United States or in other countries. While yes, perhaps the IT Supply–oriented things (like reliability) might be doing better, the business-focused measures (like functionality, ease of use, et al.) are most certainly not. Business service expectations (which are, per Chapter 11, the heart of operational expectations) are not being met.[3] However, this focus on current processes obscures the question asked earlier: What is it that characterizes an enterprise's capability for achieving operational excellence?

The End Point

The key elements of this enterprise IT capability are:

■ Service & Operational Excellence is applicable to all IT-provided services (the five service portfolios, including projects, applications, user services, direct infrastructure such as networks and workstations, and management services; see Chapter 8).
■ All IT services in the ecosystem are included; all IT sources are included.
■ IT is operated as a true service. Service performance metrics focus on the business use and impact of the services.
■ Expectations for service performance are mutually developed. Accountability for service performance and operational excellence is established.
■ The service management and operational excellence processes engage all of IT and all of business.
■ Service requirements are connected to the characteristic of the enterprise and its lines of business.
■ It includes cost and metrics reflecting the business perspective of the services.
■ It applies to all sources of IT (e.g., central IT organization, business unit activities, sourcers/cloud providers, etc.). See the IT Supply Source Profile exhibit later in this chapter.
■ Business outcomes such as those listed in Exhibit 14.4 are achieved.

Exhibit 14.4 Example Outcomes for *Service & Operational Excellence*

TVPM	Execution and Performance: The Actual Outcomes as the Basis for Credibility and Trust	
	Service & Operational Excellence **Examples: Execution and Performance Business Outcomes for "Superior Business Value"**	**Service & Operational Excellence Examples: Execution and Performance Business Outcomes for "Superior Response to Turbulence and Uncertainty"**
Project Development & Benefit Realization	• Successfully implemented and operationalized projects • Access to a domain of relevant and valuable data	• Adaptable solutions • Integratable solutions • Dynamic capabilities
Software Configuration & Development	• Successfully developed projects • Successfully acquired software and solutions	• Adaptable solutions • Dynamic capabilities
Service Delivery	• Supports cost and risk mitigation • Meets requirements • Provides cost transparency • Provides performance transparency	• Flexible and adaptable

The reader can ask whether these end-point attributes accurately describe the current practices in the enterprise and whether they apply to all IT sources in the IT ecosystem (e.g., sourcers, cloud).

A core component of strategic management is "marshaling the enterprise resources to achieve desired business strategic outcomes."[4] In *Service & Operational Excellence*, these means two things: the resources necessary for accomplishing *Service & Operational Excellence* from the supply perspective, and those resources necessary to define the requirements for IT services from the business perspective. This is reflected in the TVPM by pairing service requirements with service delivery as the foundational elements. Here we are more concerned about the former, while the latter are described aptly in the formal description of the many processes and methodologies available (e.g., ITIL, CoBIT).

Our focus here, as always, is particularly on partnership and trust. Recalling the previous chapters, we emphasize the establishment of common goals, transparency, credibility based on performance, service, and speed of response.

Over the last few years IT organizations have gone astray, adopting the mental model of "IT as a business" without thinking through the implications.

For example, this mental model puts the business enterprise in the role of a "customer" to which IT is sold and delivered as a service product. This is different from the mental model of IT as a service provider in the context of a partnership with common goals and trust. The service provider model gives good guidance for service performance, but the relationship to the business is one of jointly agreeing on goals and outcomes, costs, and performance levels. The IT-as-a-business model gives too much importance to IT's self-interests, while the IT-as-a-service-provider model gives full rein to the common goals trust, and transparency of a partnership. (See Chapter 9.)

However, the underlying requirement is true partnership with common goals. Credibility is based on service performance, of course, but this too is a part of the common goals, trust, and transparency of a partnership. Again, we are not focusing so much on the internals of IT service management (e.g., ITIL). Much goes into defining and delivering truly excellent services, and IT needs to command that. But there's even more to what constitutes good services from the business perspective. That's the message of Chapter 9; that message needs to be incorporated into the enterprise IT capability of *Service & Operational Excellence*.

There's no question about the need for credibility in IT's delivery of services to the business. As stated previously, this credibility is the foundation of trust and of the TVPM. So IT has to execute.

The focus of this execution targets service excellence from a business perspective. As Chapter 9 emphasized, this vision of service excellence is founded on business service management principles, including such concepts as empathy, reliability, responsiveness, and assurance. This is not simply based on meeting technical specifications (e.g., 99 percent uptime), but rather treating the relationship holistically as a service relationship.

Execution and performance are made more complicated by the increasing expanse of IT providers, as we've remarked about corporate, business-unit, outside sources, and do-it-yourself IT. All play a role in the delivery of IT services and, ultimately, in the IT and business partnerships. Often the end user cannot tell exactly who is involved, as several of these sources can combine to provide the end service. All of this is taken into account in the need for execution and performance, with the requisite technical (e.g., uptime) and business service (e.g., responsiveness, empathy) required.

The Processes and Methodologies in *Service & Operational Excellence*

As we've emphasized, the business–IT relationship is one of partnership (e.g., common goals) and service (e.g., IT supplying five basic services, such as projects, applications, user services). And we've also emphasized that IT is not a single organization, but embraces all sources, including business-based,

Exhibit 14.5   IT Sources/IT Supply Profile

IT Services Profile				
IT Services (Described in Chapter 8)	Provided from a Central IT Organization	Provided from Business-Based IT Activities	Provided from Sourced Providers, Including Cloud	Provided through "Do-It-Yourself" IT Activities in the Business.
Application Services				
Project Services				
Direct Infrastructure Services				
Technical (User) Services				
IT Management Services				

sourced, and do-it-yourself IT. Accordingly the assessment combines these as the Exhibit 14.5 suggests. The enterprise IT capability for *Service & Operational Excellence* capability is the sum of all these: whether the enterprise overall can perform the services with the attributes described here. Exhibit 14.5 is meant to give a context for the questions.

Consideration to all sources should be given as the assessments are made. The point is that, however IT activities occur, the enterprise needs to capably deliver services with the appropriate quality, performance, and service characteristics.

We have introduced the concept of *fit*: Do the IT services fit with the requirements and characteristics of the business? We have emphasized speed in the context of response to turbulence. We talked about a holistic perspective (e.g., covering all sources of IT) and a partnership perspective. These issues are foundational, as we emphasized in Part II.

Turbulence, however, really impacts the enterprise IT capability for *Service & Operational Excellence*. So much of the IT edifice is built around the goals of stability: a stable environment, a stable set of operational processes, a stable set of organizational relationships, a stable (predicable) set of technologies and characteristic user requirements. Turbulence—both business and technical—undercuts this stability. How can an enterprise deal with it? What is the nature of the enterprise IT capability need to continuously achieve operational excellence? Consider, for example, the recent tendency for cloud provider's services to be offered directly to the business. As a minor example, we recently worked with a manufacturing company whose products hadn't changed markedly for decades, nor had their customer requirements. Yet the business organizations imposed 67 application packages on the IT organizations and said "run them." But, you ask, what about security? Data integration? Help desk understanding of problems and solutions? This is just one example of a form of turbulence, yet it certainly undermines the stability upon which the IT organization had depended. To the extent that operational excellence includes effective performance of such things, the manufacturing company's IT was certainly challenged.

Understanding the problems is a good start. A self-assessment is helpful to position an enterprise's current situation in its capability to *Service & Operational Excellence*. We began this with the execution and performance discussion, in which the assessment is about the current actual performance in the sense of producing desired business outcomes. Here, we've noted nine factors specifically of interest. We offer our perspective on the relative importance to superior value and response to turbulence based on our research and client experience, although a particular enterprise may differ.

Chapter 11 presents a complete scorecard for enterprise capabilities. The following 10 assessment questions reflect our view of the important characteristics of *Service & Operational Excellence*. They are taken from the 22 requirements described in Chapter 11.

Exhibit 14.6 provides self-assessment for the current methodologies and processes for *Service & Operational Excellence*. Exhibit 14.7 provides the assessment for the degree for which business outcomes are achieved.

Strategic IT Management: The Systemic Capabilities for Producing the Outcomes with *Service & Operational Excellence*

Six of the 14 systemic enterprise IT capability requirements apply particularly to *Service & Operational Excellence*.

Builds Credibility through IT's Execution and Performance (A1)

As the TVPM (Chapters 2 and 4) emphasizes, service quality is the foundation for credibility and ultimately trust between business and IT. Specifically, are the "end points" listed achieved?

The challenge is defining what "execution and performance" means. It is not solely a technical matter; things like uptime and data quality are important, but are not the central concern. Rather, it is the service management aspects that form the foundation of credibility—that is, it is from the perspective of the business, not the IT providers.

Furthermore, the concept of *Service & Operational Excellence* apply to the entire service relationship between IT and business, namely the five basic service portfolios. It is not limited to the traditional, operational views of the networks and data centers; *Service & Operational Excellence* embraces systems development and project services, user services, and management services. And it applies to all IT sources, whether internal or external.

The question is whether the business and IT partnership—covering all sources of IT—is capable of performing the enterprise IT capabilities. Can the relevant IT activities execute the specific IT services, deliver value with IT, and think strategically about IT in the enterprise? In particular, can the goals for each specific capability (e.g., for *Planning & Innovation*, effective, achievable plans) be delivered? Is the enterprise capable of this?

Adds to Trust between Organizations (A2)

As IT services are delivered to the business, this question applies to the manner in which the various organizations involved interact, through processes, in management styles and decision making, in organizational approach to performance measurement and management, and in problem solving. Trust is created through transparency and through delivery on promises made.

IT Management Provides Necessary Leadership with Emphasis on Culture, Trust, and Partnership with the Business (B2)

The importance of leadership cannot be overstated given IT's 50-year history of being managed as a technology organization with an engineering-based mental model. The new mental model expressing IT as a service, with attention to the business and to traditional business service management principles, is an enormous change. It turns IT from an internally focused technical management organization to an externally focused service management organization. IT leadership must be on board as an enabler and an encourager for this culture change.

While the question focuses on the business, the same element of trust and partnership is required across the silos in IT and among the possible IT sources. A common view of the services to be provided and, more importantly, the underlying business orientation to the common goals and objectives is needed across the complete service provider landscape.

Business Management Provides Necessary Leadership with Emphasis on Culture, Trust, and Partnership with IT (B3)

While perhaps not as dramatic as the IT cultural changes, business too has a mental model change, to think of IT as a partner rather than solely a technology manager and service provider. This mental model change requires business management to set the change, define the culture throughout the business.

Similar to IT, the business too has its silos and focus on local optimization. Breaking down the walls, seeing the role and development of IT in the business as an enterprise matter, is at least as important.

Establishes Accountability for the Processes and Outcomes (B5)

When considering the possible breadth of IT sources (consider Exhibit 14.5), you may discover that accountability for service management is diffuse or nonexistent. The question here is the degree to which the enterprise is capable of managing its IT services, with focus on ensuring performance to appropriate standards and expectations.

Applies Holistically across Silos, Organizations, and Other Processes (C2)

It is common for enterprise and IT silos to impede processes, reducing understanding and trust with all the stakeholders and organizations. This particularly applies to operational excellence, where common standards of quality, performance, and service management should apply everywhere that IT service is delivered. The point applies to the different sources of IT as well, in which the business expectations for services should be applied equally.

Failure to apply service and operational excellence holistically across the enterprise ends up confusing everyone, both service providers and consumers. Difficulty in supervising the provider part, and difficulty in responding to user expectation consistently, is the result.

Strategic IT Management: The Business Outcomes with *Service & Operational Excellence*

Four of the enterprise IT capabilities apply particularly to *Service & Operational Excellence*.

Delivers or Supports Business Operational Effectiveness (D3)

This raises a key aspect of the partnership between IT and business. While providing services effectively is certainly important and is a direct factor in establishing the trust needed, the element of partnership focuses on the common goals between IT and business. It is easy for IT, in effect, to toss the services over the transom and take no interest in the achievement of the business goals, particularly the business operational effectiveness goals such as business quality, timeliness, flexibility, and responsiveness to the business's customers and clients. IT is increasingly a direct component of those business services, whether through the Internet or through processes such as kiosks and portals.

This increasing IT role in business product and service delivery demands awareness of the business and participation in the achievement of business goals for its service and product delivery.

Delivers or Supports Cost and Risk Mitigation (D4)

While arguably this is a component of business operational effectiveness, when focused on IT, the goals of cost mitigation are critically important across all IT sources. Risk, including such matters as security risk, technical risk, and supplier risk, is equally important across all IT sources.

Enables or Supports the Faster Deployment of Solutions (E3)

Sadly, it is possible that focus on operational excellence adds elements of standards and bureaucracy to IT service delivery. This can be most easily observed in pure operational services, the data center, and so on, which can tend to view new technology or new applications with some suspicion. In many respects, the mental model for IT service providers emphasizes stability as a core component of ensuring reliability.

Delivers or Supports Adaptability and Flexibility in Its Solutions (E4)

This is an extension of the issues described previously. It takes real commitment to provide flexibility in service delivery, which is also a function of leadership. Again, this becomes a question of culture and commitment.

Service & Operational Excellence Scorecard

Exhibit 14.6 and Exhibit 14.7 provide a self-assessment scorecard for *Service & Operational Excellence*. Exhibit 14.8 gives the scale.

The reader is encouraged to revisit the Chapter 11 section named "Assessing Enterprise Performance against Requirements" and apply all 21 requirements to *Service & Operational Excellence*.

Bottom Line: *Service & Operational Excellence* Performance

It comes down to three fundamental questions:

1. Do those who participate in *Service & Operational Excellence* activities (e.g., IT, business, consultants, etc.) actually perform well and produce the required business outcomes? Does IT perform?

Exhibit 14.6 Strategic IT Management: The Systemic Capabilities for Producing the Outcomes with *Service & Operational Excellence*

Requirements for Trust, Partnership, Leadership, and Services	Importance	Status
To what extent does the existing *Service & Operational Excellence* enterprise IT capability build credibility through IT's execution and performance? *Specifically, are the end points achieved?* (A1)		
To what extent does the existing *Service & Operational Excellence* enterprise IT capability enable or strengthen partnerships and collaboration at all levels and with all IT sources? (A3)		
To what extent does the existing *Service & Operational Excellence* enterprise IT capability employ methodologies that focus on specific business, strategic intentions, and goals? (B1)		
To what extent does IT management provide necessary leadership for *Service & Operational Excellence* enterprise IT capabilities, with emphasis on culture, trust, and partnership with the business? (B2)		
To what extent does business management provide necessary leadership for this *Service & Operational Excellence* enterprise IT capability, with emphasis on culture, trust, and partnership with IT? (B3)		
To what extent does the existing *Service & Operational Excellence* enterprise IT capability apply holistically across silos, organizations, and other processes? (B4)		

Exhibit 14.7 Strategic IT Management: The Business Outcomes with *Service & Operational Excellence*

Requirement for Outcomes	Importance	Status
To what extent does the existing *Service & Operational Excellence* enterprise IT capability deliver or support business strategic effectiveness? (D1)		
To what extent does the existing *Service & Operational Excellence* enterprise IT capability deliver or support innovation and change? (D2)		
To what extent does the existing *Service & Operational Excellence* enterprise IT capability enable or support the deployment of solutions faster? (E3)		
To what extent does the existing *Service & Operational Excellence* enterprise IT capability deliver or support adaptability and flexibility in its solutions? (E4)		

Exhibit 14.8   Scales for Assessment

Description	Importance Column		Status Column	
The *Importance* reflects the degree management is concerned, and the extent to which this requirement will influence business success in the future.	0	Not Applicable	0	Not Applicable
	5	This requirement is critical to the enterprise	5	Current *Service & Operational Excellence* activities often produces the required outcome
The *Status* reflects the extent to which the requirements statement is achieved today.	4	This requirement is very important to the enterprise	4	Current *Service & Operational Excellence* activities sometimes produces the required outcome
	3	This requirement is of some importance to the enterprise	3	The required outcome is not produced through *Service & Operational Excellence* activities
	2	This requirement is interesting but not important	2	Current *Service & Operational Excellence* Activities sometimes makes the outcome worse
	1	This requirement is not important to the enterprise	1	Current *Service & Operational Excellence* activities often makes the outcome worse

2. Will the *Service & Operational Excellence* activities add to trust and partnership?
3. Do the *Service & Operational Excellence* outcomes address change and flexibility sufficiently?

This is what Strategic IT Management and enterprise IT capabilities are about: getting positive answers to the three questions.

What Is the Enterprise to Do about Its Service & Operational Excellence Capabilities?

Most management attention is on the cost of services and the relative quality compared to alternatives. Yet this is an opportunity for partnership/trust development, particularly in establishing transparency on *Cost & Performance*. This becomes a good area for governance, especially providing visibility across all sources of IT services.

Implications for the Individual Manager and Professional

Everyone is either a provider or consumer of IT services. Understand the roles involved; the potential for improving the quality and (most importantly) the business impact of services is a significant contribution.

Enterprise IT Capability: *Sourcing*

Sourcing focuses on making decisions about and monitoring the many choices for obtaining IT Supply services. Exhibit 14.9 summarizes objectives, example outcomes, and methodologies commonly used in sourcing.

Sourcing applies to each of the five IT service portfolios. The range of the decisions, viewed from the business perspective, includes the internal IT organizations, outsourcing organizations, and the do-it-yourself options. A critical element is determining the balance between internal and external suppliers, meaning those activities that can be effectively sourced compared to those that cannot. Considerable attention has been paid to this question, using such concepts as sourcing noncritical activities and not sourcing core activities, as applied to IT Supply. The enterprise IT capability is about exercising that judgment about the sourcing opportunities. Methodologies partly deal with framing the issues and partly with making the determinations. Architecture, ITIL, and COBIT are examples that can help identify them.

Why is sourcing is described as an "operational" enterprise IT capability? Often it is called "strategic sourcing," and is a critical part of innovation, resource optimization, transformation, and change. That is, the ability to obtain partners to support the strategic business requirements, and the ability to enhance adaptability and responsiveness to turbulence and change, can be

Exhibit 14.9 *Sourcing*

Enterprise IT Capability	Strategic IT Management Objective	Example Outcomes for Superior Value	Example Outcomes for Superior Response to Turbulence	Example Methods
Sourcing	Match IT sourcing (internal and external) to business requirements	Sourcing matched to achieving business competitive and operational excellence, with standards	Adaptability, responsiveness, partnerships. Frameworks (e.g., responsive architectures)	Architecture ITIL COBIT

significantly enabled with the issues of sourcing. From the business perspective, sourcing covers the entire relationship between the business and all IT providers, whoever they might be. This, in the largest sense, is the meaning of Strategic IT Management, in terms of optimizing the resources available to the business to meet strategic purposes

Sourcing also has key operational aspects in terms of managing the risks, exposures, costs, and performance of all forms of sourcing. Part of the operational aspect is the ability to choose the appropriate sourcer and establish the conditions, in parallel with the *Sourcing* concerns (in the following section). This is the fundamental reason for considering the subject here, for it is the other side of the *Sourcing* coin. That is, from the perspective of transforming business in turbulent times, the unfortunate tendency of both the activity of sourcing and the enterprise IT capability of *Sourcing* can be to introduce structure, standards, and stability in ways that impede responsiveness and adaptability.

What Is the *Sourcing* Enterprise IT Capability?

We say in Chapter 1 that "an enterprise needs the capability to define, plan, acquire, manage, and effectively employ the IT services from all sources: internal IT, business-unit IT, sourcers, and 'do-it-yourself' IT activities. The core capability is reducing the risk and increasing the value of all IT services provided to the enterprise, whatever the source. As with *Operational Excellence*, the business must be capable of doing this with the right balance of adaptability and flexibility, with standards and stability.

The problem with the enterprise *Sourcing* capability is similar to those previously discussed: the lack of common standards, the lack of a point of focus for considering the alternative, the lack of inclusion of sourced IT services to be included in the holistic perspective of enterprise IT activities.

So the enterprise IT capability addresses these problems, answering key questions: How does one make the best decisions for the provisions of IT resources, as well as for sourcing (Who will be the partners? Who will provide and manage the IT services? Who will manage the relationships?), for all aspects of the business–IT relationships? This holistic vision for the enterprise is a broad perspective in which the overall capability is the enterprise's ability to make the best decisions about IT service provision, whether that solution is the IT organization, a direct service provider to the business, a "cloud" application, or the business's do-it-yourself solutions at the individual (e.g., tablets and PCs) or departmental level. These "best decisions" include all the important factors—capability, performance, risk, cost, and adaptability to change—balanced with the necessary standards and architectures.

This is not an IT organization–centric question or capability; it is an enterprise question combining the business and IT perspective. While we aren't focusing on specific processes (like ITIL's set of internal IT service management processes), it is instructive to think about the pain points in *Sourcing*. We have introduced concepts of *fit*—do the IT services fit with the requirements and characteristics of the business? We have emphasized speed in the context of response to turbulence. We talk about a holistic perspective (e.g., covering all sources of IT) and a partnership perspective. These issues are foundational. We emphasized them in Part II on Services, Partnership, and Leadership.

And as we have said before with other enterprise IT capabilities, this is not a control question. We are simply asking whether the enterprise has the *capability* to address these questions and provide a sound foundation for developing and operationalizing the answers.

Turbulence, however, really impacts the enterprise IT capability for *Sourcing*. So much of the IT edifice is built around the goals of stability: a stable environment, a stable set of operational processes, a stable set of organizational relationships, a stable (predicable) set of technologies and characteristic user requirements. Turbulence—both business and technical—undercuts this stability. And how can an enterprise deal with it? What is the nature of the enterprise IT capability needed to continuously achieve *Sourcing*? Consider, for example, the recent tendency for cloud-provider's services to be offered directly to the business.

The End Point

The key elements for the *Sourcing* enterprise IT capability include:

- The relationship with sourcers is based on partnership, trust.
- Sourcers, especially those external to the enterprise, are appropriately included in planning and governance activities.
- *Sourcing* does not inhibit flexibility and responses to turbulence and change.
- Performance and costs are transparent.
- Accountability—strategic *Sourcing* management—is effective.
- *Sourcing* extends to all forms of IT delivery, including formal outsourcing, internal sourcing of IT services, and do-it-yourself IT.
- Business outcomes such as those listed in Exhibit 14.10 are achieved.

The reader can ask whether these end-point attributes accurately describe the current practices in the enterprise and whether they apply to all IT sources in the IT ecosystem (e.g., sourcers, cloud).

Note that Chapter 6 provides considerable insight into the requirements *Sourcing* has for the enterprise and IT management. One focus here is partnership and trust. Recalling previous chapters, this emphasizes elements

Exhibit 14.10 Example Outcomes for *Sourcing*

TVPM	Execution and Performance: The Actual Outcomes as the Basis for Credibility and Trust	
	Sourcing Examples: Execution and Performance Business Outcomes for "Superior Business Value"	*Sourcing* Examples: Execution and Performance Business Outcomes for "Superior Response to Turbulence and Uncertainty"
Project Development & Benefit Realization	• Successfully implemented and operationalized projects • Access to a domain of relevant and valuable data	• Adaptable solutions • Integratable solutions • Dynamic capabilities
Software Configuration & Development	• Successfully developed projects • Successfully acquired software and solutions	• Adaptable solutions • Dynamic capabilities
Service Delivery	• Supports cost and risk mitigation • Meets requirements • Provides cost transparency • Provides performance transparency	• Flexible and adaptable

such as establishing common goals, transparency, credibility based on performance, service, and speed of response. So the set of "requirements" should be read with these overarching issues involved. That is, the enterprise IT capability for *Sourcing* is founded on the requirements of trust, partnership, and so forth.

Enterprise IT Capability Requirements

Chapter 6 provides background to the *Sourcing* enterprise IT capability discussion, particularly the issues of trust and turbulence.

Strategic IT Management: The Systemic Capabilities for Producing the Outcomes with Sourcing

Six of the systemic enterprise IT capabilities apply particularly to *Sourcing*.

The Enterprise *Sourcing* Capability Builds Credibility through IT's Execution and Performance (A1) The business–IT partnership is based on trust, which is largely a function of credible performance. From the outsourcing perspective, another organization is included in the performance issue and can greatly affect both the perceived performance as well as the process of determining what credible performance requires. This capability engages the business in the discussion as well. For other sourcing issues, such as in-business IT activities, business-acquired sourcing such as cloud, and do-it-yourself, the overall perception of performance and hence credibility and trust are just as important.

Specifically, are the "end points" achieved? The issue in this requirement is the performance itself whether those IT activities sourced meet expectations and build on credibility.

The Enterprise *Sourcing* Capability Adds to Trust between Organizations (A2)   This combines the performance/credibility issues with the governance and decision-making process. How expectations are set for IT services and translated into the sourcing requirements, is key, along with transparency of costs and performance.

The Enterprise *Sourcing* Capability Enables or Strengthens Partnerships and Collaboration at All Levels and with All IT Sources (A4)   *Sourcing* can add barriers to partnership and collaboration, particularly where external IT sourcing organizations are included. Gaining their participation in partnership building and common goals is the objective, even though Chapter 6 points out there may be incompatibilities among the organization in terms of goals. Nonetheless, the enterprise IT capability has to work toward these partnerships and collaboration, particularly as turbulence and change are in the environment.

The Enterprise *Sourcing* Capability Supports Decision Making and Overcomes Bureaucracy (A5)   While strategic sourcing is required, the additional complications of management multiorganizational relationships, costs, and contracts, and all the aspects of formal processes and relationships, can add time and reduce flexibility, in effect adding to the bureaucracy.

IT Management Provides Necessary Leadership for *Sourcing* Enterprise Capabilities, with Emphasis on Culture, Trust, and Partnership with the Business (B2)   IT management in most circumstances is the prime agent in dealing with sourcing organizations, but not always. To the extent business units get directly involved (e.g., with cloud), complexity is added. This creates a real leadership requirement—and opportunity.

The Enterprise *Sourcing* Capability Establishes Accountability for the Processes and Outcomes (B5)   Accountability is central to achieving performance and ultimately building credibility. This includes the problems of matching demand and supply and providing needed direction for future planning.

Strategic IT Management: The Business Outcomes with Sourcing

Five of the eight enterprise IT capability business outcomes requirements apply particularly to *Sourcing*.

The Enterprise *Sourcing* Capability Delivers or Supports Innovation and Change (D2) This can be a challenge, as sourcing, if not done well, adds to the inflexibility. At the same time, a strategic element of sourcing is to provide access to skills and capabilities not otherwise available and to bring these capabilities to the enterprise. Broadening the enterprise's access to new technologies and providing insights into how they may be applied can be a crucial contributor.

The Enterprise *Sourcing* Capability Delivers or Supports Cost and Risk Mitigation (D4) Cost is often the rationale for sourcing, but not to the exclusion of performance. At the same time, reducing risk to such problems as obsolescence, skills availability, and change management can also be a critical reason for sourcing.

The Enterprise *Sourcing* Capability Enables the Development of Business Solutions and Plans Quickly Enough (E2) The focus is on speed here, and the introduction of more organizations can be an impediment. The enterprise IT capability has to focus on not letting this become a problem; it combines governance issues with the whole strategic sourcing management aspects of the sourcing relationships.

The Enterprise *Sourcing* Capability Enables or Supports the Faster Deployment of Solutions (E3) Operational changes based on new developments are often an issue with external providers. At the same time, outsourced development—which can include software acquisition—can be a rational source based on flexibility and speed.

The Enterprise *Sourcing* Capability Delivers or Supports Adaptability and Flexibility in Its Solutions (E4) This summarizes the prior point, where sourcing can introduce risks to the flexibility and adaptability of future IT solutions to business issues. Turbulence and change provide the context for concern for this risk.

Sourcing Scorecard

Exhibits 14.11 and 14.12 provide self-assessment for the system and business outcome enterprise IT capability requirements. Exhibit 14.13 gives the self-assessment scales.

Exhibit 14.11   Strategic IT Management: The Systemic Capabilities for Producing the Outcomes with *Sourcing*

Requirements for Trust, Partnership, Leadership, and Services	Importance	Status
To what extent does the existing *Sourcing* enterprise IT capability build credibility through IT's execution and performance? *Specifically, are the "end points" achieved? (A1)*		
To what extent does the existing *Sourcing* enterprise IT capability add to and trust between organizations? (A2)		
To what extent does the existing *Sourcing* enterprise IT capability enable or strengthen partnerships and collaboration at all levels and with all IT sources? (A4)		
To what extent does the existing *Sourcing* enterprise IT capability support decision making and overcome bureaucracy? (A5)		
To what extent does IT management provide necessary leadership for the *Sourcing* enterprise capabilities, with emphasis on culture, trust, and partnership with the business? (B2)		
To what extent does this *Sourcing* enterprise IT capability establish accountability for the processes and outcomes? (B5)		

Exhibit 14.12   Strategic IT Management: The Business Outcomes with *Sourcing*

Requirement for Outcomes	Importance	Status
To what extent does the existing *Sourcing* enterprise IT capability deliver or support innovation and change? (D2)		
To what extent does the existing *Sourcing* enterprise IT capability deliver or support cost and risk mitigation? (D4)		
To what extent does the existing *Sourcing* enterprise IT capability enable the development of business solutions and plans quickly enough? (E2)		
To what extent does the existing *Sourcing* enterprise IT capability enable or support the faster deployment of solutions? (E3)		
To what extent does the existing *Sourcing* enterprise IT capability deliver or support adaptability and flexibility in its solutions? (E4)		

Exhibit 14.13   Scales for Self-Assessment

Description	Importance Column		Status Column	
The *Importance* reflects the degree management is concerned, and the extent to which this requirement will influence business success in the future.	0	Not Applicable	0	Not Applicable
	5	This requirement is critical to the enterprise	5	Current *Sourcing* activities often produce the required outcome
The *Status* reflects the extent to which the requirements statement is achieved today.	4	This requirement is very important to the enterprise	4	Current *Sourcing* activities sometimes produce the required outcome
	3	This requirement is of some importance to the enterprise	3	The required outcome is not produced through *Sourcing* activities
	2	This requirement is interesting but not important	2	Current *Sourcing* Activities sometimes make the outcome worse
	1	This requirement is not important to the enterprise	1	Current *Sourcing* activities often make the outcome worse

The reader is encouraged to revisit the Chapter 11 section named "Assessing Enterprise Performance against Requirements" and apply all 21 requirements to *Sourcing*.

Bottom Line: *Sourcing* Performance

It comes down to three fundamental questions:

1. Do those who participate in *Sourcing* activities (e.g., IT, business, consultants, etc.) actually perform well and produce the required business outcomes? Does IT perform?
2. Will the *Sourcing* activities add to trust and partnership?
3. Do the *Sourcing* outcomes address change and flexibility sufficiently?

This is what Strategic IT Management and enterprise IT capabilities are about: getting positive answers to the three questions.

Enterprise IT Capability: *Cost & Performance*

The purpose of the *Cost & Performance* enterprise IT capability is to make the complete set of costs and performance metrics applicable to and transparent to the complete set of IT users, with primary focus on business units, internal processes, and products/services. Exhibit 14.14 summarizes objectives, example business outcomes, and methodologies commonly used.

The processes and methodologies can range from cost allocation and assignment to chargebacks, including such activities as TCO and transaction costing. The objective is complete business-based visibility on *Cost & Performance*; turbulence and uncertainty adds both pace-of-change and performance metrics in changing conditions. Accordingly, the *Cost & Performance* enterprise IT capability focuses on providing transparent, comprehensive cost information for all IT used in the business, and on providing effective business-linked performance metrics for IT.

To provide complete pictures of costs and performance, all sources of IT are included, covering sources, cloud providers, in-house IT units, and do-it-yourself computing. This links (service) portfolio management cost information (see the *Service & Resources Optimization* section in Chapter 13) with budgeting, costing (including activities such as charge-out) and project development (see the *Development & Transformation* section in Chapter 13).

Our mantra is "If you don't know cost, you don't know anything." And it is true; a clear picture of cost throughout all elements of enterprise IT is required for transparency, trust, effective decision making, risks assessment, and planning. And yet few enterprise managements have that clear view. This is enormously problematic in building trust and partnership, for cost transparency and openness are critical components of trust. The business wants to know: Where are we spending our company's IT resources? Which are the

Exhibit 14.14 *Cost & Performance*

Enterprise IT Capability	Strategic IT Management Objective	Example Outcomes for Superior Value	Example Outcomes for Superior Response to Turbulence	Example Methods
Cost & Performance	Create trust with transparency in IT *Cost & Performance*	Complete business-based visibility on *Cost & Performance*	Comprehensive *Cost & Performance* in changing conditions	• IT Service Finance • IT Performance Metrics

poorest performing compared to cost? Who's accountable for the *Cost &
Performance* of the IT services delivered to the business? An interesting and
modest question is this: What percentage of our IT resources supports
revenue-producing activities versus supporting the back office? Typically,
less than half of IT cost—from the IT organization's perspective—supports
revenue-producing activities. However, when including other sources
of IT (sourced, cloud, do it yourself), the ratios are reversed. As one of
our CIO clients remarked, "How can you manage the place without this
information?"[5]

What Is the *Cost & Performance* Enterprise IT Capability?

In Chapter 1, we say that "an enterprise requires the capability to capture and
analyze the complete IT costs for all sources and applications of information
and IT, and describe its IT performance requirements and metrics, from the
business perspective."

The *Cost & Performance* problem is similar to those mentioned earlier for
other capabilities. First, enterprise management practices typically do not
connect appropriate cost management to IT service providers, other than
traditional cost center–based accounting. In ITIL terms, it is the equivalent of
knowing the full cost (all costs included) for the ITIL service catalog as well as
all other elements of IT services. Second, the cost reporting that does exist (or
perhaps is embodied in billing rates for services) typically does not reflect 100
percent of all IT costs, even for a central IT organization. Third, none of the
alternative sources of IT is included in consistent fashion (e.g., do-it-yourself
computing, cloud-provided services, internal business unit IT activities). Our
experience, based on research and practice, is that typically less than half of the
enterprise IT costs are included in the IT organization's budgets—and often
much less. Finally, common standards for cost identification and assignment
typically do not exist across the enterprise. So the problems with cost at the
enterprise level are based on the inability to have consistent information from
all sources of IT and for all users of IT (the business units). The enterprise IT
capability makes this connection.

But the issue is not "knowing cost "alone—it is knowing cost about things
that are relevant to the business. Knowing the cost of technology components
does not really matter to the business; rather, it is the cost of the service
delivered to the business. The unit cost of services, for example, is compelling;
yet this information typically is not available.

As an example mental model for cost, Exhibit 14.15 shows a comprehensive cost model applied in multiple organizations, using common and
standard elements and reflecting the cost of IT services tied to the
consumption of services and to the provision of those services to business

Exhibit 14.15   Example Cost Model

	Planning & Innovation	Information & Intelligence	Development & Transformation	Service & Resource Optimization	Service & Operational Excellence	Sourcing	Cost & Performance	Total
Rank: The Processes Employed Create the Trust/ Partnership/ Leadership Outcomes	2	2	1	4	6	7	5	
Rank: The Enterprise IT Capabilty Contributes to Business Outcomes	2	2	2	2	6	1	7	

activities (e.g., unit costs of business transactions). This IT cost mental model emphasizes:

- Cost of each of the basic IT services: applications, projects, infrastructures, user services, management
- Cost of these IT services to each business unit
- Transaction costs for the data acquired and managed
- Total cost of ownership for all assets, including applications

For performance, the same issues apply, namely lack of common metrics for all IT sources, the inability to combine and compare performance across the enterprise, and the limitations of perspective, say, only including the central IT organization. And in particular, metrics about IT performance in IT terms (e.g., "up time") are not nearly as helpful as metrics connected to the services actually delivered to the business, in business terms.

Cost & Performance, however, link directly to their critical enterprise IT capabilities. Without good information, planning is more difficult, resource optimization is more difficult, and operational excellence is more difficult. *Cost & Performance* is foundational, and connects into a fundamental understanding of service costing, IT budgeting, IT chargeback if used, portfolio management, and service performance.

The End Point

The key elements of the *Cost & Performance* enterprise IT capability:

1. Includes all IT costs, no matter the IT source (e.g., cloud-based, do-it-yourself IT); applies the same cost models to all sources of IT
2. Provides transparency of costs to the business, including for each business unit and function
3. Engages business in developing and applying the relevant cost models
4. Connects to the enterprise financial processes, including budgeting and general ledger
5. Provides a framework for IT budgeting, both in the IT organizations and in the relevant business units
6. Establishes a model also applicable to business processes, allowing full costing of those processes
7. Applies business-based performance metrics[6]
8. Covers the five IT service profiles: applications, direct infrastructure, technical (user) services, project services, and IT management services (see Chapter 8 for definitions)
9. Achieves business outcomes such as those listed in Exhibit 14.16

The reader can ask whether these end-point attributes accurately describe the current practices in the enterprise and whether they apply to all IT sources in the IT ecosystem (e.g., sourcers, cloud).

The key outcomes are shown in Exhibit 14.16.

The Enterprise IT Capability Requirements

Chapter 11 described the 22 enterprise IT capability requirements, in two categories: systemic requirements and business outcomes requirements.

Systemic Capabilities for Producing the Outcomes with Cost & Performance

Seven of the 14 systemic Enterprise IT Capability requirements apply particularly to *Cost & Performance*.

The Existing Enterprise *Sourcing* Capability Builds Credibility through IT's Execution and Performance (A1)   Specifically, are the end points listed in the previous section achieved?

The Enterprise *Cost & Performance* Capability Adds to Trust between Organizations (A2)   IT cost transparency provides the foundation for trust

Exhibit 14.16 Example Outcomes for *Cost & Performance*

TVPM	Execution and Performance: The Actual Outcomes as the Basis for Credibility and Trust	
	Cost & Performance Examples: Execution and Performance Business Outcomes for "Superior Business Value"	*Cost & Performance* Examples: Execution and Performance Business Outcomes for "Superior Response to Turbulence and Uncertainty"
Business Outcomes & Program Selection	• Effective business change management • Priorities based on business strategies and requirements • Clarity and agreement on business priorities	• Establish platforms for change • Adaptability beyond individual business units • Enterprise-wide applicability
Project Development & Benefit Realization	• Successfully implemented and operationalized projects • Access to a domain of relevant and valuable data	• Adaptable solutions • Integratable solutions • Dynamic capabilities
Service Delivery	• Supports cost and risk mitigation • Meets requirements • Provides cost transparency • Provides performance transparency	• Flexible and adaptable

between IT and business. Too often, the business units only know the aggregate IT budget cost for the central IT organization and do not understand the cost of IT services they consume, or the costs of internal business unit or do-it-yourself IT. All of this makes trust difficult; the key goal for this capability is to provide that information.

This may or may not drive cost allocation processes, something that depends on the enterprise culture and management team goals. But even centralized budgets can be transparent, along with the assignment of costs to the consumers of IT in the business units.

The methodologies for doing this need not be complex, but do require something more than the usual general ledger. Assigning all IT costs to the five IT service portfolios is the starting point, for achieving the goal of transparency is best met by knowing the cost of services provided and used.

The Enterprise *Cost & Performance* Capability Adds to Stakeholder Trust (A3) Cost transparency applies to each manager and executive as well.

This is particularly apparent where IT is a major component of cost in an operating unit or business unit and where business management has budget and/or bottom-line responsibility. When IT costs are subordinated to some form of corporate allocations, with no cause-and-effect between user patterns, trust plummets.

The core idea is whether costs are management and portrayed in such a way that user initiatives—affecting usage, new requirements, or strategic initiatives—demonstrably affect the IT costs assigned, or allocated to, the business management specifically and the organization in general.

The Enterprise *Cost & Performance* Capability Supports Decision Making and Overcomes Bureaucracy (B1)   We remark often: "If you don't know cost you don't know anything." This especially applies to all the elements of decision making about business performance and about IT. Exhibit 14.17 shows a generic view of where IT decisions are made, ranging from strategic planning through annual budgeting and individual project approvals. In all cases, having the relevant cost and business performance information at hand is crucial.

Exhibit 14.17 is a mental model of the (annual) planning process many enterprises follow. Often the most critical decisions are made in the areas indicated: strategic business planning, strategic IT planning, project planning, and budgeting. In all of these areas, cost is an important component, and forms the basis of management decisions.

However, such a mental model tends to imply one process, applied enterprise-wide, to one IT Supply organization. Reality is much more complicated, so care must be taken in thinking about this process as it applies to all business units and all IT sources. In particular, these steps can be bureaucratic, particularly as they are applied in a one-size-fits-all context across the

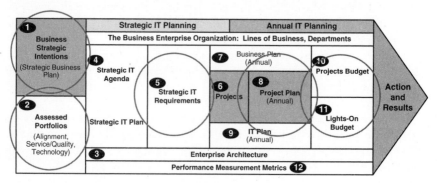

Exhibit 14.17   Example Enterprise Processes
Source: This diagram was introduced and descirbed in Robert J. Benson, Thomas L. Bugnitz, and William Walton: From Business Strategy to IT Action, (Wiley, 2004).

enterprise. This adds time and reduces sensitivity to the specific issues in each business unit and IT providing organization.

IT Management Provides Leadership for the Enterprise *Cost & Performance* **Capability with Emphasis on Culture, Trust, and Partnership with the Business (B2)**   IT management often drives these planning processes and so has a strong influence on their flexibility, speed, and applicability to the specific issues of each business unit. A strong tendency toward one size fits all can exist and needs to be overcome.

But more importantly, resistance to being transparent about costs is often observed in IT leadership. This can be seen as adding complexity to the processes of getting business management support for needed IT investments. This issue is exacerbated in issues of infrastructure investment and technology renewal and in business units' perception that they are being overlooked in favor of other business units. IT management needs to provide the leadership overcome these issues and to encourage and support the *Cost & Performance* transparency required.

Business Management Provides Leadership for the Enterprise *Cost & Performance* **Capability with Emphasis on Culture, Trust, and Partnership with IT (B3)**   Similarly, business management provides direction and leadership for working with IT *Cost & Performance* matters. Reluctance can be seen here as well, particularly when there is fear of exposing cost patterns of IT utilization in a business unit, where the visibility may prove inimical to that particular business unit. This can be seen particularly in the case of back-office business functions, where overall the idea of IT investments can be met with reluctance. Business leadership, especially the CEO and the senior leadership group, needs to provide the needed direction and leadership to overcome these problems.

The Enterprise *Cost & Performance* **Capability Produces Forecasts, Measurements, and Monitoring (C4)**   The power of *Cost & Performance* information drives forecasting and monitoring. Mentioned previously in the planning context, this capability applies across all business decision-making and planning activities.

The Business Outcomes from Cost & Performance

Three of the eight Business Outcome requirements for enterprise IT capabilities apply particularly to *Cost & Performance*.

Delivers or Supports Business Operational Effectiveness (D3)   Operational effectiveness includes cost. But it also includes making the right decisions about costs. Therefore, knowing cost and connecting the requirements to operational excellence is paramount.

Delivers or Supports Cost and Risk Mitigation (D4)   Obviously, transparency cost information is central to this.

Delivers or Supports Adaptability and Flexibility in Its Solutions (E4)   At the same time, it is not good to add bureaucracy and time-consuming processes.

Cost & Performance Scorecard

Exhibit 14.18 and Exhibit 14.19 apply the systemic and business outcome requirements in a self-assessment scorecard. Exhibit 14.20 provides the self assessment scale.

Exhibit 14.18   Strategic IT Management: System Capabilities for Producing the Outcomes with *Cost & Performance*

Requirements for Trust, Partnership, Leadership, and Services	Importance	Status
To what extent does the existing *Cost & Performance* enterprise IT capability build credibility through IT's execution and performance? *Specifically, are the "end points" achieved?* (A1)		
To what extent does the existing *Cost & Performance* enterprise IT capability add to and trust between organizations? (A2)		
To what extent does the existing *Cost & Performance* enterprise IT capability add to stakeholder trust? (A3)		
To what extent does the existing *Cost & Performance* enterprise IT capability support decision making and overcome bureaucracy? (A5)		
To what extent does IT management provide necessary leadership for the *Cost & Performance* enterprise capabilities, with emphasis on culture, trust, and partnership with the business? (B2)		
To what extent does business management provide necessary leadership for this *Cost & Performance* enterprise IT capability, with emphasis on culture, trust, and partnership with IT? (B3)		
To what extent does the existing *Cost & Performance* enterprise IT capability apply holistically across silos, organizations, and other processes? (C2)		
To what extent does the existing *Cost & Performance* enterprise IT capability produce forecasts, measurements, and monitoring? (C4)		

Exhibit 14.19   Strategic IT Management: The Business Outcomes from *Cost & Performance*

Requirement for Outcomes	Importance	Status
To what extent does the existing *Cost & Performance* enterprise IT capability deliver or support business operational effectiveness? (D3)		
To what extent does the existing *Cost & Performance* enterprise IT capability deliver or support cost and risk mitigation? (D4)		
To what extent does the existing *Cost & Performance* enterprise IT capability deliver or support adaptability and flexibility in its solutions? (E4)		

The reader is encouraged to revisit the Chapter 11 section named "Assessing Enterprise Performance against Requirements" and apply all 21 requirements to *Cost & Performance*.

Exhibit 14.20   Self-Assessment Scales

Description	Importance Column		Status Column	
The *Importance* reflects the degree management is concerned, and the extent to which this requirement will influence business success in the future.	0	Not Applicable	0	Not Applicable
	5	This requirement is critical to the enterprise	5	Current *Cost & Performance* activities often produce the required outcome
The *Status* reflects the extent to which the requirements statement is achieved today.	4	This requirement is very important to the enterprise	4	Current *Cost & Performance* activities sometimes produce the required outcome
	3	This requirement is of some importance to the enterprise	3	The required outcome is not produced through *Cost & Performance* activities
	2	This requirement is interesting but not important	2	Current *Cost & Performance* Activities sometimes make the outcome worse
	1	This requirement is not important to the enterprise	1	Current *Cost & Performance* activities often make the outcome worse

Bottom Line: *Cost & Performance* **Performance**

It comes down to three fundamental questions:

1. Do those who participate in *Cost & Performance* activities (e.g., IT, business, consultants, etc.) actually perform well and produce the required business outcomes? Does IT perform?
2. Will the *Cost & Performance* activities add to trust and partnership?
3. Do the *Cost & Performance* outcomes address change and flexibility sufficiently?

This is what Strategic IT Management and enterprise IT capabilities are about: getting positive answers to the three questions.

Summary: Operational Enterprise IT Capabilities and Competencies

We remarked at the beginning of the chapter that these three enterprise IT capabilities should perhaps have come first, before planning and tactical capabilities. The reason is that operational competence, represented in *Sourcing*, *Service & Operational Excellence*, and *Cost & Performance*, is the core of IT creditably and hence trust and partnership with the business. Placing these topics at the end perhaps sends the message that they are not as critical. And indeed, the amount of rhetoric devoted to these three in Chapter 14 is less than the rhetoric in Chapters 12 and 13 for the first four enterprise IT capabilities.

Any such interpretation is unfortunate, and this is emphasized by the TVPM introduced in Part I. As Exhibit 14.21 shows and as Chapters 2 and 3 described, the whole definition of value/performance/credibility is built on the ability to perform, and *Service & Operational Excellence* applied to all IT services is critical to this. *Sourcing* reflects competence in procuring or supplying those services, and *Cost & Performance* reflects competence and transparency in the execution of those services.

The fundamental message is, if IT can't perform, then all the discussions about strategy, development, information, and resource optimization simply are not appropriate. But the goal is not just to "perform," it is to do so with the characteristics we have emphasized, such as trust and partnership, holistically and completely engaging the business. This is, ultimately, the first and fundamental challenge, and the self-assessments should provide guidance as to the need to pay attention to these foundational enterprise IT capabilities.

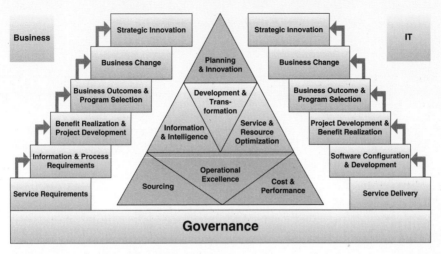

Exhibit 14.21   Total Value Performance Model

Notes

1. See our discussion of strategic effectiveness and operational effectiveness in Chapter 12 and in Robert J. Benson, Thomas Bugnitz, and William Walton, *From Business Strategy to IT Action* (Wiley, 2004).
2. See M. Treacy and F. Wiersma, "Customer Intimacy and Other Value Disciplines," *Harvard Business Review* (January-February 1993): 84–93. Also see M. Treacy and F. Wiersma, *The Discipline of Market Leaders: Choose Your Customers, Narrow Your Focus, Dominate Your Market* (HarperCollins, 1995).
3. See, for example, "Failures of IT Operations," in Charles T. Betz, *Architecture and Patterns for Services Management, Resource Planning, and Governance* (Morgan Kaufman, 2007): 6.
4. See definitions provided in Chapters 1, 11, and 12.
5. See Chapter 10, "Funding IT," in Keri E. Pearlman and Carol S. Saunders, "The Tools for Change," chapter in *Managing and Using Information Systems: A Strategic Approach*, 4th ed. (Wiley, 2010).
6. See, for example, Michael J. Mauboussin, "The True Measures of Success," *Harvard Business Review* (October 2012): 46–56.

CHAPTER 15

Managing Complex Business–IT Relationships

Tere is little research on how to manage complex business–IT relationships, neither with an internal IT department nor with external service providers. With respect to the latter, most of the literature has focused on the desirability of IT outsourcing, not on managing the relationship. It is clear, however, that relying on procedures alone, like service-level agreements (SLAs), is not sufficient for effective management of complex relationships. As part of a research program at Tilburg University, 14 case studies of European multinational companies with global or pan-European operations[1] were analyzed in order to understand what factors or conditions contribute to the success of, in particular, complex outsourcing relationships. To determine whether a case was successful, we applied 10 measures of success. The measures included both hard and soft criteria. Hard criteria encompass realization of goals, realization of service levels, expansion of the scope of the contract, absence of escalation of conflicts, and contract renewal. Soft criteria include customer satisfaction, active communication, involvement, culture fit, and trust. All the investigated cases met at least eight of the 10 criteria for success. Also, at the end of the contract period, all investigated contracts were renewed except for two cases, which were not renewed for reasons related to external market conditions.

Although this study focused typically on outsourcing, we feel the same factors that make an outsourcing relationship successful apply equally in the case of an internal IT operation. In an outsourcing cases, there is a relationship between service recipients and service providers, and the case of an internal IT operation is no different. What differs in outsourcing is that companies have their own profit and loss (P&L) statements and have no common hierarchy. Outsourcing, therefore, only makes it more difficult to create a successful relationship between two separate and distinct entities.

Complex business–IT relationships can typically be defined as multisite, multivendor, internal and external IT-service provisioning relationships. The underlying contracts and SLAs include service delivery commitments for more than one internal or external IT supplier in more than one site and involve multiple services. They often concern a contract value of at least US$20 million. The services in the investigated IT outsourcing relationships include a very broad scope of IT services. The service recipients in these cases operate in different sectors. The contract values vary from US$0.4 million total contract value to a yearly contract value of US$550 million. The IT suppliers in all cases are Atos, a French computer services provider, and Origin, the Netherlands-based IT-services subsidiary of Royal Philips Electronics, which merged on January 1, 2001. In 2011, the company showed a pro forma revenue of EUR 8.5 billion and had 74,000 employees in 48 countries. Serving a global client base, it delivers high-tech transactional services, consulting and technology services, systems integration, and managed services.[2] In addition to the case study interviews, experts from leading consulting organizations in senior positions with at least five years of experience in outsourcing were interviewed.

From these cases, three factors appear to be critical for a successful business–IT relationship: a clear strategic positioning, formal organizational arrangements that allow for adequate collaboration, and the existence of trust.

Clear Strategic Positioning

The business needs a clear vision on what it wants to accomplish with IT. Business strategies and IT strategies are closely related, and often integrated. Shaping the business and IT strategies is a matter of co-creation between business and IT and is an integral responsibility of the senior management team.

In the case of outsourcing of IT, the need for clear strategic positioning of both the service recipient and the IT services supplier is unanimously supported by all case study companies and experts. The client organizations should have a clear view with respect to their use of IT, IT services, and role these play in their company. Clear IT strategies show service providers the direction in which their clients intend to move. Formulating this strategy remains the responsibility of the client organization and, as such, is not a candidate for outsourcing. While this IT strategy is the responsibility of the CIO, the contribution of the business and in particular that of the CEO is indispensable. In addition, senior managers must be highly involved in determining the IT services that their company needs. The pressure to do so grows as IT services and business processes become increasingly interdependent. In the case of outsourcing parts of the IT operations, if the company is not clear in what it wants, many providers will react to a request for proposal with a no-bid response. On the other side, service providers, both internal and external, must be able to show their clients and potential clients what IT services they can deliver and how. This includes their plans for the future, which form the basis of any business–IT partnership. In the case of outsourcing, companies make a first selection of service providers on the basis of their profiles, focusing on information such as their vision on the future, their product portfolios, and the market segments in which they operate. Only providers who make the selection short list are sent a request for proposal.

Formal Organizational Arrangements

Formal organizational arrangements for managing and monitoring the relationship are essential. They include structural provisions to support communication and collaboration between the service recipient and supplier, such as the organization and location of the IS/IT functions (outlining clearly defined roles and responsibilities), and the diversity of IT/business committees needed to support the relationship.[3]

Structural provisions are necessary on both the recipient's and the supplier's side of the relationship. Client organizations have to adequately structure their information management function, which represents their demand management and constitutes the interface between the business processes and the IT supplier. The role of the CIO is key in this regard. (S)he is ultimately responsible for the company's IT strategy and the optimal use of the IT services delivered. In a European context, the CIO, representing the demand side of IT services, will not be the manager of the internal IT department; such a manager is responsible for the execution of IT services delivery, which is the supplier side. The two functions combined are supposed to cause a conflict of interest. As a result a separate IT director has to be appointed, one whose main responsibility is to optimize the use of internal IT capacity in terms of IT professionals, hardware, and software. It goes without saying that adequate tuning between the two functions is necessary, especially with regard to the introduction of new technologies.

Typically, the information managers report to the CIO; their main responsibility is to ensure that the information needs of the business are met by the IT services provided. They form the link between the business units and their service providers. Also, for this reason, there may be a functional accountability to business managers. Keeping internal and external IT service providers on track is a difficult task and requires significant coordination and consultation, especially with regard to aligning delivery of diverse services. Under conditions of change and turbulence, information managers can contribute to the flexibility of services provided. In this situation, the organizational position of information managers may be adapted, so that hierarchically they report to business managers, while reporting functionally to the CIO.[4] By maintaining good relationships with the business, they can react quickly and ensure adequate and up-to-date service delivery. However, success depends on the excellent communication skills of the staff directly involved.

These formal arrangements are present in all of the cases investigated in the study. Each outsourcing company had a well-developed information management (IM) function in place to represent company interests in the relationship with the suppliers. In all cases, these IM functions are independent of the internal IT department to avoid conflicts of interests. When economically feasible, the IM function is set up per business unit.

The IT services supplier, be it an internal department or an external company, has to carefully structure contract and account management (CAM), which operates as the counterpart of the IM function of the client organization. It is important that service recipients and service providers can contact each other easily. Account management is about maintaining and building one's relationship with the client. The service provider must build a network of relationships within the recipient's organization as well as staying ahead of the developments in their industry.[5] The provider's contract managers represent the second major contact for the recipient next to their specific account managers.

Contract management involves optimizing the contractual agreements between supplier and client. It also requires managing the IT professionals who execute the work, as well as taking care of the administrative aspects of the relationship, including reporting. As a result, service providers have to make allowances for substantial costs involved in ·contract management.[6] These findings are supported by all our interviews. With respect to structuring CAM, all the experts interviewed agreed: "The structure of the CAM must mirror the structure of the outsourcing company." In all of the cases studied but one, there is a mirrored structure with a consensus that this contributes to successfully managing IT outsourcing partnerships. Only in one case was CAM part of a larger CAM organization, which was responsible for a large number of complex IT outsourcing partnership contracts. The effect was a relative lack of attention from the CAM for this IT outsourcing partnership, resulting in a damaged relationship. As the CA manager said, "The responsibilities for the CAM and the service delivery are embedded in one role. This results in possible conflicts of interest. The contract manager is responsible for customer satisfaction and the service delivery manager [for] utilizing the service delivery capabilities." A major point of attention for CAM is continuity of personnel in CAM positions. Changeover results in discontinuity in the management of the partnership and endangers the continuity of service delivery.

Organizational arrangements also include a diversity of business–IT committees and coordinating roles to support communication and collaboration between service recipient and supplier. It is essential that senior managers of both provider and recipient can easily contact one another; this relates not only to the CIO but also to the recipient's business managers, who must have an easy access to the provider's senior managers. As such, these organizational arrangements facilitate active participation and cooperation between principle stakeholders, strategic dialogue, and shared learning and dialogue.[7]

Regular communication between the client organization and the IT suppliers is essential in establishing flexible partnership relationships.[8] The communication structure of most of the investigated case studies is similar and organized on three management levels.[9] There is a steering committee at the strategic level, which includes senior management and IT management for the service recipient, and senior management and account management for the IT service provider. Meetings typically take place once or twice a year. On a tactical level, there is a need for a service review meeting to monitor overall ongoing performance and to anticipate the service recipient's future requirements. These meetings usually take place on a monthly basis. Here, service provider performance is discussed on the basis of regular reporting and related to service-level management processes. On the operational level, employees of the IT supplier have daily discussions with the information managers concerning operational issues.

The case study companies with an adequate communication structure show a similarly clear and layered arrangement between the service recipient and service provider. At each level, the authorizations and topics to be discussed are detailed and described in the outsourcing contract.

A key element in communication between service provider and recipient is reporting. To track service delivery, the IT supplier must report on a regular basis regarding the IT services delivered to the service recipient and the level at which they were delivered.[10,11] For most of the outsourcing contracts studied, this required monthly reporting.[12] The report provides input for discussions between the outsourcing company and the IT suppliers. It is a critical component in managing the outsourcing relationship. In five of the investigated case studies, inadequate reporting hindered the IT outsourcing relationship. Most of the problems were related to technically oriented reporting as opposed to reporting on more business-related items using metrics such as balanced scorecards and dashboards. For all outsourcing relationships, it is essential that reporting is discussed between the parties. All cases in the study scheduled monthly meetings for this purpose.

The relationship between service recipient and provider is formalized in a contract, which may also include (multiple) SLAs. Contracts and SLAs form the basis for collaboration. It is important that the responsibilities of all players are completely clear. Contracts need to unambiguously define the IT services to be provided, including who is responsible for which tasks and deliverables.

However, business dynamics and the developments in the field of technology are such that unexpected situations will always crop up. For this reason, contract parties should include agreements on how to deal with situations not described in the contract. However, as previously stated, contracts and SLAs are not always sufficient for maintaining successful relationships in complex outsourcing relationships. There is still one element missing.

Trust

As said before, and as a key theme of this book, managing the business–IT relationship is not a matter of the "hard side" alone. Much attention must be paid to the "soft side"—especially, trust between the service recipient and their providers is of the highest importance. Such trust has to be created and maintained on an organizational level as well as between individuals. Open formal and informal communication through the structures discussed earlier is instrumental to this.

A purposeful organizational policy that contributes to the creation of mutual trust is establishing relational mechanisms at all levels.[13] The objective of relational mechanisms is to facilitate open two-way communication, active collaboration, and knowledge sharing. This may be achieved by measures like physically locating business and IT people close to each other, job rotation where business managers assume managerial responsibilities for IT and vice versa, cross-training about the value-adding role of IT in the business, and informal meetings between business and IT management. Of course this will challenge the comfort zones of all concerned. All these measures can work if and only if they are actively stimulated by the senior management team. This all starts, of course, with senior management giving a good example. Again, the case of outsourcing is no different, only more difficult. Both service recipient and external service provider have to actively assess how and what relational mechanisms may improve the collaboration on both the organizational level and personal level.

While these measures are worth pursuing under all circumstances, they are especially required under dynamic environmental conditions, which impose flexible adaptation by both recipient and provider. Trust provides the glue for a flexible relationship between the organizations concerned, allowing them to sustain the relationship over the strategic planning horizon.[14]

Notes

1. This research was done as a part of a research program at Tilburg University. For a complete report on the validation of the conclusions, we refer to E. Beulen and P. Ribbers, "Governance

of Complex IT Outsourcing Partnerships," in *Information Technology Outsourcing*, ed. L S. Rivard and B. Aubert (M. E. Sharpe, 2008). More extensive analyses are provided in E. Beulen, P. Ribbers, and J. Roos, *Managing IT Outsourcing*, 2nd ed. (Routledge, 2011).

2. http://atos.net/en-us/home/we-are/company-profile.html; consulted on August 7, 2012; verified November 19, 2013.
3. W. Van Grembergen and S. De Haes, *Implementing Information Technology Governance: Models, Practices, and Cases* (IGI Publishing, 2008).
4. E. Beulen, P. Ribbers, and J. Roos, *Managing IT Outsourcing*, 2nd ed. (Routledge, 2011).
5. G. Verra, *International Account Management* (Deventer: Kluwer, 2003).
6. S. Cullen and L. Willcocks, *Intelligent IT Outsourcing: Eight Building Blocks to Success* (Butterworth-Heineman, 2003).
7. Van Grembergen and De Haes, *Implementing Information Technology Governance*.
8. J. N. Lee and Y. G. Kim, "Effect of Partnership Quality on IS Outsourcing Success: Conceptual Framework and Empirical Validation," *Journal of Management Information Systems* 15, No. 4 (1999).
9. Beulen and Ribbers, "Governance of Complex IT Outsourcing Partnerships."
10. P. A. Palvia, "Dialectic View on Information Systems Outsourcing: Pros and Cons," *Information and Management* 29, No. 5 (1995).
11. Cullen and Willcocks, *Intelligent IT Outsourcing*.
12. W. Wallace, "Reporting Practices: Potential Lessons from Cendant Corporation," *European Management Journal* 18, No. 3 (2000).
13. Van Grembergen and De Haes, *Implementing Information Technology Governance*.
14. K. Sabherwal, "The Role of Trust in Outsourced IS Development Projects," *Communications of the Association for Computing Machinery* 42, No. 2 (1999): 80–86.

PART FOUR
Next Steps

T
hroughout the book we've introduced self-assessment instruments that we encouraged readers to apply to their specific enterprise. Taken together, they provide a significant tool for the reader to answer key questions about the current characteristics and status of the enterprise.

Exhibit IV.1, originally introduced in Chapters 2 and 3, provides the context for the next steps. As we emphasized at the end of Chapter 14, if IT cannot perform, all the strategic and tactical enterprise issues become mostly irrelevant. Yet the context for IT's performance has to be the holistic perspective of enterprise and business requirements and expectations, which have been illustrated through the many self-assessment tools provided in all the chapters.

Three business examples illustrate the outcomes of self-assessment along with commentary and recommendations. These examples, although necessarily simplistic, show how the instruments are used. Much more importantly, they demonstrate how Strategic IT Management applies in very different enterprise circumstances, along with the beginning of a roadmap for improvement.

The following questions apply the specific assessments from each chapter. We show here only the summary results here for each question. In reality, consideration of the specific details, shown in the instruments referenced in each question, would be necessary for a full picture. The fundamental importance of trust and partnership underlies these assessments. Questions 9 and 10 address the degree to which enterprise IT capabilities are based on trust and build partnership.

Question 1 from Chapter 1: What is the defining characteristic of the enterprise with respect to business and IT? See Exhibit 1.4, "Changing

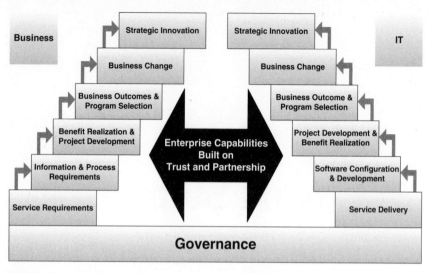

Exhibit IV.1   The Six-Step Total Value Performance Model

Enterprise Characteristics." The assessment focuses on seven specific enterprise characteristics, ranging from the business context through approach to governance, and how business views the relationship. This, overall, sets the context for the description of the enterprise. An important caution: This summary set of questions treats the enterprise as one entity without considering the differences within business units (lines of business) and business functions (e.g., finance, marketing). Our purpose is to flesh out the book's concepts with real examples/cases, but without the complexity of realistic organizations. In reality, consideration of these complexities would be necessary.

Question 2 from Chapter 8: What is the defining characteristic of the enterprise IT sources? See Exhibit 8.4, "IT Service Portfolios and Sources." The issue is the degree to which a central IT organization is the dominant provider, and consequently provides most IT services and, ultimately, the technology and service components for the enterprise IT capabilities.

Question 3 from Chapters 2 and 3: Is the IT/business actually performing? That is, where is the enterprise in terms of the performance of the Total Value Performance Model (TVPM)? How high is the enterprise on the six-step chart? See Exhibit 3.2, "Business Outcomes: Superior Value from IT," and Exhibit IV.2.

Question 4 from Chapter 4: To what extent does environmental or business turbulence determine or define the problems the business faces? The issue is the extent to which turbulence affects the business and whether it has an impact

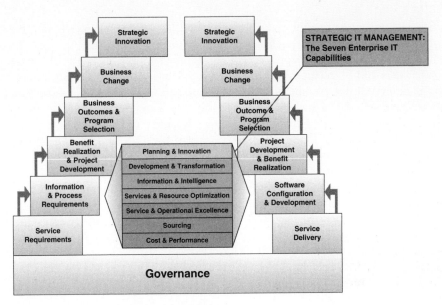

Exhibit IV.2   Seven Enterprise IT Capabilities

on the services IT needs to provide, with particular attention to flexibility and ability to change. This sets the stage for the relative importance (or not) of enterprise IT capabilities. See Exhibit 4.3, "Impact of Turbulence."

Question 5 also from Chapter 4: To what extent is the enterprise producing the business outcomes necessary to successfully cope with turbulence? If turbulence is a significant factor, then the enterprise success in employing information and IT in response is an important consideration. See Exhibit 4.4, "Business Outcomes: Superior Value from IT with Turbulence and Uncertainty."

Question 6 from Chapter 5: Is technical turbulence a defining characteristic of the new opportunities for the enterprise? See Exhibit 5.3, "Turbulence Assessment." While turbulence in IT may challenge IT providers, this turbulence may also present significant competitive opportunities to the business. This sets the stage for the enterprise IT capabilities needed.

Question 7 from Chapter 7: Does the enterprise have the IT competencies required? See Exhibit 7.6, "Strategic IT Competencies in the Enterprise." The chapter identifies 17 specific IT competencies in three groups: strategic, tactical, and operational. These represent skills the IT organization needs to command.

Question 8 from Chapter 8: Is IT managed with (business) service management principles? See Exhibit 8.10, "IT Service Management Scorecard."

This reflects the specific commitment to service delivery characteristics that underlie the competency needed to build trust and partnership.

Question 9 from Chapter 9: Is partnership a defining characteristic of the business and IT relationship? See Exhibit 9.8, "Service Portfolio Scorecard." Built on trust and credibility, commitment to partnership also requires specific management values such as common goals, transparency, and mutual respect.

Question 10 from Chapter 10: Do the CIO and CEO and all their relevant direct reports provide the leadership required? See Exhibit 9.10, "Leadership Scorecard." Addressing the major concerns of partnership and the commitments to enterprise IT capabilities requires leadership.

Question 11 from Chapter 11: Does the enterprise in general possess seven enterprise IT capabilities that build on trust and partnership? See Exhibit 11.4, "Current Enterprise Status." This question is not specific to each enterprise IT capability; rather, overall, do the critical characteristics of any of them (trust, partnership, response to turbulence, etc.) currently exist? Five groupings apply:

Strategic IT Management: The Systemic Capabilities for Producing the Outcomes

- Builds Trust and Partnership between Business(es) and IT(s)
- Provide Business and IT Leadership and Personal Responsibility
- Adapt to Enterprise and Leadership Characteristics and Culture

Strategic IT Management: The Current Enterprise IT Capabilities: The Business Outcomes

- Deliver Superior Business Value
- Deliver Superior Response to Turbulence and Uncertainty

Question 12 from Chapters 12 through 14: Does the enterprise possess each of the necessary enterprise IT capabilities, to the extent required?

Ultimately, however, the most important question is "So what?" While the data contained in these self-assessments that represent descriptions of current status for the enterprise is very interesting, what does it all actually mean to business and IT management? We'll work on some answers here.

This self-assessment process provides data to enable discussion within business and IT management groups about what needs to be done. In these cases, the data comes from the management groups themselves. Like all such data, precision is not the goal; rather, the goal is to identify exactly what the enterprise situation is, the importance of doing something to build the business–IT relationship in trust and partnership terms, and the importance of understanding and building the enterprise IT capabilities. The goal is greatly helped by having actual data. This does not overlook the tremendous opportunities IT has for responding to environmental turbulence and presenting the enterprise with dramatic transformational opportunities. Rather, this increases the chances that the enterprise is in fact capable of performing, of effectively using IT for these purposes.

Part IV goes on to provide more normative means to the same end in Chapters 16 through 19, and identifies the crucial roles the CIO and CEO play in making it all happen.

Example Enterprises

To illustrate the relevance and connection of the concepts and ideas represented by the data, we present here example results from four different enterprises. Our objective: to demonstrate the insights to be derived and the implications for action and "next steps" for each of them. (The actual data reflected here is real, but each enterprise described represents a composite of several different enterprises from the United States, Mexico, and Europe.)

Repeating our cautionary note: We present the following results for each of the four enterprises as a whole, applicable to the enterprise as a single organization, which ignores the reality that the results may be quite different for the individual business units (lines of business) and functional areas. Also we present the following results for the IT organization without considering the other sources of IT (e.g., business unit, cloud, do-it-yourself). And finally, these cases present the enterprise in an "as-is" perspective.

A secondary cautionary note: We want to illustrate the important aspects of Strategic IT Management. To review our definition, this mobilizes enterprise resources—both business and IT—to achieve superior business value and superior response to turbulence and uncertainty. These examples show where each enterprise may be weak in its ability to produce these outcomes; in effect, enterprises may be weak in how they are mobilizing their resources, providing leadership, and measuring their performance. In short, based on the data, enterprise and IT management has work to do, and the examples provide focus as to where that work is needed.

Example #1: Angus International

Angus manufactures "white" goods for retail chains that put their own brands on the product. The company is located in the United States with several manufacturing locations.

From the Strategic IT Management perspective, Angus is best described through the answers to Question 1 from Chapter 1: What are the defining characteristics of the enterprise with respect to business and IT? The self-assessment in Exhibit 1.4 asked for a 1 to 5 range between "traditional" views of the business/IT relationship and the "transformational" view. The latter view embodies the service, partnership, trust, and response to turbulence described in the book. The response for Angus, provided by its senior management team in the strategic planning workshop, is shown in Exhibit IV.3. The management team used the following interpretation of the 5-point scale:

1. Strong Traditional
2. Weak Traditional
3. Equal: Both Apply
4. Weak Transformative
5. Strong Transformative

As we noted earlier, Chapter 1 presented this table in a "From/To" perspective, which suggests that enterprises are, over time, on a journey from the "traditional" to the "transformational" characteristic. One can debate whether this is true for all, though perhaps this is a timing question. However, for our purposes in describing the enterprises in these cases, we use this as an as-is status description.

The assessment in Exhibit IV.3 gave the management team choices between a "traditional" and a "transformative" perspective. For all seven choices, the company team choices fell into the "traditional" or "equal: both apply" categories—with the exception of item seven, IT's view of the relationship. (This is a common outcome.) The answers to the other assessment questions, based on the content in the referenced chapters, are shown below in a single table. We show here only a summarized result; the details for each self-assessment are shown above.

Angus displays fairly strong "traditional" characteristics from the business–IT relationship perspective. The answers to the other 11 questions, leading to directions for addressing its requirements for Strategic IT Management, also reflect this perspective. However, the management team's response to Question 1 begs the question: What if they're wrong, particularly with respect to the statement about industry and environmental stability? For example, in their particular business of providing product to retailers, what if a) Web-enabled customer interfaces become important, b) higher supply chain integration becomes an industry direction, and c) traditional retailers become less a customer base as they themselves address Internet on-line retailers, which Angus would need to be capable of serving? In other words, turbulence always lurks, and may cause shifts in management perspectives. In

Exhibit IV.3   Angus Characteristics

Enterprise Business and IT Characteristics	Traditional Business and IT Management Perspective (the FROM)	Transformative Business and IT Management Perspective (the TO)	Management's Choice
1. Business and IT environment	The business environment is stable, static. Changes come at a relatively constant speed and are not transformational. The business and IT organizations focus on the enterprise level.	The environment is turbulent, dynamic. Change comes in unexpected ways and speeds. The business and IT organizations focus on the business unit/lines of business.	Strong Traditional
2. Management's primary focus for investment, IT business impact	Cost reduction, cost management is key.	Strategic focus, optimal (not lowest) cost is key.	Weak Traditional
3. The key attributes for "good" IT projects.	Stability, well-engineered specifications, responsive to business requirements.	Flexibility, adaptability and responsiveness, modular, meet expectations.	Equal: Both Apply
4. The enterprise approach to IT governance	Hierarchical, orientation to control.	Network, participative, orientation to business problem solving.	Equal: Both Apply
5. IT's basic culture and values	Command the technology. Respond to the business. Service an arm's-length service client.	Know the business, proactive with solutions to business, partner.	Strong Traditional
6. How business views the relationship of IT and business organizations	Business is an IT client, defines requirements. IT operates the technology, provides technical expertise. IT is a sole provider.	Business is viewed as partner, collaborative. IT as a transformative factor; IT functions as partner. Many sources of IT are possible and need management.	Strong Traditional
7. How IT views the relationship of IT and business organizations	IT is reactive to the business. Business is viewed as a client, defines requirements. IT operates the technology, provides technical expertise. IT is a sole provider.	IT is proactive, in collaboration with business partners. Focus on strategic use of IT. Need to manage the many sources of IT.	Weak Transformative

this sense, the use of Exhibit IV.3 as a FROM/TO analysis may be correct, and may suggest how the following answers identify possible problems.

The assessment data about Angus International, as shown in Exhibits IV.3 and IV.4, sets the stage for the final question 11 on Exhibit IV.4, which is the assessment of the Angus enterprise IT capabilities. Presented in Chapters 12, 13, and 14, these enterprise IT capabilities provide the ability for the enterprise to contend successfully with turbulence and, more fundamentally, obtain the best possible competitive and operational value from its IT.

Until this point, the assessments have described the as-is situation without making specific recommendations for management action or concern. Assuming change in some aspects of the current enterprise IT capabilities is necessary, the challenge is to change the existing management perspectives about the business and IT relationship, and to establish the priorities for action (e.g., which enterprise IT capabilities should be the primary focus for change?). In other words, so what?

The first challenge is addressed in Chapters 17 and 18 in terms of the roles the CEO and CIO play in affecting management perspectives. The second challenge is addressed here and in Chapter 16.

What Should Angus Do?

At the end of the enterprise IT capability description, the self-assessment focused on the *importance* this capability is to the enterprise and the *outcomes* currently produced for the enterprise. These outcomes include the business impact: superior business value, superior responses to turbulence, and the process or organizational impact: building trust, leadership, partnership culture.

To review, Angus International is a "traditional" enterprise with little current turbulence and a primarily operational relationship between IT and business. The assessment questions 1 through 11 in the prior section show this. Current IT and business management supplied the answers to the questions through the use of the self-assessment instruments described in the relevant chapters.

Exhibit IV.5 presents the self-assessment results for each of the seven enterprise IT capabilities. Chapter 11 described the complete 21 questions, and the reader is encouraged to review them. The figure below reviews the scales in use for assessing outcomes:

5. The current *Enterprise IT capability* produces the required outcome
4. The current *Enterprise IT capability* often produces the required outcome
3. The current *Enterprise IT capability* occasionally produces the required outcome
2. The current *Enterprise IT capability* rarely produces the required outcome
1. The current *Enterprise IT capability* does not produce the required outcome

Exhibit IV.4   Assessment Angus Capabilities

Q	The Question	The Assessment Issue	Current Status of Angus International
2	Chapter 8: What are the defining characteristics of the enterprise IT sources?	Reflects the degree to which the IT organization provides IT, compared to the other sources.	Almost all IT is sourced from the central IT organization
3	Chapter 2 and 3: Is the IT/Business actually performing? That is, where is the enterprise in terms of the performance of the Total Value Performance Model?	The answer is, how high is the enterprise on the six-step chart?	Angus is performing at Stair Level Two
4	Chapter 4: To what extent does environmental or business turbulence determine or define the problems the business faces?	External business and environmental turbulence. Issue is of importance to the enterprise, and has an impact on IT.	External turbulence is not (currently) a major factor External turbulence has no effect or impact on IT
		Internal (organizational) turbulence.	Internal turbulence adds to cost or decreased revenue Internal turbulence negatively affects the ability of IT to perform
5	Chapter 4: To what extent is the enterprise producing the business outcomes necessary to for turbulence?	Does the enterprise create the kind of results leading to flexibility and change?	Business–IT solutions occasionally have characteristics of flexibility and change.
6	Chapter 5: Is technical turbulence a defining characteristic of the new opportunities for the enterprise?	What is the extent to which change in IT's technology is accelerating, making new business opportunities and strategies possible?	IT turbulences does not (currently) have much effect on business. IT turbulence does not have much effect on how IT delivers services
7	Chapter 7: Does the enterprise have the IT competencies required? The chapter identifies 17 specific IT competencies in three groups: strategic, tactical, and operational. These represent skills the IT organization needs to command.	Strategic competencies: Does enterprise management attach importance to these competencies, and does the IT organization possess them?	Enterprise management is interested but with no relevant activities or initiatives. IT has some competency in the specific IT competencies.
		Tactical competencies: Does enterprise management attach importance to these competencies, and does the IT organization possess them?	These IT competencies have importance to enterprise management. IT has some competency in the specific IT competencies.

(continued)

Exhibit IV.4 *(continued)*

Q	The Question	The Assessment Issue	Current Status of Angus International
		Operational competencies: Does enterprise management attach importance to these competencies, and does the IT organization possess them?	The IT competencies are very important to enterprise management. IT is competent in the specific IT competencies.
8	Chapter 8: Is IT managed with (business) service management principles?	Application of the five service management parameters. This reflects specific commitment to service delivery.	IT services are delivered with an acceptable level of (business) service management.
9	Chapter 9: Is partnership a defining characteristic of the business–IT relationship.	Built on trust and credibility, commitment to partnership also requires specific management values such as common goals, transparency, mutual respect.	Business view: Rarely are partnership values expressed. IT view: Rarely are partnership values expressed.
10	Chapter 10: Do the CIO, the CEO, and all their relevant direct reports provide the leadership required?	Addressing the major concerns of partnership and the commitments to enterprise IT capabilities require leadership.	CEO: does not provide leadership about IT matters. CIO: does sometimes provide leadership on culture, etc.
11	Chapter 11: Does the enterprise in general possess enterprise IT capabilities?	This is not specific to each enterprise IT capability; rather, overall, do the critical characteristics of any of them—trust, partnership, response to turbulence, etc.—currently exist?	• Builds trust and partnership between business and IT: No • Provide business and IT leadership and personal responsibility: Some • Adapt to enterprise and leadership characteristics and culture: No • Deliver superior business value: Some • Deliver superior response to turbulence and uncertainty: Not applicable

Exhibit IV.5 Assessment of Angus Enterprise IT Capabilities

Enterprise IT Capabilities	Planning & Innovation	Information & Intelligence	Development & Transformation	Service & Resource Optimization	Service & Operational Excellence	Sourcing	Cost & Performance	Total
A - Builds Trust, Credibility, and Partnership	2.0	2.0	2.5	2.0	3.5	3.0	2.5	2.5
B – Provides Leadership and Personal Responsibility	4.0	2.0	3.0	2.0	2.0	3.0	3.5	2.6
C – Adapts to Enterprise and Leadership Culture	3.0	2.5	3.0	3.0	2.5	na	2.0	2.7
Total for Enterprise IT Capability—The Processes Employed Create Trust, et al.	2.8	2.2	2.8	2.1	2.8	3.0	2.7	2.6
D – Produces or supports Superior Business value	3.0	2.0	3.3	1.7	1.0	2.0	3.5	2.4
E – Produces or supports Superior Response to Turbulence and Uncertainty	1.0	na	1.5	na	1.0	1.3	1.0	1.3
Total for Enterprise IT Capability—Result in Business Outcomes	2.0	2.0	2.4	1.7	1.0	1.6	2.7	1.9

Exhibit IV.6 summarizes answers to 21 questions pertaining to each capability; see Chapter 11 for all 21. The figure codes the result for discussion. A black box/white number indicates a result of 2 or less; in other words, the capability only rarely produces the outcome. A gray box indicates a result of 3, or "occasional" production of the required outcomes.

What does this mean to Angus and its management? At one level, from the Strategic IT Management perspective, any of the "black" boxes warrants some concern: "What should we do about it?" Exhibit IV.6 provides some guidance by ranking each of the enterprise IT capabilities and highlighting with a black box those that performed the least well.

Exhibit IV.6   Ranking of Capabilities for Angus

	Planning & Innovatoin	information & Intelligence	Development & Transformation	Service & Resource Optimization	Servoce & Operational Excellence	Sourcing	Cost & Performance	Total
Rank: The Processes Employed Create the Trust/Partnership/ Leadership Outcomes	2	6	2	7	4	1	5	
Rank: The Enterprise IT Capabilty Contributes to Business Outcomes	3	3	2	5	7	6	1	

But this approach assumes everything is important to Angus, and more broadly, that every enterprise is alike. We already know the latter is not true; enterprises (and, for that matter, individual business units) vary widely. We also know that Angus, at this point, is a fairly traditional enterprise, for which operational issues (and stability) loom as the more important considerations.

What Is Important for Angus?

It is tempting to prescribe in broad strokes what a company like Angus should do. And in some ways, we do so in Chapter 16 by suggesting basic principles for setting direction for enterprises, taking into account each enterprise's specific issues.

Here, though, we look to the self-assessment process for the beginning of guidance. Just as we posed certain questions about the outcomes each enterprise IT capability produces for Angus, we also posed questions about exactly how important these things are to Angus's management. Admittedly, this depends on the perspectives management currently has about the business–IT relationship and, undoubtedly, through the CIO and CEO (and increasing environmental turbulence), these perceptions should change. On the other hand, if change must occur, working from existing management perceptions may prove helpful.

Exhibit IV.7 reports the level of importance management believes each enterprise IT capability has for the enterprise, and links this to the actual

Exhibit IV.7   Importance to Angus

	Planning & Innovatoin	information & Intelligence	Development & Transformation	Service & Resource Optimization	Servoce & Operational Excellence	Sourcing	Cost & Performance	Total
Importance to the Enterprise that Processes Employed Create Trust, Partnership	2.0	4.0	4.0	2.0	5.0	2.0	4.0	3.3
As-Is Assessment whether Processes Employed Create Trust, Partnership, et al.	2.8	2.2	2.8	2.1	2.8	3.0	2.7	2.6
Gap		x			x		x	
Importance to the Enterprise that the Processes Produce Business Outcomes	5.0	5.0	5.0	2.0	5.0	2.0	2.0	3.7
As-Is Assessment whether the Processes Produce Business Outcomes	2.0	2.0	2.4	1.7	1.0	1.6	2.7	1.9
Gap	x	x	x		x			

performance shown in the previous figures. The scale for this consideration of importance:

5. This requirement is critical to the enterprise
4. This requirement is very important to the enterprise
3. This requirement is of some importance to the enterprise
2. This requirement is interesting but not important
1. This requirement is not important to the enterprise

Again, as before, the data rolls up answers for many requirements described in Chapters 12 through 14, so the assessment scales apply to the individual requirements, and are summarized here.

Exhibit IV.7 provides guidance for areas of concern, marked with a gray X. Perhaps not surprisingly, the three areas of concern are in the operational areas of *Service & Operational Excellence*, *Sourcing*, and *Cost & Performance*.

Angus Summary

As spelled out earlier, the self-assessment process characterized Angus as a traditional firm with largely operational views of the business and IT relationship. Any roadmap would start there to fill in gaps in credibility, partnership, trust, and the elements required to do so. The lurking issues of future environmental turbulence and the likely availability of transformational IT capabilities are shown as a challenge to current enterprise IT capabilities. In short, a very good Strategic IT Management picture is drawn to guide business and IT management.

1. Do the Angus enterprise IT capabilities—engaging business and IT—perform well and produce business outcomes? Does IT perform?
2. Do the Angus enterprise IT capabilities add to trust and partnership?
3. Do the Angus enterprises outcomes address change and flexibility effectively and sufficiently?

The reader can decide based on this summary data, but the answer is perhaps not, and this should provide guidance to Angus leadership.

Example #2: Global Financial Services

The next two examples are presented in summary form.

Global operates six financial services lines of business in more than 100 jurisdictions, some with differing laws and cultures. The six businesses have different levels of IT maturity, though of course IT provides the core operational services. IT is organized into a single global organization with multiple data centers.

As we noted in Exhibit IV.3 for Angus, the assessment gave the Global management team choices between a "traditional" and a "transformative" perspective. The company team choices fell into the "strongly traditional" except for the business environment, which was "strongly transformative." The answers to the other assessment questions, based on the content from in the referenced chapters, are shown in Exhibit IV.8.

What Should Global Financial Services Do?

Exhibit IV.9 shows the relative values for the 21 questions from Chapter 11, defining the requirements for enterprise IT capabilities. As before, the numbers in gray boxes show no or very little performance in each of the capabilities.

Exhibit IV.8   Defining Business? IT Characteristics for Global Financial Services

Enterprise Business and IT Characteristics	Traditional Business and IT Management Perspective (the FROM)	Transformative Business and IT Management Perspective (the TO)	Management's Choice
1. Business and IT environment	The business environment is stable, static. Changes come in relatively constant speed and are not transformational. The business and IT organizations focus on the enterprise level	The environment is turbulent, dynamic. Change comes in unexpected ways and speeds. The business and IT organizations focus on the business unit/lines of business.	Strong Transformative
2. Management's primary focus for investment, IT business impact	Cost reduction, cost management is key	Strategic focus, optimal (not lowest) cost is key	Weak Traditional
3. The key attributes for "good" IT projects	Stability, well-engineered specifications, responsive to business requirements	Flexibility, adaptability and responsiveness, modular, meet expectations	Strong Traditional
4. The enterprise approach to IT governance	Hierarchical, orientation to control	Network, participative orientation to business problem solving	Strong Traditional
5. IT's basic culture and values	Command the technology. Respond to the business. Service an arm's-length service client.	Know the business; be proactive with solutions to business, partner.	Strong Traditional
6. How Business views the relationship of IT and business brganizations	Business is an IT client, defines requirements. IT operates the technology, provides technical expertise. IT is a sole provider.	Business is viewed as partner, collaborative. IT as a transformative factor. IT functions as partner. Many sources of IT are possible and need management.	Strong Traditional
7. How IT views the relationship of IT and business organizations	IT is reactive to the business. Business is viewed as a client, defines requirements. IT operates the technology, provides technical expertise. IT is a sole provider.	IT is proactive, in collaboration with business partners. Focus on strategic use of IT. Need to manage the many sources of IT.	Weak Transformative

Exhibit IV.9   Enterprise IT Assessments for Global Financial Services

Enterprise IT Capabilities	Planning & Innovatoin	information & Intelligence	Development & Transformation	Service & Resource Optimization	Service & Operational Excellence	Sourcing	Cost & Performance	Total
A - Builds Trust, Credibility, and Partnership	1.0	2.0	3.0	2.0	4.5	4.0	3.0	2.8
B – Provides Leadership and Personal Responsibility	1.0	1.0	3.0	2.0	4.0	4.0	4.5	2.8
C – Adapts to Enterprise and Leadership Culture	2.0	2.0	3.0	2.0	2.0	2.0	4.5	2.5
Total for Enterprise IT Capability—The Processes Employed Create Trust, et al.	1.3	1.7	3.0	2.0	3.5	3.3	4.0	2.7
D – Produces or supports Superior Business value	2.0	1.0	3.0	2.0	3.5	3.5	2.0	2.4
E – Produces or supports Superior Response to Turbulence and Uncertainty	1.0	1.0	1.0	2.0	2.0	2.0	1.0	1.4
Total for Enterprise IT Capability—Result in Business Outcomes	1.5	1.0	2.0	2.0	2.8	2.8	1.5	1.9

Exhibit IV.10 compares the results to the indicated importance to management, and identifies the gaps—that is, where performance to requirements is considerably below the importance placed on the enterprise IT capability by management.

Examining this, the gap is particularly large in the *Planning & Innovation* area in terms of business outcomes. The gaps are also large in *Development & Transformation* trust/partnership and in the *Cost & Performance* section. Both areas would appear to be of significant concern. Recall that we are not focusing on the specific technical methodologies employed in either area; rather, it is the combination of business and IT resources throughout the enterprise, involving all sources of IT, and their ability to produce trust and business outcomes.

Exhibit IV.10 Areas for Management Concern for Global Financial Services

	Planning & Innovatoin	information & Intelligence	Development & Transformation	Service & Resource Optimization	Servoce & Operational Excellence	Sourcing	Cost & Performance	Total
Importance to the Enterprise that Processess Employed Create Trust, Partnership	2.0	4.0	4.0	2.0	5.0	2.0	4.0	3.3
As Is Assessment whether Processes Employed Create Trust, Partnership, et al.	1.3	1.7	3.0	2.0	3.5	3.3	4.0	2.7
Gap	x	x	x		x		x	
Importance to the Enterprise that the Processes Produce Business Outcomes	5.0	5.0	5.0	2.0	5.0	2.0	2.0	3.7
As-Is Assessment whether the Processes Produce Business Outcomes	1.5	1.0	2.0	2.0	2.8	2.8	1.5	1.9
Gap	x	x	x		x		x	

Exhibit IV.11 ranks the seven enterprise IT capabilities in terms of trust/ partnership and business outcomes. This also provides important guidance as to where management attention may be placed.

Global Financial Services Summary

As spelled out earlier, the self-assessment process characterized Global Financial Services as a traditional firm with largely operational views of the business and IT relationship. Any roadmap would start there to fill in gaps in credibility, partnership, trust, and the elements required to do so. The lurking issue of future environmental turbulence and the likely availability of transformational IT capabilities are shown as challenges to current enterprise IT capabilities. In short, a very good Strategic IT Management picture is drawn to guide business and IT management.

1. Do the Global Financial Services enterprise IT capabilities—engaging business and IT—perform well and produce business outcomes? Does IT perform?

Exhibit IV.11   Ranking for Trust and Outcomes

	Planning & Innovatoin	information & Intelligence	Development & Transformation	Service & Resource Optimization	Servoce & Operational Excellence	Sourcing	Cost & Performance	Total
Rank: The Processes Employed Create the Trust/Partnership/ Leadership Outcomes	7	6	4	5	2	3	1	
Rank: The Enterprise IT Capabilty Contributes to Business Outcomes	5	7	3	3	1	1	5	

2. Do the Global Financial Services enterprise IT capabilities add to trust and partnership?
3. Do the Global Financial Services enterprise outcomes address change and flexibility effectively and sufficiently?

The reader can decide based on this summary data, but the answer is perhaps not, and this should provide guidance to Global Financial leadership.

Example #3: National Governmental Agency

The National Government Agency (NGA) has activities located in many jurisdictions. The agency supports five major "lines of business," that is, separate mission areas providing services to citizens and businesses. As we noted earlier, in the case of government and nonprofit we continue to use the term "business" for the agency activities. However, while we understand business as seeking profitability and return on investment, government agencies pursue mission success and efficiency. This difference does not however change any of the Strategic IT Management issues, which remain fully applicable to the government agency.

As with Global Financial Services, we present only the highest summary information.

As we noted, Exhibit IV.11 gave the management team the choices between a "traditional" and a "transformative" perspective. The answers to the other assessment questions, based on the content from in the referenced chapters, are shown in Exhibit IV.12.

Exhibit IV.12   NGA Characteristics

Enterprise Business and IT Characteristics	Traditional Business and IT Management Perspective (the FROM)	Transformative Business and IT Management Perspective (the TO)	Management's Choice
1. Business and IT environment	The business environment is stable, static. Changes come in relatively constant speed and are not transformational. The business and IT organizations focus on the enterprise level	The environment is turbulent, dynamic. Change comes in unexpected ways and speed. The business and IT organizations focus on the business unit/lines of business.	Strong Traditional Transformative
2. Management's primary focus for investment, IT business impact	Cost reduction, cost management is key	Strategic focus, optimal (not lowest) cost is key	Equally applies
3. The key attributes for "good" IT projects	Stability, well-engineered specifications, responsive to business requirements	Flexibility, adaptability and responsiveness, modular, meet expectations	Strong Traditional
4. The enterprise approach to IT governance	Hierarchical, orientation to control	Network, participative, orientation to business problem solving	Strong Traditional
5. IT's basic culture and values	Command the technology. Respond to the business. Service an arm's-length service client.	Know the business. Proactive with solutions to business, partner.	Strong Traditional
6. How business views the relationship of IT and business organizations	Business is an IT client, defines requirements. IT operates the technology, provides technical expertise. IT is a sole provider.	Business is viewed as partner, collaborative. IT as a transformative factor. IT functions as partner. Many sources of IT are possible and need management.	Strong Traditional
7. How IT views the relationship of IT and business organizations	IT is reactive to the business. Business is viewed as a client, defines requirements. IT operates the technology, provides technical expertise. IT is a sole provider.	IT is proactive, in collaboration with business partners. Focus on strategic use of IT. Need to manage the many sources of IT.	Weak Transformative

What Should the NGA Do?

At the end of the enterprise IT capability description, the self-assessment focused on the *importance* this capability has to the enterprise and the *outcomes* currently produced for the enterprise. These outcomes include the business impact: superior business value, superior responses to turbulence, and the process or organizational impact: building trust, leadership, partnership culture.

Exhibit IV.13 shows areas of concern, likely *Planning & Innovation* and *Cost & Performance*.

As was the case for Global and Angus, the question is the degree to which any of these are important to the agency. Exhibit IV.14 shows the specific enterprise IT capabilities, with significant gaps between importance and trust

Exhibit IV.13   NGA Enterprise IT Capabilities

Enterprise IT Capabilities	Planning & Innovatoin	information & Intelligence	Development & Transformation	Service & Resource Optimization	Service & Operational Excellence	Sourcing	Cost & Performance	Total
A - Builds Trust, Credibility, and Partnership	3.0	2.0	4.0	3.0	2.0	0.0	2.0	2.3
B – Provides Leadership and Personal Responsibility	3.0	4.0	4.0	3.0	2.0	0.0	4.5	2.9
C – Adapts to Enterprise and Leadership Culture	4.0	4.0	4.0	3.0	2.0	0.0	0.0	2.4
Total for Enterprise IT Capability—The Processes Employed Create Trust, et al.	3.3	3.3	4.0	3.0	2.0	0.0	2.2	2.5
D – Produces or supports Superior Business value	4.0	2.0	3.0	3.0	2.0	4.0	2.0	2.9
E – Produces or supports Superior Response to Turbulence and Uncertainty	1.0	3.0	2.0	2.0	2.0	2.0	1.0	1.9
Total for Enterprise IT Capability—Result in Business Outcomes	2.5	2.5	2.5	2.5	2.0	3.0	1.5	2.4

Exhibit IV.14 Importance and Performance

	Planning & Innovatoin	information & Intelligence	Development & Transformation	Service & Resource Optimization	Servoce & Operational Excellence	Sourcing	Cost & Performance	Total
Importance to the Enterprise that Processess Employed Create Trust, Partnership	2.0	4.0	4.0	2.0	5.0	2.0	4.0	3.3
As-Is Assessment whether Processes Employed Create Trust, Partnership, et al.	3.3	3.3	4.0	3.0	2.0	0.0	2.2	2.5
Gap		x			x		x	
Importance to the Enterprise that the Processes Produce Business Outcomes	5.0	5.0	5.0	2.0	5.0	2.0	2.0	3.7
As-Is Assessment whether the Processes Produce Business Outcomes	2.5	2.5	2.5	2.5	2.0	3.0	1.5	2.4
Gap	x	x	x		x			

and importance and production of business outcomes. Here, *Development & Transformation* and *Service & Operational Excellence*, as well as *Information & Intelligence*, come to the fore. Similarly, Exhibit IV.15 shows the relative performance of each enterprise IT capability, for trust and for business outcomes.

The reader can examine the data and come to conclusions about where management attention should be concentrated in terms of specific enterprise IT capabilities.

NGA Summary

The self-assessment process given earlier characterized the NGA as a relatively traditional organization with largely operational views of the business and IT relationship. Any roadmap would start there to fill in gaps in credibility, partnership, trust, and the elements required to do so.

Exhibit IV.15   Rank of Enterprise IT Capabilities

	Planning & Innovatoin	information & Intelligence	Development & Transformation	Service & Resource Optimization	Servoce & Operational Excellence	Sourcing	Cost & Performance	Total
Rank: The Processes Employed Create the Trust/Partnership/ Leadership Outcomes	2	2	1	4	6	7	5	
Rank: The Enterprise IT Capabilty Contributes to Business Outcomes	2	2	2	2	6	1	7	

It comes down the three questions.

1. Do the NGA enterprise IT capabilities—engaging business and IT—perform well and produce business outcomes? Does IT perform?
2. Do the NGA enterprise IT capabilities add to trust and partnership?
3. Do the NGA enterprise outcomes address change and flexibility, effectively and sufficiently?

Note that only the final three figures of analysis are shown; Chapter 11 stated all 21 questions the NGA answered for each capability.

Summary

Our purpose is not to show a consulting process to examine these three organizations. Rather, we want to show how the specific issues of importance to us—namely trust, partnership, performance, response to turbulence, value—apply to three quite different organizations. This carries out the mantra "one size doesn't fit all," since we do not assert that each enterprise IT capability is equally important to all organizations. Rather, our point is that the specified capabilities and their performance for an organization can be described, and conclusions drawn, as to the areas of concern for business and IT management.

CHAPTER 16

What Should Be Done?

The broad questions now are:

1. Now what?
2. What needs to be done?
3. Who needs to do it?

The answers, of course, depend on the specifics of the enterprise and the current conditions of the enterprise IT capabilities throughout the enterprise. We offer here a multistep approach to assessing those specific and conditions, all pointed toward achieving the basic goals of Strategic IT Management.

Two points to get started. First, significant overlap occurs among within the tools and assessments suggested in the following. Each reader will need to determine those that are most helpful. Second, we consistently emphasize that Strategic IT Management is not about the technical details for managing IT nor, for that matter, managing business. Rather, it is the crucial piece of fitting business and IT together, in partnership, to achieve the common goals of value from IT and response to turbulence and uncertainty.

But why are we taking this trip? The question applies not only to Chapter 16 but also to the discussion of the self-assessments described in the Part IV Introduction. After all, the reader might exclaim, we certainly know our own enterprise! And, more to the point, we'll be told what to do by senior leadership. And is all this too simplistic? Our enterprise is an organic, complicated thing. Yet our experience has been that most managers and professionals really haven't considered the specifics of the organizations for which they work. This probably is not true for senior managers, but the people in the organization have typically not considered the environment, particularly in terms of the many alternative ways of doing so. This trip is a very positive thing, and contributes to insight as to what exactly needs to be done and, as importantly, what can be done.

However, a more fundamental issue is that our presentation of Strategic IT Management and the seven enterprise IT capabilities could sound a lot like a process/methodology discussion, and even worse, like a IT process discussion to be performed by the IT organization. The risk is that we—both IT and business managers—tend to think that processes and methodologies are good, and we need all of them. And while we've worked hard to state—repeatedly—that one size does not fit all, it still is very easy to slip into the perspective that we do, in fact, need to do everything: planning, operational excellence, service management, development—the whole lot of IT management processes.

But Strategic IT Management steps back and asks a fundamental question: Is the enterprise mobilizing its business and IT resources optimally to achieve value and response to turbulence? This is not a process or methodology question; it's a management leadership and partnership question.

We suggest three fundamental questions that override everything else:

1. Do the *enterprise IT capabilities*—engaging business and IT—perform well and produce valuable business outcomes? Does IT perform?
2. Do *enterprise IT capabilities* add to trust and partnership?
3. Do *enterprises IT capabilities* address change and flexibility, effectively and sufficiently?

Through self-assessment, we can begin to obtain the answers. For example, we do know one important thing: Performance leads to credibility, trust, and partnership, and consequently we must perform! It is helpful to return to the self-assessments in Chapter 11 and consider question A1 about each of the seven enterprise IT capabilities: To what extent does the *existing enterprise IT capability* build credibility through IT's execution and performance?

In effect, do we perform? Take a look at the three cases that we introduced in the Introduction to Part IV. The three examples show some of the possible variations in responses: To remind ourselves, the responses are for each of the 21 requirements described in Chapter 11 (in the section "Assessing Enterprise Performance against Requirements").

5. Produces the required outcomes
4. Often produces the required outcomes
3. Occasionally produces the required outcomes
2. Rarely produces the required outcomes
1. Does not produce the required outcomes

Exhibit 16.1 shows the current performance as determined by the self-assessments by the enterprise managers, based on the provided five-point scale. But so what? How should the relative importance and priority of these areas be considered? The Introduction bases the answer on a self-assessment basis.

Exhibit 16.1   Enterprise Performance Profile

	Strategic	Tactical			Operational		
	Planning & Innovatoin	*information & Intelligence*	*Development & Transformation*	*Service & Resource Optimization*	*Service & Operational Excellence*	*Sourcing*	*Cost & Performance*
Angus International	3.0	3.0	2.0	3.0	4.0	3.0	4.0
Global International	1.0	1.5	3.0	2.0	4.5	3.0	3.0
National Gov. Agency	4.0	4.0	4.0	2.0	2.0	2.0	2.0

Here we go beyond that and suggest ways to consider priorities for attention. The basic rule: not everything is necessary, not everything is priority.

We also know a second important thing: whether the enterprise is capable of coping with the turbulence and change affecting it. We go back to the Chapter 11 assessments, which include the following requirements: *Recognize projects and requirements faster. Develop solutions and plans faster. Deploy solutions faster: Business and technical solutions emphasize adaptability and flexibility.*

It comes down to the capacity to change in response to turbulence, to respond to change. Looking at the three example cases shows the issues; Exhibit 16.2 shows how the three example enterprises can respond to turbulence and change.

Exhibit 16.2   Enterprise IT Capability to Respond to Turbulence

	Strategic	Tactical			Operational		
	Planning & Innovatoin	*information & Intelligence*	*Development & Transformation*	*Service & Resource Optimization*	*Service & Operational Excellence*	*Sourcing*	*Cost & Performance*
Angus International	1.0	na	1.5	na	1.0	1.3	1.0
Global International	1.0	1.0	1.0	2.0	2.0	2.0	1.0
National Gov. Agency	1.0	3.0	2.0	2.0	2.0	2.0	1.0

Exhibit 16.3 Enterprise IT Capability to Build Partnership and Trust

	Strategic	Tactical			Operational		
	Planning & Innovatoin	*information & Intelligence*	*Development & Transformation*	*Service & Resource Optimization*	*Service & Operational Excellence*	*Sourcing*	*Cost & Performance*
Angus International	2.0	2.0	2.5	2.0	3.5	3.0	2.5
Global International	1.0	2.0	3.0	2.0	4.5	4.0	3.0
National Gov. Agency	3.0	2.0	4.0	3.0	2.0	2.0	2.0

We know a third thing as well: how well the enterprise in its IT capabilities builds trust, credibility, and partnership. This has a terrific impact on the ability of the enterprise to accomplish responses to turbulence and improve value delivery. Comparing the three examples in Exhibit 16.3 shows the contrasts among the three example enterprise cases.

All of these examples emphasize the not-one-size-fits-all characteristics of enterprise and, accordingly, the Strategic IT Management directions to be taken.

The Part IV Introduction applies the self-assessment instruments from each chapter to answer the current status question. We used the results to give direction for next steps, dependent on the outcomes of each self-assessment activity. However, they may not convey the entire picture, considering their dependency on current management perspectives. While we engage business and IT management in the Strategic IT Management discussions, in some ways they are part of the problem. We can benefit from also taking an external view of the enterprise; that is, by applying more normative sources to help determine the status. By this we mean applying various mental frameworks to characterize the enterprise and consequently clarify what would be important for the enterprise to consider.

Applying Frameworks to Describe the Enterprise

Every enterprise and government agency is different. We have consistently remarked that one size does not fit all. While true, this begs the very important question: exactly what do we mean, and how should this be applied in working with enterprise IT capabilities? We've said this catchphrase perhaps too many times. But it is really true: while the simple diagrams we'll apply in this chapter are applicable to all in some way, the specifics underlying them certainly are not. For example, the characteristics of a particular enterprise's competitive position in its industry greatly affect the specific requirement for the *Planning & Innovation* enterprise IT capability. That is, the specifics of what a given enterprise needs to be able to command and do well are quite different, and have different urgencies.[1]

For discussion purposes, we've found it very helpful to apply simple classifying frameworks as a means to describe the differences in enterprises. We have also found it helpful in practice to use these frameworks with business and IT executives—really, with anyone who is concerned with and involved with *Planning & Innovation* (and the other enterprise IT capabilities). These turn into simple self-assessments. The frameworks describe the nature of the enterprise itself and the characteristics of the IT activities supporting the enterprise. These are used for assessing what is most important to a particular enterprise.

We show here a number of tests based on differing frameworks. They may not be consistent with each other. But they most certainly have the power to direct the attention to a sense of priority for enterprise IT capabilities. Our objective is primarily to encourage readers to consider exactly the circumstances of the particular enterprise. Even more important is to consider whether change—particularly in turbulent times—causes a shift in the enterprise characteristics described.

The Power of Frameworks

We describe eight ways to think about an enterprise's characteristics as they apply to Strategic IT Management and trust and partnership. These are simplistic and do not reflect rigorous analysis: they are simply descriptive. But they are powerful, especially in terms of defining the effects of change on the enterprise. The question, in addition to how well the characteristics apply to the enterprise, is: *How will the enterprise change in the near future?* That is, what is the characteristic today, and how will environmental business and technical change result in a different characteristic tomorrow?

The idea of change in enterprise characteristics has been held out as a particularly powerful idea, as it implies that the ripple effects of change will extend, at the least, to how the IT organization is run and its interactions with the business. That's the sense of what we are doing here. We aren't specifying exactly what all the implications will be, although we will point out some of the more important ones. We particularly want to encourage readers to take a what-if posture, especially as readers might perform one or more of the self-assessment exercises we suggest in each of the enterprise IT capabilities.[2]

Four important ground rules must be clarified for this discussion. The *first* is that most of the classifying frameworks we describe are decades old and, over time, have been elaborated on and extended by many academicians, practitioners, authors, and consultants. The ground rule is that this is certainly okay, as our goal is not to perform, for example, business strategic planning or organizational design. Rather, our goal is to stimulate discussion and, through obvious though perhaps simplistic characterization, suggest that the implications may be quite different for one enterprise compared to another. We encourage readers to pursue these characterizations with further reading and research, applied to the particular enterprise.

The *second* ground rule is that these certainly are not the only pertinent frameworks. The literature and consultant practices are replete with many wonderful and useful frameworks: contingency theory is alive and well! But the frameworks we present here have proven to be helpful in client and student situations.

The *third* ground rule is more fundamental. From the beginning of these kinds of frameworks, the implication has largely been that they apply to the enterprise as a whole. For simple enterprises with one dominant line of business, this is pretty much true, although there can be differences between front-office and back-office characteristics even in these simple enterprises. But most enterprise and government agencies have multiple lines of business and/or well-defined business units or business functions. For many of the frameworks we apply here, the results can be markedly different among the multiple units and functions. If we were dealing with a single IT organization providing services to all the units, that's one thing (complicated in its own right). But so many organizations have an IT ecosystem featuring multiple IT organization providers (some embedded in business units), sourcers (e.g., cloud-provided applications), and what we've called do-it-yourself IT, where hardware and software are acquired independently by individuals and/or components of the business units. Our point is that the use of these frameworks to describe each major enterprise component yields insights into the risks and challenges of successful Strategic IT Management. In particular, what if the enterprise has several business units with vastly different characteristics (definable with these frameworks)? Consequently, how can each enterprise IT capability successfully cope with these differences?

The *fourth* ground rule emphasizes that individual readers—managers and professionals—can apply the frameworks to consider how these situations may apply to them and to chart a course for individual development. In our experience, many mid-level staff have never thought through the character of the enterprise for which they work. This can be an enlightening and helpful experience.

Finally, why are we doing this in the first place? This is not an exercise in business or IT planning per se. Rather, these frameworks are helpful in guiding the reader to that which is most important in a Strategic IT Management perspective for a particular enterprise of particular characteristics.

We make suggestions as to the priorities an enterprise might choose among all enterprise IT capabilities, based on the enterprise characteristics. These are suggestions based on our consulting and management experience and observations of enterprises as revealed in workshops and academic courses. The fundamental point is that one size does not fit all. This is something that most books or practitioners do *not* completely appreciate: specific tools and methodologies, and in our case the importance of enterprise IT capabilities, are not the same for everyone. Even within a given relatively complex enterprise, parts of the enterprise will be different from other parts. This makes a common approach to management, governance, and application of specific (common) methodologies problematic. We believe, through experience, that the approach taken needs to fit with the character of the enterprise.[3]

However, we do not expect these directions we suggest for priorities (in, for example, Exhibit 16.8) *to be prescriptive.* Each reader—CEO, CIO, manager, professional, student—should apply the frameworks with the idea that a) the enterprise is unique, b) by understanding the uniqueness, good priority decisions can be made, and c) the self-awareness earned enables you to make the appropriate priority decisions. But most importantly, readers should reject the notion that one single solution—methodology, process, IT strategy, and so on—applies to every enterprise. It all depends; our proposition is that it depends on the characteristics of the enterprise. We offer eight ways to think about that.

Organizational Context

As mentioned earlier, a key issue is the number of separate business units (or lines of business) and the relationship among them. If the enterprise is a single dominant line of business, these models do not apply to distinguish lines of business within the enterprise.

There is an important overriding consideration, however. While we talk about the enterprise IT capabilities as the focus for Strategic IT Management, in some very large enterprises that are essentially holding companies, there is little or no relevance to adopting the holding company as the "enterprise." Individual business units—wholly separated except for the ownership by the holding company—otherwise have no other connection. A large government

Exhibit 16.4 Organization Framework: The Operating Model

Operating Model for the Enterprise	Mark Which Is the Dominant Model from the Enterprise Perspective
Unification	
Diversification	
Replication	
Coordination	

Adapted from Jeanne W. Ross, Peter Weill, and David C. Robertson, *Enterprise Architecture as Strategy: Creating a Foundation for Business Execution* (Harvard Business School Press, 2006).

agency with very separate agency divisions can fall into this category. This is tricky, though, because there could be some elements of IT still provided globally by service organizations (e.g., networks). This overall consideration is included in one of the models that follows, but take care to be sure the unit of analysis (the enterprise) is at the right level of the organization.

Frameworks One and Two: Organization and Governance

Exhibits 16.4 and 16.5 give guidance as to the unit of analysis for thinking through Strategic IT Management and in particular the scope of each enterprise IT capability. Ross and Weill also introduced an important concept with "reach and range" in their presentation of infrastructure and governance.[4] There are also an "as is" and "to be" to this assessment, although these intrude

Exhibit 16.5 Governance Framework

Operating Model for the Enterprise	Mark Which Is the Dominant Model from the Enterprise Perspective
Integrated	
Allied Related	
Allied Unrelated	
Holding Company	

Adapted from Leonard Wrigley, *Divisional Autonomy and Diversification* (doctoral dissertation, Harvard University, 1970); Richard P. Rumelt, *Strategy, Structure, and Economic Performance* (Harvard Business School Press, 1974; rev. ed. Harvard Business School Press, 1986); and Kenneth R. Andrews, *The Concept of Corporate Strategy* (Irwin, 1986).

more into the realm of business and strategic planning. Nevertheless, it is a dynamic to be considered. However, this can't be a simple discussion when, in conditions of turbulence, a structuring of the operation model or governance relations among otherwise autonomous business unit is part of the enterprise response. For some, this is a significant dynamic in the environment and strongly suggests the value of an "as is" versus a "to be" character of the relevant self-assessment.

Again, the point here is not to provide planning or organizational design direction; rather, it is to diagnose the current situation for purposes of thinking through the scope of Strategic IT Management and the application of the self-assessments presented in Part III.

Framework Three: The IT Strategy Process[5]

Although the current planning process is more properly considered in the *Planning & Innovation* enterprise IT capability discussion, it does reflect the current structure of relationships between IT and the business, and consequently is helpful in thinking through the Strategic IT Management implications.[6]

The framework connects with the description of the enterprise business structure, particularly one in which many separate business units exist with very different characteristics (as we've discussed before). The challenge is more than just the IT side of things; it connects to how the business units themselves do their business planning, whether at the enterprise level or in parallel, separately within the business unit. A similar distinction about strategic versus annual/operational planning occurs, where the enterprise characteristics may determine the consistency across these planning variables (Exhibit 16.6).

The issue covers consistency/comparability of the processes employed, but as referred to earlier, the changes in these characteristics occur through the impact of turbulence.

Exhibit 16.6   Organization Classifying Framework

The IT Strategy Process	Mark the Dominant Characteristic of the Process
Siloed	
Reactive	
Proactive	
Integrated with Business Planning	

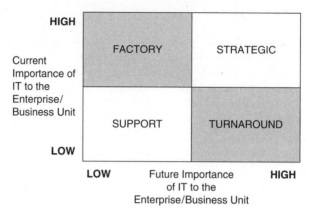

Exhibit 16.7   Role of IT in the Enterprise/Business Unit: Current and/or Planned

Framework Four: The Role of IT in the Enterprise

Perhaps the most famous framework, Exhibit 16.7, is more than three decades old but maintains its descriptive powers. This is the "role of IT in the business unit" model (our title) initiated by MacFarlan and colleagues[7] and adapted by many other authors. A lot of the power is based on the sense of change that would occur as an enterprise might move from one to another quadrant based on changing conditions. One example is airlines; when frequent flier programs were new, the classifications would have been *Turnaround* moving to *Strategic*. Now that they are simply the price of doing business in that industry, frequent flier programs have moved to *Factory*, or maybe even *Support*. From our perspective, the question is how these simple characteristics translate into consequences for the enterprise IT capabilities required.

Undoubtedly this framework is the most recognized and continues to be used by many. We note that many authors have adapted this and altered the names of the quadrants.[8] The core idea—the role of IT in the enterprise and, more importantly, to each business unit within the enterprise—leads to significant differences in management requirements and in the priority of enterprise IT capabilities.

In Exhibit 16.8, we offer our consulting and teaching experience in suggesting which enterprise IT capabilities are especially important, given the character of the enterprise reflected in the framework. One complexity—and this is an important one—is that individual business units or lines of business may be characterized by location in different quadrants. This presents challenges to the enterprise governance processes and the sense of priority for reviewing and improving enterprise IT capabilities. As the title of Exhibit 16.7 suggests, it can be applied in an as-is or in a to-be mode. Obviously, if known,

Exhibit 16.8   Possible Priorities for Enterprise IT Capabilities

	Strategic	Tactical			Operational		
	Planning & Innovation	Information & Intelligence	Development & Transformation	Service & Resource Optimization	Sourcing	Service & Operational Excellence	Cost & Performance
Factory				High	High	High	High
Support						High	High
Turnaround	High	High	Medium	High			
Strategic	Highest	Highest	Highest		Medium		

the "to-be" is at least as important in terms of assessing which of the enterprise IT capabilities requires the more urgent attention.

We remind the reader of the power of these frameworks, which lead to understanding the priorities the enterprise or business unit may have, the implications of change (e.g., moving from *factory* to *strategic* because of response to turbulence), and the implications of variability, with individual business units or functions in different areas of the quadrant.

We also remind the reader that the expressions of priority shown in Exhibit 16.8 and in subsequent exhibits are not prescriptive. They result from our many years of experience as CIOs, academics, and consultants.

Framework Five: Business and IT Management and Governance Culture[9]

A lot of the angst of IT and business relationships is found in the patterns of governance and management found in the business and, to a lesser extent, in the IT domains (Exhibit 16.9). This extends to the ability of the enterprise to deal with turbulence (unanticipated change) and uncertainty. Recall the requirement of increasing speed in decision making proposed in Chapter 7 as a consequence of turbulence. This speed is required to detect the problem, plan a solution, and deploy the solution.

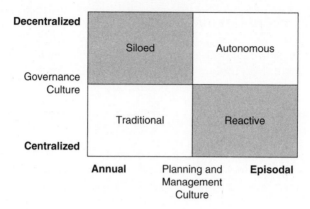

Exhibit 16.9   Planning and Governance Culture

But what if the culture does not make that possible (or, at least, easy)? The question can apply to the IT organization as well, for which the culture and process might be quite different from the business.

Note that Exhibit 16.10, Classifying Framework Five, applies separately for the enterprise and for the IT providers (the IT organization, or perhaps the main sourcers).

Exhibit 16.10   Classifying Framework Five

Management and Decision-Making Culture	Strategic	Tactical			Operational		
	Planning & Innovation	Information & Intelligence	Development & Transformation	Service & Resource Optimization	Sourcing	Service & Operational Excellence	Cost & Performance
Siloed	High	High	High	Medium		Medium	
Traditional				Medium	High	High	High
Autonomous			High	High		High	
Reactive	High		Medium				High

Turbulence and Change

These models help define the economic and technical context within which the various types of organizations, as described earlier, operate.

Framework Six: The Nature of Turbulences Affecting the Enterprise[10]

Turbulence, of course, is a central theme for us, as reflected in the book's subtitle: *Strategic IT Management for Turbulent Times*. But as Chapters 4 and 5 point out, many sources of turbulence affect business and technology, and these might apply differently to different enterprises or (as pointed out in Framework One) differently in different business units and functions of the enterprise.

From our perspective, the question is how these simple characteristics translate into consequences for the enterprise IT capabilities required. The framework shown in Exhibit 16.11 focuses on the degree to which current conditions in the business and/or the technology environment are turbulent. Chapters 4 and 5 give additional self-assessments about the nature of turbulence and its primary drivers and characteristics.

Note that the Part IV Introduction, in describing the application of self-assessment for four cases, highlights the description of the enterprise context. Angus International, for example, would likely fall into the Stable/Stable

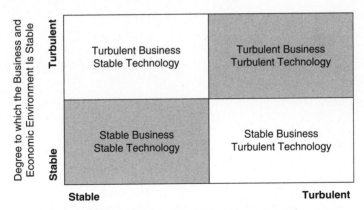

Degree to which the Information Technology Enviornment
Available to the Business Is Stable or Turbulent
(can be the technology itself; can be the providers (e.g., cloud))

Exhibit 16.11   Enterprise Status for Turbulence

Exhibit 16.12   Priorities Based on Status of Turbulence

	Strategic	Tactical				Operational	
	Planning & Innovation	*Information & Intelligence*	*Development & Transformation*	*Service & Resource Optimization*	*Sourcing*	*Service & Operational Excellence*	*Cost & Performance*
Turbulence in both business and technology	High	High	Medium				
Turbulent business, stable technology	High	High		Medium		High	High
Stable business, turbulent technology	High		High			High	
Stable in both business and technology	Medium		Medium	High	High	High	High

category, at least for the moment. So this framework works well with the self-assessment instruments shown throughout the book.

As before, we offer our consulting and academic experience to suggest the priorities. Note that Exhibit 16.12 in particular can—and should—be applied to the enterprise as a whole and to individual business units/lines of business.

Framework Seven: Enterprise Business Response to Turbulence

Ansoff began the discussion of organizational response to environmental turbulence in the 1970s. He suggested a five-element classification of the enterprise in terms of turbulence, in terms like these:[11]

- *Relatively unchanging.* Management values stability, best practices.
- *Growth, without disruptive change.* Management values application of enterprise experience in promoting continues growth, ability to respond to growth without disruption.
- *Fast changing in known directions.* Management values capability to predict changes, flexibility to respond.

- *Discontinuous, entrepreneurial.* Management values flexibility to adapt to new conditions.
- *Discontinuous, unknown, disruptive.* Management values the ability to adopt new contexts and directions effectively.

Thinking about the dominant structure for the enterprise provides guidance as to the priorities for Strategic IT Management.

Framework Eight: Enterprise Culture and Response to Change

While the enterprise business environment and industry conditions form a primary influence on the priorities for Strategic IT Management, so do management culture and personality, especially of the senior leadership of CEOs and CEO equivalents in the business units (see Exhibit 16.13).

Many books have been written on the subject, sometimes under the heading of leadership, sometimes on change, sometimes on what constitutes

Exhibit 16.13 Business Environment Frameworks

Business Environment	Strategic	Tactical		Operational			
	Planning & Innovation	Information & Intelligence	Development & Transformation	Service & Resource Optimization	Sourcing	Service & Operational Excellence	Cost & Performance
Relatively unchanging				Medium	High	High	High
Growth, without disruptive change			Medium	Medium	High	High	High
Fast changing in known directions	Medium	Medium	High			Medium	
Discontinuous, entrepreneurial	High	High	High				
Discontinuous, unknown, disruptive	High	High	High				

a highly effective enterprise. A lot of the discussion of CEO leadership personality develops five basic themes, or values. Each of these represent an unstated filtration system, used to guide decisions and responses to circumstances and new proposals. Each can be reflective of a spectrum of characteristics; taken together, the five reflect a strong statement of managerial culture. The following statements are expressed in terms of the CEO but are equally applicable to business unit executives and senior leadership team (SLT) members (e.g., the CFO).[12]

- *Uncertainty Avoidance.* One end of the spectrum: The CEO does not like uncertainty and works to reduce it in every possible context. Decisions tend to avoid conditions of uncertainty. The other end: The CEO understands uncertainty and works to assemble data and insights to reduce risks associated with uncertainty.
- *Risk Propensity.* One end: The CEO almost relishes risk as an important component of the business; he/she does not throw out circumstances or proposals solely on the existence of risk. The CEO works to mitigate risk. Other end: The CEO avoids circumstances or decisions that contain high risk levels.
- *Openness to Change.* One end: The CEO accepts and promotes change, and provides environmental and cultural support for the successful achievement of change. The other end: The CEO values stability and prefers things to remain unchanged, and it takes a strong proposal to get acceptance for the need for change.
- *Time Orientation.* One end: Actions and events occur over a reasonable time frame. Other end: Speed is essential.
- *Perception of Control over the Environment.* One end: The CEO can directly change the conditions that pertain to the enterprise as necessary, whether in competitive, customer expectations, regulatory, technology, and so on. The other end: The CEO is not capable of changing the conditions and must respond directly to turbulence.

Classifying the current management teams in these elements of culture provides strong insight into the current circumstance and, along with it, the challenge of introducing new Strategic IT Management requirements. Exhibit 16.14 shows one way of doing this. One of the interesting outcomes is seeing the differences in culture between corporate, business unit executives, and IT management.

The Strategic IT Management priorities depend, of course, on the answers. If the defining cultural responses were all at the "other end" description, the priorities might look like Exhibit 16.15.

Exhibit 16.14   Management Culture

	CEO	CFO et al.	Business Unit Executives	IT Executives
Uncertainty Avoidance				
Risk Propensity				
Openness to Change				
Time Orientation				
Perception of Control over the Environment				

If, on the other hand, the defining culture responses are at the "one end," the priorities might look like Exhibit 16.16.

The exercise in matching the management cultures with the Strategic IT Management directions can be very productive.

What Needs to Be Done?

In some ways this is an exercise in change management that begins with accepting that change is necessary. This can mean change in IT itself, in how business deals with IT (e.g., governance), and in how the enterprise understands the role that IT plays. This is why we spend so much attention on the self-assessment material, to provide data about whether change really is needed. Of course, anecdotally, everyone has a perspective on the need for change. Now, however, we can structure that sense and work on acceptance on the part of all concerned.

To do so, though, requires some additional acceptances:

- First, understand that business is an equal partner in this process. As we remarked in the book's beginning, it is too easy to think that all this is strictly IT's problem and that it is strictly the CIO's mandate to do something about it.
- Second, accept that existing technical competencies (see Chapter 7) are not enough to address the issues of dealing with turbulence and delivering superior value from IT.
- Third, accept that traditional practices are not sufficient and that current "best practices" typically have gaps in their effectiveness in building trust and partnership, increasing the business value of the IT

Exhibit 16.15 Management Culture and Strategic IT Management

	Circum-stance	Strategic	Tactical			Operational		
		Planning & Innovation	Information & Intelligence	Development & Transformation (Change)	Service & Resource Optimization	Sourcing	Service & Operational Excellence	Cost & Performance
Uncertainty Avoidance	Accepts and manages	Medium	High		High		Medium	
Risk Propensity	Accepts and manages	Medium	High		Medium	Medium	Medium	
Openness to Change	Accepts and manages	High	Medium	High		Medium	Medium	
Time Orientation	Short-term for actions			Medium			Medium	
Perception of Control over the Environment	Little control	High	High	Medium		Medium	Medium	Medium

Exhibit 16.16   Management Culture and Strategic IT Management

	Circumstance	Strategic	Tactical			Operational		
		Planning & Innovation	*Information & Intelligence*	*Development & Transformation (Change)*	*Service & Resource Optimization*	*Sourcing*	*Service & Operational Excellence*	*Cost & Performance*
Uncertainty Avoidance	Does not like uncertainty		Medium		High		High	High
Risk Propensity	Does not like risk		Medium				High	High
Openness to Change	Not open to change						High	High
Time Orientation	Long-term perspective			Medium				
Perception of Control over the Environment	High degree of control						High	High

deployed in the business, and coping with turbulence and uncertainty. The discussions in each chapter outline both evaluative methods for determining whether this is in fact the case in a particular organization and steps that can address the gaps.

- Fourth, accept that better approaches to these activities are based on fundamental principles about trust, partnership, business value, turbulence, and uncertainty. These are described as the foundation activities in Strategic IT Management, in the respective chapters listed earlier.
- Fifth, accept that one size does not fit all and that a critical element of transforming business in times of turbulence is matching Strategic IT Management to the enterprise profile and culture.

Consequently, the initial steps are to evaluate and assess the current enterprise IT capability for the organization, determine where the gaps are, and make the appropriate investments and changes.

The second part is to prepare the organization for Strategic IT Management. For example, we have had significant experience in strengthening the enterprise IT capabilities of enterprises across the seven areas. We've called this the *IT University*; it is focused on all IT managers and professionals as well as related business unit managers and staff. The purpose is to elevate the understanding of each enterprise IT capability, particularly to recognize the connection to business strategies and goals, and overall to build the ability of the enterprise as a whole to deploy their IT resources most effectively. This is what Strategic IT Management, ultimately, addresses.

Finally, the company must mobilize the leadership of the CIO and CEO and the rest of senior management, a process we'll cover in Chapters 17 and 18.

A Risk

Throughout this book we run the enormous risk of sounding like the focus is on IT processes and that the desired outcome is simply a transition from some as-is situation in IT management to a better to-be situation. Part of this comes from the propensity of IT folks to seek stability. This is not unlike an earlier discussion about IT's comfort with engineered outcomes and meeting 100 percent of requirements, rather than accepting the concept of continual change. Of course, having infrastructure (and enterprise IT capabilities) that enable change, promoting flexibility and agility, is the real point.

The risk, though, is the tendency to view the end point as itself being stable even if it has desirable flexibility and agility characteristics. Consider Hagel, Brown, and Davison's statement that it is "not about seeking incremental growth opportunities that afford periods of stability . . . we must reconceive changes as part of a grand adventure and be at peace with fluidity, even though it may defy our natural inclination to reach a steady state." While they are speaking of a broad transformational enterprise and business context, these words apply with equal force to the context and goals of Strategic IT Management. The risk lies in forgetting this and striving for that "steady state" which, we believe, is at least elusive and perhaps impossible.[13]

How Does Strategic IT Management Connect to Governance?

Strategic IT Management builds on the governance and decision-making processes the enterprise uses to determine IT's direction and use. Chapter 2 introduced a governance diagram (Exhibit 2.6) and the main areas about which decisions are central to the governance process. *Service & Operational Excellence* is certainly a part of this, particularly in setting performance standards and assessing/mitigating risk and cost. Exhibit 16.17 shows the six governance decision categories in which the *Service & Operational Excellence* enterprise IT

Exhibit 16.17 Assessment of Governance Decisions

Governance Decision Categories	Importance to the Enterprise	Status Governance	Governance Role and Mission
Project/ Program Selection			Ensuring that projects and programs are ranked according to their delivery of business value, response to business needs, overall risk profile, probability of success, and cost. Ensuring that resources are assigned to initiatives that support the expected timing of improved investments
Technology Selection			Ensuring that technology sources and technology decisions meet functional needs while conforming to the usability, performance, operability, security, and integration standards needed by the business.
Financial Constraints			Monitoring and determining cost levels for business units, investments, and the IT organization.
Organization Structure			Establishing an organization design that promote accountability and effectiveness for all the enterprise IT capabilities, regardless of source (in the ecosystem) that are necessary to create superior business value and superior responses to turbulence.
Performance Requirements			Establishing business-based metrics and appropriate standards; monitor ongoing performance of the IT services delivered to the business. Determine and monitor sourcing.
Risk Management			Identifying and monitoring the threat landscape to include risks that affect strategies, operations, customers, suppliers, and employees. Included in this category are business continuity planning and information security. Overview and monitor risk mitigation actions.

capability is engaged. The key question: Is the enterprise capable of making decisions in its governance processes about:

- Project/Program Selection
- Technology Selection
- Financial Constraints
- Organization Structure
- Performance Requirements
- Risk Management

A critical point must be emphasized here. That is, governance is not a matter of control or hierarchy (or at least not completely). Rather, it is more about the relationships between and among business and IT managers and organizations. It is through this governance relationship that many of our goals of trust and partnership are accomplished (or not).[14] In effect, governance is integral to change management.

The self-assessment in Exhibit 16.17 gives guidance to where the particular enterprise stands and where the gaps are in its *Service & Operational Excellence* enterprise IT capability. Scales for the assessment are in Exhibit 16.18 and Exhibit 16.19. Decision making, of course, is central to the capability of the enterprise to deal with turbulence and uncertainty.

Governance is a foundation for Strategic IT Management but is also the context for the necessary partnerships. Governance by its nature—and its origins—is the decision-making process by which business guides the deployment and spending of IT resources.[15] The capability for doing this, however, is a joint activity, a partnership, with the stakeholders including IT. So the basic

Exhibit 16.18   Scale One for Assessment of Governance Decisions

Description	Current Importance to the Enterprise	
The *Importance* reflects the extent to which the status of this governance role	0	Not Applicable to this enterprise
	1	Not important to the enterprise
	2	Management is interested, but with no relevant activities
	3	Some importance to the success of information and IT in the enterprise
	4	Very important to the success of information and IT in the enterprise
	5	Critical to the success of information and IT in the enterprise

Exhibit 16.19 Scale Two for Assessment of Governance Decisions

Scale	Current Status of Governance	
0	Not Applicable	Don't know or not applicable
1	Ineffective	Governance (corporate, or business unit–based, or sourced/cloud) is ineffective, with bad results
2	Mostly Ineffective	Governance (corporate, or business unit–based, or sourced/cloud) is mostly ineffective, with bad results
3	None	No competence, but without good or bad results
4	Some Effectiveness	Governance (corporate, or business unit–based, or sourced/cloud) has some competence
5	Effective	Governance (corporate, or business unit–based, or sourced/cloud) is effective

question implied by Exhibit 16.17 is: *Is the enterprise capable—in its governance processes—of making the decisions necessary in the deployment and management of information and IT?*

This begs a number of related questions and issues, such as dealing with silos, dealing with the many suppliers of IT, fitting the process to the nature of the enterprise, and so forth.[16] At bottom, it is the point of these enterprise IT capabilities to determine whether they can be accomplished in the context of all these related factors.[17]

How Does Strategic IT Management Connect to Innovation?

As we were preparing this book, many individuals commented that perhaps we were slighting the important role of creating business opportunity, responding to new circumstances, and on and on—in short, have we shorted *innovation*? In most ways, no, as the seven enterprise IT capabilities are judged by how well they allow response to turbulence and change. But in one other way, yes: We don't, for example, have a chapter that specifically addresses innovation.

A number of important books do focus on innovation in general and with respect to IT in particular. We like Gary Hamel's *What Matters Now: How to Win in a World of Relentless Change, Ferocious Competition, and Unstoppable Innovation*[18]—just reading that subtitle is inspiring. He does emphasize the practical problems, though. For example, he remarks, "Few, if any employees have been trained as business innovators [or] have access to the sort of customer and technology insights that can help to spur innovation. [They] face a bureaucratic gauntlet." Hamel points his readers to another book as an example a good innovation approach.[19]

Our bottom line, however, is that *everything* about Strategic IT Management ultimately ends in innovation—change in response to turbulence, change in response to the imperative for greater value from IT. So we don't have an innovation chapter—we have a whole book.

What Needs to Be Done?

We tend to commit the continuing IT sin of promoting a solution (in this case, Strategic Information Management) in search of a problem. Well, of course, real problems exist: lack of trust, partnership, performance, and so forth. To clarify whether the problem exists in your enterprise, we have previously offered a whole series of assessments and several case examples of their use. But these are detailed and have some complexity.

To simply the assessment, consider two simple questions: 1) Are these outcomes important to me and my enterprise? and 2) Are we performing sufficiently well to produce the outcomes?

Summary

In this chapter we turn our focus on the next steps to be taken by an enterprise, its business units, and IT providers. Or, more to the point, the next steps to be taken by the reader.

First and foremost is self-assessment about the current circumstances found in the reader's enterprise. Without this self-knowledge, knowing what to do next is difficult. Second is stepping back to think about what is possible. We've tried here to suggest priorities that differ based on enterprise circumstances and the readiness of the business and IT to move forward. Leadership is a consideration of course, and our next two chapters deal with the CIO and CEO in particular.

Third is to consider what might be done in the form of training and development for managers, supervisors, and professionals. As we've mentioned, we have a program called *IT University* that teaches professionals about the issues facing anyone attempting a partnering and trusting relationship between business and IT. Again, self-awareness is the starting point, particularly in considering Part II's messages about service, partnership, and leadership. But simply getting started in developing the staff and organization is a good thing.

But finally it comes down to a simple issue: Is any of this important to the reader and the reader's enterprise? If not, well, we hope it is all interesting. But if it is important, then the next step is to get started.

Notes

1. Martin Reeves, Claire Love, and Philipp Tillmanns, "Your Strategy Needs a Strategy," *Harvard Business Review* (September 2012): 76–80.
2. See, for example, the discussion of strategic context in Marianne Broadbent and Peter Weill, "Management by Maxim: How Business and IT Managers Can Create IT Infrastructures," *Sloan Management Review* (Spring 1997): 77–92.
3. The notion of "strategic fit" as described by many authors applies. Again, the idea is that one size simply does not fit all.
4. Peter Weill and Marianne Broadbent, *Leveraging the New Infrastructure: How Market Leaders Capitalize on Information Technology* (Harvard Business School Press, 1998).
5. Observation: Different frameworks are available for this kind of classification. For example, Joe Ward and John Peppard, *Strategic Planning for Information Systems* (Wiley, 2002), present a view on the evolution of strategic planning in general and strategic IT planning in particular. Another classification set could be (referring to the interdependence between business and IT): pooled, sequential, reciprocal, integrated: which relates to siloed autonomous, siloed directed by business, simultaneous business and IT planning, and business–IT co-creation of the business plan.
6. See, for example, Thompson S. H. Teo and William R. King, "Assessing the Impact of Integrating Business Planning and IS Planning," *Information and Management* 30 (1996): 209–321. Framework based on W. R. Synott, *The Information Weapon: Winning Customers and Markets with Technology* (Wiley, 1987).
7. F. W. McFarlan, "Information Technology Changes the Way You Compete," *Harvard Business Review* (May 1984). See also the extensive adaptation of the framework in Robert J. Benson, Thomas L. Bugnitz, and William Walton, *From Business Strategy to IT Action* (Wiley, 2004): 80–84.
8. See, for example, Ward and Peppard, who carry the analysis one step further to the specific composition of the application portfolio: even if a company (or business unit) is "strategic," some of the portfolio will still be support, key operational, and so on.
9. Robert Benson and Thomas Bugnitz, "Transformative IT: Creating Lean IT Portfolio Management . . . or Not," in *Cutter IT Journal* 22, No. 1 (2009): 31–39.
10. Robert J. Benson.
11. Igor Ansoff and Edward McDonell, *Implanting Strategic Management*, 2nd ed. (Wiley, 1990).
12. We encountered the concept of a management culture profile in a research paper. As the authors put it: "a managerial profile based on established cultural characteristics and a strategic posture profile based on the perceived environmental volatility." Our point is not to take a rigorous research perspective, but to apply this as a very useful profile (which we've done with clients) in the challenge of fitting IT's strategic capabilities to the character of enterprise management. Found in and adapted from Robert C. Moussetis, Ali Abu Rahma, and George Nakos, "Strategic Behavior and National Culture: The Case of the Banking Industry in Jordan," *Competitiveness Review: An International Business Journal* 2, incorporating *Journal of Global Competitiveness* 15 (2005): 101–115.
13. Jon Hagel III, John Seely Brown, and Lang Davison, *The Power of Pull: How Small Moves, Smartly Made, Can Set Big Things in Motion* (Basic Books, 2012), xi.
14. Ryan Peterson, Pieter Ribbers, and Ramon O'Callaghan, "Information Technology Governance by Design: Investigating Hybrid Configurations and Integration Mechanisms," *ICIS 2000 Proceedings* (2000), Paper 41. http://aisel.aisnet.org/icis2000/41
15. Peter Weill and Jeanne W. Ross, *IT Governance: How Top Performers Manager IT Decision Rights for Superior Results* (Harvard Business School Press, 2004).
16. See Chapter 5, "Create Clear and Appropriate IT Governance," in Marianne Broadbent and Ellen Kitzis, *The New CIO Leader: Setting the Agenda and Delivering Results* (Harvard Business Review Press, 2004): 105. This does not emphasize our perspective governance as essential to

partnership development and change, but it does have a deep presentation of the key ideas. See also Weill and Ross, *IT Governance*.

17. See Gad Selig, *Implementing IT Governance: A Practical Guide to Global Best Practices in IT Management* (Van Haren, 2008).

18. Gary Hamel, *What Matters Now: How to Win in a World of Relentless Change, Ferocious Competition, and Unstoppable Innovation* (Wiley, 2012): 52.

19. Nancy Tennant Snyder and Deborah L. Duarte, *Unleashing Innovation: How Whirlpool Transformed an Industry* (Jossey-Bass, 2008). Mentioned in Hamel, *What Matters Now*, 53.

CHAPTER 17

Requirements for CIO and IT Leadership

W e stated our Principles for Strategic IT Management in the introduction to Part II. One specifically targets CIOs and leadership:

Senior business and IT management provides support for the business–IT relationship and provides leadership throughout the life of the relationship. IT leadership creates business-focused culture and nurtures the best relationships within IT and with the business. The CEO and business leadership establish the environment for the partnership, the roles to be played, and the necessary commitment and motivation.

This chapter summarizes this book from the CIO perspective, and makes seven basic statements, or messages, to the CIO, IT management, and IT professionals.

1. The CIO and IT managers have important "to do's" on their lists.
2. The business–IT partnership requires CIO and IT management leadership.
3. Enterprises need Strategic IT Management and the aptitudes described by the seven enterprise IT capabilities. Coping with business and technology turbulence requires these capabilities.
4. The CIO needs to manage the technology well; this is necessary, but not sufficient.
5. Authority, control, and "reporting to the CEO" are not sufficient to produce the required results.
6. Be faster. Be flexible.
7. A proactive leadership approach and vision are required.

In addition to these messages, this chapter will ask the CIO and IT managers several questions (see, for example, Exhibits 17.2 and 17.4). These

Exhibit 17.1   Performance Outcomes for CIOs

Outcomes for CIOs
Improve Trust
Strengthen Partnerships
Fit to the Business
Perform to (Service) Expectations
Perform to Create Superior Business Outcomes

questions sum up the messages here and the assessments done in all the other chapters. In short, these questions set the stage for deciding on actions required. These questions, however, also apply to every IT and business professional. It will be a great exercise to think through the current status of the enterprise and the IT activities.

Consider the sense of performance expressed at the end of the previous chapter. It comes down to five basic imperatives, as shown in Exhibit 17.1.

These five outcomes are, fundamentally, the job description for IT managers and professionals. Underneath these very short titles, of course, are all the details represented by IT competencies, such as strategic planning, operational excellence, software development, and so forth.

The question for the reader is simple: Are we performing each of these five imperatives to the extent needed by the enterprise?

Message #1: The CIO and IT Managers Have Important "To Do's" on Their Lists

Overall, the CIO (and by extension the entire IT governance and management process) has these critical "to do's" to achieve.

1. Work to build trust within IT and with business. This is accomplished through transparency and addressing the IT culture barriers, as described in Chapters 10 and 11.
2. Build a partnership with the key business executives, particularly in the business units, to achieve the critical enterprise IT capabilities as described in Chapter 12. Work with them to achieve their roles as shown in the Total Value Performance Model (TVPM; Exhibit 17.2).
3. Fully accept and acknowledge that IT is in the service business—but service as defined by the business. This means service management

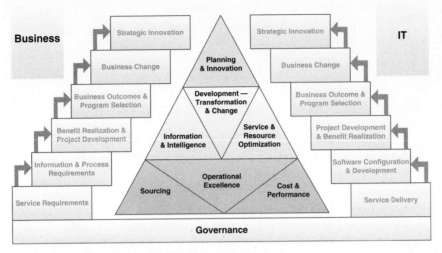

Exhibit 17.2   The Total Value Performance Model

emphasizing personal relationships, common culture, and common goals with the business, as described in Chapter 8.

4. *IT has to perform!* Achieve the six-level TVPM capabilities for the IT organization (see Exhibit 17.2 and Chapters 2 and 3). Chapter 19 lays out the specific targets, the things to be accomplished, while Part II characterizes the importance of partnership, trust, and leadership in achieving these results.

5. Talk business to business executives and the board. Nothing less will work.[1]

6. Talk to customers.[2]

As a guide, revisit each of the self-assessments in the several chapters, particularly Chapters 9 (Partnership), 10 (Leadership), and 12 (the enterprise IT capabilities).

Consider how well your IT is performing, per Exhibit 17.2, and consider the self-assessment results per Chapter 3, Exhibit 3.2 (Business Outcomes: Superior Value from IT), and Chapter 4, Exhibit 4.4 (Business Outcomes, Turbulence and Uncertainty). All this leads to possible answers and conclusions to the fundamental questions that every CIO and IT manager really has to be able to answer (see Exhibit 17.3).

The answers to these questions will begin to set the stage for actions to be considered.

Exhibit 17.3   Questions for the CIO and IT Managers

Strategic IT Management	Questions for Which CIOs and IT Managers Need Answers
IT Performance (TVPM)	At what level (on the stair steps) is IT performing? At what level (on the stair steps) is business performing? What business risks exist in current performance levels?
Service Management in IT	To what extent is IT managed as a service?

Message #2: The Business–IT Partnership Requires CIO and IT Management Leadership

This leadership focuses on setting the culture (within IT and with business partnership) and on making the changes in the relationships with business. We focus here on IT managers and professionals and what they need to be capable of doing with respect to working with the business. We characterize this working relationship as a partnership, built on mutual trust and willingness to participate in the processes (Exhibit 17.4).

This puts real responsibilities on the IT folks, and as Chapter 8 pointed out, real hurdles stand in the way of achieving success. Achieving the end points requires the leadership to proactively accomplish basic outcomes:

- IT's culture, behavior, and performance need to focus on business.
- The CIOs and management staff need to provide the leadership to establish trust and partnerships.

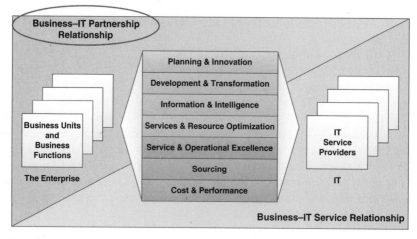

Exhibit 17.4   The Partnership Relationship

- Business managers need to fully participate in the IT processes, producing trust and partnership.
- CEOs and SLTs need to provide the right context and leadership, and the CIO needs to help this to happen.
- IT processes that engage business need to create and nurture the conditions for trust and partnership, and not to act as further inhibitors.

These outcomes are necessary. The CIO and other relevant IT managers need to produce them. This is, in one sense, the job description for IT leadership. And we have to remember that this applies to the processes of oversight and leadership for all IT in the enterprise, whatever the sources (e.g., IT organizations, business unit–based organizations and activities, sourcers, or "do-it-yourself" IT.) To achieve this in this disparate and expanding context requires real leadership, not simply supervision of IT activities. It is on the CIO's plate.

Providing the Needed Leadership

In Chapter 10 we noted the two elements of leadership as (proactive) transactional and transformational. The former is task and achievement oriented, the latter is vision and direction-setting oriented. CIOs, by their nature—and given the importance of operational performance as the foundation for credibility and trust—can be strongly focused on operations and tasks and performance. While important, this limits the CIO's leadership effectiveness.

We quoted John Kotter earlier: "Management is coping with complexity; leadership is coping with change."[3] We also said at that point that it is more than coping; it is proactively doing something in response. Recall that in Chapter 10, we defined leadership in terms of setting vision and persuading others to work toward accomplishing the vision. This is the cornerstone of the CIO's role in Strategic IT Management.

But there are also general characteristics of managers—not just IT managers—that can be problematic, a barrier to achieving leadership (and trust, and partnership, etc.). Michael Watkins described the process of change from good management capabilities to necessary leadership characteristics.[4] He describes seven fundamental shifts or, as he puts it, "seismic shifts of perspective and responsibility." Now, of course, his article is targeted toward individuals who become CEOs and senior business unit leaders, and highlights what is required for success in that transition.

But these ideas are equally effective in describing the challenges of moving from IT management roles to partnership development roles with

Exhibit 17.5 Questions for the CIO and IT Managers

Strategic IT Management	Question CIOs and IT Managers Need an Answer To
The Partnership Relationship	How strong is the business–IT partnership?

business. Consider several of the management "classifying framework" shifts he outlines:

- Specialist to Generalist
- Analyst to Integrator
- Tactician to Strategist
- Bricklayer to Architect
- Problem Solver to Agenda Setter

This shift is more than style; it is fundamental change in the role being played, a fundamental shift in the framework for the CIO in terms of the roles to be played. Again, leadership is at its heart persuasion. These basic shifts parallel the behavior shifts we described in Chapter 8, namely Closed to Open, and so forth.

The Watkins article goes on to identify behaviors needed. Some of them are:

- Understand the frameworks, tools, and terms used in key business functions
- Integrate the collective knowledge of partners
- Shift to the larger (business) picture so that strategy, structure, operating models, and skill bases fit together
- (Identify) what the organization should focus on
- Proactively shape . . . (the partnership)

The result gives the CIO the answer to Exhibit 17.5 question, about the strength of the Business/IT partnership. The answer, like the Exhibit 17.3 questions, sets the stage for further action.

Message #3: Enterprises Need Strategic IT Management and Enterprise IT Capabilities

Coping with business and technology turbulence requires these capabilities.

The enterprise needs the seven capabilities, but one size does not fit all, whether at the enterprise level and within the enterprise, for each line of business and functional area. We emphasize that Strategic IT Management engages both business and IT, in all its organizational and ecosystem complexities. This requires both business and IT leadership.

IT, in particular, provides a significant context for achieving the seven capabilities. The complex ecosystem involving more than simply the IT organization complicates it, and the CIO and IT managers provide much of the energy and culture needed.

The Enterprise IT Capability for Strategic Thinking and Action about IT in the Business

Planning & Innovation. An enterprise requires the capability for business and IT (together) to define the future of the business and its use of information and IT.

This requires the ability to: establish strategies, products/services, and business models; describe the turbulence and uncertainty affecting the business; forecast its requirements or means for reacting to uncertainty; understand competitive and performance requirements; and respond to its requirements and uncertainty with viable plans, goals, and roadmaps for all its IT, and do so successfully in conditions of turbulence.

The Enterprise IT Capability to Deliver Value through Information and IT

Service & Resource Optimization. An enterprise requires the capability to optimize its sourcing, development, and application of all its IT services and resources, from all sources: internal IT, business unit IT activities, sourcers, and do-it-yourself IT activities.

Development & Transformation. An enterprise requires the capability develop, implement, and apply information and IT capabilities to change and transform business with superior returns

Information & Intelligence. An enterprise requires the capability to acquire, manage, analyze, and apply its vast information resources in all relevant enterprise areas

The Enterprise IT Capability for Strategic Thinking and Action about IT in the Business

Planning & Innovation. An enterprise requires the capability for business and IT (together) to define the future of the business and its use of information and IT.

This requires the ability to: establish strategies, products/services, and business models; describe the turbulence and uncertainty affecting the

Exhibit 17.6 Questions for CIOs and IT Managers and Professionals

Strategic IT Management	Questions CIOs and IT Managers Need Answers To
The Enterprise IT Capabilities (Chapter 11)	Does our enterprise have the enterprise IT capabilities required? What business risks exist in the level of our current enterprise IT capabilities?

business; forecast its requirements or means for reacting to uncertainty; understand competitive and performance requirements; respond to its requirements and uncertainty with viable plans, goals, and roadmaps for all its IT; and do so successfully in conditions of turbulence.

The questions in Exhibit 17.6 need answers, and guidance is found in the self-assessments and classification of the enterprise and its lines of business.

The CIO/IT manager to-do list includes steps to clarify the enterprise requirements for Strategic IT Management, chiefly though instruments such as described in Chapter 16. This should provide a sense of priority among the seven enterprise IT capabilities. The individual assessments in Chapters 12 to 14 provide the specific as-is context for each of them and together provide a sense of direction that should show where emphasis should be place.

The first step, though, is acceptance of the requirement that the current as-is probably is not sufficient to deal with the issues of IT value and, in particular, effective response to turbulence and uncertainty. Looming large throughout is the partnership and relationship with business, which the seven enterprise capabilities focus on achieving and strengthening.

A key issue is the enterprise's capability to deal with turbulence, uncertainty, and change. You can explore these topics using the questions in Exhibit 17.7.

Message #4: The CIO Needs to Manage the Technology Well; This Is Necessary, but Not Sufficient

As Exhibit 17.8 shows, the service relationship creates the foundation for the CIO and IT management role in providing IT to the business. The (business-focused) service management component requires CIO leadership, which emphasizes service, not technology (see Chapter 8).

Exhibit 17.7 Questions for the CIO and IT Professionals and Managers

Strategic IT Management	Questions CIOs and IT Managers Need Answers To
Turbulence in Business	To what extent is IT a part of enterprise capabilities for dealing with turbulence in the business environment? What business risks exist due to current involvement of IT in responding to IT business turbulence?
Turbulence in Information Technology	To what extent is IT turbulence bringing new business opportunities to the enterprise, and is business capable of exploiting them? To what extent is IT turbulence affecting IT performance in the enterprise? What business risks exist due to IT turbulence?

But managing the technology well is also a requirement. IT does require the specific competencies to carry out the development and deployment of its services. IT has to perform.

Chapter 7 described these IT competencies in detail; we show them in summary form in Exhibit 17.9.

Yet technology itself can be more of a focus than necessary. It continues to be apparent that CIOs and IT professionals face the "trend of the month" or "fad of the month" on an ongoing basis. Simply reviewing the many blogs and publication web sites devoted to IT and CIOs confirms this. CIOs are

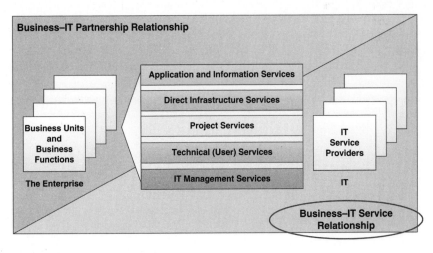

Exhibit 17.8   Service Relationship

Exhibit 17.9   IT Competencies

IT Strategic Competencies	IT Tactical Competencies
Strategizing	Portfolio Management
Innovation	Cost & Performance Management
IT Leadership	Formulating Information Needs
Strategic Outsourcing	Service Management
Architecture Planning	Supplier Management
Strategic Planning	**IT Operational Competencies**
Relationships Building	Service Delivery
	Accountability
	Application
	Software Development and Maintenance
	Professionals Management

challenged to adopt the latest and greatest flashy ideas and hopefully produce value. The challenge is to put these trends on the back burner and concentrate on what is really critical. But the core point is assuring credibility! Performance at each level of the TVPM (see Exhibit 17.2) is vital. Review Chapter 7 for specifics and Chapter 19 for the necessary outcomes.

On the CIO to do list is the assessment of current competences as shown in Chapter 7, together with the question of whether they are up to the requirements of Strategic IT Management (Exhibit 17.10). This is made more complicated by the complexity of the IT ecosystem, but needs doing nevertheless.[5]

Considerable advice to the CIO is available on the technical management aspects but more importantly on the relationships with business.[6]

Exhibit 17.10   Questions for the CIO and IT Managers and Professionals

Strategic IT Management	Questions CIOs and IT Managers Need Answers To
The IT Competencies (Chapter 7)	Is the service relationship with business strong? Does IT have the technical competencies required? What business risks exist in the level of our current IT competencies?

Message #5: Authority, Control, and "Reporting to the CEO" Are Not Sufficient

We're often asked: Does reporting to the CEO fix all these things?

This is an ongoing IT wish: "The CIO needs to be at the table." This is believed to fix all things: visibility, relationships, partnerships, direction-setting, and authority.[7] But it is not completely clear that reporting to the CEO is a good thing. Achieving this carries baggage—in effect, it makes partnerships and relationships harder. It can inhibit trust with peer business managers and organizations. It also may not be good in the sense of weak business-related oversight: CEOs do not necessarily know what is appropriate. Reporting to the CEO requires a culture change for the CEO to pay attention to IT. He/she really needs to pay attention and to the larger issues, not just the interesting technology issues. Otherwise IT's hopes for reporting to the CEO founders on inattention.

Strategic IT Management leads to a new adaptation of the overall organization model of where IT reports. That is, reporting to the CEO creates new issues of where reporting lines go between business units and IT itself. If there's great diversion (business units report up to the CEO through one line, IT through another), IT reporting to the CEO can lead to the creation and increase of gaps between business and IT rather than increasing partnership and trust. Among other things, this can complicate the processes for chartering the partnerships, resolving disputes, and receiving guidance about appropriate actions and directions.

It is unusual when IT is an unfettered, unguided organization, working solely with business managers on a service/partnership relationship. The right people can do it, of course, but this can be difficult and can lead to unresolved issues. This is not an argument for the CIO reporting to the CEO. It is an argument for the effectiveness of any reporting relationship to be measured by the success in creating of partnerships and trust with the business.

The point is simple: The important thing for CIOs is trust, partnership, and leadership with the business. Not authority. Hence the reporting to the CEO may be a diversion from the main challenges and actually make things more difficult. But the more important point is the need for CIOs and IT managers to understand the need for business partnership and trust, rather than authority. Our recommendations at the end of this chapter reflect this.[8]

The bottom line: The CIO and IT reporting line should maximize partnership and trust, not emphasize authority and control.[9]

One other factor is finding the right business partner, potentially a CxO or business unit executive. One compelling partner (if not a reporting line) is the

CFO. It is instructive to read CFO leadership articles and books about what *they* want. See for example, a list of possibilities:

- CFO as Architect of Adaptive Management
- CFO as Warrior against Waste
- CFO as Master of Measurement
- CFO as Regulator of Risk
- CFO as Champion of Change

These are chapter titles from Jeremy Hope's book, *Reinventing the CFO*.[10] A recent *Wall Street Journal* article echoed many of these points.[11]

From the CIO and IT's perspective, and from the larger Strategic IT Management stage, these are key, critical elements of the issues to be pursued and the goals to be achieved. What better than partner with a part of the enterprise with perhaps exactly the same goals? This is what an enterprise IT capability in, say, playing, or operational excellence, or resource management, should be about.

Message #6: Be Faster; Be Flexible

Our recurring theme of turbulence and uncertainty leads to an IT imperative to produce faster results and flexible results (infrastructure, applications, information resources).[12] This requires accepting the idea that accommodating continual change, often transformational, is central to the IT role in the enterprise.[13] We noted earlier that IT's instincts are for well-engineered, stable outcomes, and that change is considered to be something of an enemy. Recall that in traditional systems development, "freezing requirements" is thought to be a critical step.

Here, the mantra becomes "stability is dangerous." The drive for stability comes in many forms: architecture, operational processes, systems development methodologies, governance, annual planning, and budgeting cycles are just a few means of preserving stability. These are not bad per se; rather, they can very much get in the way of reality—that environmental turbulence and uncertainty require a faster, more flexible IT capability.

Preparing for the prospect of continual change can have a stability of its own. For example, technical architectures can have as their overriding goal the accommodation of change, and this would create a context that at one level is stable, but at the level of the activities and systems and data to be supported has a dynamic nature. We mentioned "Dynamic IT" in a previous chapter, which is part of the picture.

The bottom line: The CIO and IT managers face the challenge of being faster, being flexible. To deal with turbulence and uncertainty, this is a requirement.[14]

Message #7: An Active, Proactive Leadership Approach Is Required, with Clear Vision

In a recent management summit, one person remarked that "IT is the hardest filter" for prospective projects. He meant that the IT organization can erect barriers—sometimes called architecture reviews, sometimes experienced as IT misunderstanding of the business importance of the required, and most often reflecting an IT disinterest in the core business issues (and the people in the business). This says important things about the hurdles to establishing partnerships. But he went on to remark that IT has never found its place in the organizational chart. It has migrated from general administration to CFO and sometimes to CEO, which depends on that individual's interest.

IT is a relatively new service function in the business compared to other service functions that have been around for a while, such as legal. But (and this was a wonderful observation from a recent workshop attendee) IT is now the wheels of the organization. Unfortunately, IT is also the last to know about the business. And business often does not know what it needs. It comes down to business and IT leadership, or the lack of it. Certainly the CEO and SLT play roles here, but without clear IT leadership from the CIO and others, the culture that encourages IT to be separate, not involved in the business, will continue.

IT's Vision: History Is Not Kind to CIOs

In August 1994, Bob Benson made a presentation to a national conference of CIOs focused on what they needed to address.

> *We need an IT vision.* More accurately, we need a re-vision because our old ones aren't generally adequate for today's enterprises and tomorrow's competitive circumstances. Why aren't our old visions adequate? It's partly because IT organizational and professional roles are in the midst of radical and fearful change. Technology changes which emphasize IT dispersion are partly to blame; business demands for more flexible and responsive IT services are also partly to blame. At the same time, the typical enterprise needs to invest in new IT forms that require new, and not-well-understood, IT roles. The sense of business demand (senior manager demand) for IT

change grows. In the middle of all this we're stuck with our old visions and consequences (legacies), an operational focus (the existing systems must continue to run well), a strong set of values (e.g., change management, systems development methodologies), fear about IT disaggregation throughout our enterprise, and our innate distrust (or perhaps fear as we don't yet get it) of the viability of the new ways to do things.

Why don't we have a vital, business-based, future-based vision today? When we look at the IT profession as a whole we observe possible patterns that have served as inhibiting factors.

1. *Perhaps we have learned to be helpless.* We have approached senior management and our peer managers before with our visions and proposals and hopes for significantly reshaping how the enterprise functions—many times before—with less success that we would like. Perhaps this has taught caution and given us a *passive* approach to business.

2. *Perhaps we do not believe any longer.* Perhaps we don't have the sort of committed belief in the role and mission of IT that we used to have, particularly as we see skill sets no longer appropriate, ways of doing IT business becoming unnecessary. *Perhaps we believe the rhetoric about the dinosaur IT organizations, the irrelevant IT initiatives.*

3. Perhaps we are tired. *Technology is bubbling up around us*, and it is difficult to keep in front of it all, particularly the new ways of doing things.

4. Perhaps we have fallen into *the reactive trap*: we only do what the user wants. We only understand what the user understands. We perhaps have lost the ability to promote technology and have become incapable of thinking and acting on business- or enterprise-related issues for ourselves. Perhaps we rely on reactivates and user direction rather than providing leadership and direction and *energy. Perhaps we are no longer capable of acting productively.*

5. Perhaps we are reluctant to press what we have been perceived as promoting: our self-interest as an IT profession, as an *IT organization and its role and mission.*

These are possibilities, but the real reason for needing a revitalized IT Vision is that the opportunities and contributions IT can make have changed just as dramatically as the underlying technology has. In many ways any malaise in the current IT Vision lies in the success enjoyed in achieving the significant operational systems that we now call the legacy. In most enterprises, main business processes have had a considerable history of automation and computer applications. In many ways, we have automated all the major business processes. This can lead to the feeling that there is nothing left to be done, and the related feeling that initiatives like reengineering threaten to undo what has been accomplished.

In the narrow sense, regenerating the IT Vision is one way to combat the class of problems described above. In the broader sense, the ReVisioning of IT is an integral step in positioning IT as the primary contributor to future enterprise development. In fact, IT is a vital force for business change. In fact, IT is growing in most enterprises. In fact, new intellectual and leadership challenges exist.

A new view of the IT role. Technology is changing, offering powerful tools and capabilities to managers and organizational units throughout the enterprise. Business is changing too; one needs only to read the latest *Fortune* or *Business Week* or *Economist* to recognize the wide range of management initiatives and business themes. Taken together, a new set of management paradigms are available to enterprises. A short list of examples include the horizontal corporation, total quality management, strategic alliances, and partnerships. In many cases enterprises strive to apply them to strengthen their business performance, but without the dimension of success hoped for.

The phenomena of new management paradigms and the related issues of change and change management—the processes by which enterprises reenergize themselves by applying new ways of management and structure—offer one major hook for IT re-visioning, for IT can be a main, if not the main tool for adopting the management paradigms. An interesting challenge: What role should IT have in leading the movement toward adopting the new management paradigms?

It is interesting: The IT ReVision may have close links to the values and practices we learned in the 1960s and 1970s. Then, the new management paradigms focused on task automation, cost reduction and efficiencies, and integration of information used in multiple business functions. It may be that now, the ReVision is not something new in kind, but a return to our roots and initial values.

Normally, we would take the IT view on the issue of vision. It is easy to focus on technologies, organizations, methods, themes like business process reengineering (BPR), and so forth. It is easy to take defensive positions like the business value of IT, IT is a service, let us get senior management support for IT-enabled business change, and so on. These defensive positions offer neither leadership nor vision. We need to take the enterprise view first: What are the core things that have to be accomplished for the enterprise? What are the core things underlying successful adoption of new management and new business paradigms? Some of these things might be technical in nature (e.g., achieve the enterprise-wide common network). These things are much more likely to be business in nature (e.g., radical restructuring of service/product delivery to customer to slash cost/time and increase flexible response to customer requirements). This is more than BPR and business value; this is a vision, a reaffirmation of how IT fits into achieving those core business requirements.

Having a vision gives coherence to the actions, decisions, and strategies we have to have to make anything happen. Two themes can be advanced to justify this statement. First, IT is complex and multifaceted. A vision gives a sense of common direction for all the facets. A vision is important if we want to change what we are doing. A vision is particularly important in our business, for (business) change is what we are about. To do change effectively demands a clear vision as to where we are going, why we want to, what we want to do to get there.

We could look at this from the IT perspective. Right now, we need a vision because IT is changing and expanding. In part we need a vision to cope with the increasingly complex mix of technologies being applied in the enterprise. Perhaps we need vision that results in usable architectures, standards, and similar attributes of effective technology management.

We do face new directions for technology, including technology patterns with which we are unfamiliar (e.g., imaging, expert technologies, various communications technologies). Perhaps new skills and organizational roles. The change includes recycling our own staff, restructuring how we relate to the business. We do not, however, need a vision that's "just another IT initiative" similar to ones we have mounted in the past (e.g., the power of relational databases, the convergence of communications and computing, the excitement of expert systems and/or decision-support systems). These were okay, but they focused on technology delivery, not business impact.

We can look at this from the CEO or enterprise perspective. Right now, we need vision because the business is telling us we have to change how we are doing IT. We have a lot of technology changes (e.g., client-server and open systems architectures), but these are merely symptoms and tool-set opportunities. Their purpose is to improve our ability to change the business. Our competition is, we have things like total quality management and reengineering and the virtual enterprise (actually, none of these things is more than a slogan . . . but we surely have to slash costs, slash cycle times, add flexibility and customer care.) However, this view possibly overlooks the IT role in basic and fundamental business change, represented by management and business paradigms.

Once we take the CEO/enterprise perspective, we then need to express the vision in ways that allow us to accomplish it. This is the change-management issue; once we have identified where we have to go, how, exactly, can we get there? This problem reintroduces technology and technology management, in terms of formalizing the vision in ways we can deal with.

To accomplish this, the CIO and the IT Organization must do these things:

- Recognize the new management and business paradigms.
- Recognize the role IT plays in getting it done.
- Define the role the senior IT executive plays in marketing the position.
- Define the role the IT organization plays in organizing work.
- Find success in getting the resulting projects accomplished and change managed.

So, finally, the problem of this presentation is this. We need vision of two kinds: a destination (end-point) vision and a change-management/directional vision. These two kinds are not only related, but they are "two sides of the same coin." We have to articulate this vision in ways that link the technology opportunities to where we need to take IT as a whole in the enterprise. We have to avoid the trap of making the driver for this be technology for its own sake.

Back to the Future for Vision

Regrettably, it feels as though the presentation could have been made yesterday. The recommendations made in 1994, on balance, were not followed—which is, of course, why we wrote this book. We are talking about the framework for the CIO (and for IT managers), about the role they play and the leadership characteristics they need to achieve. The need for the

Exhibit 17.11   Questions for the CIO and IT Managers

Strategic IT Management	Questions CIOs and IT Managers Need Answers To
The Roadmap for Strategic IT Management	Do we have a roadmap for filling the gaps in addressing the questions raised earlier? Are the CIO and IT management defining the IT vision?

two kinds of vision remain: the vision for the end point, and for how to get there.

But things have changed. In some ways, IT has grown more sophisticated in the management of IT Supply with maturing tools such as enterprise architecture and agile development. This is however an IT organizational view; the changing IT landscape is one of ubiquity and for many purposes, dispersion.

Another component of change is whether the business side, the CEO and business executives, have an improved vision for the importance of IT both operationally and strategically. Certainly in many enterprises they do, but the evidence is that this is not widespread. This is part of the vision and leadership mandate: ensuring that vision is articulated and understood throughout the enterprise.

Of the five expressions of CIO leadership requirements, "recognize the role IT plays in getting it done" is perhaps the biggest need. This describes CIO's leadership role, both in IT itself and throughout the business. And again, this applies to all aspects of IT use and sources, whether from the traditional IT organization or from the many other sources available to the business.

Exhibit 17.11 completes the questions for the CIO and IT managers, focusing on what might come next.

Conclusions: For the CIO, What Does Strategic IT Management Offer?

So what do we recommend about reporting lines and the CIO leadership role? Every enterprise is different, of course, and the issue of reporting lines and control is surely dependent on the enterprise history, culture, and CEO/business unit executives/CIO personalities. But there are things to be done irrespective of reporting line and lines of authority.

First, accept that CIO (and IT) leadership is not to control, but to encourage the conditions we have emphasized here, the partnership relationships among the many IT providers/sources and the many components of the business. The challenge is not authority; it is having the right platform and relationships for exercising leadership.

Second, behave as a transactional leaders and accept that performance is the basis for credibility and trust. If IT is broken, fix it. If IT outside the purview of the IT organization is broken, help to fix it.

- Achieve performance success according to the six-level Total Value Performance Model.
- Establish the conditions necessary for the success of Strategic IT Management, namely the seven enterprise IT capabilities. Partner with whoever is needed to achieve the performance for each of these capabilities.

Third, behave as a partner. As Chapter 9 emphasizes, this means adopting common purpose and goals, providing transparency, and so forth.

Fourth, behave as transformation leaders and establish and communicate the vision for the role of IT.

Fifth, communicate with the business, the CEO, and the board. Nothing less will do.

Sixth, clarify all roles to be played, particularly in the IT organization.

And seventh: Ensure that all IT understands these requirements and performs appropriately. Proactively work toward IT's culture change. Accept nothing less in culture and performance. *That is, lead!*[15]

Every IT person, trained now to be specific and technology focused, is challenged to become a business problem solver. IT leadership is more than specific problem solvers, simply delivering technology. And this is why we include IT staff in the set of actors requiring leadership skills, for the IT people—as part of partnerships in project teams, in planning groups, in service-providing roles—are charged to provide this kind of leadership to allow us to achieve our goals: superior response to turbulence, superior value delivered to the business.

To the IT manager and professional: Go back and read the Preface.

Self-Assessment for IT Leadership

As stated earlier in the chapter, every IT professional has the opportunity to lead, for example as part of project teams, performing operational activities with the business, introducing technology, and all the responsibilities included. This is a self-assessment for both the enterprise and for the individual reader.

Exhibit 17.12 along with the scale on Exhibit 17.13 provide a final self-assessment for the CIO and IT management.

Exhibit 17.12   CIO and IT Leadership

CIO and IT Leadership Role	Enterprise	IT Organization	Personal
Not to control, but nurture the partnerships.			
Performance is the basis for credibility and trust.			
Behave as a partner.			
Establish and communicate the vision for the role of IT.			
Assure that all IT understands these leadership requirements.			
See that IT performs appropriately.			
Proactively work toward IT's culture change. Accept nothing less in culture and performance.			

Exhibit 17.13   Scale

0	Not applicable
5	This leadership role is understood and proactively addressed
4	This leadership role is somewhat understood
3	Do not know, or not a factor
2	This leadership role is lacking
1	This leadership role is lacking and impedes the achievement of goals

Notes

1. See, for example: Kim S. Nash, "Clueless in the Board Room," *CIO* (November 15, 2012): 22–28.
2. See, for example, Kim S. Nash, "Customers F2F," *CIO* (March 1, 2012): 37–44.
3. See John P. Kotter, *Leading Change* (Harvard Business Review Press, 1996).
4. Michael D. Watkins, "How Managers Become Leaders," *Harvard Business Review* (June 2012): 65–72.
5. See Keri E. Pearlson and Carol Saunders, *Strategic Management of Information Systems*, 4th ed. (Wiley, 2009). See Chapter 8, "Governance of the Information Systems Organization" for section "What Managers Can Expect from IS," 224.

6. Examples from which we have benefited include: Lane Dean, *The Chief Information Officers' Body of Knowledge: People, Process, and Technology* (Wiley, 2011); Richard Hunter and George Westerman, *The Real Business of IT: How CIOs Create and Communicate Value* (Harvard Business Press, 2009); Marianne Broadbent and Ellen S. Kitzis, *The New CIO Leader: Setting the Agenda and Delivering Results* (Harvard Business Press/Gartner, 2004): 23–45; Martha Heller, *The CIO Paradox: Battling the Contradictions of IT Leadership* (Bibliomotion, 2013); Keri E. Pearlson and Carol Saunders, *Strategic Management of Information Systems*, 4th ed. (Wiley, 2009).

7. See, for example, Chapter 1, "Get the CIO on the Executive Team," in *Managing IT as a Business: A Survival Guide for CEOs*, ed. Mark D. Lutchen (PriceWaterhouseCoopers/Wiley, 2004).

8. See Larry Tieman, "Why CMOs and CFOs Will Rule Above CIOs," *Information Week*, July 9, 2012, www.informationweek.com/gloval-cio/interviews/why-cmos-and-cfs-will-rule-above-cios/240003340

9. For a more contemporary view, see Peter S. Delisi, Dennis Moberg, and Ronald Danielson, "Why CIOs Are Last among Equals," *Wall Street Journal*, May 24, 2012. They argue that CIOs typically fall behind other CxOs in abilities such as synthesis, communication, and relationship skills.

10. Jeremy Hope, *Reinventing the CFO: How Financial Managers can Transform Their Roles and Add Greater Value* (Harvard Business School Press, 2006).

11. Matthew Quinn, "What the CFOs Want," *Wall Street Journal*, June 27, 2011. See also any issue of *CFO Magazine* or other publications targeted toward financial management.

12. Gary Hamel, *What Matters Now: How to Win in a World of Relentless Change, Ferocious Competition, and Unstoppable Innovation* (Jossey-Bass, 2012).

13. See, for example, Gary Hamel, with Bill Breen, *The Future of Management* (Harvard Business Review Press, 2007): 19.

14. See John P. Kotter, *A Sense of Urgency* (Harvard Business Press, 2009).

15. See Graham Waller, Karen Hollenbeck, and George Rubenstrunk, *The CIO Edge: 7 Leadership Skills You Need to Drive Results* (Harvard Business Review Press, 2010). See also "The Elements of Leadership," an extensive part of Chapter 1, in Broadbent and Kitzis, *The New CIO Leader*: 23–45.

CHAPTER 18

Requirements for CEO and Business Leadership

This chapter talks to CEOs and all business managers and professionals. The first part emphasizes the important messages and roles for CEOs. The second part speaks to all business managers and professionals, as partners with the IT leadership and organizations.

Practically everyone—authors, CIO organizations, CIOs—believes the CEOs (and CEO equivalents in lines of business and large functional areas) need to provide the leadership and support for IT in the business. Why is this? Primarily because IT represents change and perhaps transformation in the business, and change requires vision, motivation, encouragement, cheerleading—all of which are elements of leadership. And it is the role of the CEO to motivate and provide all this.

We stated this principle in Chapter 11:

> *Leadership*: Senior business and IT management provides support for the business–IT relationship and provides leadership throughout the life of the relationship. IT leadership creates business-focused culture and nurtures the best relationships within IT and with the business. The CEO and business leadership establishes the environment for the partnership, the roles to be played, and the necessary commitment and motivation. Chapter 10 describes the leadership required.

This chapter summarizes this book from the CEO perspective and makes seven basic messages to the CEO and business leadership. The importance of the CEO's role in enabling the culture and commitment to Strategic IT Management cannot be overstated.

Exhibit 18.1   Questions for CEOs and Business Leaders

Key Topics	CEOs and Business Leaders Need Answers To These Questions
Turbulence in Business	To what extent is IT a part of our capabilities for dealing with turbulence in our environment? What business risks exist due to current involvement of IT in responding to IT business turbulence?
Turbulence in Information Technology	To what extent is IT turbulence bringing new business opportunities? To what extent is IT turbulence affecting IT's performance in the enterprise? What business risks exist due to IT turbulence?

Seven Messages to CEOs and Business Unit Executives (CEO Equivalents)

1. The enterprise needs Strategic IT Management.
2. Strategic IT Management requires CEO leadership for organizational context, culture, and change.
3. The CEO provides the enterprise leadership to generate and actively communicate the business vision and IT's role.
4. The CEO builds and supports the environment for partnership, teamwork, collaboration.
5. Building and supporting IT governance is critical to change management.
6. Engage the CMO, CFO, and the Board in Strategic IT Management.
7. Good IT is necessary; do not accept poor performance.

In addition to these messages, this chapter poses questions the CEO and business leadership need to answer—or at least need the capability to answer. Exhibit 18.1 begins these questions, and each section of CEO Messages concludes with important questions.

Message #1: The Enterprise Needs Strategic IT Management

No senior executive can be unaware of the business and technology turbulence affecting business in general and the enterprise in particular. Of course, the details of how turbulence affects the individual enterprise depends on a lot of variables, many of which are senior leadership's vision, strategies, and plans.

At the same time, senior executives understand the role IT plays in the enterprise and the requirement for great IT performance.

Information technology is both a cause of and a response to turbulence. Current IT management organizations and processes are resources for improving IT performance, and also a cause of difficulty in improving.

Strategic IT Management is the framework for addressing turbulence and effective IT performance. The key concepts (Exhibit 18.1) are partnership (business and IT), trust among all the players, speed of response to environmental changes, and flexibility of the results. Strategic IT Management requires the CEO and senior leadership for understanding, support, and proactive actions.

Message #2: Strategic IT Management Requires CEO Leadership for Organizational Context, Culture, and Change

Much leadership literature focuses on the up-front role the CEO plays in driving the enterprise forward with vision and strategic actions. Certainly a great deal of management literature is written to and about the CEO. But for those of us interested in IT and its role in the enterprise, there is a nuance to this. Leadership is challenged to create the management climate that allows all the other actors—business unit executives, for example—to play their roles in the development, use, and management of IT in the enterprise. This is a major challenge and typically requires the CEO to create and sustain that climate.

This is not new. From the beginning of IT (in the 1950s and 1960s), the clarion call was always, "We need to get senior management support." Practically every book written since 1960 has a chapter or section that identifies the importance of CEO support for IT. This has morphed into the call for the CIO to report to the CEO, one of the reasons being the opportunity to create that necessary leadership context.

This leads to two somewhat independent thoughts about the CEO and IT. The first is that the CEO's leadership is needed to provide support for mobilizing business unit leaders' and managers' participation in the necessary planning, management, and guidance roles in deploying IT . . . sometimes called *alignment*. The second is the need for the CEO to generate the business vision for the use of IT—often a competitive or industry transformational vision—that can provide the incentive to use IT in a dramatic, competitively effective manner (Exhibit 18.2). This is sometimes termed *innovation* in the context of new IT roles in the enterprise strategies.

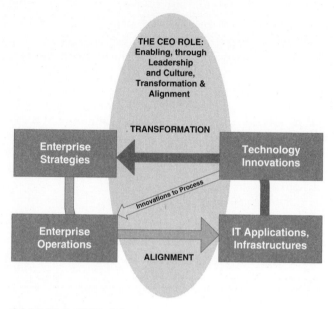

Exhibit 18.2   CEO's Role

These two thoughts mirror the business–IT relationship diagram introduced in Chapter 2 and shown in Exhibit 18.2 to define the CEO's role; we need CEOs setting the context for each of those relationships to enable the direct development of IT as a contributor to transformational responses to competitive and industry changes, and to enable the opportunity for IT to provide those transformational visions about the possibilities for business.

Our experience is the former is the most prevalent: Almost every enterprise has the problem of deploying IT in an innovative and transforming way to support the use of information and IT for operationalizing new business strategies and new operational configurations. This is the *alignment* portion of leadership, something we referred to as *transactional* in Chapter 10. On the other hand, there are certainly examples of IT leading the charge, the "impact" or innovation side of things, which requires the CEO to be the cheerleader, the supporter of the transformational opportunities in business. This is the *transformational* part of leadership, from Chapter 10.

Someone has said that the CEO is, ultimately, about change. The CEO energizes fundamental change in strategy and operations, and in the ways IT is exploited in transformational ways. If one reads the business and technology journals, it would seem that every technology opportunity and "new thing" applies to everyone—for example, cloud, big data, analytics, customer engagement, and so forth. But it is not so, and the CEO plays an important role in

Exhibit 18.3   CEO and Business Leader Questions

Key Topics	CEOs and Business Leaders Need Answers to These Questions
The Enterprise IT Capabilities (Chapter 11)	Does our enterprise have the enterprise IT capabilities required? What business risks exist in the level of our current enterprise IT capabilities?

clarifying exactly what the business vision and role of technology will be. The questions in Exhibit 18.3 should help.

Message #3: The CEO Provides the Enterprise Leadership to Generate and Actively Communicate the Business Vision and IT

Weill and Ross's book[1] states a number of IT key leadership roles for the CEO and business executives, such as communicating the enterprise operating model, building the culture, assigning accountabilities, and establishing appropriate governance. The key thought is changing the behavior of the actors, requiring clear direction and leadership. The CEO needs to clarify the vision and consider how organizational and management roles will play in Strategic IT Management and how the IT environment continues to change.

A shorthand statement of the requirement for CEO leadership in communicating the business vision and connection to IT:

- Review the business capabilities the enterprise requires, and determine how to address the gaps. See Exhibit 19.1 in Chapter 19 for these capabilities.
- Define the role and mission for participants in the business–IT partnership.
- Set the expectations.
- Encourage participation; in particular, overcome the legacy of silos both in business and in IT.
- Set the business vision and IT's role in it.
- Require superior performance.

We've already explored the role of CEOs in clarifying IT's role in the enterprise. This is important, to be sure. But the other elements are at least as important. This applies to all of the senior leadership team (SLT) members, particularly the CFO. Without clear support for the transformational aspects

Exhibit 18.4 CEO Culture

Uncertainty Avoidance	The degree to which this affects CEO plans and decisions
Risk Propensity	The degree to which the CEO is comfortable with taking on and managing risk.
Openness to Change	The degree to which the CEO embraces business change
Time Orientation	The horizons affecting plans and decisions: short term vs. long term
Perception of Control over the Environment	The degree to which the CEO believes the enterprise can control the key variables affecting it

of IT in the enterprise, little gets done. And this is even more severe in times of turbulence and uncertainty. It is only natural: All involved fear for the future.

The CEO shapes the culture. But the CEO also has a culture, or context, as well (Exhibit 18.4). We introduced some of this in Chapter 16, where we cast the discussion as characteristics of the enterprise and its leadership team. The reader is encouraged to go back to Chapter 16 and apply the frameworks to the CEO, to gain a better understanding of culture driving the CEO (and the senior leadership team as well).

Is the CEO really that important? Some years ago, a *Harvard Business Review* article titled "What Only the CEO Can Do"[2] made clear that, indeed, the CEO is the driving force for setting an enterprise's direction, its culture, and the pathways it takes in negotiating turbulence. The CEO is in fact critical, in ways both positive (enabling things to happen) and negative (setting limits on what can happen).

Much is written elsewhere about the CIO–CEO relationship, and this chapter is not intended to focus on that per se. Rather, the point here is to focus on what business leadership needs to do to enable Strategic IT Management and its role in dealing with business turbulence and uncertainty, and generally improving the outcomes for IT in the enterprise. And setting the culture is a critical component.

But this is not an independent variable; much of this flows from the CEO as well as from the character of the enterprise itself, as discussed in Chapter 16. One of the simple frameworks introduced there works here to help understand where the CEO is and hence the starting point for the culture affecting IT.[3]

We applied this set of ideas as a framework in Chapter 16, but it has special importance for understanding the role the CEO is likely to play. The answers to the question in Exhibit 18.5 certainly affect the ways in which IT—and the

Exhibit 18.5   CEO and Leadership Questions

Key Topic	CEOs and Business Leaders Need an Answer to This Question
The Roadmap	Do we have a roadmap for filling the gaps in addressing the questions raised?

Strategic IT Management's enterprise capabilities—function, and even more importantly, their priorities. For example, a CEO with limited Time Orientation and a Low Risk Propensity will set a different climate for IT innovation and business transformation than one with a different set of perspectives.

Message #4: The CEO Builds and Supports the Environment for Partnership, Teamwork, Collaboration

Achieving the goals for Strategic IT Management requires partnership and trust between IT and business. The CEO sets the expectations for this, emphasizing its importance. The questions in Exhibit 18.6 should set you on the right track.

The expectations include:

1. Partnership and teamwork is important.
2. Everyone (senior business management, IT management, professionals) participates.
3. Overcoming the challenges of silos is imperative.
4. Accept no poor partnership, participation, or performance.

Exhibit 18.6   CEO and Business Leadership Questions

Key Strategic IT Management Topics	CEOs and Business Leaders Need Answers to These Questions
Trust and Partnership between Business and IT	What is the level of trust and partnership? Does this apply to all business units? Does this apply to all IT sources? What business risks exist in the current level of trust and partnership?
The Partnership Relationship	How strong is the business–IT Partnership?

Message #5: The CEO Builds and Supports IT Governance as Critical to Change Management

Governance provides the context for defining priorities, the importance of partnership, performance monitoring, and development and adherence to the business and IT visions.

Governance is, fundamentally, the mechanisms for achieving change in both business and IT. Several principles apply:

- The CEO encourages governance as a core part of building the business–IT partnership development, not control.
- One size does not fit all. Accordingly, the nature of the governance processes depends on the enterprise characteristics, as Chapter 16 discussed.
- The CEO considers the roles that various senior leaders play as the technology and its use evolves. This particularly involves the changing role of many IT providers.
- Stability is dangerous. While this can be a natural goal for governance processes, the underlying objective is enabling good responses to turbulence and change. Good architecture done with this in mind is a form of stability, but practically everything else gets in the way and should be a core element of the governance discussion.
- Speed and flexibility are the paramount characteristics of IT investment solutions.

Message #6: Engage the CMO, CFO, and Board in Strategic IT Management

The CEO does play the leading role, but other senior executives also set the culture and expectations and context for partnership and governance. Chiefly, the CFO and CMO fall into this category; the CFO because this often is a normal reporting line for IT, and the CMO because so much of the aspects of turbulence, and the enterprise responses, fall within the CMO purview.

The board, too, is a player, and should be engaged in the Strategic IT Management considerations.

While the CEO is a vital leadership player, realistically the CFO also has a considerable role to play as well. One of the ironies is that CFOs are seeking some of the same relationship characteristics as the CIO, namely a strategic role or something similar.[4]

But the CFO often is in the reporting line for the CIO and certainly is involved in the financial, risk, and perhaps security management of IT functions. This means the CEO should have visibility into the CFO–CIO relationship and help establish the appropriate expectations and context for the IT activity.

Message #7: Good IT Is Necessary; Do Not Accept Poor Performance

The CEO should focus on three dimensions of "good" IT, as shown in Exhibit 18.7. First is IT performance, as represented by the Total Value Performance Model (TVPM). Note this includes both IT and business performing their respective roles. Second is the availability of IT competencies in the IT organization(s) providing services to the enterprise. The checklist in Chapter 7 is a good place to begin. Third is IT's participation in the business–IT partnership and the building of trust with business.

The bottom line, though, is that the CEO cannot accept poor performance from IT, particularly as measured against the requirements of Strategic IT Management.

Messages to Business Managers and Professionals

Each manager can begin by reviewing the messages to CEOs, as they can be applied to everyone in business. In particular, business managers can consider the "CEOs and Business Leaders Need Answers to These Questions" and how the answers describe the business unit/organization in which they function.

Chapter 17 offered six messages to CIOs and IT professionals. Mirror-image questions equally pertain to the business partners. The principle of business–IT partnership sets the requirements, and the business managers/

Exhibit 18.7   CEO and Leadership Questions

Key Strategic IT Management Topics	CEOs and Business Leaders Need Answers to These Questions
IT Performance (TVPM)	At what level (on the stair steps) is IT performing? At what level (on the stair steps) is business performing? What business risks exist in current performance levels?
Service Management in IT	To what extent is IT managed as a service?
The IT Competencies (Chapter 7)	Does IT have the competencies required? What business risks exist in the level of our current IT competencies?

professionals need play their full partner role. Recall Chapter 9's section on reasons for the business–IT partnership, which emphasizes the roles both IT and business play. In other words: Partnership requires partners.

> *Message 1*: The CIO and IT managers have important "to do's" on their lists. The question for business managers is: What role should they play for each of the "to do's"?

> *Message 2*: The business–IT partnership requires CIO and IT management leaderships. Just as importantly, the partnership requires the full participation of business managers and professionals.

> *Message 3*: Enterprises need Strategic IT Management and the aptitudes described by the seven enterprise IT capabilities. Business and technology turbulence requires these capabilities. Each business manager should consider how to best enable and participate in these enterprise IT capabilities.

> *Message 4*: Managing the technology well is not sufficient. The business is the recipient of technology and of the additional IT activities.

> *Message 5*: Authority and control (and "reporting to the CEO") are not sufficient to produce the required results. This characterizes the essence of the partnership: working together to achieve the desired business outcomes, particularly in response to turbulence and uncertainty. Business managers should question how they participate in the partnership.

> *Message 6*: A proactive leadership approach and vision are required. This equally true for business managers.

Concluding Message to the CEO

The topic of this book, transforming business with IT in turbulent times, puts a lot on the plate of the CEO. With its enabling role as an integral part of the business organization, IT is in the heart of what the enterprise does. No wonder that the management of IT is a critical success factor (or failure factor) for reaping business benefits from IT investments. We have tried to make clear that IT has become (or if not yet, is becoming) too important to be left with IT people. The business is supposed to pick up its responsibility at every level of management, including at the level of the CEO.

We are not going to repeat the messages of this book here in this concluding paragraph; just remember that turbulent times require agility and that the business–IT relationship is a service relationship, embedded in a partnership. Remember that turbulence, service, and partnership have implications for both sides. Turbulence demands agility and swift reactions of business functions and IT; services cannot be produced or delivered well without them being defined well; and trust and partnership need two to tango. What about the CEO? The CEO is the eventual responsible person for the success of the enterprise; he/she sets objectives, decides on plans, establishes the right organization, controls outcomes against plans, and the like. We believe that three major responsibilities stand out.

First, the CEO is the organizational architect. Creating an agile organization with appropriate structures, processes, and relational mechanisms requires a purposeful design, selecting the right people with right skills and mind-set (or retraining them in the right way).[5] This is, for most cases, a transformation, which without the drive of the CEO will not take place.

Second, the CEO drives and sets the culture in which there are no IT plans as isolated plans, but in which there are only business plans. Business (strategic) planning is a matter of co-creation where business and IT, under the drive of the CEO, collaborate to define the future business plans. At the highest level, this collaboration implicates the CEO and the highest IT leadership (CIO).

Third, the CEO establishes a culture of "no-excuses management."[6] There are, throughout the business, no excuses to not deliver on expectations and to not deliver value.[7] As we have pointed out throughout this book, performance is *the* foundation of trust: without performance, no trust, and as the saying goes, "without trust, no trade." Performance relates to all levels of our staircase: to the foundational levels of service delivery and project definition and management, but also to the growth levels of transformation and innovation. And for each of these levels, performance not only relates to technically delivering what is expected, but also to an open, transparent, and caring attitude between the service provider and the recipient. This change to an organization of trust does not take place by lip service only: It requires supporting changes in reward and recognition systems. For each of these elements, it is the CEO who sets the stage.

Henry Mintzberg[8] distinguished interpersonal, informational and decisional roles for managers. In each of these roles, the CEO has activities that he/she is expected to perform, as well as with regard to Strategic IT Management in turbulent times. The need for agility, service relationships, and trust and partnership should be repeatedly and clearly communicated to all levels. Lower-ranked business and IT managers should be held responsible for establishing this culture in their respective units. Up-to-date information about initiatives and policies that proved to work should be provided to those who need to be aware of them. Finally it is the CEO's responsibility to ensure that necessary decisions are being made. He/she allocates the necessary resources, is in the midst of possible conflicts, and so forth.

We said it before, IT is too important to be left solely to IT people; however, here we add: Strategic IT Management cannot be done by the CIO

Exhibit 18.8   Self-Assessment

CEO/Business Leadership Role	Enterprise	Personal
Acknowledge that the enterprise needs Strategic IT Management.		
Strategic IT Management requires CEO leadership for organizational context, culture, and change.		
The CEO provides the enterprise leadership to generate and actively communicate the business vision and IT.		
Building and supporting the environment for partnership, teamwork, collaboration is critical.		
Build and support IT governance as critical to change management.		
Engage the CMO, CFO, and the board in Strategic IT Management.		
Good IT is necessary; do not accept poor performance.		

alone; he/she needs top-level support. In a recent panel discussion with CIOs in which we participated, in answer to the question "What is your biggest threat?" one of CIOs answered: "I am sad to say, it is my CEO; he does not like change." As we hope we have convinced our readers, this is the wrong message.

Self-Assessment for Business Leadership

As stated earlier, CEOs (and CEO equivalents) have the opportunity to lead. Exhibit 18.8 is a self-assessment for both the enterprise and for the individual reader, with Exhibit 18.9 providing the scale.

Exhibit 18.9   Self-Assessment Scale

0	Not applicable
5	This leadership role is understood and proactively addressed
4	This leadership role is somewhat understood
3	Do not know, or not a factor
2	This leadership role is lacking
1	This leadership role is lacking and impedes the achievement of goals

Notes

1. Peter Weill and Jeanne W. Ross, *IT Savvy: What Top Executives Must Know to Go from Pain to Gain* (Harvard Business Press, 2009): 142.
2. A. G. Lafley, "What Only the CEO Can Do," *Harvard Business Review* (May 2009): 55–61.
3. Adapted from research papers: See our discussion of this framework in Chapter 16.
4. See, for example, Matthew Quinn, "What the CFOs Want," *Wall Street Journal*, June 27, 2011.
5. Robert Howard, "The CEO as Organizational Architect: An Interview with Xerox's Paul Allaire," *Harvard Business Review* (September–October 1992).
6. T. J. Rodgers, "No Excuses Management," *Harvard Business Review* (July–August 1990).
7. Graham Waller, George Hallenbeck, and Karen Rubenstrunk, *The CIO Edge: 7 Leadership Skills You Need to Deliver Results* (Harvard Business Review Press, 2010).
8. Henry Mintzberg, *The Nature of Managerial Work* (Harper & Row, 1973).

CHAPTER 19

Reflections and Recommendations

C hapter 1 introduced the notion of capability the enterprise should have, needs to have.

By now the reader should have clear understanding of what is meant for each of the bullets in Exhibit 19.1. The IT Perspective list has some parallel to the IT Competencies, but adds the working together with business. The Business perspective and the Turbulence and Uncertainty list are key points, the real contributions Strategic IT Management makes to the enterprise.

Summarizing the Enterprise IT Capabilities and Their Importance

Broadly, of course, the enterprise IT capabilities connect the things that IT organizations and business organization must do.

To review previous chapters, we developed the Total Value Performance Model (TVPM) shown in Exhibit 19.2 to convey three basic ideas. First, is that both business and IT have things they should do (perhaps must do) to ultimately create business change and strategic innovation. This is a stair-step concept: they must perform the first step (e.g., service delivery/service requirements) well in order to be able to perform requirements/configuration, and so forth. The TVPM communicates this stair step, a "Mastery" model perhaps, as we introduced in Chapter 2.

The second concept is that these steps are completely connected. Both business and IT must do their part. For IT to provide service delivery (the first step), business must define its service requirements. And so on up the respective staircases.

The third concept is that the seven enterprise IT capabilities connect them, coordinate them, and create the context in which they can be done successfully. Without the enterprise perspective, these activities are done in

Exhibit 19.1   Enterprise Capabilities

Enterprise IT Capability	The Enterprise— business and IT working together—is capable of this (from IT perspective)	The Enterprise— business and IT working together—is capable of this (from business perspective)	The Enterprise is capable of this (to deal with turbulence and uncertainty)
Planning & Innovation	Planning for the use of information and IT Matching IT Supply to IT Demand	• Seeing the potentially massive disruptions in business and technology • Understanding the potential for IT as transformational force • Moving beyond business as usual • Taking a holistic perspective of the business: overcoming the silos • Business and IT working in partnership • Understanding the business • Thinking strategically • Finding business innovations through the use of information and IT • Adopting sense and respond—to fast moving business requirements • Seeing and understanding industry patterns • Rising above the IT-centric perspective • Planning for adaptive/dynamic IT	• Performing faster, producing quicker responses, enabling dynamic business changes • Adopting enabling architectures and capabilities necessary for dynamic IT
Development & Transformation	Maximizing project value		
Information & Intelligence	Applying analytics and data		
Service & Resource Optimization	Managing IT assets Strategic sourcing		
Sourcing	Making the best decisions among the alternatives for IT sourcing Managing sourcing decisions		
Cost & Performance	Knowing and managing costs Understanding the cost and value of all information and IT		
Service & Operational Excellence	Performing service excellence in all five IT service portfolios Delivering IT services to the business		

silos and without reference to the other activities and knowledge needed. Without the enterprise perspective, ultimately, it becomes significantly more difficult to achieve our overall goals: superior business value and superior responses to turbulence.

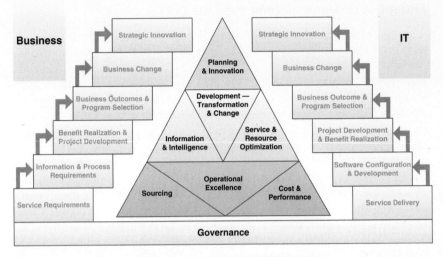

Exhibit 19.2   Total Value Performance and Enterprise IT Capabilities

In looking over the seven enterprise IT capabilities, it is clear that all are critical to the overall IT performance in the enterprise. Again, we are not talking narrowly about the process and methodologies themselves. Those are within the province of the technology manager in the IT organization or in the business domain. Recall our observation that there are different practices, for example between the United States and Europe, as to who is primarily engaged in the oversight and the enterprise IT capabilities. The crucial idea is that the enterprise, taken as a whole, possesses and performs each of these enterprise IT capabilities. And, moreover, that the multiplicity of activities in the enterprise, the business units on the business side, and all the sources of IT on the IT side, are engaged in and participate in the execution of the activities within each of the enterprise IT capabilities.

But So What? What Is the Business Outcome of Having Enterprise IT Capabilities?

The ultimate question is what the enterprise can expect if it indeed possesses—and executes—the enterprise IT capabilities. One way of looking at it is from the achievement/mastery perspective. We recall a CEO telling us, "Don't talk to me about better processes, or increased IT value. Talk to me about increases in sales." In other words, the enterprise overall needs IT (all its sources) to perform in business terms. Business outcomes, not technology outcomes, are required.

Enterprise Outcomes: Connecting the Dots

The application of information and IT is important and represents the real enterprise maturity. Specifics of what each IT maturity stage entails provide a guideline for determining the current as-is for a particular enterprise and a sense of the goals that lie ahead. One difficulty, however, is that much of the rhetoric in the "typical outcomes" is focused on the central IT organization. Artifacts like service-level agreements (SLAs) may not exist for, for example, directly purchased cloud SaaS solutions (e.g., Sales Force Automation purchased directly by the marketing organization).

But this is part of the point, a major part actually. The notion of enterprise IT capability is that all of the enterprise and its IT activities have the capabilities of maturity. Indeed, a major challenge in IT's dispersion is providing the necessary elements of IT maturity for IT not sourced from the central IT organization. This does not make the identified outcome less important; rather, it strengthens the case for thinking about these issues not so much as an IT organizational capability but as an enterprise IT capability.

Service Delivery/Service Requirements

At this level, the IT function strives for operational excellence. The IT organization has to ensure that basic IT services are delivered against the service levels agreed on, and at an acceptable cost. In addition, the right technology has to be in place or must be sourced, and appropriate standards, methods, and procedures for the utilization of IT resources must have been developed and are applied. Available staffs possess the skills to answer the organization's needs. Typical outcomes include:

- Services meet SLA specifications, including cost, performance, and quality.
- Services meet agreed-upon technology standards (e.g., vendor risks, integration, common technologies).
- Service risks are mitigated (e.g., skill sets to support the services are available).
- Security risks are mitigated.

Software Configuration and Development/Information and Process Requirements

IT can develop software on time, on budget. Software can be specified for acquisition. Software services can be acquired from the Internet or other sources. The software developed, acquired, or obtained as a service is competently specified as to business requirements. Typical outcomes include:

- Projects are completed on time, on budget.
- Projects meet business requirements.
- Project development risks are mitigated.

Project Development & Benefit Realization

Typically at this level, management recognizes the critical nature of IT in providing and contributing to successful business operations. Software, applications, and acquired services are easily implemented and integrated into the overall IT structure. Data integration is enabled. Typical outcomes include:

- Projects are easily integrated into infrastructure and operational environments.
- Project information can be integrated with other information.
- The promised business benefits are accomplished.

Business Outcome and Program Selection

This level on the stairway refers to the IT organization's ability to translate business strategy and intentions into strategic IT intentions and solutions, in close collaboration with business management. IT trends are actively followed by the IT organization and form an input for business strategic planning, including decisions concerning the strategic sourcing of IT. Typical outcomes include:

- Business planning focuses on business requirements and new technology opportunities.
- IT planning is integrated with business management and planning.
- Strategic prioritization is done.

Business Change

This level refers to the ability to implement business strategy through change plans that affect structures, processes and procedures, and IT investments. IT plans are thoroughly integrated with business change plans. This stair step includes the ability to prioritize IT investments across the organization according to business objectives. Typical outcomes include:

- Business change initiatives formally apply IT to support the process innovations.

■ Business organizational and process changes are achieved with use of IT.

■ Business innovations to products and services are achieved with use of IT.

Strategic Innovation

At this level, an organization develops unique uses of IT that form the basis for a radical change in its business model: IT as the driver of innovation. Business strategy development is the result of co-creation. The business vision impacts the IT solutions to be applied, and new IT solutions impact the business's vision. Typical outcomes include:

■ Competitively distinctive IT innovations are adopted.

■ IT is integral to business strategic initiatives.

These descriptions largely focus on processes. But the real questions are: What are the business outcomes? and Which enterprise IT capabilities are required to produce them? That is, what can an enterprise expect if the maturity level has been achieved? So much of IT is focused on the IT supply processes—and the maturity model is no different. We can see the operational excellence, the project development, the planning and information management aspects, all defined from the standpoint of how they are produced and the enterprise IT capability and excellence of the processes that produce them. So some of the outcomes are in fact based on business, but probably not enough.

Strategic IT Management looks at it from the results perspective. For example, if there is operational excellence—so what? Does what is produced actually meet the business needs? Are the business processes and management activities actively supported in meeting their goals? That's the business organization's problem to work out. One might say IT is in the business of delivering what's requested. No, we say. Strategic IT Management is about delivering what's required in business terms—meaning addressing the business requirements.

Exhibit 19.2 connects the outcomes at each level of maturity with the enterprise IT capabilities necessary to achieve them. The table gives an indication of what's needed to produce the outcomes, to improve the maturity level of the enterprise IT. Note though that these outcomes are described from the IT Supply perspective. That is, it takes the point that indicators of maturity are specific to the IT capability: for example, if IT can maturely perform "Business Change"—the fifth level—then outcomes like "Business innovations to products and services" are achieved with the use of IT. That's nice, but it does not necessarily address directly the main theme our book, namely *Transforming Business in Turbulent Times*.

This table, however, does help in demonstrating what IT processes are necessary for effective IT delivery of services through the maturity cycle. As we have mentioned, irrespective of the issues of turbulence and the like, there are important issues with the delivery of IT services in general. Enterprise IT capabilities are a primary solution to those problems, and the maturity model shows where those capabilities provide leverage in terms of improvement.

The Bottom Line

For everyone concerned, whether CEO, CIO, IT professionals, business executives, or managers, the bottom line comes down to three basic questions.

1. Do the *enterprise IT capabilities*—engaging business and IT—perform well and produce business outcomes? Does IT perform?
2. Do *enterprise IT capabilities* add to trust and partnership?
3. Do *enterprises IT capabilities* effectively and sufficiently address change and flexibility?

We all need "yes" answers to these questions!

ABOUT THE AUTHORS

Robert J. Benson applies his more than 45 years of academic and corporate experience to assist nearly 100 companies and government agencies in understanding the business value of IT, strategic and financial IT management, strategic IT planning, effective IT application development, and IT governance. He has consulted for and conducted workshops with clients in the United States, Mexico, Europe, and the Pacific Rim. He has written more than 150 short advisories on business technology strategy and IT governance as well as executive reports, executive updates, and *Cutter IT Journal* articles. He is a Fellow with Cutter Consortium's Business Technology Strategies and Government & Public Sector practices. He is also a Principal with The Beta Group.

Bob Benson taught computer science and information management at Washington University in St. Louis (USA) for 40 years, where he also served as Associate Vice Chancellor for Computing and Communications, Dean, and in various financial executive positions. He has also taught information systems and management at Tilburg University (the Netherlands) and is a member of its faculty. Mr. Benson has appeared in numerous keynotes at executive conferences, including Cutter's *Summits* in the United States and Mexico, *Gartner Symposium/Expo* events, *Information Management Forum CIO*, *Enterprise Architecture Conference*, IQPC-sponsored *Summits*, and others. He is coauthor of several books, including *From Business Strategy to IT Action: Right Decisions for a Better Bottom Line*; *Information Economics: Linking Information Technology and Business Performance;* and *Information Strategy and Economics: Linking Information Systems Strategy to Business Performance*. Mr. Benson holds a bachelor of science degree in engineering science and a law degree, both from Washington University.

Prof. Dr. Pieter M. Ribbers holds the chair of Information Management at the School of Economics and Management, Tilburg University, in the Netherlands. He has served as dean, head of department, academic director of graduate and executive programs in Information Management, author and consultant for almost 30 years. At TiasNimbas, the Executive Business School of Tilburg University, he has been and is responsible as academic director for executive programs in Information Management, which he developed in close collaboration with the Dutch and European CIO community. He has conducted executive seminars and has taught graduate courses in schools of business and engineering throughout Europe and the United States. From

1991 until 1995 he held a position as affiliated Professor in Information Management at Washington University in St. Louis, MO.

His interests span management of information technology (in particular questions related to alignment and information economics), inter-organizational systems (in particular e-business), and the strategic and organizational consequences of the use of information technology. He supervised over 30 PhD theses and has contributed articles in this field to professional national and international journals and (co-)authored several books. His most recent books, are *e-Business: Organizational and Technical Foundations*, co-authored with Mike Papazoglou (Wiley, 2006), and *Managing IT Outsourcing*, co-authored with Eric Beulen and Jan Roos (Routledge, 2011), 2nd edition. He is a member of the editorial board of *Information and Management — The International Journal of Information Systems Applications*. He combined his academic career with consulting; as a consultant he worked for national and international companies like Brunel Financial Consultants, Nolan Norton, Ordina, Philips, and ING-group, especially in outsourcing, scenario development, and information economics.

Ronald B. Blitstein is Director of Cutter's Business Technology Strategies practice. He is also a Fellow of the Cutter Business Technology Council. His 30 year career includes extensive international operations experience and spans all aspects of information management. This includes technology strategic planning, program management, mergers and acquisitions, IT turnarounds, business process reengineering, software solutions development, ERP deployment, security/risk management, outsourcing negotiation, and network/operations management.

As a senior technology executive, Ron Blitstein has been a hands-on change agent working in companies across several industries, including office products, chemicals, medical systems and pharmaceuticals, and consumer products. He has held senior leadership positions at Xerox Corporation, Ohmeda, BOC Group, Pitney Bowes, and Revlon, in addition to providing consulting services at several *Fortune* 500 companies as Managing Director of IMprove Technology Advisors. His operating roles included direct leadership of global organizations based in the United States, United Kingdom and Germany, South Africa, Australia, Japan, China, Singapore, and India.

INDEX